THE
DECISION
MODEL

A Business Logic Framework
Linking Business and Technology

IT MANAGEMENT TITLES
FROM AUERBACH PUBLICATIONS AND CRC PRESS

The Executive MBA in Information Security
John J. Trinckes, Jr
ISBN: 978-1-4398-1007-1

The Decision Model: A Business Logic Framework Linking Business and Technology
Barbara von Halle and Larry Goldberg
ISBN: 978-1-4200-8281-4

The SIM Guide to Enterprise Architecture
Leon Kappelman, ed.
ISBN: 978-1-4398-1113-9

Lean Six Sigma Secrets for the CIO
William Bentley and Peter T. Davis
ISBN: 978-1-4398-0379-0

Building an Enterprise-Wide Business Continuity Program
Kelley Okolita
ISBN: 978-1-4200-8864-9

Marketing IT Products and Services
Jessica Keyes
ISBN: 978-1-4398-0319-6

Cloud Computing: Implementation, Management, and Security
John W. Rittinghouse and
James F. Ransome
ISBN: 978-1-4398-0680-7

Data Protection: Governance, Risk Management, and Compliance
David G. Hill
ISBN: 978-1-4398-0692-0

Strategic Data Warehousing: Achieving Alignment with Business
Neera Bhansali
ISBN: 978-1-4200-8394-1

Mobile Enterprise Transition and Management
Bhuvan Unhelkar
ISBN: 978-1-4200-7827-5

The Green and Virtual Data Center
Greg Schulz
ISBN: 978-1-4200-8666-9

The Effective CIO
Eric J. Brown, Jr. and William A. Yarberry
ISBN: 978-1-4200-6460-5

Business Resumption Planning, Second Edition
Leo A. Wrobel
ISBN: 978-0-8493-1459-9

IT Auditing and Sarbanes-Oxley Compliance: Key Strategies for Business Improvement
Dimitris N. Chorafas
ISBN: 978-1-4200-8617-1

Best Practices in Business Technology Management
Stephen J. Andriole
ISBN: 978-1-4200-6333-2

Leading IT Projects: The IT Manager's Guide
Jessica Keyes
ISBN: 978-1-4200-7082-8

Knowledge Retention: Strategies and Solutions
Jay Liebowitz
ISBN: 978-1-4200-6465-0

The Business Value of IT
Michael D. S. Harris, David Herron,
and Stasia Iwanicki
ISBN: 978-1-4200-6474-2

Service-Oriented Architecture: SOA Strategy, Methodology, and Technology
James P. Lawler and H. Howell-Barber
ISBN: 978-1-4200-4500-0

Service Oriented Enterprises
Setrag Khoshafian
ISBN: 978-0-8493-5360-4

THE
DECISION
MODEL

A Business Logic Framework
Linking Business and Technology

Barbara von Halle and Larry Goldberg

CRC Press
Taylor & Francis Group
Boca Raton   London   New York

CRC Press is an imprint of the
Taylor & Francis Group, an **informa** business

Auerbach Publications
Taylor & Francis Group
6000 Broken Sound Parkway NW, Suite 300
Boca Raton, FL 33487-2742

© 2010 by Taylor and Francis Group, LLC
Auerbach Publications is an imprint of Taylor & Francis Group, an Informa business

No claim to original U.S. Government works

Printed in the United States of America on acid-free paper
10 9 8 7 6 5 4 3 2 1

International Standard Book Number: 978-1-4200-8281-4 (Hardback)

Library of Congress Cataloging-in-Publication Data

Von Halle, Barbara.
  The decision model : a framework for business logic and business-driven SOA / authors, Barbara Von Halle, Larry Goldberg.
      p. cm.
  Includes bibliographical references and index.
  ISBN 978-1-4200-8281-4 (hardcover : alk. paper)
  1. Industrial management--Decision making--Data processing. 2. Business--Decision making--Data processing. 3. Business logistics--Data processing. 4. Service-oriented architecture (Computer science) 5. Decision making--Mathematical models. 6. Expert systems (Computer science) I. Goldberg, Larry, 1946- II. Title.

HD30.2.V67 2010
658.4'03--dc22   2009026784

Visit the Taylor & Francis Web site at
http://www.taylorandfrancis.com

and the Auerbach Web site at
http://www.auerbach-publications.com

Contents

Foreword: Business Rules and the Real World...vii

Preface and Acknowledgments...xi

About the Authors xxiii

Contributors' List...xxv

About the Contributors xxvii

SECTION I   THE DECISION MODEL IN CONTEXT

1   Why the Decision Model?...3

2   An Overview of the Decision Model...13

3   The Business Value of Decision Models...37

4   Changing the Game: BPM and BDM..63

5   SOA and the Decision Model 91

6   How the Decision Model Improves Requirements,
     Business Analysis, and Testing..103

7   Getting Started...139

SECTION II   THE DECISION MODEL IN DETAIL

8   The Structural Principles..167

9   The Declarative Principles...211

10   The Integrity Principles..231

v

11 At a Glance: The Decision Model and the Relational Model..............271

12 The Decision Model Formally Defined 301

SECTION III COMMENTARIES

13 Enterprise Architecture: Managing Complexity and Change............ 319
    JOHN ZACHMAN

14 Opportunities in Enterprise Architecture 329

15 Service-Oriented Architectures 359
    MIKE ROSEN

16 Specifications, Standards, Practices, and the Decision Model 385

17 Integrating the Decision Model with BPMN 421
    BRUCE SILVER

18 The Case for the Physical Decision Model 427
    DANIEL J. WORDEN

19 Enterprise Decision Management and the Decision Model 441
    JAMES TAYLOR

20 Introducing the Business Decision Maturity Model 455

21 The Decision Model and Enterprise 2.0: Enabling Collaboration 481
    BRIAN STUCKY

22 A Management Perspective...493
    DAVID L. HASLETT AND TRACY WILLIAMS

23 Better! Cheaper! Faster! 501
    DAVID PEDERSEN

Bibliography...507

Index 511

Foreword: Business Rules and the Real World

This is an important book: it has important things to say about an especially important set of real-world problems—business rules. Clearly, business rules represent one of the 21st century's major technological challenges, and if we are to create a new generation of large-scale information systems that are agile, adaptable, and predictable, then we must have repeatable methods for developing consistent business rules. Here, this book makes a contribution: it describes an approach (theory and method) that is easy for business users and IT professionals to create consistent sets of business rules and, at the same time, is easy for them to adapt as marketplaces, laws, regulations, and technologies change.

Down the hall from my office there is a law library. It contains national and state laws, agency rules, and pending legislative issues. Recently, it occurred to me that this library was not so much a law library as it was a library of business rules: rules governing taxation, rules governing the construction of roads, rules governing the support of children and families, rules governing the incarceration of criminals, etc. The business rules in this library are encoded in an archaic language called legal English, and despite the enormous amount of money spent on legal fees and research that goes into the creation and maintenance of this library, the business rules found there are only generally consistent with one another. And each year new cases and new laws arise that make even the most learned jurists' heads swim. To resolve this enormous set of new or inconsistent laws, regulations, etc., society has found it necessary to create a legal system made up of lawyers, law clerks, prosecutors, judges, appeals courts, and supreme courts. You would think with all the smart people and sophisticated technology involved, society could do better—this book suggests that they could.

But as useful as this approach will be in helping people developing computer systems, this book is not really about technology. This book is really about consistent rules that govern how an enterprise acts under specific situations. This book is about a common, consistent language and method for defining rules that can be used by either humans or computers. In the end, the approach described here can help both the users and the computer folks.

There are some things that computers do better than people and some things that people do better than computers; the trick is knowing which is which. Given the right set of consistent business rules, computers can come up with the same answer time after time, and do so not in months or years (or sometimes decades), but in microseconds. Clearly, one of the reasons that computer systems have become so important in advanced organizations everywhere is this ability to get the right answer instantly. But getting the right answer is only possible if one has a consistent way to define and implement business rules within an organization. Anyone can develop a simple business rule or a small set of business rules; as the number of rules and decisions grows, the problem gets exponentially more difficult.

What about the method itself? Well, for one thing, it is elegantly simple. This is vitally important because in today's fast paced world, it is particularly important that organizations and enterprises be able to define large bodies of business rules in a manner that is at the same time clear, concise, minimally redundant, and also easy to modify. This, as we've learned, is by no means a simple task. Indeed, business rules are perhaps the most important unresolved problem facing business and IT professionals today. One of the reasons that business rules remain a problem is that developing consistent business rules involves both knowledge of semantics and logic, as well a deep understanding of business and of communication skills. And for large business rule bases, it demands an organized method.

There are a great many approaches to developing business rules, but too much of this writing is a rehash of logic programming or expert systems. Because these approaches were largely developed by and for programmers, they don't really provide business professionals and business analysts a usable methodology for developing a large business rule base. The reason is simple: the key knowledge needed for defining business rules almost always resides in the minds of a wide assortment of nonprogrammers—business managers, lawyers, accountants, engineers, and scientists.

Like the law library, today's large organizations have tens of thousands of business rules expressed in hundreds of different ways. These business rules fall into any number of major categories: national and international legal restrictions, company policies, privacy and security rules, rules for computing key formulas, and so on. Like the law library, these rules are expressed (locked up) in dozens, sometimes hundreds, of obscure documents, formulas, and drawings. History suggests that coming up with a common formal set of business rules from all of this encoded information is a very tough chore indeed.

The world of business rules today is not unlike that of a database 40 years ago. In the late 1960s a large number of different approaches to database design were competing for recognition when Ted Codd and his associates at IBM Research came up with what we now call relational database theory. Codd, a mathematician by training, was able to develop a rigorous, consistent approach for defining sets of relational tables that would provide the requisite answer sets, were internally consistent, and were minimally redundant.

Codd and his associates conceptualized a way of looking at that data that was not only mathematically consistent, it was also maximally flexible and scalable. Codd's approach made possible the complex systems that exist today. Because it was so straightforward and simple, it greatly aided the communication between different systems and different databases. Even though relational database theory is being challenged by other forms of data storage and manipulation approaches today, it still provides the gold standard upon which a database is judged.

One of the secrets of Codd's great success was his focus on elegant simplicity along with mathematical rigor. What Barb and Larry have done is to come up with an analogously elegant and simple approach for defining large sets of business rules that has mathematic rigor as well. Then, starting with this compelling conceptual model, they have been able show how to build a broad methodology for capturing, analyzing, and using those business rules, whether for a small departmental application or for an entire line of business.

One of the most important characteristics of the model presented here is that it is truly a logical model, i.e., it is technology independent (or technology agnostic, if you will). It leverages technologies, but it doesn't require them. Over time this will pay off because the history of computing over the last half century has shown that logical models have a much longer life than technology-based ones. This has been true of database modeling and design, it has been true of workflow modeling, and I think that time will show that it is equally true of business rule modeling as well.

One of the obvious advantages that good, logical models have is that they are clearer and more consistent, they make it easier to define large problems, and, at the same time, to recognize broad, logical business patterns. Too often business rules are buried in complex, unintelligible language or complex flowcharts of complex code. In addition, it makes it particularly difficult to make sense of the underlying rules. Moreover, this complexity makes it difficult to understand the rationale (semantics, ontology intent) behind the rules. Clarity improves our ability to quickly see a rule and understand whether it is correct and consistent. This kind of insight is after all often one of the most valuable byproducts of well run business rule projects.

The authors should be complimented on their ability to specify how their business rule methodology fits together with the whole complex of other major business/technology concerns, including business decision modeling, business process management, SOA, and requirements definition. This is especially important because business rules occur in a variety of shapes and sizes: business process rules, data rules, computation rules, application rules. The book shows how, for example, using business rules located in common evaluation modules can greatly simplify a business process model and make it far easier to modify these models when the business rules change.

A great many organizations are not so much the masters of their business rules but prisoners of them. They have woven a web of complexity that no one really understands but is so daunting that no one dares to change it either. That is unfortunate. A great deal of this is a result of a modern education system that fails to teach people either the careful use of language or the fundamentals of logic. Natural language is great for ordering hamburgers or proposing marriage, but it is not well suited for describing complex decisions. And as we have seen programming logic is often not all that logical. The methodology presented hints at some of the major problems that organizations face in defining and implementing their business rules. Every so often a book comes along that reminds us that the purpose of business rules is to take a complex issue and produce a simple logical solution. All this looks easy, but it is not. For those who read this book, it can be a great help.

So is this book the last word on business rules? By no means. This book is not the end of research and discussion about business rules any more than Ted Codd's initial paper was the end of research and discussion regarding databases, or Crick and Watson's initial paper on the structure of DNA was the end of research and discussion regarding molecular genetics. Important books are not an end; they are a framework for others to build on.

Ken Orr
Topeka, Kansas
kenorr@kenorrinst.com

Preface and Acknowledgments

Edwin Abbott, in his classic *Flatland* (Abbott, 1884), points out that if we viewed our universe in two dimensions, we would detect only length and breadth. That means we would see directly only points and lines. We could, however, infer the existence of two-dimensional shapes, like triangles and squares. But no spheres. No cubes. Such things would exist, of course, but we could not see them or even suspect their existence.

For those of us quite comfortable with cubes and spheres, Abbott explains how a three-dimensional artifact appears to a Flatlander, who recognizes only two dimensions. Put a penny on a table. If we view it from a position above the table, we perceive a circle. Now, if we view it from a position where our eyes are even with the table's edge, the penny suddenly appears as a simple straight line. The same would be true of other two-dimensional shapes. Squares, hexagons, and triangles all appear as lines when viewed from the table's edge. In fact, Flatland, to its inhabitants, is an entire universe of points and simple straight lines. Even people, houses, food, and other everyday items are reduced to points and lines.

Residents of Flatland navigate their world successfully, though, by distinguishing among the shapes they can't see based on the behavior of the lines. For example, if such a shape, which they cannot see directly, moves closer or further away, the line becomes shorter or longer. Abbott brilliantly illustrates that there are disadvantages to viewing a world in fewer dimensions than really exist. Yet, surely, some Flatlanders sense another dimension. Abbott cautions that they do so not based on lucid observation but on belief alone.

In our world, we actually see directly two dimensions (i.e., planes) and infer three dimensions (i.e., solids). We are able to infer that the planes we see directly are really solids through the perception of shadows, for example, but we don't really see the solids. We simply infer and believe they are there.

It seems like business rules and business logic are much like a dimension we can't quite distinguish. Like Flatlanders, we navigate our world successfully (i.e., our business processes and systems) without the benefit of seeing a business logic dimension. It remains invisible, buried in program code, manuals, or peoples' heads. But it's still there, nonetheless. In fact, it runs most aspects of our businesses. Unable to perceive it, we bump into it from time to time in the form of system errors, inconsistent conclusions, or those based on business logic that is unsound or even unknown. We develop explanations for its influence on our lives, such as unclear requirements, out-of-date documentation, prepackaged inflexible software, or loss of business knowledge. If Abbott is correct, there are disadvantages to viewing our world without this dimension if it really exists.

But some of us have long sensed that a business logic dimension really exists. We try to bring it into direct focus when we discover a single business rule and add it to a list of other ones. Or, we diagram a business rule on top of a data model or add it as a miscellaneous note to a business process model or use case. Sometimes, we automate it diligently in special technology, but it has been known to disappear even there. It seems like we aren't really seeing the business logic directly. We only infer its existence when its behavior influences our world.

Therefore, do we sense a business logic dimension based only on belief? Or is it possible to observe it directly as having a distinct structure and behavior? After all, Abbott implies that "dimension implies direction, implies measurement, the more and the less ..." (Abbott, 1884). Is it really there?

This book declares that it is really there. In this book, the Decision Model gives the business logic dimension a formal, recognizable structure along with behavior that is explained through principles belonging to this dimension. Through the Decision Model, we are able to see directly that business logic has an existence of its own that transcends the perception of one business rule at a time. This idea is intriguing because moving from lower to higher dimensions brings new awareness and opportunities. Once we can see what was previously invisible, we are positioned to harness it to our advantage. Moreover, it will advance our knowledge of other dimensions (e.g., business processes) so we can simplify them.

It is natural, at first, to feel a bit uncomfortable at the thought of a whole new dimension. Detecting a new dimension can be overwhelming. In fact, a Flatlander, upon perceiving Spaceland for the first time, was understandably bewildered, wondering if it were madness or hell. A voice, emanating from a sphere, nevertheless, offered consolation, "It is neither.... It is knowledge; it is Three Dimensions: open your eye once again and try to look steadily" (Abbott, 1884).

We hope you enjoy the journey into the business logic dimension and the Decision Model. May it be the beginning of new awareness, technology, and other opportunities.

> ... It is as natural for us Flatlanders to lock up a Square for preaching the Third Dimension, as it is for you Spacelanders to lock up a Cube for preaching the Fourth. (Abbott, 1884)

How This Book Came About

This book truly began a decade ago in conventional time (but eons in Information Technology time) when Barbara founded Knowledge Partners Inc. (KPI). Well-known for coauthoring *The Handbook of Relational Database Design* (Addison-Wesley, 1989), she intended to further her pioneering work in data architecture, focusing on the importance of business rules. She participated in the GUIDE Business Rules Project in its early meetings and contributed to its Final Report published in October 1997. She began to work with clients in this area, researching not only the subject but advancing the practice. This ultimately led to the publication of *Business Rules Applied* (Wiley, 2002), which she authored with contributions from several of her colleagues at KPI.

At that time, the practice around business rules was focused on separating them from the rest of the artifacts in business system development in the firm belief that "It can help you build better, easily changeable systems faster than any previous approach" (von Halle, *Business Rules Applied*, 2002).

It was shortly after the publication of that book that Barbara and Larry met at a major U.S. federal agency. KPI was consulting on methodology for a business rules approach in a modernization effort. Larry was the business sponsor for the business rule technology vendor and for the team implementing the technology. This meeting led to an exchange of experience in business rules, and the realization that we shared a similar vision about the subject.

Larry, a serial entrepreneur in the IT arena, had built a software application company around technology that externalized business rules, which allowed the resulting application to be highly configurable. He had sold this company to a niche global software vendor in the hope of broadening the market for the application technology. It was in the pursuit of this endeavor that he was working on business rule technology and introducing it into the federal agency.

We exchanged ideas for several years, which culminated in a business partnership through KPI, now renamed Knowledge Partners International, LLC. Our intention was to develop our ideas into tangible products for the business rules market. Our focus quickly became the recurring patterns in business rule structures that had become evident as we utilized the methods in *Business Rules Applied*. These patterns gave rise to the idea that there is, within business logic, an inherent structure, just as there is an inherent structure that Dr. Codd had detected in data almost 40 years earlier.

With large organizations integrating a business rules approach into their standard business systems projects, we created such inherent business logic structures across industries. A goal was to provide a means of representing business logic in one and only one correct way, such that it was not left to chance or preference. This worked well but was just the beginning.

An epiphany came when Barbara was working with a large U.S. retailer. The team was largely a business group with a representative from information technology (IT). At a certain point the team developed the base structure for a particular "rule family" (our grouping of business rules at the time.) The IT person remarked that, with the base structure, the IT group could design the code, even before the business rules were populated into the structure. We talked about this after the session with the added insight that the emerging business logic structures not only have one correct representation; they have a value that transcends the intuitive expression and organization of business rules as a precursor to automation. The deeper we looked, the greater appeared the utility of such structures to business people, to faster iterative development methods, and even to system architecture.

Shortly, we began to sense some parallels with the early usage of the Relational Model, especially the value of rigorous principles. In late 2006 we issued a paper to formalize the ideas. Over time, the Decision Model emerged, and the paper was extended to become the seed of this book. It is important to note that the Decision Model was not contrived to embody the rigor of mathematical set theory as is the Relational Model. However, as a humble beginning, it embraces some of the concepts introduced by Dr. Codd but applies them to the business logic dimension. So, by design, this book is a mixture of Decision Model principles, giving the model rigor, and actual experience, proving that it is teachable and practical in the everyday world.

We began using the Decision Model in practice, with results that exceeded our expectations. People found the Decision Model intuitive to interpret and predictable to create. At the same time, the Decision Model resulted in a dramatic improvement in the productivity of harvesting and automating business rules compared to the classical methods used in previous projects.

Because of the desire to test and prove the Decision Model, initial progress on the book was slow. We joked that we wrote the book twice—once for us and once for others. But, in fact, by the end, we had probably written it at least three times. As experience revealed useful advances in the Decision Model principles, we revisited chapters in the book to accommodate those enhancements.

As we reach the end of this long period of development, we believe that more is to be discovered and improved about the Decision Model. But we have confidence that it reflects a simple nature of business logic, as a starting point, and will continue to be of value over time. Readers of this book will realize that the methodology and techniques in *Business Rules Applied* remain valuable, but are enhanced significantly by the introduction of the Decision Model as an important additional deliverable.

Edmund Phelps, a professor of economics from Columbia University and a Nobel Laureate, is fond of observing that it is not the great scientific discoveries that advance productivity in economies. Phelps says that it is actually the practical knowledge that is learned when implementing those discoveries, the "tweaking" that the practitioners are able to achieve that is the cause of the great leaps in value in economies (Tilman & Phelps, 2008). Evidence of this is the passage of several decades from Codd's initial publication of the Relational Model in 1970, to the emergence of commercial relational database management systems in the 1980s, to their final ascendancy in the 1990s. This timeframe from invention to adoption reflects that successful practice is valuable to the adoption of a new idea.

We placed great emphasis on the use of the Decision Model in real projects, by us and by others, over the last two years, and have learned much from that use. More work still lies ahead. John Zachman said "It occurs to me that once the underlying structure of a discipline is discovered, friction goes to zero! The processes (methodologies) become predictable and repeatable" (Zachman, 2006). We have seen this in the dramatic improvement in productivity and quality that has been achieved in actual projects using the Decision Model, giving our convictions quite a good deal of courage.

Ironically, this book was completed in the middle hours of the global economic panic of 2008. Imploding property, credit, and stock markets were wreaking financial havoc on great and small alike. Much ink has been spent on the causes and the possible cures. One compelling fact is that regulators, managers of banks, and insurance company executives placed blind faith in computer models to quantify, reduce, or even eliminate risk from complex financial instruments. Instead, it turns out that they amplified risk, and to levels that were unsustainable. On the other hand, managers who knew and understood the capabilities, limitations, and true content of their computer models also understood what limits could be placed on their efficacy. Their institutions will likely survive and prosper.

The object lesson to be learned is not to accept the output from automated systems as having value unless the business logic in those systems is known, understood, tested to be correct, and is able to be adjusted quickly to reflect changing conditions. Unfortunately most modern enterprises have, and continue to build, systems in which the business logic becomes lost or is not well-managed. Trusting the future to a black box is likely to result in unpleasant surprises. It is time that the business logic in business systems is given recognition as something worth managing well. This is ultimately the goal that we believe the Decision Model can help achieve.

Who Should Read This Book

Because the Decision Model has an impact on business and technology practices, this book is written for both business and technology professionals. For academic audiences the book serves as a reference for curriculums covering relevant aspects of software engineering and enterprise architecture.

None of these audiences is likely to read the book in its entirety—nor perhaps all of every section—as some chapters are business oriented and others are technically oriented. The book is written in three sections—the first being an overview, the second being a detailed technical treatment, and the third being aspects of special interests. Each chapter in the first two sections contains discussion points and exercises that may be of interest to academic and professional audiences in testing their understanding of the chapter. Therefore, below is a brief guide for navigating the book, based on personal objectives.

How to Read This Book

Because the book introduces a new model with tentacles in many disciplines, it is divided into three sections:

Section I: An executive summary followed by a survey of business, technical, and methodology implications of the Decision Model. A general reader will get a complete overview of the Decision Model and its place in the business and technology world by reading this section.

Section II: A detailed treatment of the foundation of the Decision Model and a formal definition of the model. Those who wish to understand the Decision Model in depth would read this section. Also, the section could be used as a reference for practitioners when working with the Decision Model in practice.

Section III: Specialized topics of interest in the Decision Model, including both business and technical topics. Readers with particular interests will find details on them in this section. While it is possible to read the book from cover to cover, we have prepared a set of navigation charts for readers with different backgrounds and objectives. Some of the categorization in these charts is somewhat arbitrary, such as the definition of "business interests" and "technical interests."

All Readers and Those Desiring an Executive Summary

All readers should read Chapter 1, which justifies the need for a new model, and Chapter 2, which introduces the nature and notation of the Decision Model. These two chapters constitute the executive summary of the book. Readers with additional objectives can consider the paths below.

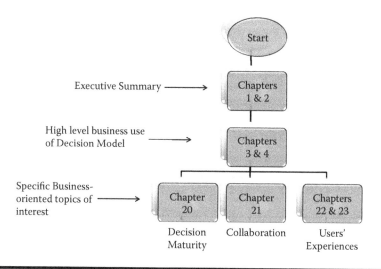

Figure P1   How to read about business relevance and benefits.

Readers Interested in Business Relevance and Benefits

If you are interested in the business ramifications of the Decision Model, after Chapters 1 and 2, read Chapter 3 for an approach to determine its tangible business value and Chapter 4 for how it simplifies business processes.

After Chapter 4, you may want to read selected chapters in Section III for more details on specific business-oriented topics of interest.

If you are interested in understanding organizational maturity levels related to the adoption of the Decision Model, read Chapter 20. If your interest is in the Decision Model and enterprise collaboration, read Chapter 21. Finally, if you are interested in advice from people like yourselves, read Chapters 22 and 23. Refer to Figure P1.

Readers Interested in Technical Relevance and Benefits

If you are a reader interested in the technical implications of the Decision Model, after reading Chapters 1 and 2, continue with Chapter 4 on Business Process Management (BPM) and Business Decision Management (BDM), Chapter 5 on Service Oriented Architecture (SOA), and Chapter 6 on Requirements, Business Analysis, and Testing.

After Chapter 6, you may choose to read more detailed chapters in Section III on specific technology topics of interest.

If you are a technical reader with an interest in the Decision Model in Enterprise Architecture, read Chapters 13 and 14. If your interest is the Decision Model in

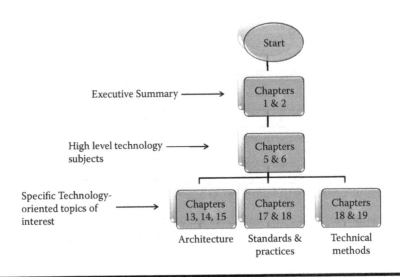

Figure P2   How to read about technology relevance and benefits.

SOA, read Chapter 15. If your interest is in the Decision Model's improvements in current and emerging standards, read Chapter 16 on standards and Chapter 17 on Business Process Management Notation (BPMN). If you are an advanced technical reader, read Chapter 18 on the idea of physical Decision Models. If you are interested in learning more about BDM, or as it is called in this chapter, Enterprise Decision Management (EDM), read Chapter 19. Refer to Figure P2.

Readers Interested in Technical and Business Relevance

In Chapter 21 Brian Stucky discusses the "Purple People," those who are not necessarily purely business professionals or IT professionals, but who move effortlessly from one world to the other (read the chapter to discover the origin of the term "Purple People.") For those Purple People, we suggest reading Section I from start to finish, read Section II to the extent that you desire to learn the full rigor of the Decision Model (or use the section for reference when necessary), then read chapters of topical interest in Section III. Refer to Figure P3.

Readers Interested in Conducting a Decision Model Project

If you are interested in managing or participating in a Decision Model project, after Chapters 1 and 2, proceed to Chapter 7 on Getting Started and use Chapter 12 as a handy reference during the life of the project. Refer to Figure P4. In addition, some

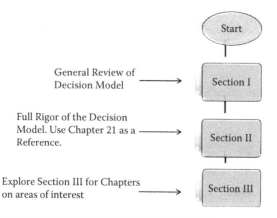

Figure P3 How to read about both business and technology relevance and benefits.

project team members may choose to read other chapters relevant to the members' role on the project.

Readers Wanting Full Technical Details

If you are interested in detailed rigor and have an analytical or technical background, follow Chapters 1 and 2 with Chapters 8, 9, and 10 on the Decision Model Principles. If you have experience with the Relational Model, you may find Chapter 11 interesting. Use Chapter 12 as a convenient reference. You may wish to read several chapters in Section III. Refer to Figure P5.

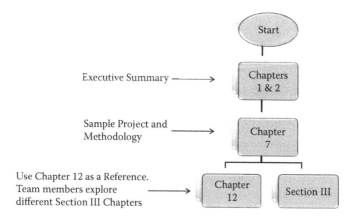

Figure P4 How to read about managing or participating on a Decision Model project.

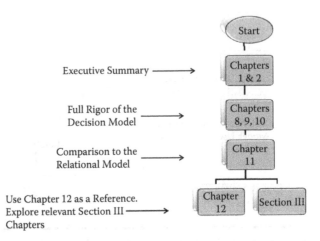

Figure P5   How to read about the full technical details of the Decision Model.

Readers Wanting a Reference

Chapter 12 provides a complete reference of terms and principles of the Decision Model. It supplements any of the previous paths through the book, but is most useful for a detailed review or for use during the progress of an actual project.

Those to Be Thanked

We gratefully acknowledge the support of our clients who trust us with some of their most precious assets, and who had faith in the quality of our ideas. Without them this book would not exist. For confidentiality reasons, we cannot acknowledge you by name, but you know who you are and hopefully you know that we are grateful to you.

During the research and writing we were honored that several professional colleagues (some using the Decision Model in practice) offered to read and comment on many of the Decision Model principles. Our thanks to Mishka Ilmer, Bob Evory, Gil Segal, and Bill Shaffer, who were the patient readers of our early drafts.

A special thanks to the eclectic group that made up our second group of readers, because for their pain they were rewarded with the task of writing a contribution to the book! These contributors came from several different disciplines and backgrounds. Their contributions to the third section of the book are invaluable in placing the Decision Model into the perspective of a wide range of different audiences and specialties. Our thanks to John Zachman, Ken Orr, Bruce Silver, James Taylor, Mike Rosen, Brian Stucky, Dave Haslett, Tracy Williams, Dave Pedersen, and Daniel Worden. And yet, we also owe thanks to those who comprised our third group of readers who reviewed the completed manuscript—some providing detailed comments and all providing endorsements. Our thanks to Dave Hay, Dr. Opher Etzion, Nadav Hashon, Mannes Nauer, Bob Schork, Robert S. Seiner, Carol-Ann Matignon, Carlos Serrano-Morales, Arne Herenstein, Professor William Miller, Len Silverston, Andrew Spanyi, and Tom Wolfe.

Finally, a special note of thanks to our publisher, Auerbach, and editor, John Wyzalek. John was more than anyone could ask in an editor—supportive, helpful, and remarkably patient. In particular, he reacted quickly to our book proposal with enthusiasm for its potential in the marketplace. A note of thanks also goes to the editorial staff at Taylor & Francis, Stephanie Morkert, Amber Donley, Karen Schober and, most especially, our Project Editor, Andrea Demby, who made it all happen.

A Personal Note from Barb

As always, I owe so much to my husband of more than 30 years, Mike. He has, at all times, supported me in every way on many projects. This book is no different. He generously gave of his time, edited hundreds of manuscript pages, and provided useful insights into how best to reach the reading audience.

A Personal Note from Larry

As I think about the dislocation that my attention to this book caused my family for the last two years, I gratefully dedicate it to my long-suffering but always loving wife of 40 years, Jillian, and our wonderfully supportive children and grandchildren, Nina, Parke, Chloe, and Betsy, and Rafael, Ashlyn, and Julian. But that hardly reaches the measure of my indebtedness to family and is an insufficient acknowledgment of the importance that family has played in my life, especially during these pressured years.

Quite by coincidence, during the development of these pages, I became involved in a broad effort across a wide group of cousins on both Jill's side and mine to build a family tree on the community-based Web site, Geni.com. Sadly, during this time my mother passed away, and she will be unable to share further in the coming together of this extraordinary family far-flung across four continents in the United States, the United Kingdom, Europe, Africa, Israel, and Australia, whose roots lay in the Pale of Europe. The forebearers we celebrate came from humble beginnings and sought freedom in distant, forbidding, and strange lands in order to escape a very cruel tyranny. Thanks to their prescience and courage, many of us were saved from the Holocaust. We remember with reverence those who perished in the slaughter. Those who survived were scattered across the face of the globe. Through the effort on Geni we are trying to rebind precious ties.

As the Geni project matured, the scope and scale of our ancestors' sacrifice became evident to me, exciting my wonder and admiration. The project became my escape—in late night sessions of research into old shipping manifests and archives—from the unrelenting pressure of the book deadline.

So I broaden the dedication—to family, but in the widest sense, to the group that truly delineates family. First to my father, whose 95th birthday, fate willing, we will celebrate this year, and whose life is an example to us all; to my brothers Norman and Trevor, and to Jill's brothers Jonni and the late Shalom, all of whose closeness and love are and have been a constant in our lives; and to their families, and our aunts, uncles, and cousins across the globe (numbering, now in the thousands!), and in memory of our ancestors who set the bar so high for us all. Of them all I must single out Raymond and Selwyn Haas, and their late parents Gertie and Ivor, who reached out a hand of help when it was most needed, and no other was offered; it was, and will always be deeply appreciated, even though it cannot ever be repaid in full measure.

And finally to that most distant of relatives, but closest of kin, mentor, foil, and beloved friend, the late Dr. Jos Gerson. He achieved much in life as a world-renown economist. However, his most important mark may be the impression he made among the wide, but close, circle of friends that he made across the world. This was an eclectic group of economists, rabbis, humanists, liberals, and conservatives, ranging across several generations and continents, united by his magnetic and compelling personality, and challenged by his extraordinary intellectual energy. He was also a deeply loving—if ever challenging—husband and father to Kirsi, Daniel, Miriam, and Julian. Over time he taught us a great deal, but the last three years of his life were a living lesson in honesty, grace, and courage. Jos will never be forgotten.

> As long as lips can breath, or eyes can see,
> So long lives this, and this gives life to thee

William Shakespeare

About the Authors

Barbara von Halle, cofounder of Knowledge Partners International LLC, is coinventor of the Decision Model and co-owner of its patent. She is also the 1995 recipient of the Outstanding Individual Achievement Award from International DAMA.

An early career highlight was Barbara's role as the project manager overseeing one of the first installations and tests of DB2. She assisted many corporations in adopting and leveraging the Relational Model and related technology. Her early exposure to the Relational Model enabled her to coauthor, with Candace Fleming, the *Handbook of Relational Database Design* (Addison-Wesley Publishing Company, 1989), which still serves as the most critical reference book for relational design methodology and implementation.

She was a popular columnist in *Database Programming and Design* magazine for years. She also served as the editor of the popular Auerbach series *Handbook of Data Management* from 1993–1995.

Other book publications include *Business Rules Applied* (John Wiley & Sons, 2001), which was a finalist for the 2002 Software Development Jolt Award. She also co-edited an anthology called *The Business Rule Revolution* (Happy About, 2006). Her recent article in *Intelligent Enterprise* magazine, "Business Rule Maturity: Roadmap to an Agile Enterprise," was one of the top 20 most popular articles of the year.

As a pioneer in data architecture, business rules, and the Decision Model, Barbara has consulted and offered training to clients and appeared as a keynote speaker at conferences in the United States and Europe.

Barbara has a bachelor's degree in mathematics and was the recipient of Fordham University's Mathematics Award, graduating as class valedictorian. She also holds a master's degree in computer science and electrical engineering from Stevens Institute of Technology.

Larry Goldberg, cofounder of Knowledge Partners International LLC, is co-inventor of the Decision Model and co-owner of its patent.

Larry has spent many decades in the IT industry, and has created several companies focused on developing and marketing business applications, based on business rules technology. He led the development of several successful commercial enterprise applications, including applications in the healthcare, insurance, and supply chain domains, and was active on the board of several industry bodies.

In 1999 he sold the PowerFlex company to a global software company. From 1999 to 2004 he led the business rules activities of that company, and was the principal for several major business rules product developments in both government and the insurance industry. He has consulted with clients and appeared as speaker in conferences in the United States and Europe as a thought leader in the application of business rules.

In recent years, Larry has been the editorial director of the *BDM Bulletin*, an electronic publication of the BPMInstitute.org, and has been the track chair of the BDM track at Brainstorm Conferences throughout the United States. Larry also coedited an anthology called *The Business Rule Revolution* (Happy About®, 2006).

Contributors' List

Chapter 13

John A. Zachman
Zachman International
La Cañada, California
http://zachmaninternational.com

Chapter 15

Mike Rosen
Chief Scientist
Wilton Consulting Group
Wilton, New Hampshire
mike@mikerosen.com

Chapter 17

Bruce Silver
Principal
Bruce Silver Associates/BPMessentials
Aptos, California
bruce@brsilver.com

Chapter 18

Daniel J. Worden
Principal
RuleSmith Corporation
Toronto, Canada
daniel@worden.net

Chapter 19

James Taylor
CEO
Decision Management Solutions
Palo Alto, California
james@decisionmanagementsolutions.
com

Chapter 21

Brian Stucky
Managing Director, Business Decision
Management
Allegiance Advisory Group
Reston, Virginia
bstucky@allegianceag.com

Chapter 22

David L. Haslett, PMP
Blue Cross Blue Shield of Kansas, Inc.*
Topeka, Kansas
davhasl@gmail.com

---

* Blue Cross and Blue Shield of Kansas, Inc.
is not connected to this book project in any
way.

Tracy Williams
Blue Cross Blue Shield of Kansas, Inc.*
Topeka, Kansas
tracy.matthias@ymail.com

Chapter 23

David Pedersen
Senior Decision Analyst
Knowledge Partners International
Mentor, Ohio
dpedersen@kpiusa.com

---

* Blue Cross and Blue Shield of Kansas, Inc. is not connected to this book project in any way.

About the Contributors

John A. Zachman

John A. Zachman is the originator of the Framework for Enterprise Architecture, which has received broad acceptance around the world as an integrative framework, or "periodic table" of descriptive representations for enterprises. He is not known only for this work on Enterprise Architecture, but also for his early contributions to IBM's Information Strategy methodology (Business Systems Planning) as well as to its executive team planning techniques (Intensive Planning).

In 1990 he retired from IBM, having served them for 26 years. He is chief executive officer of Zachman International. He has spoken to many thousands of enterprise managers and information professionals on every continent.

Mr. Zachman serves on the Executive Council for Information Management and Technology of the United States General Accounting Office. He is a fellow of the College of Business Administration of the University of North Texas. He serves on the Advisory Board, Data Resource Management Program, University of Washington, and on the Advisory Board, Data Administration Management Association International (DAMA-I), which awarded him its 2002 Lifetime Achievement Award. He was the recipient of the 2004 Oakland University Applied Technology in Business (ATIB) Award for IS excellence and innovation.

Mike Rosen

Mike Rosen is chief scientist at Wilton Consulting Group, which provides expert consulting in Service-Oriented Architecture (SOA), Enterprise Architecture (EA), and Model-Driven Solutions. Mr. Rosen is also director of Enterprise Architecture for the Cutter Consortium and editorial director for SOA Institute. His current emphasis is on the implementation of agile, flexible, enterprise SOA solutions, and on education and training for SOA and EA.

Mike Rosen has more than a dozen years of experience with SOA applications in the finance, insurance, and telecom industries, and more recently, in government agencies and technology product companies. He has helped many different organizations initiate and implement SOA architectures, solutions, and programs, and get beyond the simple Web-service-enabling approach to actually create more flexible, consistent systems.

Much of Mr. Rosen's work is also in the area of Enterprise Architecture. Given the dozens of questions and choices about EA programs, frameworks, governance, processes, and artifacts, Mike helps organizations cut through the clutter and focus their EA activities toward creating value immediately and over time.

As a student of computer architecture, Mike has spent years understanding, developing, writing, and teaching about the principles, practices, and skills of an architect. He has years of experience in the architecture and design of applications for global corporations and was a product architect for several major middleware vendors. Prior to consulting, Mike had 20+ years of product development experience for distributed technologies including DCE, CORBA, DCOM, J2EE, Web Services, Transaction Processing, and Messaging.

Mr. Rosen is an internationally recognized speaker and author of dozens of papers and several books including *Applied SOA: Architecture and Design Strategies* (Wiley, 2008) *Developing eBusiness Systems and Architecture: A Manager's Guide* (Morgan Kaufman, 2001), and *Integrating CORBA and COM Applications* (Wiley, 1998).

Bruce Silver

Bruce Silver is an independent industry analyst and consultant focused on business process modeling and management. He is the author of *BPMN Method and Style* (Cody-Cassidy Press, 2009, www.bpmnstyle.com), and delivers BPMN training through BPMessentials.com, the BPM Institute, and other channels. He is the author of the popular BPMS Watch blog (www.brsilver.com/wordpress) and of the BPMS Report series of product evaluations.

Daniel Worden

Daniel Worden has worked with Decision Support Systems since the early 1980s. He has held management positions in private and public sector organizations, and has been responsible for design, development, deployment and support of database and Web-enabled solutions.

The author of five books on a range of topics from relational database technology to storage networks and Java, he has written and presented on best practices for adopting IT tools and techniques.

In his capacity as a consultant to management, Mr. Worden has focused on uncovering hidden business value in information systems, as well as on leveraging information as an asset.

Current areas of interest include Emergent Strategy, Adaptive Systems, and, naturally, Decision Models.

James Taylor

James Taylor is a leading expert and visionary in Decision Management Solutions, helping companies build decision-centric organizations, processes, and information systems. He actively maintains two blogs on decision management, and has been published and quoted in a wide range of magazines from *BusinessWeek* to *Intelligent Enterprise*. He is a frequent speaker at conferences. Previously, he was a vice president of product marketing at Fair Isaac Corporation, and he has held posts in software research and consulting at PeopleSoft and at Ernst & Young Management Consulting. A graduate of the University of London, James lives with his family in Palo Alto, California.

Mr. Taylor is a highly sought-after speaker and appears frequently at industry conferences, events, and seminars, as well as in university lecture halls. Along with writing numerous contributed articles for industry publications and reports, he has contributed chapters to *The Business Rule Revolution* (Barbara von Halle and Larry Goldberg, Happy About, 2007) and *Business Intelligence Implementation: Issues and Perspectives*. Working with Neil Raden, he has published the definitive work on decision management: *Smart (Enough) Systems* (Prentice Hall, 2007).

James' blogs can be found at

http://jtonedm.com

http://www.ebizq.net/blogs/decision_management/

David L. Haslett, PMP*

David L. Haslett's career spans 32 years in Information Systems working for a large health insurance company in Kansas. He started his career in March 1975 as a computer operator and today is Manager of Systems Support. Mr. Haslett's experience has included a wide range of professional titles and responsibilities over the years, and he has been instrumental in the successful implementation of numerous large projects. He is currently responsible for 29 professional Information Services staff dedicated to Enterprise Decision Management Services, Enterprise System Services (Business Rules Engine, Imaging, OnDemand, OCR, secured transactional pages on the company Web site, company intranet, Legal Services), Electronic Data Interchange (EDI), e-mail, and IS division planning. Mr. Haslett graduated from Electronic Computer Programming Institute in 1974, has attended Washburn University in Topeka, Kansas, earned his Project Management Professional (PMP) certification in May 2002, and was Information Technology Infrastructure Library (ITIL) Foundation Certified in December 2006. He is a member of the Project Management Institute, the PMI Kansas City Mid-America Chapter, and the local Chamber of Commerce in Topeka, Kansas.

---

* PMP™ (Project Management Professional) is the trademark of PMI, Project Management Institute.

Tracy Williams, BPMP*

Tracy Williams has enjoyed a diverse career in information systems, working for a Midwest health insurance company. Her 9-year career has encompassed roles as systems analyst/developer, business/rule analyst, and project manager. She is currently team leader of the Enterprise Decision Management Services unit. This team works with many business areas throughout the organization, leading rules-related projects from a business perspective.

Ms. Williams holds a degree in computer information systems from Washburn University, and has been certified as a Business Process Management Professional, BPMP.

Brian Stucky

Brian Stucky is Managing Director of Business Decision Management at Allegiance Advisory Group. A recognized thought leader in the area of business rules, Brian brings over two decades of experience designing and implementing business rule and process management systems for both commercial and federal clients. Prior to joining Allegiance, Brian was Vice President of Decision Management Solutions at InScope Solutions, Inc. where he directed the company's technology practice area.

Prior to joining InScope, Mr. Stucky served as the Enterprise Rule Steward at Freddie Mac, where he set the business and technology strategy for business rule development across the corporation. These efforts resulted in Freddie Mac winning a 2005 *Application Development Trends* Magazine Innovator Award in the category of Component-Based Development ("Freddie Mac redesigns its processes to satisfy new customer needs") and being named a finalist for a 2005 *Mortgage Technology Magazine* "10X" Award.

Mr. Stucky also cofounded two companies that specialized in the design and implementation of intelligent systems. He has implemented and managed business rule development efforts in a variety of domains, including the secondary mortgage market, credit card marketing and processing, and mutual fund portfolio analysis.

Mr. Stucky works closely with a number of business rule vendors and speaks internationally at conferences and professional events. He has given presentations at the Business Rules Forum, European Business Rules Conference, Mortgage Bankers Association Technology Conference, the Brainstorm Business Process Management Conference Series, and was an invited panelist at a Gartner Group Financial Services Summit. He was also a contributing author to *The Business Rule Revolution*. Mr. Stucky holds a BS in computer science from the University of Kansas and an MS in computer and information science from the University of Massachusetts at Amherst.

---

* BPMP™ (Business Process Management Professional) is the trademark of the BPMInstitute. org.

David Pedersen

David Pedersen has more than 25 years of IT experience and is a Certified Public Accountant (CPA). He began his career as a CPA and quickly moved to developing and implementing Information Systems in a variety of industries.

He has enjoyed a diverse career serving in various roles: programmer, business analyst, Senior Decision Analyst, CFO, Director of Global IT and managing partner. His experience includes co-founding a technology company, successfully developing and implementing enterprise systems, and leading large global business process and business decision management initiatives.

Mr. Pedersen is currently a Senior Decision Analyst at KPI where he leverages his diverse background and experience to implement BPM and BDM solutions in a variety of industries. Prior to KPI he served as a Director at Ernst & Young, LLP, where he led the development, implementation and support of a portfolio of enterprise applications. His work included Enterprise Architecture and the development and implementation of complex global business processes re-engineering/improvement initiatives that were among the firm's top global priorities. Prior to joining Ernst & Young, LLP, he developed enterprise solutions for the hazardous waste industry, legal profession, insurance and printing industries, and nonprofit organizations.

Mr. Pedersen has a degree in business administration from the University of Texas. His education includes engineering and math. He is an author of many papers, a frequent contributing writer for the BPM Institute, BPTrends and a conference guest speaker.

THE DECISION MODEL IN CONTEXT

Intended for all readers, this section is an introduction to the Decision Model and the opportunities it offers both business and technology audiences.

Chapter 1 is a brief introduction to the motivations for the Decision Model. These motivations explain why the Decision Model has a broad impact on management practices and on business systems development and technology.

Chapter 2 provides a general understanding of the look and feel of the Decision Model. The chapter is a prerequisite for interpreting the diagrams throughout the book. The chapter references, but does not pursue in depth, the 15 principles of the Decision Model and the concept of Decision Model normalization.

The four chapters that follow explore the impact and value of the Decision Model for various disciplines. These disciplines include determining the business value of Decision Models (Chapter 3), Business Process Management (Chapter 4), Service-Oriented Architecture (Chapter 5), and business system requirements gathering (Chapter 6). Each discipline is presented in light of the Decision Model at a level appropriate for all audiences. These chapters enable the reader to understand, and perhaps share, the excitement that has greeted the adoption of the Decision Model among the current practitioners.

Chapter 7, the final chapter in the section, pulls together all ideas of the section in a realistic project. Although fictional, different aspects of the project are drawn from several real projects that helped deliver and automate the Decision Model. This chapter is vital for readers familiar with a traditional business rule approach. It reveals significant advantages that the Decision Model brings to the management and success of real-world business rule projects. Readers can find more information on the Decision Model at www.TheDecisionModel.com.

THE DECISION MODEL IN CONTEXT

Chapter 1

Why the Decision Model?

Contents

How It Began 4
    Automated Business Systems: The Beginning 5
    The One Dimension Left Behind 6
        What Is Business Logic? 6
        Why Separate Business Logic? 6
    A Disruptive Solution from the Past 7
The Current Separation of Business Logic 7
    The Need for a New Model 8
        The Advent of the Decision Model 8
        Underlying Premise of the Decision Model 8
        Five Most Interesting Characteristics of the Decision Model 10
    Rigor of the Decision Model 10
The Decision Model as an Impetus for Change 10
Summary 12
New Vocabulary Introduced in This Chapter 12
And What about the Quote 12
Discussion Points and Exercises 12

> Business rules have always represented one of the knottiest problems in application development. ... In recent years, there has been a rediscovery of the importance of business rules, and exciting research has been working to make business rules as independent as, say, database management.
>
> **Ken Orr, Chief Scientist, Ken Orr Institute**

The Decision Model is a new model that impacts not just technology trends, but also business management practices. It brings to the world of business rules a well-defined structure based on the inherent nature of logic, extended with integrity and normalization principles. This is similar in concept to what the Relational Model brings to the world of data.

This chapter is an introduction to the reasons for the development of the Decision Model. It begins with a historical perspective of the reasons leading to the model, and continues with a brief review of the role of the model in both a business and a technology context. Finally, the chapter closes with insights into the potential opportunities offered by adoption of the Decision Model.

In Chapter 2 there is an overview of the structure of the Decision Model and its notation.

How It Began

Since the inception of computer systems in the early 1950s,* there has been a constant expansion of the functionality of computerized business systems. This expansion has resulted in their playing a central role in the enterprise. Even a medium-sized organization has hundreds of discrete applications. Large organizations have thousands of applications, each succeeding application more complex than the last. Today, there are few systems in an enterprise that are not at least partially automated.

Before the advent of commercially available computers, a business carried out its processes through human effort guided by human thinking and logic. In many cases, critical processes were documented as a set of tasks and important checkpoints, along with guidance for carrying out decisions along the way. Indeed, such documentation exists today for many processes that are partly or wholly carried out by humans. The documentation together with training informs the processes and evolves them over time.

In the age of commercial computer processing, important business processes, or parts thereof, have become ideal targets for automation. The sequences of steps along with the business logic for making decisions behind those steps have been translated into program code.

Businesses have gained a great deal by automating business processes. The ability to process transactions quickly, in greater volume, and with more

---

* And even earlier, beginning with the advent of card-sorting machines.

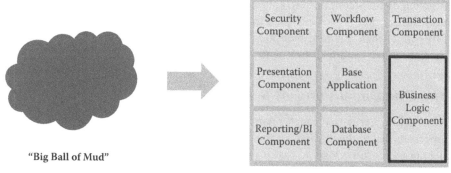

Security Component	Workflow Component	Transaction Component
Presentation Component	Base Application	Business Logic Component
Reporting/BI Component	Database Component	

"Big Ball of Mud"

Separated Application Component

Figure 1.1 Teasing out the big ball of mud. (Source: Adapted from Ken Orr "Putting Data into SOA," Cutter Consortium, Business Intelligence Vol. 7, No 11. Used with Permission.)

consistency has made all the difference in the world to most businesses. The gains have been enormous and, consequently, the wave of business automation has grown beyond initial expectations. So, too, have the sophistication of technology and the way automated systems are designed. However, a price has been paid for these great advances. That is, many, if not most, enterprises have lost track of and control over the business logic that is embedded in these systems. This is a natural result of how the design and development of automated systems have evolved.

Automated Business Systems: The Beginning

Ken Orr explains the evolution of automated business systems: "In the beginning, individual programs and systems resembled a big ball of mud* (Figure 1.1). All the

---

* "A big ball of mud is haphazardly structured, sprawling, sloppy, duct-tape and bailing wire, spaghetti code jungle. We've all seen them. These systems show unmistakable signs of unregulated growth, and repeated, expedient repair. Information is shared promiscuously among distant elements of the system, often to the point where nearly all the important information becomes global or duplicated. The overall structure of the system may never have been well defined. If it was, it may have eroded beyond recognition" (Foote and Yoder, 1999). What the authors of this famous passage left out is "logic is shared promiscuously among distant elements of the system, often to the point where nearly all the important logic becomes global or duplicated."

functionality was contained in a single framework: dimensions like reporting, database, transaction processing, presentation, workflow, security, and business rules. Over time, these major dimensions have been teased apart so that they can be developed (and modified) independently" (Orr, 2007).

The One Dimension Left Behind

Although it is true that much progress has been made in teasing out the distinct aspects buried in the big ball of mud, there has not been widespread success in teasing out the business logic so that it can be developed and modified independently. Ironically, the business logic is the very heart of automated business systems.

What Is Business Logic?

For the purpose of this chapter, business logic is simply a set of business rules represented as atomic elements of conditions leading to conclusions. As such, business logic represents business thinking about the way important business decisions are made. Examples of business decisions include the decision to grant an education loan or to pay a claim. The business logic behind such business decisions includes evaluation of a student's academic and financial status or a claim's eligibility for payment. So, business logic is the underpinning of an organization's identity, integrity, innovation, and intelligence. Business logic represents the "rules of the business" that operate perhaps thousands of times a day in service to customers and partners. They are the present and the future of the company.

Why Separate Business Logic?

Yet, many "rules of the business" are buried in program code or in people's heads. Sometimes, the business rules executing in program code are not what the business thought they were or even what the business needs them to be. They are an important consideration in implementing change and delivering enterprise agility. However, today they operate as a silent, invisible business asset rather than one worthy of being managed separately from other dimensions. As a result, they remain buried, scattered, and resistant to change.

Even when captured separately from models and requirements, the technology for storing business logic ranges from documents, spreadsheets, modeling tools, repository tools, and proprietary software, to home-grown databases. They are managed as a catalog or list of business rule statements, tied in one way or another to related deliverables. They are not managed in a common model as data is managed today. The historic impact of a common model for data is worth contemplating.

A Disruptive Solution from the Past

One of the earliest aspects teased out of the ball of mud was data. In the late 1960s and early 1970s, there emerged the recognition that data should be separated from process. An early attempt at separation was the introduction of data dictionaries or data catalogs. However, the mere separation of data into a list of data elements was not sufficient for delivering the anticipated benefits of increased data sharing and data quality. That's because design approaches still varied and were influenced by proprietary database technology. So, separation alone proved to be insufficient. There arose the need for a common design approach.

Success came with the introduction of a model for data that was different from existing models. In 1970, Dr. E. F. Codd wrote of a model (Codd, 1970) that changed forever the way the world thinks about, manages and leverages data stored in databases.* His model led to revolutionary advances in technology, methodology, career paths, academic programs, and almost every aspect related to the building of automated systems.

Codd's model, the Relational Model, is significant for many reasons, but what led to its endurance is that it provided the database field with a stable, scientific foundation. It was based only on the inherent nature of data itself, and nothing more.† Adoption of the Relational Model along with related technology and best practices significantly improved the quality of data stored in database technology. Consequently, data is now a well-recognized business asset supported by a multibillion dollar industry. Today, there are data standards, commercial data models, and a universal way of structuring most data that is a "relational way."

Nevertheless, the success of the Relational Model was not an overnight phenomenon. The model had its critics. It stirred the kind of resistance that accompanies the introduction of a disruptive invention. Yet, the eventual adoption of the Relational Model by software vendors and practitioners has been a significant contributing factor to the advent of the Information Age and the related advances in global productivity.

The Current Separation of Business Logic

Returning again to Ken Orr's insight, recent years have seen a rediscovery of business rules as an important asset worth teasing out from the ball of mud. A desire has arisen to separate business rules and make them as independent as database

---

* An analysis of the Relational Model and the Decision Model is found in Chapter 11.
† To be more accurate, the Relational Model is based on a rigorous theory (including functional dependency, normalization, and set theory) applied to the characteristics of data.

management. In fact, over the past ten years or so, books have emerged on the topic of "business rules," and adoption of business rule technology (e.g., business rule management systems) has increased. More recently, major vendors are endorsing, introducing, or acquiring business rule management system software.

As with data in the 1970s, the mere separation of business logic into a list of business rules has not proved sufficient for delivering the anticipated benefits. Again, current technical solutions play a role analogous to the proprietary database management systems of the 1970s. That is, the products themselves are excellent and mature, but proprietary. As a result, design approaches vary and are highly influenced by proprietary target technology. Although vendors are making advances in managing and maintaining such business rules in a business-friendly manner, each vendor does so in its own way. Standards and specifications groups are addressing common languages or grammars for business rules, but there is no universal model that serves as a starting point independent of language and target technology. The lesson from the data separation precedent is that large-scale success is more likely to come with the introduction and adoption of such a model.

The Need for a New Model

So, a very simple question comes to mind: Is there a model of business logic that is simple to create, interpret, modify, and automate? Is there a rigorous, repeatable, and technology-independent model that is based only on the inherent nature of business logic itself and nothing more?

Such a model would provide a missing link in today's technologies, methodologies, and business practices and also lead to technology advances that preserve the technology-independent view of business logic. As the Relational Model did for data, it would enable the separation of business logic from other concerns by providing a very specific representation for its maintenance and automation.

The Advent of the Decision Model

These possibilities instigated several years of research. The Decision Model was tested and refined, which resulted in the writing of this book. The goal now is to promote wide-scale usage of the Decision Model and continue its evolution.

Underlying Premise of the Decision Model

The Decision Model structure is based on the premise that business logic has its own existence, independent of how it is executed, where in the business it is executed, and whether or not its execution is implemented in automated systems. The Decision Model has a recognizable structure that is not the same as the structure of other kinds of models. Refer to Figure 1.2 for a quick glance at obvious visual differences among data, process, and Decision Models. With the introduction of the

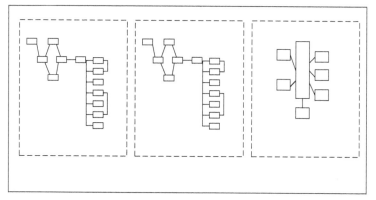

Data Models

Process Model

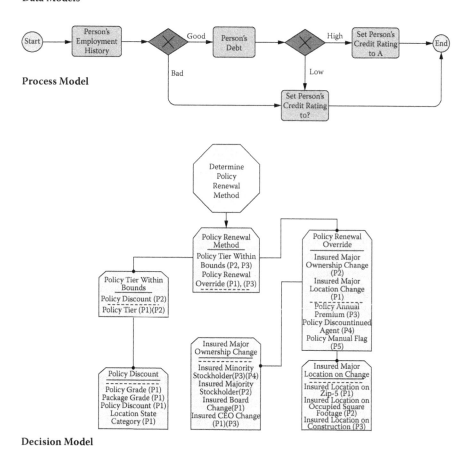

Decision Model

Figure 1.2 A glance at some models for a simple visual comparison.

Decision Model, it is improper to impose (and thereby bury again) business logic onto other kinds of models because business logic now has its own model.

Five Most Interesting Characteristics of the Decision Model

It is important that the Decision Model have its own notation and principles that make it a totally different model from other kinds of models. Five overall characteristics that make it interesting are as follows:

1. It defines a technology-independent way of organizing an important, somewhat intangible business intellectual asset. That asset is business logic.
2. The Decision Model is a pure representation of business logic. That is, it is devoid of biases from process, data, or technology. It possesses three significant features of technology-independent models: a simple structure, declarative nature, and optimal integrity.
3. Despite being independent of technology, it is easily implementable in technology and transcends current and future technology products.
4. The Decision Model is neither a language nor a grammar. It is a model. Yet, languages and grammar can be defined over the Decision Model in much the same way that SQL, as a language, was built over the Relational Model.
5. It is a model that addresses an important unsolved problem: how to effectively manage business logic and business rules, not as lists or annotations attached to or buried in other models, but in a model of their own.

Rigor of the Decision Model

Rigor is introduced into the model through a set of 15 principles, detailed in Chapters 8, 9, and 10, that define the model's structure, its declarative nature, and its integrity. These principles ensure that the model is stable, flexible, and remains technology-independent. They also introduce the concept of normal form to the model. This ensures that each business logic statement, that is, each business rule, is atomic and is placed in the one and only one proper place in the model.

The Decision Model as an Impetus for Change

The Decision Model has the potential to change current business management practices and future technology, enabling both business and IT professionals to rethink the way they view, design, execute, and govern business logic. Practice indicates that the Decision Model makes it possible for nontechnical business people to interact intuitively with their own business logic. This leads to natural business governance over business directions and agility.

Industry analysts predict significant growth* in the technology areas of Service-Oriented Architecture (SOA), Business Process Management (BPM), and Business Decision Management (BDM—also, and interchangeably, referred to as Enterprise Decision Management (EDM)). Major corporations investing in one or more of these technologies span all industries. The interest in these areas stems from a growing need to enable business agility, leverage current investments in IT infrastructure, and gain control over IT governance.

Each of these trends promises to deliver supporting infrastructure around an important and proprietary business asset: the business's logic that should drive its operational transactions in the most desirable manner. Therefore, a model of such business logic is at the center of all of these emerging areas. Industry analysts, vendors, and practitioners proclaim that such business logic today needs to be separated from other logic so as to be reusable, changeable, and deployed in corresponding technology. It needs to be delivered in appropriate technology and made available to all business processes and systems that need it and across emerging SOAs. However, without a well-formed model of business logic, there is little rigor and no solid roadmap for achieving this.

Based on experience, the Decision Model has the potential to bring about the following kinds of changes:

- IT and business management methodologies that promote business decisions and corresponding Decision Models to the level of prominent management levers
- Commercial automation software that supports decision services derived from Decision Models
- Commercial modeling and requirements software that enable specification and governance of Decision Models from business to technology
- Delivery of domain-specific decision logic that become standard commodities
- Business leaders who will view, value, challenge, and simulate their own business logic, before, after, and even if it is not, automated

This book sets out not only to present the details of the Decision Model, but also to explain how it integrates with emerging management methods.

---

* "The pure-play business process management and business rules engine software markets will outpace other software infrastructure markets from 2005 through 2010, growing by 11.8 % and 9.2 % for license revenue, respectively" (Cantara, 2006); "Web services and Web 2.0 technologies are features in many current software products deployed in Service-Oriented Architecture environments. By 2011, 63% of products in the software infrastructure market and 56% in the software application market will support Web services and Web 2.0 technologies" (Dataquest Insights, 2007).

Summary

The Decision Model is a new model aimed at representing business logic. The Decision Model is based only on the inherent characteristics of business logic itself; therefore, it is unbiased by other concerns and is very easy to create and manage.

The important points in this chapter are the following:

- There has not been wide-scale success in teasing out the business logic so that it can be developed and modified independent of other concerns.
- The Decision Model structure is based on the premise that business logic has its own existence, independent of how it is executed, where in the business it is executed, and whether or not its execution is implemented in automated systems.
- Business logic has a recognizable structure that is not the same as the structure of other assets for which there are models.
- Although the Decision Model fills a missing gap in today's technology trends, its greatest significance may be its potential to give birth to new, related directions.

A general overview of the Decision Model is presented in Chapter 2.

New Vocabulary Introduced in This Chapter

- big ball of mud
- business logic
- Relational Model
- Decision Model

And What about the Quote

The quote at the beginning of the chapter speaks of the emergence of business rules (and business logic) as a separate asset of business concern. The Decision Model is a solution to the long-standing issue of separating business logic from other dimensions in business systems, automated or not.

Discussion Points and Exercises

1. Discuss why people often resist new ideas such as the Relational Model.
2. If you want to introduce the Decision Model to an organization but suspect some people will resist it, how would you proceed?
3. Discuss symptoms you have seen or experienced indicating that business logic is mismanaged or not managed. What do you believe may have been the consequences?

Chapter 2

An Overview of the Decision Model

Contents

What Is the Decision Model? 14
   The Decision Model as an Intellectual Template 15
   The Decision Model as a Model...15
      Examples of Business Logic 16
From Business Logic to Decision Model Structure 17
   Gathering Business Logic Input...18
   Creating the Decision Model Structure..18
   Populating the Decision Model Content...18
   Distilling Sentences from the Decision Model 20
   Changing the Decision Model Content 21
   Relating Decision Model Structures...22
   The Role of Rule Patterns 24
   Not Just a Set of Decision Tables 25
Decision Model Notation and Supporting Software Tools...................................25
   The Decision Model Diagram..26
   Rule Family Table 27
   Software for Building Decision Models and Diagrams 29
The Decision Model Has Principles..30
   A Glance at Decision Model Normalization...30
Business Logic and Business Rules..31
   Consideration #1: The Logic Is of a Purely Business Nature............................32

Consideration #2: The Logic Is Intuitively Represented as Conditions and
Conclusions..33
Consideration #3: The Logic Has a Natural Boundary....................................33
Consideration #4: The Logic Is Not Known Otherwise 33
Consideration #5: The Logic Needs to Change Often.....................................34
Summary.. 34
New Vocabulary Introduced in This Chapter...35
And What about the Quote..35
Discussion Points and Exercises..35

Logic is the beginning of wisdom, not the end.

Leonard Nimoy as Dr. Spock in Star Trek

This chapter is a brief overview of what the Decision Model looks like and its graphical notation. Readers should note that the populated Rule Family structures in this chapter are not necessarily meant to be fully populated. This means that readers ought not to be concerned that the Rule Families are not complete. They are simply populated with instances that illustrate a particular point about Rule Families.

Readers interested in the full rigor of the Decision Model will find a detailed explanation in Chapters 8, 9, and 10. Definitions of all Decision Model components are summarized in Chapter 12.

What Is the Decision Model?

The *Decision Model* is an intellectual template for perceiving, organizing, and managing the business logic behind a business decision.* Chapter 1 introduced an informal definition of business logic as a set of business rules represented as atomic elements of conditions leading to conclusions. A more formal definition of *business logic* is "a means by which a business derives a conclusion from facts." So, business logic is a prescription for the way business experts want to evaluate facts in order to arrive at a conclusion where the conclusion has both meaning and

---

* The concept of a business decision is discussed later in this chapter and covered in more detail in the next chapter. For now, it is sufficient to recognize that a Decision Model is the business logic behind one business decision, and hence has very specific boundaries.

value to the business. Therefore, a business decision is defined as a conclusion that a business arrives at through business logic and which the business is interested in managing.

It follows then that business logic itself is intellectual in nature because, as Chapter 1 also points out, it represents business thinking about the way important decisions are to be made.

To make business logic tangible, common practice is to translate the business thinking into a visible, communicable form, which often is a set of business rules or business statements. These vary in format: free-form text, fill-in-the-blank templates, decision tables, decision trees, or sentences adhering to specific syntax or grammar. Regardless, it is these business rules or statements (more accurately, their intended logic) that are modeled in a Decision Model structure adhering to the Decision Model principles.

First, it is important to understand what it means for the Decision Model to be an intellectual template.

The Decision Model as an Intellectual Template

As an intellectual template, the Decision Model is a logical representation of business logic. It is, by deliberate intent, not a physical model of how that business logic is to be implemented in specific technology. It is not even a model for how that business logic is to be communicated through procedure manuals or training materials. Instead, it is an intellectual template for the full and rigorous specification of that logic. From this full and rigorous specification, if the goal is to automate it, a Decision Model can be translated into one or more target technologies through appropriate design methodologies. If the goal is for humans to follow it, a Decision Model can be translated into whatever format is most easily referenced by humans.

It is also important to understand that the Decision Model is a model and not just a list.

The Decision Model as a Model

The Decision Model is not simply a list of business rules or business statements. Rather, it is a model representing a structural design of the logic embodied by those statements.

As a model of business logic, the Decision Model is a unique representation of business logic, unlike other representations. For example, it is, by deliberate intent, not a model of how that business logic relates to processes, use cases, information, or software models. It is not a notation added to data models, fact models, process models, or any other kind of model. Instead, it is an independent representation of business logic based on the premise that business logic has its own existence, independent of how it is executed, where in the business it is executed, and whether or not its execution is implemented in automated systems. The Decision Model can be anchored to any and all other kinds of models, but maintained independently of them.

Having its own existence implies that a model of business logic has a recognizable structure that is not the same as the structure of other kinds of models.* Not only that, the Decision Model is distinct in its representation of business logic because a Decision Model aims to be

- Simple to interpret and manage
- Declarative so as to be independent of technology or processing requirements
- Optimal in integrity, meaning that its business logic is consistent within itself and aligns with business direction

As a separate model with these characteristics, the Decision Model elevates business logic to the status of a valuable organizational asset that would remain elusive without such a representation.

Examples of Business Logic

Earlier, this chapter defined business logic as a means by which a business derives conclusions from facts. The following are statements by which conclusions can be reached from facts:

- A person who has not had any jobs in the past five years is considered to have a poor job history.
- A person with more than ten jobs in the past five years is considered to have a poor job history.
- A person with a poor job history, a large mortgage, and a significant number of miscellaneous loans is considered very likely to default on a loan.
- A person with a low credit rating must not be granted an unsecured loan.
- A person's credit rating is computed according to proprietary formula A154.

First of all, each of these statements is expressed in the way that a business person might express it. None is stated in terse, forced, unnatural, or pseudocode format. The expressions are business-friendly and serve as a starting point. The goal is to discover the intended business logic behind the statements and translate it into a more rigorous form in a Decision Model. In fact, a natural language statement can

---

* Examples of other kinds of models include process models, data models, object models, and other kinds of architectural models (e.g., enterprise architecture, system architecture, and technology architecture models).

be generated from the Decision Model that is more precise than the raw material from which it started.

For now, each of the foregoing statements is, simply, one business conclusion. That is, each statement comes to a simple or complex conclusion (e.g., a loan applicant is considered to have a poor job history) based on facts (e.g., how many jobs a person has held in the past five years).

The first two statements come to a conclusion about a person's job history. The third one arrives at a conclusion regarding a person's likelihood of defaulting on a loan. The fourth comes to a conclusion about granting an unsecured loan. And, the fifth comes to a conclusion about the value assigned to a person's credit rating.

In the fourth statement, the conclusion seems like an unconditional constraint because it defines a situation that must never be true. In the fifth statement, the conclusion is the result of a computation because it provides a specific formula. Regardless, each of these statements still arrives at a conclusion using certain facts as input (i.e., conditions) specified by business leaders.

Capturing business logic, from conditions to conclusions, and refining it until it is atomic, precise, unambiguous, and aligned with business objectives is what the Decision Model and its principles are all about. A Decision Model is a prescription for how the business arrives at fact-based conclusions that collectively represent the intended business logic behind a business decision.

These individual conclusions and their representation in a Decision Model are independent of whether they support complex custom software, purchased software packages, or processes carried out by humans. In fact, a Decision Model conforms to all Decision Model principles regardless of type of automation or lack thereof. In practice, it is best to develop a Decision Model up front and then determine whether the Decision Model is best carried out by technology or by humans. If technology is most appropriate, the Decision Model can assist in selecting the technology that best fits the characteristics of the business logic behind the business decision.*

The next section introduces the basic concepts about Decision Model structure.

From Business Logic to Decision Model Structure

A quick way to learn about the Decision Model is to start with a business statement and translate it into a structural element of a Decision Model.

Suppose a financial institution provides various kinds of loans. Recently, the number of customers defaulting on loans has increased so significantly that the

---

* One characteristic of business logic, for example, is whether it is very computation-oriented or more inference-oriented. Therefore, the characteristics of the business logic behind a business decision, its complexity, and its political sensitivity should be understood up front so that the most appropriate technology for its automation can be selected.

business experts want to sharpen the business logic that determines the likelihood of such default. The business experts, therefore, need a Decision Model that comes to a conclusion about a person's likelihood of defaulting on a loan. This new Decision Model needs to be put into action. The business then needs to monitor the frequency and magnitude of subsequent loan defaults. A comparison of past to future defaults measures the effectiveness of the new Decision Model. If the improvement is not what the business anticipated, the business logic within the Decision Model will be changed, perhaps tested against sample loan applications, put into play in the business, and the results measured again.

Gathering Business Logic Input

So, experts gather for a meeting to provide insights into what the new business logic ought to be. There is much discussion. The following statement represents a conclusion reached about the likelihood of defaulting on a loan based on certain business facts:

> A person who has a poor employment history, a poor mortgage situation, and a high miscellaneous loans assessment is highly likely to default on a loan.

Creating the Decision Model Structure

The next step is to translate this free-form textual sentence into a representation in a Decision Model. The fundamental structural element of a Decision Model is a two-dimensional table relating conditions to one—and only one—corresponding conclusion. So, which part of this statement is the conclusion and which parts are the conditions?

Apparently, this statement evaluates three business facts (i.e., conditions): a Person's Employment History, Mortgage Situation, and Miscellaneous Loans Assessment. The statement comes to a conclusion about a Person's Likelihood of Defaulting on a Loan.

So, the two-dimensional structure is created, called a Rule Family, as shown in Table 2.1, representing three condition columns that are tested to arrive at the conclusion column. Rule Families throughout the book adopt a naming convention for column headings that does not include the apostrophe.

Populating the Decision Model Content

In Table 2.1, the first column contains the phrase "Rule Pattern," which is explained later in this chapter. For now, note that Table 2.1 has one column heading "Conditions" and another heading "Conclusion." Therefore, it is obvious where

Table 2.1 Simple Rule Family

	Conditions			Conclusion
Rule Pattern	Person Employment History	Person Mortgage Situation	Person Miscellaneous Loans Assessment	Person Likelihood of Defaulting on a Loan
1	Is | Poor	Is | Poor	Is | High	Is | High

to put the conditions and the conclusion. Looking closer at Table 2.1, each column has another heading. Under "Conditions," the column headings contain the name of the fact being tested: Person Employment History, Person Mortgage Situation, and Person Miscellaneous Loans Assessment. Under "Conclusion," the column heading contains the name of the conclusion being reached, Person Likelihood of Defaulting on a Loan.

The rows below these column headings are populated using two cells for each label. The first cell is for an operator to apply against the column heading and the second cell is the operand for that operator. The first condition column in the first row has an operator of "Is" and an operand of "Poor." Because this is a condition column, these are interpreted as testing whether Person Employment History is Poor. If this test is true and if the corresponding tests of Person Mortgage Situation and Person Miscellaneous Loans Assessment are true, the conclusion column delivers a conclusion that the Person Likelihood of Defaulting on a Loan is High.

It is easy to see that additional rows can be added to the Rule Family in Table 2.1, each of which will test Person's Employment History, Mortgage Situation, and Miscellaneous Loans Assessment and come to a conclusion about the Person's Likelihood of Defaulting on a Loan. Likewise, it is easy to imagine deleting rows and updating rows until the business logic conforms to what the business experts prescribe.

However, although it is possible to populate the condition columns with rows that evaluate the Person's Employment History, Mortgage Situation, and Miscellaneous Loans Assessment, it is not possible to add a row that tests Person's Credit Rating. If a Person's Credit Rating is to influence the conclusion about a Person's Likelihood of Defaulting on a Loan, another condition column is needed. So, the column headings restrict the kinds of evaluations that can populate them.

Now, some questions arise about the Rule Family in Table 2.1:

■ Do all decision makers agree with these conditions leading to this conclusion?
■ What exactly is meant by Person Employment History? What are values other than Poor?

- What is meant by Person Mortgage Situation? What are its other possible values?
- What about Person Miscellaneous Loans Assessment? Which kinds of loans are included and excluded?
- What is mean by Person Likelihood of Defaulting on a Loan and what are its possible values?
- What if Person Employment History is not Poor? What rows are needed in this Rule Family?

The answers are needed so that the Rule Family can be interpreted properly and so that its business logic is complete and consistent. Naturally, some questions may spark interesting political discussions and debates, depending on the importance and sensitivity of the conclusion itself. If there are disagreements among business experts, appropriate accountability and stewardship will need to be established for resolving these.

Distilling Sentences from the Decision Model

As mentioned earlier, it is possible to convert each row in a Rule Family into a sentence that sounds natural to a business audience and is more precise and correct than the statement from which it is derived. That's because the translation from the original statement to its representation in a Rule Family requires analysis leading to properly named labels as well as adherence to the remaining Decision Model Principles.

For now, the row in the Rule Family in Table 2.1 can be translated into any one of the following expressions:

- If/when Person Employment History is Poor and Person Mortgage Situation is Poor and Person Miscellaneous Loans Assessment is High, then (the business concludes that) the Person Likelihood of Defaulting on a Loan is High.
- A Person with Poor Employment History and Poor Mortgage Situation and High Miscellaneous Loans Assessment has a High Likelihood of Defaulting on a Loan.
- A Person has a High Likelihood of Defaulting on a Loan if all of the following are true:
    - Person Employment History is Poor
    - Person Mortgage Situation is Poor.
    - Person Miscellaneous Loans Assessment is High.

All of these expressions are equivalent to the row in Table 2.1. These expressions are referred to as the natural language form of a business logic statement. There is no need, from a Decision Model perspective, to enforce one particular kind of natural language expression over another, as long as the expression is equivalent to the representation in the Rule Family. What is important is that the labels be named and defined correctly and the corresponding conditions and conclusions be expressed correctly. It is not intended that the natural language form will be executable by a computer, but it should be well understood by a human who may be validating the business logic or even carrying it out manually.

Changing the Decision Model Content

Suppose that tomorrow, the business experts want to change some of the business logic in Table 2.1. In particular, the business experts decide that a Person whose Employment History is Poor, Mortgage Situation is Poor, but whose Miscellaneous Loans Assessment is Medium (instead of High) is highly likely to default on a loan. Where would this change be made? The answer is easy. The Decision Model will have only one Rule Family for each type of conclusion column. So, there is only one place to make this change in Table 2.1 because there is a Rule Family that already makes conclusions about Person Likelihood of Defaulting on a Loan. It already has columns for these conditions. So the change is simply made in the appropriate row.

Suppose that after more discussion, the business experts decide that a conclusion about a Person's Likelihood of Defaulting on a Loan really ought to consider an additional fact: the Person's Outside Credit Rating. Where is this condition added? Fortunately, again, the change occurs in this Rule Family because it reaches conclusions about Person Likelihood of Defaulting on a Loan. No other Rule Family is needed. However, a new condition is needed, as shown in Table 2.2.

It soon becomes obvious that there is more to know about this new fact, such as what should be its name and what kinds of values it can have. And, working with the partly populated Rule Family in Table 2.2, questions arise about how the new condition impacts the values in the already populated rows.

Table 2.2 Adding a New Condition to a Rule Family

Rule Pattern	Conditions								Conclusion
	Person Employment History		Person Mortgage Situation		Person Miscellaneous Loans Assessment		Person Outside Credit Rating		Person Likelihood of Defaulting on a Loan
1	Is	Poor	Is	Poor	Is	High	?	?	Is	High

These examples illustrate that changing business logic in a Decision Model is straightforward. That's because a Decision Model is constrained such that each conclusion has a home in one—and only one—place.

The next section looks at the need for more than one Rule Family in a Decision Model and how Rule Families relate to one another.

Relating Decision Model Structures

We return to the example of the financial institution. Table 2.2 raises the need for more information about its condition columns. Starting with the first condition, where do the values for Person Employment History come from? Does someone simply provide the values, such as Excellent, Good, or Poor? Or do the values come as input from a Web page or a file? Or are the values the results obtained by evaluating other facts?

At this point, assume the business experts point out that the value for this condition column is actually determined by evaluating other facts. The business experts come to a conclusion about Person Employment History based on facts such as a Person Years at Current Employer and the Person Number of Jobs in the Past Five Years. So, an additional Rule Family is created in which these two facts form condition columns and where the conclusion column contains the heading "Person Employment History" as shown in Table 2.3. In this way, the Decision Model now contains two Rule Families.

It is worth noting that Table 2.3 introduces the concept of an interim decision. An interim decision is a conclusion determined during the course of a transaction but which may not be permanently stored in a database.* In this case, the interim decision is Person Employment History. Its value is determined by executing the corresponding Rule Family, but the value may never be stored permanently. The value may simply serve as input to another Rule Family, sort of an in-flight conclusion.

As discussions continue with the business experts, the need arises for yet another Rule Family. This one comes to a conclusion about Person Miscellaneous Loans Assessment, which is based on two facts: a Person's Student Loans and a Person's Business Loans. Table 2.4 illustrates the three Rule Families.

It is critical to note that the conclusions in the first and third Rule Families also serve as conditions in the second Rule Family. There is a need to show these relationships. The best way is to create lines that connect related Rule Families. However, a diagram showing the full content of a Rule Family and the relationships among all Rule Families in a Decision Model quickly becomes unmanageable. It is easy

---

* Such interim decisions turn out to be important and are the glue that ties together a Decision Model. Interim decisions do not usually show up as attributes in a data model or fields in a database, if their values are not stored in a database. They may, however, be part of an object model.

Table 2.3 Building Up to Two Rule Families

Rule Pattern	Conditions									Conclusion	
	Person Employment History		Person Mortgage Situation		Person Miscellaneous Loans Assessment		Person Outside Credit Rating			Person Likelihood of Defaulting on a Loan	
1	Is	Poor	Is	Poor	Is	High	?	?		Is	High

Rule Pattern	Conditions		Conclusion
	Person Years at Current Employer	Person Number of Jobs in Past Five Years	Person Employment History

Table 2.4 Three Rule Families

Rule Pattern	Conditions		Conclusion
	Person Student Loans	Person Business Loans	Person Miscellaneous Loans Assessment

Rule Pattern	Conditions									Conclusion	
	Person Employment History		Person Mortgage Situation		Person Miscellaneous Loans Assessment		Person Outside Credit Rating			Person Likelihood of Defaulting on a Loan	
1	Is	Poor	Is	Poor	Is	High	?	?		Is	High

Rule Pattern	Conditions		Conclusion
	Person Years at Current Employer	Person Number of Jobs in Past Five Years	Person Employment History

to imagine rapidly creating many Rule Families and soon being unable to fit them into an easily viewed whole. So, another kind of diagram is needed, as illustrated later in this chapter.

For now, the next section emphasizes two more points about Rule Families: the role of Rule Patterns and a comparison to decision tables.

The Role of Rule Patterns

Suppose business experts in the financial institution continue to populate the Rule Families. As some point, the populated Rule Family is as shown in Table 2.5.

Table 2.5 comes to a conclusion about a Person's Miscellaneous Loans Assessment and requires careful inspection to understand its business logic.

First, there are three types of conditions that influence this conclusion: Person Student Loans, Person Business Loans, and whether a Person is a current customer. For now, for the sake of simplicity, the value of a Person's Student Loans and Business Loans is a simple yes or no, rather than loan amounts. However, not all three conditions contribute together to the corresponding conclusion. The first and third rows consider only whether a Person has student loans and is a current customer. In fact, if a person is a current customer and has a student loan, the business considers this as carrying a low risk (probably because the financial institution is involved in these loans). If a person is not a current customer and has a student loan, the business considers this as carrying a medium risk (perhaps because the financial institution is not able to know much about those loans).

Table 2.5 Populated Rule Family with Two Rule Patterns

Rule Pattern	Conditions						Conclusion	
	Person Student Loans		Person Business Loans		Person Customer Status		Person Miscellaneous Loans Assessment	
1	Is	Yes			Is not	Current customer	Is	Medium Risk
2			Is	Yes	Is not	Current customer	Is	High Risk
1	Is	Yes			Is	Current customer	Is	Low Risk
2			Is	Yes	Is	Current customer	Is	Medium Risk

The second and fourth rows only consider whether a person is a current customer and whether the person has business loans. A person who is not a current customer with a business loan carries a higher risk than does a person who is a customer with a business loan.

The point is that not all three types of conditions need to be evaluated to reach a conclusion about Person Miscellaneous Loans Assessment. In fact, rows two and four evaluate two conditions. Rows one and three evaluate a different set of two conditions.

In the Decision Model, a set of Rule Family rows with a common set of condition cells that are populated is called a Rule Pattern. Therefore, Table 2.5 is a Rule Family comprising two Rule Patterns. Rows one and three form one Rule Pattern, and rows two and four form another. Rule Patterns become important when the Decision Model Principles are applied to Rule Families.

The second point about Rule Families is a comparison with the traditional notion of decision tables.

Not Just a Set of Decision Tables

At first glance, the Rule Families of a Decision Model appear to be nothing more than familiar decision tables, but this is not so. A common definition of a decision table is "a table of all contingencies and the actions to be taken for each" (Wordwebonline "Decision Table"). It is true that a Rule Family in a Decision Model resembles a decision table in that both are two-dimensional structures of contingencies leading to actions or conclusions. However, the Rule Family in a Decision Model differs from a decision table in two important ways.

First, each Rule Family adheres to a full set of principles whereas a traditional decision table does not do so.* Second, not only may each Rule Family be related to other Rule Families, but Rule Family relationships are managed carefully. Traditional decision tables are not so related. So, out of these disciplined and related Rule Families, a Decision Model is formed.

Decision Model Notation and Supporting Software Tools

To fully represent the Decision Model and its principles, a Decision Model notation is needed for at least two different kinds of diagrams: the Rule Family table and the Decision Model diagram.

---

* One of the principles, for example, prescribes that a Rule Family have only one conclusion column.

The Decision Model Diagram

The Decision Model diagram depicts only the Decision Model's structure and not the detailed content of its Rule Families.

A Decision Model diagram, such as the one in Figure 2.1, begins with an octagonal shape that represents the entire business decision. It is this shape that relates to tasks within business process models and to steps within use cases, precisely at places in those models where the business decision is in play. The business decision shape also connects to business objectives, business tactics, and business requirements.

The other shapes in the Decision Model diagram represent Rule Families. The Decision Model in Figure 2.1 has six Rule Families.

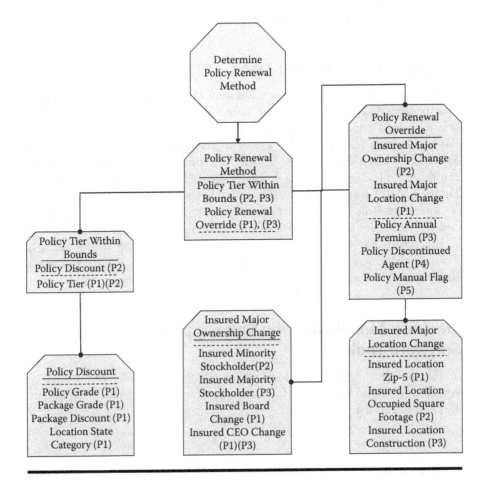

Figure 2.1   Decision Model diagram.

The Rule Family directly connected to the business decision shape is called the Decision Rule Family because its conclusion is the conclusion sought by the entire Decision Model.

The name of each Rule Family is simply its conclusion column heading. (This is possible because one of the principles of the Decision Model limits a Rule Family to having only one conclusion column). Therefore, the name of the Decision Rule Family in Figure 2.1 is "Policy Renewal Method."

All labels below the Rule Family name are the condition column headings that contribute to that conclusion. So, the Decision Rule Family in Figure 2.1 has two conditions, one named Policy Tier Within Bounds and the other named Policy Renewal Override.

The labels below the solid line but above the dotted line denote condition column headings that serve as a conclusion column heading in another Rule Family. Therefore, in Figure 2.1, the Rule Family named Policy Renewal Override has a condition column heading of Insured Major Ownership Change, which is a conclusion column heading elsewhere in the Decision Model.

The labels below the dotted line denote condition column headings that do not serve as a conclusion column heading in another Rule Family. These condition column values will be provided by known fact values (e.g., persistent data).

The solid line terminated by the dot connects Rule Families that have an inferential relationship—meaning that the conclusion of one Rule Family is used as a condition in another. The dot appears at the end of the line connecting the Rule Family whose conclusion serves as a condition in the Rule Family at the other end of the line.

The (Pnumber) denotes Rule Pattern numbers within a Rule Family. So, the Decision Rule Family in Figure 2.1 contains three Rule Patterns.

A summary of this explanation is shown in Figure 2.2, which contains the complete Decision Model diagram in the upper-left corner. The circle in that complete Decision Model diagram shows the area of the model that is magnified in the figure.

Rule Family Table

A Rule Family table provides a complete view of the content of a Rule Family. Clearly, each Rule Pattern in the diagram may represent from one to many rows of business logic statements. The Decision Model diagram enables a view of the structure of the model without having to deal with the detailed content.

Figure 2.3 shows a Rule Family table within the context of a Decision Model diagram. Again, the Decision Model diagram in the top left carries out the decision to Determine Policy Renewal Method. The circle shows the portion of the Decision Model that is magnified. The Rule Family table is the populated Rule Family named Policy Renewal Method, and this view enables a drill down to the details of all the business logic statements of that Rule Family.

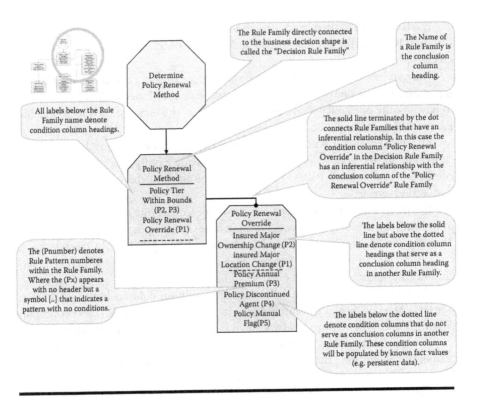

Figure 2.2   Explanation of Decision Model diagram.

The rows are the set of business logic belonging to the Rule Family. So, each business logic instance is represented by a single row in the Rule Family table. The condition and conclusion columns participate in logical expressions in the body of the Rule Family. This Rule Family has two condition columns and one conclusion column. The order of these columns is unimportant, but they are shown in a convenient way whereby the condition columns are on the left and the conclusion column is on the right. Because both these condition columns serve as conclusions in other Rule Families, the condition columns are shown below the solid line and above the dotted line. The actual business logic instances appear as if they were data in the Rule Family. A natural language translation of this Rule Family would be: "If the Policy Renewal Override is … and the Policy Tier Within Bounds is …, then Policy Renewal Method is …"

Hopefully, it has become clear that the Decision Model serves as a universal communication of business logic, regardless of industry. In fact, the person creating a Decision Model need not be an expert in the underlying industry, business, or even business decision. Access to business expertise is always needed, however.

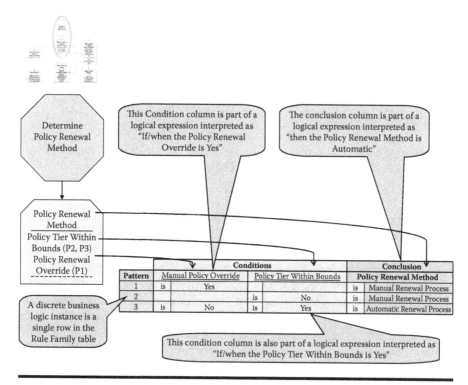

Figure 2.3   **Rule Family table in the context of a Decision Model diagram.**

Software for Building Decision Models and Diagrams

Ideally, Decision Modeling software* allows the creation of a Decision Model diagram even before it is populated. On the other hand, such software also allows for the population of Rule Families first and automatic generation of the corresponding Decision Model diagram. In either case, robust Decision Modeling software allows the viewing of the Decision Model diagram and drilling down into its Rule Family tables. Such software also allows the viewing of business objectives that drive the Decision Model and where in processes and systems that Decision Model is in play. This kind of traceability is extremely important because it enables evaluation of the impact of proposed business logic changes on processes, systems, and business objectives.

---

* The Authors retain the rights related to "Business decision modeling and management system and method, as U.S. Patent Application No. 12/130,605" for certain of the intellectual property represented in the Work. Readers interested in use of the patent should contact the authors at www.kpiusa.com.

The Decision Model Has Principles

This chapter has introduced the structural look and feel of the Decision Model and alluded to the idea that this structure adheres to specific principles. The principles of the Decision Model are divided into three groups, where each group supports a common goal from the list of characteristics at the beginning of this chapter. These goals and groups are as follows:

- Goal 1: Structural simplicity (The Structural Principles in Chapter 8)
- Goal 2: Declarative nature (The Declarative Principles in Chapter 9)
- Goal 3: Optimal integrity (The Integrity Principles in Chapter 10)

Some of the principles address Decision Model normalization, which is summarized in the next section. Some of them define the various pieces that comprise an atomic business logic representation, because a business logic statement is represented in a Decision Model in its most atomic (hence, most manageable) form.

An ideal Decision Model is one that adheres to all Decision Model principles. Yet, in reality, practitioners are often constrained by time, money, or access to knowledgeable resources. As a result, it may not be possible to ensure adherence to all of the principles. The good news is that, by understanding each principle and its goal, practitioners can understand, ahead of time, the compromises that are made in the quality of business conclusions and the repercussions that may result.

A Glance at Decision Model Normalization

Decision Model normalization is an advanced topic, covered in detail elsewhere.* It is introduced here because it is fundamental to the quality of Decision Models. That is, normalization principles applied to a Decision Model ensure that it meets a certain level of integrity. Fortunately, readers should be able to understand and apply the Decision Model principles without a comprehensive understanding of Decision Model normalization.

In a nutshell, Decision Model normalization is a philosophy for analyzing and decomposing Decision Model structures into a different set of structures that are technology independent, process independent, and more desirable than the unnormalized structures. This book introduces three basic forms of Decision Model normalization: First, Second, and Third.†

The purpose of first normal form for the Decision Model is to impose a discipline on the content so that the model can be represented and interpreted in one and only one way. Loosely speaking, first normal form for the Decision Model

---

* More information on Decision Model normal forms is found in Chapters 8 and 10.

† It is probable that higher normal forms exist, but they are beyond the scope of this book.

simply means that, in terms of the tabular picture of a Rule Family, each Rule Family row cannot be decomposed into more than one row reaching the conclusion. In other words, a Rule Family row makes one conclusion and does not contain any conclusions nested inside it. This means that a Rule Family row cannot be decomposed into more than one such judgment, which has implications for how to represent OR, OTHERWISE, and ELSE among conditions.

The purpose of second normal form for the Decision Model is to eliminate functional dependencies (i.e., inferential dependencies) involving only part of the condition key of a Rule Pattern. A Rule Pattern is in second normal form if the conclusion is fully functionally dependent (i.e., inferentially dependent) on the entire condition key.

The purpose of third normal form for the Decision Model is to eliminate functional dependencies (i.e., inferential dependencies) among conditions. A Rule Pattern is in third normal form if it is in second normal form and none of the conditions are transitively functionally dependent on other conditions. In other words, there are no hidden interim decisions in the Rule Family. All interim decisions are represented in their own Rule Family structure. Third normal form makes sure that changes are made to one and only one place in the model.

Although it is beyond this chapter to describe these normal forms in more detail, suffice it to say that they purify a set of Rule Families by removing the risk of logic errors and anomalies. So, Decision Model normalization results in one—and only one—place in the Decision Model for each atomic statement of business logic (and the correct place). Decision Model normalization also delivers a Decision Model structure whose content is semantically correct, consistent, and complete.

Business Logic and Business Rules

Chapter 1 indicated that, informally speaking, business logic is nothing more than a set of business rules represented as atomic elements of conditions leading to conclusions. For the most part, this is true, although there are various definitions for the phrase "business rules."* For the purpose of this book, the Decision Model constrains atomic elements expressed within business rules or expressed in other ways and their arrangement to produce one and only one proper structure. This means that any business rule or statement that can be expressed in a language or diagram as atomic elements of conditions leading to conclusions can be depicted in

---

* Some definitions limit business rules to constraints on data stored in databases. To avoid confusion and to be more selective, most of the chapters in this book use the phrase "business logic." The exception is where chapters contributed from other authors use the phrase "business rules." Essentially, the phrase "business logic" refers to the kinds of logic most beneficial to represent in a Decision Model, regardless of whether results of that logic are stored in a database or anywhere.

a Decision Model. Yet, it is important to note that not all such statements are created equal. Specifically, some have more value to the business than others.

So, in practice, the Decision Model is most useful for business rules or statements that can be expressed as conditions leading to conclusions that are of measurable business impact.* The reason for this distinction is that there are many kinds of statements and rules that are sometimes called business rules but which are not the ideal target for a Decision Model (even if it is possible to put them in a Decision Model).

Business logic best targeted for a Decision Model is of a purely business nature, involves evaluation of facts leading to a conclusion, represents one business decision, is not easily represented by another means, and is subject to change. These considerations lead to a model that is of high and measurable value to the business.

Each is explained in more detail in the following subsections.

Consideration #1: The Logic Is of a Purely Business Nature

Logic of a purely business nature does not include logic for determining data quality, data transformations, workflow routing, or driving interface sequences.

Data validation rules are an example worth exploring.† Most often, data validation rules are not the optimum target for a Decision Model. One reason is that they do not arrive at a business-oriented conclusion. Rather, data validation rules ensure that data meets certain requirements so that it is of good quality. Once data validation rules have been applied to data, the data can be used as facts leading to a conclusion in a Decision Model. However, the data validation rules themselves are typically not part of the Decision Model, but external to it.‡

Transformation rules contain logic for translating data from one format and representation to another. Data transformation rules do not result in a business-oriented conclusion.

Workflow or process-routing rules contain logic regarding where to send work. However, this conclusion is about managing workloads, not making purely business-oriented conclusions.

User or system interface rules come to conclusions about a particular navigation sequence through Web pages or some other interface, but do not result in a purely business-oriented conclusion.

---

* Techniques for determining the measurable business impact of a Decision Model are discussed in Chapter 3.
† In practice, many organizations select data validation rules as the target of a first Decision Model project. Sometimes these rules are chosen because the project team has a strong data background. However, in reality, these rules are not the optimum target for a Decision Model because they are usually simple, well-known, static, and documented elsewhere. Simply put, usually there is not much business value to creating a Decision Model for these rules.
‡ In a business process model, most likely there will be a task that executes data validation rules prior to a task that calls a Decision Model which relies on that data.

Consideration #2: The Logic Is Intuitively Represented as Conditions and Conclusions

When this is so, an entire web of interconnected logic emerges based on the very nature of the logic itself.

For example, data validation rules for an address are usually a list of constraints for each field in an address. A state code must be two characters drawn from the set of standard state codes. A zip code has its own type, length, and domain. The same is true for street number, street name, and town name, and other possible pieces in an address. Although it is possible to express these data validation rules as conditions leading to a conclusion of either "valid field" or "invalid field," this is not the most intuitive way to represent them. Further, most data validation rules are simple, and the set of validation rules for one field may be unrelated (or minimally related) to the validation rules for other fields. Therefore, they do not form a very interesting cohesive logic model.

Consideration #3: The Logic Has a Natural Boundary

The Decision Model captures business logic bounded by the limits of a business decision. This means that the logic is about business reasoning, not other kinds of reasoning.

In this book, **business decision** is defined as a conclusion that a business arrives at through business logic and which the business is interested in managing. So, Characteristic #3 institutes a realistic boundary around a Decision Model. Characteristic #3 requires that an entire web of business logic (i.e., a whole Decision Model) arrive at an externalized conclusion worth managing. It is the notion of business decision that elevates business logic to its highest business value.

Consideration #4: The Logic Is Not Known Otherwise

This may include logic that lies buried within system code, peoples' heads, or in imprecise, outdated manuals.

On the other hand, logic that stems from a reliable, proven representation, such as data validation rules, is not the optimum choice for a Decision Model. For example, logic that can be derived from a data model (i.e., "the brother of my father is my uncle") is best ascertained by following relationships in a data model that provide the definition of uncle. A Decision Model, while it can represent this logic, is probably not needed.

Security and authorization rules are sometimes considered as business logic for a Decision Model and sometimes not. One reason they are usually not the optimum choice for a Decision Model is they come to a conclusion about a very narrow type of judgment. The conclusion is about access to systems, data, or other resources. There are other more common and practical ways to manage these kinds of rules, usually within security and authorization software.

Data validation rules are most often represented as part of data-oriented deliverables (e.g., data models, database Data Definition Language), data transformation rules in Extract Transform Load (ETL) deliverables, workflow rules in BPMS, and so on. There is usually no pressing need to represent such rules in two different ways when current practice suffices.

Consideration #5: The Logic Needs to Change Often

The Decision Model is for managing important business logic, especially the business logic that enables enterprise agility. If target business logic hardly ever changes, other forms of documentation may suffice. Again, an example is data validation rules. These tend to be very static, once defined. So, these are not the optimum target for a Decision Model.

However, for business logic that changes, a Decision Model (and Decision Modeling tool) provides traceability for impact analysis. This traceability includes connections to other Decision Models, business process models, use cases, systems code, and business metrics impacted by changes.

Summary

This chapter presented a justification for, and brief introduction to, the Decision Model. Specifically, the chapter covered the following important concepts:

- The primary structural feature of a Decision Model is a two-dimensional structure consisting of column headings representing types of conditions and one column heading a representing a type of conclusion.
- The two-dimensional structures, when adhering to Decision Model principles, are called Rule Families.
- Rule Families connect to each other in a natural way, by means of a conclusion in one structure serving as a condition in another structure.
- The Decision Model is populated with specific instances of its conditions and conclusions.
- A Rule Family comprises Rule Patterns, which become most obvious when the Rule Family is populated.
- Anyone can interpret a Decision Model without knowing much more than the diagram and its supporting definitions.
- Decision Model normalization refines a Decision Model to minimize the risk of logic anomalies.
- The Decision Model adheres to a full set of principles.

New Vocabulary Introduced in This Chapter

- business logic
- business decision
- Decision Model
- Rule Family
- natural language form of business logic
- Rule Pattern
- interim decision
- decision table
- Decision Model normalization

And What about the Quote

One definition of wisdom is "accumulated philosophical or scientific learning" and another is the "ability to discern inner qualities and relationships" (Merriam-Webster Online Dictionary "wisdom"). The quote suggests that logic is the beginning of such wisdom. Indeed, a Decision Model represents accumulated learning about the logic within it, especially as that logic is changed over time to better achieve intended objectives. A Decision Model also allows someone to discern visually the inner details and relationships of the logic as well as its relationships to other models and considerations. So, if logic is the beginning of wisdom, the Decision Model is a mechanism for improving on that wisdom.

Discussion Points and Exercises

1. Give advantages and disadvantages of representing business logic in a model that is independent of target technology. Discuss reasons why a technology-independent and technology-specific representation may be needed.
2. For each business statement listed in the section "Examples of Business Logic," identify conditions and conclusions.
3. Create a Rule Family for each of the statements listed in the section "Examples of Business Logic."
4. What kinds of facts did you use to select your college (if you are a student) or your current employer (if you are employed)?
5. What kinds of facts do you think your college (if you are a student) or your employer (if you are employed) used to select you?

6. Discuss why you think the business logic in a Decision Model is confidential and proprietary to the business that owns it. Why would some Decision Models within a business be more proprietary than others?

7. Discuss whether you think an off-the-shelf software system would be of greater or lesser value if it came with a fully disclosed set of Decision Models. What if such software allowed purchasers to customize the business logic within those Decision Models—would that be of value?

Chapter 3

The Business Value of Decision Models

Contents

The Nature of a Decision Model's Business Value 39
Examples of Business Decisions..39
The Three Characteristics That Are Important to a Business Decision's
Business Value 41
 Characteristic #1: Its Operative Context 42
  A Business Decision in the Simple Operative Context................................43
  An Example of Business Decision in a Simple Context..............................44
  A Business Decision in the Complicated Operative Context 44
  An Example of a Business Decision in a Complicated Context.................46
  A Business Decision in the Complex Operative Context 47
  An Example of a Business Decision in the Complex Context 47
  A Business Decision in the Chaotic Operative Context 49
 Characteristic #2: Its Volume-Based Economic Impact 49
 Characteristic #3: Its Complexity of Business Logic 52
Putting the Characteristics Together 54
Applying the Business Value Characteristics: Some Practical Ideas.....................57
 Case Study..57
  Solution for Business Decision and Business Motivation 58
 Operative Context 58
  Solution for Operative Context...58
 Usefulness of the Decision Model 58
  Solution for Usefulness of the Decision Model...59

Volume-Based Economic Impact 59
    Solution for Economic Impact 59
The Business Logic Complexity 59
    Solution for Business Logic Complexity of Decision Model Pieces.............60
Summary...60
New Vocabulary from This Chapter 61
And What about the Quote? 61
Discussion Points and Exercises..61
Case Study 62

No trumpets sound when the important decisions of our life are made.
Destiny is made known silently.

Agnes de Mille

This chapter focuses on the business value of business decisions, with
emphasis on advantages of using the Decision Model to fully realize that
value.

The chapter first explains, from a business perspective, examples of business decisions and the characteristics important to their value. From here,
the chapter categorizes business decisions according to three different ways of
assessing business value and identifies those most appropriate for a Decision
Model.

Historically, business logic has been taken for granted. It operates in enterprises
today without a great deal of thought given to it, hidden from sight. It could even
be thought of as a liability rather than the powerful asset it ought to be.

The Decision Model gives form, function, and a tangible visual representation
to business logic. Business leaders can use it to expose and manage the business
logic as an instrument of business agility both in normal changing times as well as
in tumultuous crises.

So, the Decision Model emerges as a new business asset of high business value.
Further, each Decision Model has its own unique characteristics and, therefore,
each delivers different business value. Like all business investments, it is important
to understand and assess that value before embarking on the development and
management of a particular Decision Model.

The Nature of a Decision Model's Business Value

This chapter uses the phrase "business value" to denote all considerations by which a Decision Model aims to contribute to the health and well-being of a business. These considerations include the following:

- How much the Decision Model accelerates business agility
- How the Decision Model proves useful in normal, complicated, and threatening times, and in times of crisis.
- How much profit, reputation, consistency, and quality the Decision Model delivers to the marketplace
- How much valuable, expensive, and rare business knowledge the Decision Model secures
- How much the Decision Model corrects shortcomings in today's best practices, such as Business Process Management (BPM) and Business Decision Management* (BDM).

The remainder of this chapter addresses the second, third, and fourth bullets. The others are addressed in Chapter 4.

Examples of Business Decisions

According to the definition given in Chapter 2, a business decision is "a conclusion that a business arrives at through business logic and which the business is interested in managing." Table 3.1 contains seven examples of business decisions. The first column of the table shows that each business decision has a name that begins with a "deciding word" (e.g., calculate, estimate, determine) and the object of that deciding word. Further, the object of that deciding word is correlated to a conclusion fact type, which is simply the piece of information about which the conclusion is made. And, third, the business decision and its conclusion fact type belong within a business context (i.e., a business concept), the latter usually being a business object, data entity, input form, Web page, etc.

The business concepts in this table are person, claim, insurance policy, loan, inventory item, and vendor. The second row in the table denotes a business decision that comes to a conclusion about a particular attribute of the business concept of Claim. This business decision comes to a conclusion about the amount to pay on a claim, and this judgment is probably based on a complex evaluation of business criteria.

---

* BDM is also sometimes referred to as Enterprise Decision Management (EDM). This book uses the acronym BDM instead of EDM because decision management needs to be business-focused and its scope need not always be enterprisewide.

Table 3.1 Examples of Business Decisions

Business Decision	Business Concept or Context	Conclusion Fact Type
Calculate the BMI of person	Person	Person BMI (Body Mass Index)
Estimate the payment amount that should be paid on this claim	Claim	Claim Payment Amount
Determine payment eligibility of claim	Claim	Claim Payment Eligibility
Determine whether the insurance policy renewal method is to be automatic or manual	Insurance Policy	Insurance Policy Renewal Method
Determine whether this customer meets the loan prequalification requirements	Loan	Customer Loan Prequalification Status
Assess the minimum stock level for this inventory item	Inventory Item	Inventory Item Minimum Stock Level
Calculate the Vendor's Performance Index	Vendor	Vendor Performance Index

Why are business decisions, such as those in the table, so important? Taylor and Raden state that "organizations are perceived through the lens of the decisions they make" (Taylor and Raden, 2007).

However, not all business decisions are equal in value. Some are of high value, others of less value. Some are automated, others may never be automated. Any one of these business decisions, taken by itself within the context of one transaction, may seem to have a low value. However, a new realization is that the high volume of these operational decisions, taken as a group, has a huge cumulative effect on an organization's health. Other business decisions of low volume but of a strategic nature also can have a huge impact on an organization's health.

This means that there is an emerging business focus on how to better manage and automate business decisions. This is the practice of BDM. Not only does BDM focus on the business value of business decisions (and their Decision Models), BDM also advances Business Process Management (BPM) and Service-Oriented Architecture (SOA) by promoting business decisions to the status of a visible asset worthy of management. The latter topics (BDM and SOA) are covered in other chapters. The remainder of this chapter provides a means for determining the business value of business decisions whether or not they are part of BPM or SOA.

The Three Characteristics That Are Important to a Business Decision's Business Value

Business decisions vary in character a great deal, and are not made in a vacuum. There are three characteristics of a business decision that are important to its business value as well as to the applicability of the Decision Model:

Characteristic #1: Each business decision has an operative context. The operative context is the complexity of the business environment in which the business decision is made. The complexity of the business environment may range from simple to very complex. Some business decisions are made in the course of everyday business processes. Some are made during a business crisis. Some are made when relevant facts are available, whereas others are made in the "fog of war," when relevant facts are not available and intuition must substitute for them. The value of a Decision Model must take into account its operative context.

Characteristic #2: Each business decision varies in its volume-based economic impact. Each instance of a business decision has an economic impact on the business. An instance of a business decision that is strategic in nature—to acquire another company, for example—may have a greater economic impact on the organization than an instance of a business decision to grant a particular level of discount to a given group of customers. Each business decision also has a frequency of how often it is made, which is called its volume. For example, a business decision to acquire another company may only be made on a rare occasion, but business decisions about customer discounts are likely made many times a day. The collective economic impact of a business decision, then, is a combination of the economic impact of each individual instance and its volume. If a business decision granting discounts is made millions of times a day, the actual financial impact of that business decision may be equivalent to that of a major acquisition decision. The full value of a Decision Model must take into account both volume and individual financial value.

Characteristic #3: Each business decision varies in the complexity of its business logic. Some business decisions may have one or two Rule Families, each of which may contain only one or two business logic statements. On the other hand, there are business decisions that contain many Rule Families, and many hundreds, even thousands of business logic statements. Some Rule Families may contain as few as no condition columns, or perhaps only a single condition column, while others may contain many condition columns. The value of a Decision Model must take into account its complexity and the ease with which its business logic is understood and managed.

The impact of business decisions on a business is a function of all three characteristics. Each characteristic measures a different aspect of a business decision and assists in maximizing the usefulness of the corresponding Decision Model.

The following sections explain how the three categories determine the business value of business decisions and Decision Models as follows:

- The operative context determines how a Decision Model solves a business problem or opportunity.
- The volume-based economic impact provides insight into the financial value of the Decision Model.
- The business logic complexity assists in understanding the cost of developing and managing a Decision Model.

Characteristic #1: Its Operative Context

The definition of business decision given earlier stated that business decisions are conclusions arrived at through business logic, and hence derived from facts. Yet, not all business decisions made in the course of business can be made based on facts alone, because sometimes the facts are just not available. When events do not follow an expected course—due to opportunity, crisis, or unforeseen events—decisions must be made in the absence of desired facts.

These decisions have to be made by relying on the decision maker's intuition or expertise instead of some or all of the facts. These types of decisions are referred to as "pattern based" or "event based." To the extent that they are not fully fact based, they cannot be fully modeled by a Decision Model. However, in these circumstances the Decision Model still plays an interesting and important role.

The concept of operative context is explained in "The Cynefin Framework"* (Snowden and Boone, 2007). This is a "Leader's Framework for Decision Making", formulated by David J. Snowden and Mary E. Boone. The framework defines an operative context in which business decisions are made, representing these operative contexts as a continuum of "contexts."

---

* "*Cynefin*, pronounced ku-*nev*-in, is a Welsh word that signifies the multiple factors in our environment and our experience that influence us in ways we can never understand" (Snowden and Boone, 2007).

Snowden and Boone define four different operative contexts for business decisions based on the input to them, as follows:

- The Simple context, where the input consists of "Known knowns." All parties share an understanding of the facts required to make a decision.
- The Complicated context, where the input consists of "Known unknowns." This is the domain of experts, where there may be a need to work in unfamiliar environments. More than one correct answer may exist for the same input.
- The Complex context, where the input consists of "Unknown unknowns." This is when there is incomplete data, and there may be no correct answer for some or all inputs.
- The Chaotic context, where the input consists of "Unknowables." Here, the fabric of order is more than disheveled; it is rent. The events of September 11, 2001, is the example given by Snowden and Boone as requiring a series of decisions in the chaotic context based on unknowables. The financial panic of September 2008 may be another such case.

The first two contexts, the Simple and Complicated, are in the Ordered Domain, whereas the Complex and the Chaotic are in the Unordered Domain.

Although the Decision Model is obviously quite appropriate for decisions occurring in the ordered domain, it also proves useful in the unordered domain.

A Business Decision in the Simple Operative Context

In the Simple context, the "known knowns" form the natural foundation of a Decision Model because not only are the fact types known, the fact values* are also known. In other words, it is possible to identify the column headings for Rule Families, as well as the condition and conclusion expressions for each business logic statement or row.

In this context, the parties come to agreement on the Decision Model, deploy it, and measure it against relevant business objectives. Business decisions in this context are typically those that guide business processes. The sequence of tasks in the business process is purposely designed to ensure that the facts necessary for making the business decision are available when the business decision is to be made.

The usefulness of the Decision Model in this context is that it provides a shared understanding of the logic behind the business decision, ensures a complete

---

* In this chapter, we use the phrase "fact value" to mean a business logic expression for a fact type (i.e., an appropriate operator and operand). That is, a "fact value" is simply the population of a Rule Family cell.

and accurate set of logic, and enhances the agility of the corresponding business processes.

An Example of Business Decision in a Simple Context

Consider the example of a ticket-pricing decision in the airline business. Most likely, the Decision Model may be fairly large. The Decision Rule Family is likely to include fact types related to cost factors and revenue. Sample fact types for cost factors are route distance, standard cost per passenger mile, airport operation costs for each airport, and crew positioning. Sample fact types for revenue are service class, potential load factors, rates offered by competitive airlines, feeder and impact on other routes.

In many full-service airlines, such a Decision Model provides a different price for each flight, based on flight days and times. In discount airlines, the rate may be static as to flight times, and perhaps even flight days. This implies that additional condition fact types include day of year, day of week, and time of day. In the case of full service and discount airlines, additional fact types may be needed to include the impact of a return journey on the pricing decision.

Without modeling the complete business decision, the Decision Rule Family will have a large number of condition fact types, and many dependent Rule Families. However, once modeled, it will become relatively stable as, with experience, all considerations become understood and tested. The Decision Model enables all stakeholders to understand clearly the structure of the business decision and to communicate about it in common terms.

Over time, the airline can measure the profitability of the airline and of each flight to evaluate the efficacy of the pricing decisions, adjusting fact values to perfect them. So, even though the business decision itself is quite complex, it operates in the simple context because its fact types and values are known and agreed upon. Figure 3.1 is a depiction of a fictional Decision Model for the Airline Ticket Price, operating in the simple context. It shows only the Decision Rule Family, no supporting Rule Families, or the details of the Rule Patterns. This is a sufficiently detailed view of the model for the purpose of sharing an understanding of its content.

> In the Simple context, the Decision Model emerges as the primary business construct allowing capture, understanding, communication, and consistency of the business logic behind an important business decision.

A Business Decision in the Complicated Operative Context

In the Complicated context, the business decision operates with "known unknowns." In this situation, specification of the fact types or fact values requires expert advice and assistance.

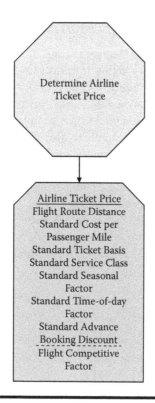

Figure 3.1 Airline ticket price Decision Model.

Typical of business decisions in the Complicated context is that the fact types (i.e., column headings), are known, but there may not be sufficient information to populate the condition or conclusion cells for those headings. The usefulness of the Decision Model, then, is that it highlights the unknowns that help to identify the kind of business expertise needed. When and if those experts are included in development of the Decision Model, it will represent content that is shared from expert to nonexpert.

Often a business decision operating in a Complicated context may need to allow for more than a single solution for the same input. If so, the usefulness of the Decision Model is that it provides a clear understanding of those multiple solutions and simplifies the comparative analysis among them. Business decisions in the Complicated context sometimes provide guidance for business processes, but are more likely to do so in Complex Event Processing (CEP),* and in other event-driven contexts.

---

* Complex event process deals with identifying meaningful events within a cloud of events using special detection mechanisms. An example is recognizing a wedding event by identifying a series of meaningful smaller events.

An Example of a Business Decision in a Complicated Context

Consider the dramatic business changes that occur when a new airline competitor enters the market, a regulatory action introduces a new type of tax, or there is a sudden increase in fuel costs. Suddenly, the previous Decision Model is no longer sufficient to come to a conclusion about ticket price because its operative context has changed from Simple to Complicated, or complex.

The airline will have to move rapidly to discover whether new fact types or fact values are necessary to reach an optimum conclusion under the new circumstance. Additional fact types may include the new tax type or a separate fuel surcharge. The second Decision Model in Figure 3.2 contains only the Decision Rule Family but with a new fact type for Fuel Surcharge Factor.

The second Decision Model in Figure 3.2 is specific enough for one to understand that the value of the Fuel Surcharge Factor is determined by a supporting Rule Family because the Fuel Surcharge Factor is above the dotted line within the

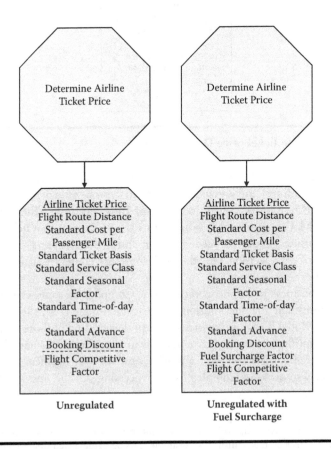

Figure 3.2 Airline ticket price Decision Model adding fuel surcharge.

Decision Rule Family. Once added, the supporting Rule Family can be developed that determines the appropriate value of the Fuel Surcharge Factor.

By using the Decision Model to understand how to integrate new fact types and fact values, the business decision is reduced to the Simple context.

In many respects the role of the Decision Model in the Complicated context is to ensure that the context is reduced to the Simple context as much as possible. When conditions change and business decisions have to be adjusted for new circumstances, the operative context threatens to become complicated. The Decision Model helps expedite the changes and avoid unnecessary complications.

> In the Complicated context, the Decision Model emerges as the primary business construct to review when conditions change, to change, extend, add, or remove columns (fact types), rows (business logic statements), or even whole Rule Families.

A Business Decision in the Complex Operative Context

In the realm of the "Unknown Unknowns," the Complex context, the Decision Model is more difficult to construct. The fact types are as yet unknown. There may be no clear solution for some or all inputs. Experimental solutions may be necessary. The usefulness of the Decision Model is that it is an aid for inventing solutions.

Business decisions in complex contexts are found in fluid circumstances such as business mergers and acquisitions, disruptions in the marketplace, major changes in regulatory environments, unexpected litigation, and similar events.

An Example of a Business Decision in the Complex Context

Continuing with the airline example, imagine the complexity that arose when deregulation was introduced. During the long history of airline regulation, the Decision Model for ticket pricing was easy to construct because ticket prices were mostly preset by regulation with only a few additional variables having to do with season, class of service, and so on. However, with deregulation, the number of additional considerations to be factored into the pricing decision were not fully known or understood at the time, even by the experts.

Airline experts had to construct business decisions based on their knowledge of markets where there was limited regulation* and by looking at economic patterns in free markets with similar characteristics as the airline market. This was truly the world of "unknown unknowns." Business decisions had to rely on pattern matching and intuition. The usefulness of the Decision Model in the Complex context is to serve as the foundation for iterative development of a solution, starting with

---

* Very few of those existed anywhere in the late 1970s when the U.S. market was deregulated.

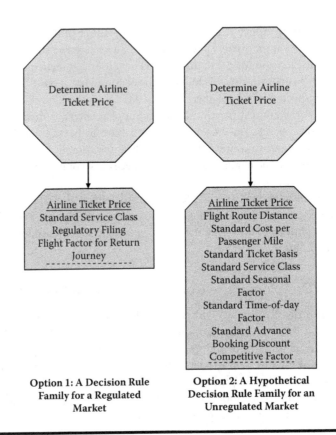

Figure 3.3   Airline ticket price Decision Model from regulated to unregulated.

what is known.* The iterative development begins with a Decision Rule Family and discovers, one at a time, the conditions (fact types) that may lead to that conclusion. In the Decision Model, the values of the fact types that form these conditions need not be immediately obvious or available. Instead, they may be discovered by the logical construction of a dependent Rule Family in a further iteration.

In Figure 3.3, Option 1 illustrates how a Decision Model may have looked in a regulated environment. Option 2 contains a hypothetical set of conditions to test (or use in a formula) to reach a conclusion in an unregulated environment. At first, these will be based on experience, advice, and best guesses of experts. As the rows of the Decision Rule Family are populated and as the supporting Rule Families are built, the condition fact types will be corrected and improved until a potentially

---

* In order to better understand problems that appear complex, unsolvable, and incomprehensible, it is useful to begin with the simple things that are known, using them as a starting point for teasing out the unknown. The Decision Model enables this path for business decisions operating in complex contexts.

stable model emerges. Once the Decision Model is tested in the marketplace, new conditions will probably be discovered and these conditions will likely evolve as competitors show their hand. This in turn will add new fact types, fact values, or new rows to the Decision Rule Family.

This is the process by which a Decision Model in the Complex context is reduced first to a complicated, and then, possibly, to a simple context. Over time, by measuring business performance, the Decision Model is improved to optimize the business decision.

> In the Complex context, the Decision Model emerges as the primary business construct for iterative invention of experimental solutions in fluid environments.

A Business Decision in the Chaotic Operative Context

The complexity and unknowns in the Chaotic context are beyond those even of the Complex context. In the Chaotic context, the business needs to make decisions in the realm of "unknowables." In this operative context, there is little applicability for a Decision Model that addresses the entire business decision. However, the Decision Model still plays an important role.

The Chaotic context is improved by finding areas within the chaos that can be separated from the chaos and developed into an area of relative order. It is in these areas that the Decision Model proves useful in bringing order to the chaos.

> In the Chaotic context, the Decision Model emerges as the primary business construct by which business leaders carve out islands of order from chaos and develop Decision Models for them.

Table 3.2 summarizes the usefulness of a Decision Model based on the operative context.

The next characteristic of a business decision that aims to contribute to the health of a business is its volume-based economic impact.

Characteristic #2: Its Volume-Based Economic Impact

Taylor and Raden (2007) state that a key factor in the categorization of a business decision is the number of times it is made in a given period, such as per day, month, or year. For example, a discount decision for customer orders may be made many times a day based on the quantity of daily customer orders. On the other hand, a business decision to upgrade the product's current features may be made as infrequently as once a year or less often. In general, operational decisions,* those guiding

---

* Sometimes called *transactional decisions*, because they guide daily business transactions.

Table 3.2 The Usefulness of the Decision Model Based on Operative Context

Operative Context	Characteristics of Inputs	Typical Characteristics of Corresponding Decision Models	Usefulness of the Corresponding Decision Model
Simple	Known knowns	• Known fact types • Known fact values • Related to business process models	• Delivers and deploys agreed-upon and shared business logic • Ensures complete and accurate business logic • Is measurable against business objectives • Enhances agility in business processes
Complicated	Known unknowns	• Known fact types (not always) • Unknown fact values • More than one possible solution for the same input • Related to complex event processing	• Identifies unknown fact types and values • Ascertains areas needing specific expertise • Delivers business logic shared from experts to nonexperts • Provides clarity to available solutions and simplifies comparative analysis • May reduce complicated business decisions to simple ones • Expedites changes when events dramatically change business conditions
Complex	Unknown unknowns	• Unknown fact types • Unknown fact values • Unclear solutions for some or all inputs • Related to fluid circumstances	• Aids in developing solutions • Delivers business logic in a form amenable to iterative development • May reduce complex decisions to complicated or simple ones

Table 3.2   The Usefulness of the Decision Model Based on Operative Context (Continued)

Operative Context	Characteristics of Inputs	Typical Characteristics of Corresponding Decision Models	Usefulness of the Corresponding Decision Model
Chaotic	Unknowables	• Any of the above • Related to crisis • Applies to islands of order within chaos	• Aids in delivering order where order can be envisioned

core business transactions on a day-to-day basis, are made in the highest volumes. In contrast, the business decisions made at the strategic level of the business are typically the lowest volume of frequency. An example of a strategic-level business decision is a merger decision which, in some businesses, may be made only once in an entire business lifetime, if ever.

An interesting observation about business decision volume is that it often occurs in inverse proportion to its individual economic value. For example, although a customer order discount decision may be made many times a day—perhaps in some businesses thousands of times an hour—the economic value of each by itself is relatively inconsequential to the enterprise as a whole. The opposite is also true. A strategic business decision may be made only once in a long period of time, but a single strategic business decision may have a profound economic value. The overall economic impact of a business decision to the enterprise is the product of its volume and its individual economic value. So, in the discount example, the value of the discount decision taken as a whole is the product of the inconsequential impact of its single execution and the thousands, perhaps millions, of times that it is invoked in a given time frame.

Thus, a business decision on one side of the volume continuum may be as important to the economic health of the enterprise as one on the other side. Indeed, Taylor and Raden point out that while a great deal of support for strategic business decision making is available, very little is provided for those operational business decisions that are made daily in the business, and that this is at the peril of the enterprise. The Decision Model provides tangible support in the management of operational business decisions—an area where such support is lacking.

Taylor and Raden (2007) highlight the importance of operational decisions and the need to better manage them in "Smart Enough Systems Manifesto." They argue as follows:

- Operational decisions are important.
  - Organizations are perceived through the lens of the decisions they make.
  - Lots of small decisions add up.
  - All decisions an organization makes should be managed as though they are deliberate.
- Operational decisions can and should be automated.
  - High-volume, operational decisions especially can, and should, be automated.
  - Traditional technology approaches will not succeed in automating decisions.
  - The overall effectiveness of automated decisions must be measured, tracked, and improved over time.
- Taking control of operational decisions is increasingly a source of competitive advantage.

As discussed, operational decisions are primarily decisions made in the simple context, and are —or should be—intrinsic to an organization's business processes.

Table 3.3 summarizes the value of a Decision Model based on the management level and volume-based economic impact of its corresponding business decision.

Table 3.3 indicates that the operational business decisions that are the subject of Taylor and Raden's book fit into the simple operative context. Hence, the corresponding Decision Models deliver the same values as any Decision Model operating in that context.

Table 3.3 highlights the fact that strategic and tactical decisions referenced in Taylor and Raden, although of high economic value, are likely to span operative contexts. Thus, the value of their corresponding Decision Models is the same as described in Table 3.2 for those contexts.

For operational business decisions, Table 3.3 notes that the Decision Model is traceable to business metrics. This is especially helpful for those business decisions that, if not done properly, result in loss of revenue, loss of customers, significant fines, reprocessing of transactions, or the need to reclaim money incorrectly paid out. All of these have individual economic value that can add up to significant economic impact.

The third way of categorizing a business decision is by the complexity of its business logic.

Characteristic #3: Its Complexity of Business Logic

The word complex means "a whole made up of complicated or interrelated parts." (Merriam-Webster Online Dictionary "complex") For a business decision, the whole is its corresponding Decision Model. Its complicated or interrelated parts are

Table 3.3   The Value of the Decision Model Based on the Management Level and Volume-Based Economic Impact

Management Level	Typical Characteristics and Economic Impact of Corresponding Business Decisions	Business Value of the Corresponding Decision Model
Strategic	• Low volume • High individual economic value • Spans simple to chaotic operative context	• Delivers the same value as its operative context; see Table 3.2
Tactical	• Medium value • Medium individual economic value • Medium collective economic value • Spans simple to chaotic operative context	• Delivers the same value as its operative context; see Table 3.2
Operational	• High volume • Small individual economic value • High collective economic value • Mostly operates in the simple operative context	• Provides a management approach for the small decisions that add up to high economic impact • Provides a starting point for high-volume operational decisions to be automated • Provides traceability to business objectives and metrics—especially relating to business decisions that result in fines, reprocessing, and reclaiming of money • Serves to provide competitive advantage and agility.

its Rule Families of conditions and conclusions and the relationships among Rule Families. So, in order to categorize a business decision by the complexity of its business logic, it is necessary to understand the quantity of Rule Families, conditions, conclusions, and the relationships among Rule Families.

The complexity of the business logic of a Decision Model is most often considered to be high when there is a large quantity of Rule Families (e.g., 10 or more), where each single Rule Family consists of a very large quantity of fact types (e.g., 10 or more), and many logic statements in a Rule Family (e.g., 50 to 100s and 1000s). On the other hand, the complexity of the business logic of a Decision Model is considered low when a Rule Family contains few fact types (e.g., fewer than 5) or perhaps only a single formula for its conclusion fact type. In between, these are the Decision Models of medium business logic complexity.

Some industries operate with very complex Decision Models, where the quantity of Rule Families and business logic statements is higher than indicated in the previous paragraph and where the relationships among them are many and complex. This is often true of the insurance and financial services industries.

Table 3.4 provides a summary of the value of Decision Models when viewed through the complexity of their business logic. Essentially, for the simplest business logic complexity, the Decision Model provides a means for documenting, sharing, standardizing, and changing that logic. As the complexity of the business logic increases, the Decision Model also serves as a mechanism for discovering that complexity, possibly simplifying it, and positioning parts of the Decision Model for appropriate automation or for human handling.

Putting the Characteristics Together

Each of the three characteristics of a business decision that contribute to its business value evaluates a different aspect of the corresponding Decision Model. Whereas assessing each of these characteristics individually provides insight into the cost and value of one aspect of the Decision Model, putting them altogether conveys a holistic view of the worth of the Decision Model to the business.

In this regard, Figure 3.4 depicts the interplay among the three major categorization schemes.

The horizontal axis represents the operative context, from Unordered on the extreme left to Ordered on the extreme right, divided into the Cynefin Framework gradations of Chaotic, Complex, Complicated, and Simple.*

The left portion of Figure 3.4 represents business decisions that operate in the unordered context and are primarily pattern based. The right portion of the figure represents business decisions in the ordered context that are primarily fact based.

The vertical axis of the graph demonstrates the volume-based economic impact as discussed by Taylor and Raden. Because the axis represents two values that are inverses of each other, Figure 3.4 represents them by a split bar. The split bar on the right indicates the relative frequency of business decisions where the frequency rises from top to bottom. The split bar on the left represents the economic value of each

---

* There is a fifth context, Disorder, but it does not apply to this analysis.

Table 3.4   The Value of the Decision Model Based on Complexity of Business Logic

Measure of Business Logic Complexity	Characteristics of Corresponding Decision Model	Business Value of Corresponding Decision Model
Simple complexity	Low quantity of: • Fact types (columns) • Business logic (rows) • Rule Families (tables) • Inferential relationships (connections) • Fact types known • Fact values known	• Delivers the same value as Decision Models operating in the simple context. • For Decision Models that are very simple in business logic complexity, the main value is in communicating and standardizing on the business logic.
Medium complexity	Medium quantity of: • Fact types (columns) • Business logic (rows) • Rule Families (tables) • Inferential relationships (connections) • Fact types known • Fact values known or require human expertise	• Delivers the same value as Decision Models operating in the complicated context. • Serves as a mechanism for discovering, gaining clarity, and standardizing business logic with medium complexity, ensuring the greatest degree of simplicity of the business logic as possible. • Serves as a basis for determining which parts of the Decision Model can be automated and which ought to be handled by humans.
High complexity	High quantity of: • Fact types (columns) • Business logic (rows) • Rule Families (tables) • Inferential relationships (connections) • Fact types unknown • Fact values unknown or require rare human expertise	• Delivers the same value as Decision Models operating in the complex and chaotic context. • Highlights the value and competitive advantage of strategic human expertise • Serves as a mechanism for discovering, gaining clarity, and standardizing business logic with high complexity, ensuring the greatest degree of simplicity of the business logic as possible.

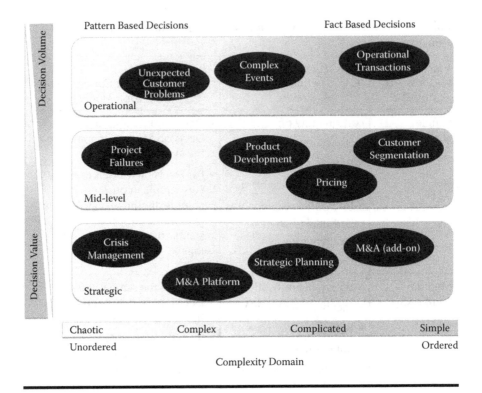

Figure 3.4 Categorizing business decision.

business decision that rises from top to bottom. Therefore, the business decisions higher on the vertical axis occur in the most volume and have the lowest individual economic impact. Conversely, the business decisions lower on the vertical axis occur in the least volume and have the highest individual economic impact.

Each bubble represents a "business decision type." A "business decision type" is simply a named set of business decisions guiding a specific business activity. For example, the business decision type named Operational Transactions represents all business decisions that come to conclusions during the execution of daily business transactions. Another example is the business decision type named Crisis Management, which represents all business decisions that come to conclusions during emergency business situations. The business decision types in the diagram are broad in nature and illustrative only. Obviously, there are unique business decision types with corresponding positions on the grid for different industries and different organizations.

Also, Figure 3.4 arbitrarily divides the business decision types among strategic, midlevel, and operational management levels.

The size of the bubble is indicative of the business logic complexity of its business decision. Figure 3.4 shows all business decisions types as the same relative size, indicating that the business logic behind each is roughly equivalent in complexity. By representing business logic complexity as the relative size of the bubble, such a diagram becomes useful in comparing the level of effort required for different business decisions in different areas of the enterprise.

The business decisions ideally suited for complete coverage in a Decision Model are those that operate in the simple or complicated domain, hence are fact based, and provide guidance in business processes. These are the business decisions on the right side of the diagram. Their corresponding Decision Models are useful for documenting, sharing, measuring, and managing changes in such business decisions.

On the left of the graph are decisions that arise from unforeseen events or complex changes in the business. The usefulness of corresponding Decision Models is to reduce complexity and invent decision solutions in unordered environments.

Applying the Business Value Characteristics: Some Practical Ideas

It is important to determine the potential business value of a business decision to understand fully the usefulness, participants, cost, effort, and benefits of its corresponding Decision Model. This chapter has provided insights into how to assess three characteristics of business decisions where the Decision Model can contribute to their value. An approach to assessing such business value is to identify, for each characteristic, where the Decision Model fits, followed by how it influences the use, participants, cost, and effort. An example is helpful in clarifying this.

Case Study

A financial institution is reevaluating its loan approval process, which is partly automated and partly handled by loan officers. The system seems to operate well in making most decisions involved in approving loans except in the area of the possibility of the applicant's defaulting on a loan. A disturbing organizational issue is that the evaluation of an applicant's likelihood of defaulting on a loan often differs depending on who the loan officer is, because different loan officers use different criteria. Another disturbing issue is that the quantity of defaulted loans over the past six months has significantly increased.

The institution wants to automate the business decision involving the applicant's likelihood of defaulting on a loan to enforce consistency and so that only exceptional situations in this regard require immediate handling by a loan officer. Therefore, new objectives are set: to decrease by 60% in one year the number of loan applications evaluated by a loan officer regarding the likelihood of default and to reduce by 25% in one year the quantity of defaulted loans.

The task is to identify a target business decision. The business decision is named starting with an appropriate deciding word and followed by the fact type to which the conclusion applies. Business motivations are identified for why it is important for the business to manage it.

Solution for Business Decision and Business Motivation

The solution consists of the following:

■ Target business decision: Determine Applicant's Likelihood of Defaulting on a Loan
■ Business Motivations
  – General
    • Greater consistency in loan approvals by automating the business decision
    • Less time spent by humans making this business decision; 60% reduction in one year
■ Fewer defaulted loans; 25% reduction of quantity of loans in one year

Operative Context

The next task is to determine the operative context for the business decision by using Figure 3.4 as a reference or the definitions in this chapter for Simple, Complicated, Complex, and Chaotic operative contexts.

Solution for Operative Context

The primary operative context for this business decision is the Simple context because the business decision is related to a business process. Most likely, the fact types can be known, but may need to be gathered from various loan officers to study a complete set of fact types. The same is true of the fact values. The business decision has some characteristics of the Complicated context because it probably will be easy to determine the most important fact types, but the fact values used by the different loan officers may be more unknown. The loan officers may not remember the fact values they use, may not be consistent in the fact values they use, or may not want to participate. However, there should be only one solution for a given loan request, and the business decision is not part of complex processing. Therefore, a reasonable use of the Decision Model is to reduce the business decision to the Simple operative context.

Usefulness of the Decision Model

The next task is to determine the usefulness of the corresponding Decision Model. To determine how much of the Decision Model can be populated and what levels of expertise need to be involved in doing so, Table 3.2 serves as a reference.

Solution for Usefulness of the Decision Model

The Decision Model will represent agreed-upon, shared, complete, and accurate business logic for determining an applicant's likelihood of defaulting on a loan that can be measured against business objectives. As a Decision Model separated from the Loan Approval Process Model, agility is increased because the business logic for the decision can be changed without changing the Loan Approval Process itself.

The Decision Model will point out which fact types and values are not well known, needing more expertise so that expert knowledge (when automated) will be in place for the nonexperts using the system.

Identification of the most appropriate fact types and fact values will probably require the involvement of those loan officers who have been approving the least number of defaulted loans.

Volume-Based Economic Impact

The next task is to identify the volume-based economic impact of the corresponding Decision Model. This involves estimating its value, based on the value of its individual conclusions as well as how frequently it is executed.

Solution for Economic Impact

The business decision of determining an applicant's likelihood of defaulting on a loan is made 25 times a day and the average loan is for $100,000. If it is assumed that 5% of the loans default, it means that 1.25 loans approved in a day will default. The business people need to provide information on how much money is lost on average for each defaulted loan. Then, the product of number of defaulted loans per day times the amount of money lost for each will provide the volume-based economic impact of improving this business decision. Assuming this can amount to hundreds of thousands of dollars very quickly, the savings due to reduction in the quantity of defaulting loans by 25% can be calculated.

Depending on the volume-based economic impact of the Decision Model, the stakeholders determine that it makes economic sense to proceed with estimates for creating and maintaining this Decision Model. Estimates involve understanding the business logic complexity.

The Business Logic Complexity

It is now necessary to determine the business logic complexity of the Decision Model so that the cost/benefit analysis of developing the Decision Model can be performed. Estimations for the quantity of Rule Families, business logic statements, and fact types are needed.

Solution for Business Logic Complexity of Decision Model Pieces

Early estimations are that there will be fewer than five Rule Families, approximately 200 business logic statements, and possibly 25 fact types. This indicates that the business logic is expected to be simple.

Based on the business logic complexity of the Decision Model, the effort is assessed by estimating the time required to define fact types, Rule Families, populate Rule Families, and resolve conflicts, confusion, and unknowns.

If the IT group already has experience in automating Decision Models in target technology, estimates can be made for incorporating the automated Decision Model into a business application.

Summary

This chapter presented various tangible ways that a business decision and Decision Model bring value to a business. The chapter concludes with some suggestions for assessing that value in planning for the development of the corresponding Decision Model.

The most important concepts in this chapter are as follows:

- As with any business investment, it is important to understand and assess the business value before investing in the development of a particular Decision Model.
- The three characteristics of a business decision that determine its business value are its operative context, volume-based economic impact, and complexity of its business logic.
- The operative context determines how a Decision Model solves a business problem or opportunity.
- The Simple operative context is when the input consists of "Known knowns."
- The Complicated operative context is when the input consists of "Known unknowns." More than one correct answer may exist for the same input.
- The Complex operative context is when the input consists of "Unknown unknowns." There may be no correct answer for some or all inputs.
- The Chaotic operative context is when the input consists of "Unknowables."
- The volume-based economic impact provides insight into the financial value of the Decision Model.
- The overall economic impact of a business decision to the enterprise is the product of its volume and its individual economic value.
- Categorizing a business decision by the complexity of its business logic means understanding the quantity of Rule Families, conditions, conclusions, and relationships among the Rule Families.
- The business logic complexity assists in understanding the cost of developing and managing its Decision Model.

New Vocabulary from This Chapter

- business value
- business concept
- operative context
- Simple operative context
- Complicated operative context
- Complex operative context
- Chaotic operative context
- volume-based economic impact
- pattern-based or event-based business decision
- fact-based business decision
- business logic complexity

And What about the Quote?

The quote warns that some of the most critical decisions of our lives are made without fanfare. Unfortunately, the same is true of critical business decisions in the lives of enterprises, sometimes putting enterprise directions at risk. By identifying those business decisions worth managing, thoughtfully analyzing the business logic behind them, and measuring their results against the changing circumstances, an enterprise can gain more control over its fate. The Decision Model provides a way to achieve that goal if it is put into place for business decisions that deliver the most business value. The task of determining the business value for each candidate business decision will highlight those for which Decision Models deliver the most business value to the enterprise, its customers, and its partners.

Discussion Points and Exercises

1. Identify a recent business decision in your organization and consider whether it operates in a simple, complicated, or complex (or perhaps even chaotic) operative context.
2. Identify at least three high-volume business decisions made in your organization, and describe why a Decision Model would be beneficial.
3. Identify a business decision that is buried within an operational system and discuss the following:
   a. What objectives the business decision aims for
   b. Whether the business decision, as currently implemented, meets the business objectives
   c. How the business logic for the business decision can be improved

4. Identify a high-value business decision that your organization may have made recently, and describe what a high-level Decision Model for that decision may have looked like.
5. For the following case study, do the following:
   a. Identify the target business decision. Name it, and make a note of business motivations for it.
   b. Determine the operative context in which the business decision operates.
   c. From the operative context, determine the usefulness and participants in the creation of the Decision Model.
   d. Discuss how to determine the volume-based economic impact of this business decision.
   e. Discuss what percentage of the volume-based economic impact to invest in the Decision Model.
   f. Estimate the business logic complexity for the Decision Model.
   g. Based on the business logic complexity, estimate a time frame for developing the Decision Model.
   h. Suggest a time frame for a pilot.
   i. Extra credit: What kinds of business metrics can be used to measure the effectiveness of the Decision Model over time?

Case Study

An etail/retail institution seems to have a problem with filling duplicate orders. Orders are submitted via e-mail, mail, fax, a phone call to customer service who places the order through the Internet, and via the Internet by the customer directly. Sometimes, customers place an order more than once if they think it didn't go through the first or subsequent time. Orders entered through the Internet directly are placed on a queue for the Order Validation System. Orders not entered via the Internet are scanned into the Order Validation System. This system generates a report of groups of orders that are candidate duplicates. Order processing clerks then process these groups to determine the actual duplicates and make sure the nonduplicates are placed on the Order Fulfillment system queue.

The disturbing business issues are as follows:

- Humans handle every possible duplicate order.
- Humans make mistakes 40% of the time.
- The company incurs great cost when shipping and paying returns on duplicate orders.
- Customer satisfaction is declining because customers are frustrated by receiving and returning duplicate orders.

Chapter 4

Changing the Game:
BPM and BDM

Contents

How the Decision Model Simplifies Business Processes 64

Definition of a Business Process 64

Example of a Business Process... 65

Definition of a Decision-Aware Business Process... 66

Distinguishing a Procedural Task from a Declarative Decision 67

Example #1: Separation of Business Decisions from Business Process 68

Example #2: A Business Process Model Never Reveals All Business Logic 70

The Secret of the Missing Business Logic 72

Example #3: Simplicity, Productivity, and Cost Savings 73

Example #4: When Business Logic Requires Deliberate Sequence 75

Example #5: Separation of Business Decision for Nonoperational
Business Decisions 77

More Real-World Examples 78

Example #6: When Business Process Excellence Alone Is Insufficient
for Competitive Advantage 78

Example #7: The Power of Smart Decisions behind Business Processes 80

How the Decision Model Advances BDM 82

Definition of BDM 83

Establishing BDM 84

More about Modeling Tools for Creating and Managing Decision Models 85

Decision Modeling Tools for Business Analysts 85

Decision Modeling Tools for Business People..86
Decision Model Tools for Enterprise Architects...87
Decision Modeling Tools for Everyone...88
Summary...88
New Vocabulary from This Chapter 89
And What about the Quote? 90
Discussion Points and Exercises.. 90

In virtually every industry, companies of all sizes have achieved extraordinary improvements in cost, quality, speed, profitability, and other key areas by focusing on, measuring, and redesigning their customer facing and internal processes.

Michael Hammer
(Hammer, 2007)

This chapter points out that the Decision Model not only changes some of today's best practices, but it also actually advances these practices in business-changing ways.

The chapter specifically addresses the impact of the Decision Model on business processes, Business Process Management (BPM), and Business Decision Management (BDM or EDM). The benefits of the Decision Model for these practices include simplification, increase in quality, savings in time and money, and strategic competitive advantage.

The previous chapter showed that business decisions made in the simple and complicated operative contexts are likely to serve as elements of guidance in business processes. Further, when those business processes are executed in high volume, the business decisions have a significant economic impact on the enterprise.

How the Decision Model Simplifies Business Processes

Therefore, this chapter introduces the important role of business decisions and the Decision Model in guiding business processes. First, a common definition of business process is needed.

Definition of a Business Process

For the purposes of this chapter, a business process is defined as a series of repeatable, defined activities taking place in a planned sequence by actors (being individuals or systems) within a defined scope of organization where the tasks add value to a good or a service for a customer.

Business processes are important; some more than others. A business designs, implements, manages, monitors, and optimizes them to obtain advantage. The goal in managing business processes is to provide customers with outstanding products or services, or to lower costs. In short, improvement in business processes aims to perfect business performance.

A business process is wide in scope, an end-to-end chain, rather than a functional narrow view. So a business process is less concerned with the functional departmentalization (functional silos) of the organization, than with the breadth of business processes that deliver value to the customer. So, a business process exists regardless of, and spanning, the functions of the organization. In this way, the focus is on the value chain of the organization. The value chain is simply the set of steps by which the business adds value to the goods or services delivered to customers.

Example of a Business Process

For example, within an airline, one business process is the customer's interaction from the moment the customer inquires about a flight to that customer's completion of the journey, referred to as the "Customer Trip Process." It involves many steps, including inquiring about flight times and cost, completing the reservation process, arriving and waiting at the airport, boarding the plane, and so on until the end of the trip. Of course, this business process involves many different departments and personnel from the airline. It may also include the hiring of a car from one of the airline's rental car partners because wide business processes may cross the boundaries of the organization to include partner and customer organizations.

In addition to spanning multiple departments or functional silos of an organization, business processes also span a significant period of time. The whole "Customer Trip Process" can take days, weeks, or months from start to finish. Hence, business processes are "long-running transactions."

To improve business processes, a business designs, implements, possibly automates, and continually improves them. A whole theory of process improvement has evolved, using techniques for creating an abstract visual representation called a business process model. This assists in gaining a shared understanding of the business process among stakeholders. Today, automated modeling tools for producing business process models can simulate the business process and serve as a source of building blocks when automating it. There are many different diagrams that represent parts of business process models, including flowcharts and activity diagrams, swim lanes and process charts, and process and functional decomposition diagrams.

Regardless of which types of diagrams are preferred, most business process models today do not separate business decisions from the business process. Instead, the business logic of the business decisions is merged into the visual representation of the business process flow. This leads to the creation of inefficient processes that are difficult to modify. Such business processes do not enable optimum business agility even when agility is the main objective. That's because such business processes are not decision aware.

Definition of a Decision-Aware Business Process

This book defines a decision-aware business process as one that is designed to distinguish between tasks that perform work (i.e., process tasks) and tasks that come to conclusions based on business logic (i.e., decision tasks). Because a decision-aware business process makes this distinction, the details behind a decision task are separated from the details behind the process task. This separation enables the details behind a decision task (i.e., business logic) to be represented in a different kind of model, specific to business logic.

However, most business processes today are not designed to be decision aware. Taylor and Raden describe the problem as follows: "Although organizations have automated standard processes with enterprise software, these operational decisions haven't been the focus of investment. They are overwhelmingly made manually or automated poorly, which is a mistake. Embedding business processes in systems to streamline operations but not managing and improving these decisions leaves half the opportunities for improvement untouched" (Taylor and Raden, 2007).

To manage and improve business decisions, they need to be separated from the business processes that rely on them. To separate business processes and business decisions, they must somehow be different from each other in a recognizable way. It turns out that they are truly different in a very significant way. In fact, the inherent nature of a business process is very different from that of a business decision. To date, however, this difference has not been well understood, but the advent of the Decision Model brings this difference to the forefront.

Essentially, a business process is procedural in nature, but a business decision is declarative in nature. However, without a clear understanding of declarative versus procedural nature, common practice involves creating business process models in which business decisions are loosely represented as just another part of the business process. In other words, it is common practice to model business processes and business decisions in a procedural manner rather than modeling the latter in a declarative manner. This common practice not only constrains the business decision unnecessarily, it seriously hinders agility for both the business process and the business decision. Understanding the difference between a business process and a business decision means distinguishing and preserving the difference between a procedural versus declarative solution.

Distinguishing a Procedural Task from a Declarative Decision

A procedural solution specifies how, in a step-by-step manner, something is to be done. So a business process model is a procedural solution because it prescribes a set of tasks that are carried out in a particular sequence. The business process model is the "How" of a unit of work.

A declarative solution, on the other hand, only specifies what needs to be done, with no details as to how, in a step-by-step manner, it is to be carried out, because sequence is irrelevant to arriving at the correct result. A Decision Model is a declarative solution because it is a set of unordered business logic, not a set of ordered tasks. A Decision Model is the "What" of a special kind of unit of work. "HOW means saying how, step by step, the work is to be done; WHAT just means saying what the work to be done is" (Date, 2000).

The declarative Decision Model for a business decision should be removed from the procedural business process so that it can be managed separately in a declarative form.

Figure 4.1 summarizes the visual distinction between a procedural business process model and a declarative Decision Model.

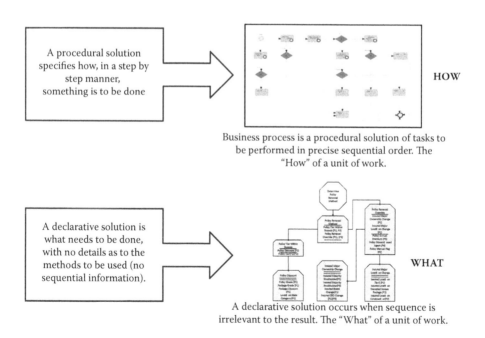

Figure 4.1   Distinction between procedural and declarative models.

Separating business decisions from business process tasks simplifies the business process model, offers more creativity in organizing the business logic, and delivers the business logic in a form that transcends technology options. These advantages become clear in the following examples.

Example #1: Separation of Business Decisions from Business Process

Consider a small piece of a business process model to determine a person's credit rating.

Option 1 in the business process models* in Figure 4.2 prescribes that first the process determines a person's employment history, and then if the result is good, the process next determines the person's debt. If the debt is low, the process sets the person's credit rating to "A." However, if the results are bad and high, respectively, the process branches elsewhere. In this business process flow, the sequence of evaluating the business criteria or conditions is set in a specific order. The process flow is rigidly specified, not allowing for alternative sequencing.

Yet Option 2 prescribes a different sequence that also works, although this process flow likewise does not allow for alternative sequencing.

Option 3 offers a significant improvement simply by removing the declarative business decision from the procedural process flow. It represents a simpler process flow consisting of only one task. That task combines the whole previously sequential set of tasks into one task, denoted as a decision task, behind which a business decision executes in a declarative fashion. Within the process flow, the decision task looks like any other task but contains a decision shape within the task box. Option 3 also includes the Decision Model diagram, which puts the Decision Rule Family in context with its related Rule Families, and Option 3 includes a Rule Family table for the Decision Rule Family. Neither the Rule Family table nor the Decision Model diagram is embedded in the process flow. They are separate deliverables, anchored to the process flow by the decision shape.

The Rule Family, by definition, implies no particular sequence among the conditions to be tested. The Rule Family in Figure 4.2 also indicates via the "?" that there are other possible combinations of conditions to consider. The Rule Family can contain as many rows as are needed to reach the correct conclusion. For that matter, it can contain additional columns if other conditions are needed to determine a person's credit rating. The Rule Family table also contains business logic for

---

* The figure uses OMG's BPMN notation for business process models, but the same principles of separating business decisions from business process tasks apply no matter what notation is used. It is important to note that the diamond shape in BPMN does not represent the idea of decision (as the diamond may in other notations) but denotes a gateway, a branching of execution. BPMN notation is discussed in Chapter 17.

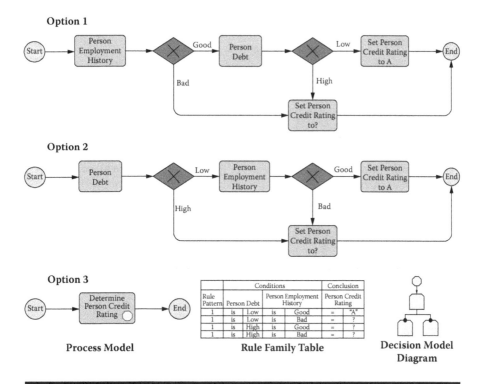

Figure 4.2 Procedural versus declarative solutions.

the logic not modeled in the business process models of Option 1 and Option 2. These include the adjudication of the credit rating for all values of person's debt and employment history other than "low" and "good." Incorporating these into the business process model rather than in the Decision Model would have enlarged and added unnecessary complexity and unnecessary sequence information to the business process model. To change or add conditions in such a business process model is far more cumbersome than doing so in the corresponding Rule Family.

Immediate observations are that Option 3 is an improvement over Options 1 and 2 because it

- Allows a much simpler business process model
- Easily highlights all possible combinations of conditions
- Permits changes in the Decision Model without changing the business process model
- Permits changes in the business process model without changing the Decision Model (supporting the principle of separation of concerns, or teasing apart the ball of mud)

Table 4.1 Important Distinctions between Business Process and Business Decision

Business Process	Business Decision
• Procedural in nature	• Declarative in nature
• Consists of tasks connected by sequence	• Consists of Rule Families connected by inferential relationships (all independent of sequence)
• Is all about how (step-by-step sequence to carry out work)	• Is all about what is to be concluded (the logic leading from conditions to conclusion)
• Improvements in business process aim for increased work efficiency	• Improvements in a business decision aim for smarter business logic
• Represented best in a procedural business process model	• Represented best in a declarative Decision Model

The differences between a business process and business decision is summarized in Table 4.1.

Table 4.2 summarizes the disadvantages of not separating business decisions from business processes.

Example #2: A Business Process Model Never Reveals All Business Logic

The previous example illustrated that business process models that do not separate business decisions from process tasks bury some business logic in the

Table 4.2 Disadvantages to Burying Decisions (Business Logic) in Business Processes

1	Forces unnecessary sequence and constraints on business logic
2	Makes changes to business process and business logic difficult
3	Adds unmeaningful complexity to business logic and business process
4	Fails to deliver a visual representation of all business logic
5	Makes governance of business process and business logic difficult to manage
6	Results in business logic and business processes that are not reusable
7	Compromises SOA

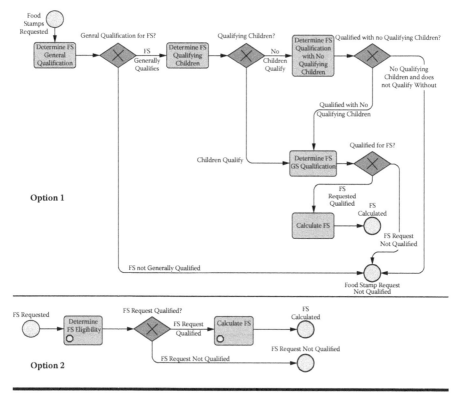

Figure 4.3   Imaginary food stamp (FS) processes.

business process model itself. Example #2 now illustrates that, even when this is so, it is usually impossible to resurrect all business logic from such a business process model.

Figure 4.3 shows two business process models for determining Food Stamp (FS) eligibility.* Option 2 depicts a much simpler business process model than does Option 1. That's because Option 1 depicts a sequence of process tasks that are forced to occur in a particular sequence but for which such sequence is actually not required. The business process model is simplified by removing parts of it that can be represented in a declarative Decision Model. So, the high-level Decision Model in Figure 4.4 represents the business decision "Determine FS Eligibility." Although the Decision Model contains business logic from several of the tasks in Option 1, namely, FS Eligibility and Children Qualification, it also contains several Rule Families that are not represented by process tasks in the business process model:

---

* This is an entirely imaginary process, and one that has no bearing on an actual food stamp eligibility process. It is, in fact, drawn from an eligibility process for a completely different federal program, but has been changed to preserve the anonymity of the real process.

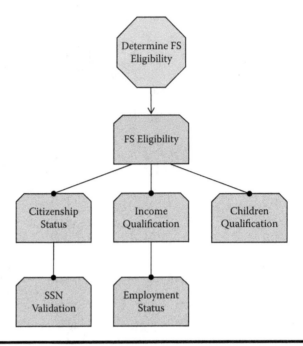

Figure 4.4 Imaginary FS Decision Model.

Citizenship Status, SSN Validation, Employment Status, and Income Qualification. So, mingling business decision logic with process flow as in Option 1 does not necessarily expose all of the business logic in that process flow.

The Secret of the Missing Business Logic

But then where is the missing business logic in business process models like those in Option 1 of Figure 4.3? Apparently, because all of the business logic is not directly visible in the business process model, some of it must be buried in one or more of the tasks. In fact, it probably is buried in many places, because some of it may be used in several of the tasks (which is the case in this business process model).

So, it is likely that some of the business logic is hidden from view in a procedural business process model such as in Option 1. Further, it is difficult, if not impossible, to resurrect all of it in one visual artifact—not even by drilling into the detail behind each of the process tasks. Therefore, the business logic is rendered unmanageable.

On the other hand, the Decision Model, by definition and purpose, resurrects all of the business logic in one visual artifact. In a populated Decision Model, all business logic is clearly visible in one place and assists in rapidly and accurately gauging the impact of suggested business logic changes without reviewing every task in which some portion of that business logic may reside.

In a Decision Model, the business logic in one business decision is a chain of inferential dependencies. The inferential nature of business logic within a business decision makes it amenable to having its own model, with distinct boundaries and distinct connections to business processes as needed. In this way, the Decision Model can be viewed, managed, and executed as one whole set of business logic, as a black box evaluating conditions and reaching a conclusion.

Example #3: Simplicity, Productivity, and Cost Savings

The business process model in Figure 4.5 is based on a real project and is a typical representation of a business process model when it is depicted without regard for whole business decisions. Some of the tasks evaluate one condition, so the sequence of such tasks imposes a sequence on the evaluation of those conditions. Further, the model contains textual annotations in red representing other business logic (or business rules) that are not represented as tasks in the model itself. So, the business logic has two different kinds of representations, neither of which seems optimal. It is not difficult to imagine that producing such business process models is time consuming, and they quickly become complex. Management of the business logic and business rules becomes tedious, if not impossible, because some of it is stated explicitly, some is buried in the business process model itself, and some is probably missing. In fact, this business process model became so unmanageable that the client gave up maintaining it, the typical result for models that mix process and logic, because they are not decision aware.

However, the business process model in Figure 4.6 is a reengineering of the one in Figure 4.5, but with one subtle and important difference: The business decisions are noted simply by the decision icon within decision tasks. (The notation style difference between the two diagrams may be ignored.) The corresponding business logic statements or business rules are nowhere on this diagram. This solution depicts tasks in a prescribed sequence, differentiating those tasks representing a conclusion carried out through business logic. The detailed business logic is captured in corresponding Decision Models.

Simplification became obvious when the quantity of business process models for the entire project was reduced from approximately 25 to 10. Additionally, at least 5 of those business process models were reused elsewhere because removing business logic resulted in more generic business process models. Most of the Decision Models also became candidates for reuse.

The diagram in Figure 4.7 illustrates one of the project's business process models and how its Decision Models represent all of the business logic alluded to in the original deliverable but more completely, accurately, and visually. The business process model, devoid of business logic in Figure 4.6, contains visible anchor points (e.g., decision shapes within task boxes) for five Decision Models. One of those Decision Models is shown in Figure 4.7, complete with its Decision Rule Family and five other Rule Families. Three of those Rule Families appear as Rule Family tables.

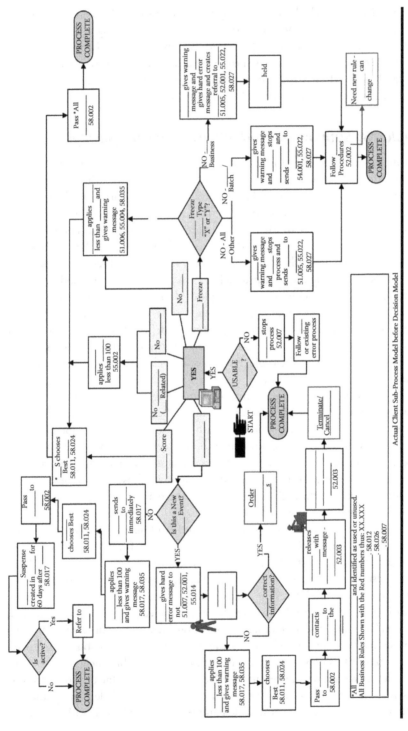

Figure 4.5 Business process model without regard for business decisions.

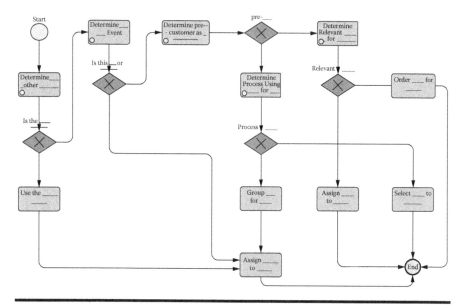

Figure 4.6   Business process model with business decisions separated.

With these deliverables, the original set of approximately 250 random groups of business rules was reduced to approximately 20 business decisions totaling 51 Rule Families in third normal form. It took much less time to create the revised business process models, new Decision Models, and populated Rule Families, compared to the original "combined" deliverables that were ultimately abandoned as unmanageable. Further, the "pure" business process models, Decision Models, and Rule Families in Figure 4.7 were dramatically easier to implement in the target technology than the original deliverables.

Example #4: When Business Logic Requires Deliberate Sequence

There are, however, certain circumstances when sequence of business logic execution is relevant to arriving at the correct conclusion. In such circumstances, a single Decision Model does not suffice. The business logic must be divided into multiple Decision Models, each linked to a separate process task. In this way, the deliberate sequence of the process tasks enforces the sequence of Decision Model execution because business process models enforce sequence and Decision Models do not.

For example, in Figure 4.3 (Option 2) the process flow has two process tasks, each one a decision task. The first task calls a decision to Determine FS Eligibility, whereas the second task calls a decision to Calculate FS. The question

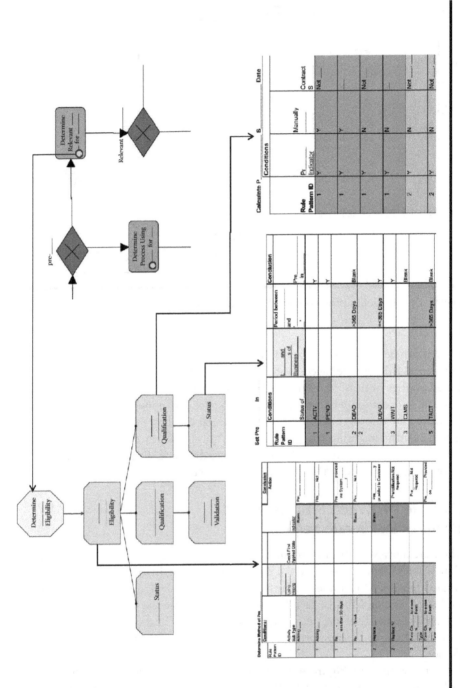

Figure 4.7 Business process model, Decision Model, and Rule Families.

is: Can this business logic be combined into a single business decision, and hence a single Decision Model? If so, then the business process model needs only one decision task, not two. Therefore, why separate the two business decisions when it is possible to calculate the value of the food stamps and set the value to zero for those who are not eligible? At first glance, this appears to be a reasonable question.

However, there are business circumstances that require separate business decisions and Decision Models. First, each business decision may be governed by a different group, hence having separate Decision Models facilitates separate governing bodies for the business logic. Second, there may be a process task that needs to take place after one conclusion based on the first conclusion before arriving at the other conclusion (i.e., sequence!) such as sending a message based on the first conclusion. These are some of the circumstances that dictate a required sequence (even if the pure business logic itself does not require a sequence).

So, the business process model is simplified and collapsed by removing business decisions from the business process model when sequence is not required within the business decision logic. Business decisions are therefore represented, not by spreading or diluting them across process tasks and imposing unnecessary sequence, but by separating them in declarative Decision Models that sit behind a decision task. In this way, the business decision is represented as a separate model from that of the business process model, can be managed independently, and can share its conclusions with business processes. This also implies that a business process model is not the optimum way to visualize the business logic of a business decision.

The previous examples dealt with operational business decisions (i.e., guiding operational business transactions). The next example illustrates that separating business decisions from business process is also powerful when dealing with strategic business processes and corresponding business decisions.

Example #5: Separation of Business Decision for Nonoperational Business Decisions

In 2000, Pitney Bowes, a $7 billion U.S. corporation, made a strategic business decision to transform itself from a hardware-oriented provider of mail-room equipment to a software and service-oriented provider. The tactical approach for achieving this was to do so through acquisitions.

So, Pitney Bowes purposely formalized its acquisition business process, identifying places where important business decisions were needed, and creating rigor around corresponding fact-based business decisions. Over time the acquisition business process and corresponding business decisions have been improved based on experience, but the essentials have remained constant. (Nolop, 2007)

The Pitney Bowes case not only better defined a strategic business process, but also developed fact-based business decisions that likely are worth tens or hundreds of millions, or even billions, of dollars and which are only executed a few times a year. By elevating the acquisition business process to a formally defined business process, and managing the business decisions separately from the business process, Pitney Bowes were able to place these strategic business decisions into the simple operative context. This enabled them to manage the business process and corresponding decisions in much the same way they manage operational business processes and business decisions.

Eight years later, the company had made 83 acquisitions, a rate of over 10 per year, while investing $2.5 billion. The acquisitions have caused revenue to grow by 25%, substantially accelerated organic growth, and made a positive contribution to net income and cash flow.

This example confirms what Chapter 3 pointed out—that the management of business decisions and Decision Models is valuable for decisions made at various management levels: strategic, tactical, and operational. Of importance is the Complex operative context and how much that may be reduced to a Simple context. If all the facts can be known, the business decision functions in the orderly operative context and can be modeled fully in a Decision Model.

More Real-World Examples

A great deal has been written about the use of Business Process Management (BPM) to achieve business objectives and to transform the enterprise into a customer-focused value chain. Organizations adopt BPM to achieve operational excellence, the epitome of which is the lowest possible cost of providing a given level (presumably high) of service. This is commendable, but is often insufficient for the truly competitive organization. After all, squeezing inefficiency out of a business process is a tactic available to all competitors in the marketplace. All other things being equal, the most efficient operator will, over time, inevitably be challenged by a competitor who achieves or exceeds the same level of efficiency. The key differentiation then becomes the organizational intelligence that operates behind critical business processes. This means that competition is not only about how efficient a business process is but also how smart its business decisions are.

Example #6: When Business Process Excellence Alone Is Insufficient for Competitive Advantage

An excellent example of business process excellence alone being insufficient for competitive advantage is Dell. Long the dominant PC company, Dell had achieved leadership through the creation of an outstanding supply chain, coupled with a razor-sharp focus on their peerless direct sales channel. With every possible cent squeezed out of their cost, and the ability to deliver attractive product at the lowest conceivable cost directly to the consumer, they dominated the PC world for

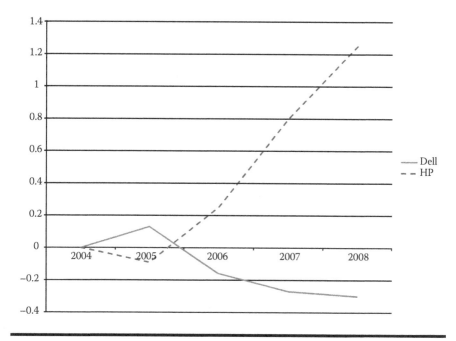

Figure 4.8   Dell versus HP stock price January 2004–January 2008.

many years. However, in the space of four short years Dell slipped to second, perhaps third, place in computer sales and their stock price has halved, as shown in Figure 4.8. What happened?

It appears that Dell's operational excellence, delivered through its hyper-efficient business processes, failed to provide the feedback that would warn of the changes in the marketplace. Even when Dell finally read the signals (in some cases only after outside analysts had pointed them out publicly), its business processes appear not to have had the ability to make the necessary adjustments.*

Most analysts today agree that Dell's failure could be attributed to several specifics, chief among which were the following:

■ Dell failed to recognize that the general consumer was transitioning to laptop computers, and so Dell remained focused on desktop computer sales.

---

* Dell likely did not realize that the business decision context in which the company was entering in late 2005 was becoming complicated, if not complex. Perhaps they did not realize that they were making business decisions with many unknowns, such as the change in the market demographics (the growth in the emerging markets), the change in the product mix (the growing popularity of the laptop market), and so on. Perhaps this was because they were not managing the business decisions separately from the business processes. By the time Dell finally took action, they were several years behind the market.

- Hewlett-Packard and other computer manufacturers were able to achieve and exceed the efficiencies of Dell's supply chain and direct supply model. Competitors retained major sales in the retail and other channels, giving them the advantage of cumulative volume through multiple channels as volume is an important element in the cost calculus of PC manufacturing.
- Dell remained focused on the U.S. market, and failed to recognize that the international market was rapidly catching up to the U.S. market in size and importance. Again, competitors were able to build volume in those markets that positioned them to exceed Dell.
- Dell's response to its cost and product disadvantage was to continually ratchet margins down to meet the competition, which it was unable to offset by any further saving in operational expense. Eventually, the point was reached when the gross margin slipped below operational cost, and the model broke completely. The company was forced, from a weak position and by 2006—very late in the cycle (some think too late)—to rethink their strategy and reorganize.
- After the first round of reorganization, by early 2008, Dell's recovery is faltering. It appears that the company has not been able to fully embrace the essential transformation they needed to make, and they remains mired in problems.

The lessons from Dell—and many others—are that key business processes must not only be efficient and consumer-friendly, they must also be smart and agile. Business processes become agile when declarative business decisions are separated from procedural business process tasks. Business processes become smart when the business decisions are governed appropriately by business leaders. Business decision governance involves monitoring the business decision performance against objectives and recognizing when events occur that raise the operative context of a business decision into the complicated, complex, or chaotic realm. When the business leadership clearly understands the business logic behind the business decisions, the impact of those decisions can be ascertained, and the business can quickly and easily make adjustments. Then, those decisions are smart and serve as intelligent business levers.

Example #7: The Power of Smart Decisions behind Business Processes

To understand the idea of smart decisions, consider the case of Parker Hannifin, a U.S.-based Fortune 500 manufacturer of motion and control equipment (Aeppel, 2007). In 2001, a long-time employee, Donald Washkewicz, became president of the company. He very soon realized that the company's pricing policies were flawed:

managers would simply pitch their prices to earn the company a gross margin of 35%, considered an industry standard.

Washkewicz realized—with the help of outside consultants—that this failed to capture the value that the company was adding for their customers. He began to understand that by being able to price according to a formula that recognized this value, he could transform the company. It took a major reorganization of the company's business processes (and a very significant change of culture) to engineer this capability. The reengineered business processes separated price, tying it to a system of intelligence gathering to accurately determine the appropriate price for a given product.*

This was not easily achieved. The old pricing rules were deeply buried, hard-coded in computer systems, many of them as recently deployed as the 1990s. But management persevered and eventually succeeded, despite the impediments created by automation itself.

Today, Parker Hannifin researches the pricing of each and every product it manufacturers, and tracks feedback on those products from its customers over time to constantly validate and adjust the price. It works closely with its customers in helping them understand the price/performance advantage of its products compared to the competition, and constantly improves the products in ways that can save the customers money.

At the same time, Parker Hannifin refined its other processes, including its "buy side" value chain (how it purchases products from suppliers), and adopted lean manufacturing. The results have been dramatic.

Parker Hannifin today is a leader in its industry, in fact a leader in almost any category of U.S. business. Between 2002 and 2007, its stock rose 160%, exceeding twofold the rise of the high-tech NASDAQ, and eightfold the growth of the Dow Jones Industrial index. Other key numbers:

- **Revenue**—Just topping the $5 billion mark in 2001; analysts estimate $12 billion for 2008.
- **Profits**—In 2002, the company achieved a profit of $130 million; in 2008, analysts estimate profit will be closing in, on $1 billion.
- **Fortune 500 Ranking**—In 2001, the company was ranked 330; in 2008, it was ranked 247.

Figure 4.9 compares the performance of Parker Hannifin against the Dow Jones Industrial Average, where they have handily and consistently beaten that average from 2003 to January 2008.

---

* When Parker Hannifin decided to pursue a "value pricing" strategy, they placed themselves into a complex operative context, and they may not have recognized, at the time, the methods of dealing with this context. Having a Decision Model, and knowing something of their context, may have shortened the cycle and reduced the difficulty of implementing this strategy.

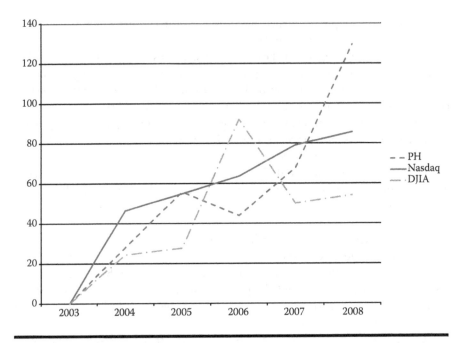

Figure 4.9 Parker Hannifin (PH) stock prices compared to NASDAQ and Dow Jones Industrial Average (DJIA).

Parker Hannifin took several of the major steps necessary to create smart processes. They separated the business decisions from the business processes, tied specific targets of performance to the business decisions, and implemented the means to measure that performance. In their case, the focus was the added value of the product to their customer. Not only did they determine this value, but actively worked with the customer to understand this value, and worked with the customer to improve the value by improving the design of the product.

Today, Parker Hannifin continues to monitor the value of products to ensure that the price remains competitive while delivering a good return to the company. As a company, it has achieved some of the highest gross profits in their sector of industry.

How the Decision Model Advances BDM

Business processes that meet the criteria of being smart and agile are those for which the business decisions have been separated from the business process, are represented in Decision Models, whose impact on the business is monitored, and whose business logic is adjusted to remain aligned with business objectives.

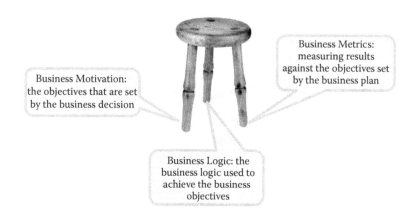

Business Metrics:
measuring results
against the objectives set
by the business plan

Business Motivation:
the objectives that are set
by the business decision

Business Logic: the
business logic used to
achieve the business
objectives

Figure 4.10   The three legs of Business Decision Management.

Definition of BDM

The practice of managing smart, agile decisions is called Business Decision Management (BDM). BDM is often referred to as Enterprise Decision Management—these terms can be used interchangeably.

Figure 4.10 summarizes the three elements of BDM: business motivation, business logic, and business metrics.

These three elements interact to create "smart" business systems, which is the goal of BDM:

- **Business Motivation:** This is the general business plan, and the specific business objective/s within that business plan, that the business decision is meant to implement.
- **Business Metrics:** These are the measurements and time periods that are set by the business objectives, and that must be achieved by the business. These metrics are arrived at in the business planning phase, and may be supported by predictive modeling techniques.
- **Business Logic:** This is the logic underlying the business decision that is implemented to achieve the business objective. This business logic is formulated to best deliver the business metrics set by the business objectives. The role of the Decision Model in BDM is to maintain a stable, normalized and complete representation of that logic.

BDM, and the role the Decision Model plays in BDM, are discussed in greater detail in several different chapters of this book:

■ Chapter 19, contributed by a foremost thought leader on the subject, is a detailed examination of EDM (Enterprise Decision Model) (EDM and BDM are essentially the same thing.)

■ Chapter 20 contains an explanation of the BDMM (Business Decision Maturity Model), which is used to assess the appropriate level of maturity in a BDM approach, taking into account risk and intended return on investment.

■ Chapter 16 includes an introduction into the BMM (Business Motivation Model), the OMG (Object Management Group) model used for business planning, and a discussion of the relationship between the BMM and the Decision Model.

■ Chapter 16 also includes a discussion of STEP, a methodology for implementing Decision Models in a BDM approach.

Establishing BDM

Early adopters of the Decision Model have begun to adopt best practices for BDM. From an organizational perspective, doing so requires seven important considerations:

■ Consideration #1: Recognize business decisions as key business assets that drive business processes. Success begins with the recognition that business decisions and corresponding business logic should be made explicit and agreed upon by relevant business stakeholders.

■ Consideration #2: Adopt the Decision Model as a separate, cohesive representation for the detailed business logic behind business decisions. The Decision Model provides a graphic representation of this business logic. The Rule Families provide a means to explore the complete logic behind the Decision Model in a clear and simple manner. In other words, the Decision Model can be used to achieve a shared understanding of the business decisions and reach a consensus around them.

■ Consideration #3: Define the active role of business people in creating, changing, and governing the important Decision Models.

■ Consideration #4: Use the Business Decision Management Maturity Model (BDMM) to develop a road map toward implementation of BDM. This will help to reduce risk and to maximize the return on investment. (See Chapter 20 for details on the BDMM.)

■ Consideration #5: Establish a center of excellence for BDM to outline methodology, deliverables, standards, and training.

■ Consideration #6: Evolve the current state of business requirements to include Decision Models.

■ Consideration #7: Prepare the technology. Select a modeling tool for creating and managing important Decision Models. Invest in specific technology for automating selected Decision Models. Consider technology to provide the necessary modeling tools to project performance and analytic tools to track the performance of business decisions. Start to build the architecture to support BDM.

More about Modeling Tools for Creating and Managing Decision Models

Decision Models may be drawn with paper and pencil. Often, a more robust solution is preferred, particularly when a Decision Model is to be shared among many stakeholders. An electronic storage medium can be as simple as a Microsoft Excel spreadsheet containing the Rule Families and Decision Models. But these options fail to provide adequate support as the quantity and complexity of the business logic grows. These options are also inadequate as changes in business logic increase.

Therefore, other than pilot or small projects, more sophisticated decision modeling tools are needed. An array of such tools, each aimed at a different level of modeler, is expected in the future as the practice of BDM matures across industries. Insights and examples are discussed in the following subsections.

Decision Modeling Tools for Business Analysts

Business analysts are most often the people who capture business logic and business rules and create Decision Models, usually for a particular project. Although many business analysts do so using spreadsheets, documents, or requirements tools, a better alternative is a product like Rule Guide from New Wisdom Software, LLC, as shown in Figure 4.11.

This figure contains a Rule Family with multiple columns and rows. Each row is a logic statement (or business rule) that can be separately maintained. The tool has features for maintaining the glossary of fact types, and other metadata that is important to the business logic, such as version, status, and business motivation. RuleGuide supports a true enterprise environment.

A business analyst can create a Decision Model diagram using a diagramming tool such as Microsoft Visio, but such a diagram lacks Rule Family content and metadata. Therefore, the business analyst can next enter Rule Family content into Rule Guide to better manage the content and add relevant metadata.

The advantage of emerging tools like this one for business analysts is that they deliver functionality specific to the Decision Model and Rule Families. Therefore, use of these tools is superior to paper and pencil, spreadsheets, or extensions to requirements tools.

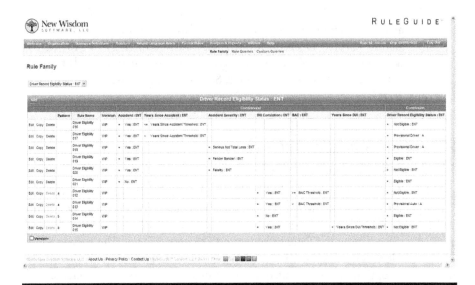

Figure 4.11   Sample screen from Rule Guide by New Wisdom Software. (Source: New Wisdom Software, LLC. Used with permission.)

Decision Modeling Tools for Business People

On the horizon are tools that enable a person who is neither a business analyst nor a technical person to create simple models and simple business requirements, probably for a particular project. Using one of these tools, a business person can create a simple business process model and a set of requirements using an interface much like that of Microsoft Visio and Microsoft Excel. However, such tools would not provide sophisticated modeling or requirements capabilities or store extended metadata.

The purpose of these new tools is to enable a business person to initiate the creation of business process models, corresponding requirements, and ideally, Decision Models. Once in these tools, such artifacts can be passed onto business analysts, enterprise architects, or technical people, who embellish them with technical considerations. It is expected that requirements tools will also be Decision Model enabled. This would enable a functional requirement in the requirements tool that is implemented by a Decision Model to be traced to the relevant Decision Model. Decision Models could either be created within the requirements tool, or in an external tool.

At the time of this writing, such tools for business people are just emerging, so functional details are not yet available. RuleGuide is a step in this direction, and it will be interesting to see if the product evolves to fulfill this promise.

The advantages of software tools for business people are that these people can drive the creation and management of Decision Models, at least up to a certain point. They can do so with minimal reliance on a business analyst or technical support.

Decision Model Tools for Enterprise Architects

Another kind of tool is a Decision Modeling tool aimed at enterprise architects. These tools integrate Decision Modeling with a business process modeling tool such as an Enterprise Architecture (EA) repository. This combination enables a sophisticated modeler to switch among views of the business process model, a decision task, and a corresponding Decision Model and Rule Families. In addition, an EA repository provides the ability to trace the business decision to its corresponding business objectives and the target metrics for that business decision. This can occur for a particular project or at an enterprise level. An example of extensions for Decision Model capabilities in an EA repository, System Architect, is shown in Figure 4.12.

There are two advantages to EA repositories as Decision Modeling tools: the ability to trace from business process models to Decision Models to business objectives to metrics, as well as the ability to drill down into Rule Families and fact types. These capabilities evolve the business decision and Decision Model into a new business asset and revolutionize business requirements and systems development.

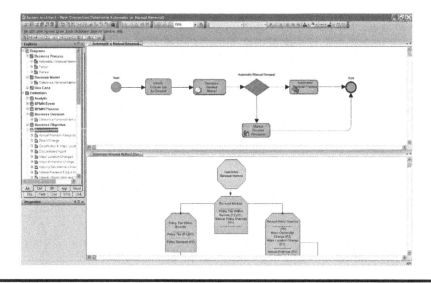

Figure 4.12 The Decision Model in extensions to an Enterprise Architecture Repository Tool (Source: Telelogic System Architect is a product of International Business Machines Corp. (IBM). Screenshot used with permission.)

Chapter 14 explains the functionality of a BDM or Decision Model tool based on EA considerations.

Decision Modeling Tools for Everyone

A vision arises for a full spectrum of Decision Modeling software.

Ideally, the creation of Decision Models is initiated by business people using a very simple and intuitive modeling tool. Such a tool supports only what pure business people want to capture about their business process models, Decision Models, and Rule Family content.

From here, Rule Family content is shared with a more sophisticated tool for use by business analysts, who manage the content regarding versions, stewardship, and perhaps automated analysis, usually on behalf of one project.

From here, the Decision Models and Rule Family content are shared with a requirements tool, or a sophisticated tool for use by enterprise architects. Within this tool, the Decision Models and Rule Families are connected to other related artifacts, including the generation of executable code, perhaps for a project or for the enterprise. Comparisons to and integration with enterprise artifacts are possible. Such a tool provides support for translating business process models and Decision Models into deliverables for SOA.

Summary

Because business logic is such an important but overlooked business asset, the Decision Model delivers significant value to all activities that involve important business decisions. Therefore, the Decision Model's impact is significantly wide—spanning business and IT projects and strategic to operational business issues. This chapter presented insights into the impact that the Decision Model has had on BPM and BDM and some insights into the future.

The most important concepts covered in this chapter are the following:

- A business process is wide in scope, an end-to-end chain, rather than a functional narrow view.
- Most business process models today do not separate business decisions from business process, and thereby fail to deliver maximum business agility.
- A decision-aware business process distinguishes between process tasks that perform work from those that carry out business decisions, and separates the details of the business decisions from the business process model into their own model.
- A business process model is a procedural solution because it prescribes a set of tasks that are to be carried out in a particular sequence.

- A Decision Model is a declarative solution because it is a set of unordered business logic, not a set of ordered tasks.
- There are, however, certain circumstances when sequence of business logic execution is relevant to arriving at the correct conclusion. In such circumstances, a single Decision Model does not suffice.
- The management of business decisions and Decision Models is valuable for business decisions made at various management levels: strategic, tactical, and operational. The operative context and how much it can be simplified are important aspects.
- Squeezing inefficiency out of a business process is a tactic available to all competitors in the marketplace.
- Competition is not only about business process efficiency but also about the smart decisions behind those business processes.
- Business processes become agile when declarative business decisions are separated from procedural process tasks.
- Business processes become smart when the business decisions are governed appropriately by business leaders.
- Separating business decisions from process tasks dramatically simplifies the business process model, offers more creativity in organizing the business logic, and delivers the business logic in a form that transcends technology options.
- The practice of managing smart, agile decisions is called "Business Decision Management" (BDM).
- A whole array of new tools to support creation and maintenance of Decision Models is likely.

This chapter has pointed out that the Decision Model changes everything about how business logic is managed. These changes begin with the way business requirements are captured and managed and continue into related methodologies, modeling paradigms, and industry specifications. Chapter 6 discusses what becomes of business requirements in light of the Decision Model. Chapter 16 discusses the impact of the Decision Model on specifications, standards, and industry practices.

New Vocabulary from This Chapter

- business process
- business process model
- decision-aware business processes
- wide and long-running processes
- procedural solution
- declarative solution
- smart processes
- Business Decision Management

And What about the Quote?

The quote tells us that reengineering business processes is an important formula for success. But implementing business process correctly is as much (and perhaps more) about managing business decisions as it is about business process. By ensuring that a business pays attention to both sides of this symbiotic relationship, the business is more likely to achieve the greatest gains from business process improvement.

Discussion Points and Exercises

1. Describe the characteristics of a business process that is agile and smart.
2. Consider a game of American baseball. What parts of the game are procedural and what parts are declarative? What is the role of the official rulebook?
3. If the example shown in Figure 4.2 were to consider a third condition for Person's Net Worth, how would you make that change to Option 1, Option 2, and Option 3?
4. Draw a high-level process model of a business process in your organization until you identify business decisions. Name the business decisions and determine what the business objectives of each may be.
5. Document a use case or business process model (the successful scenario) by which an applicant can check out his or her qualifications for a loan from the Web, based on the following business expert interview:

   > "A typical customer would like to begin by first selecting the type of loan he or she is interested in.
   >
   > Of course, if the system can determine that the customer is already a known customer, it can automatically know some of the information about him or her.
   >
   > It then presents the customer with the loan-specific screen, but allows the customer to change some of the information about himself or herself.
   >
   > The system would then determine whether the income is valid with respect to the loan.
   >
   > It would then determine if there are any factors that might impact the customer's ability to repay the loan, such as the existence of other loans.
   >
   > Finally, it evaluates all of these results and determines if the customer prequalifies for the loan.
   >
   > If so, it determines the interest rate."

Chapter 5

SOA and the Decision Model

Contents

What Is SOA? 92
    What Is a Service? 92
    SOA's Broad Perspective and Details 93
    SOA as the Next Generation of Computer Systems Architecture 93
    Why Is SOA Important? 93
    SOA as a Layered Architecture 94
    SOA's Service Inventory 95
SOA Service Roles 95
    Why Businesspeople Should Care about SOA Service Roles 96
What Everyone Needs to Know about SOA and the Decision Model 96
    How the Decision Model Makes SOA Even More Important 98
Summary 98
New Vocabulary Introduced in This Chapter 99
And What about the Quote 100
Discussion Points and Exercises 100
    Exercises Based on Chapter 5 100
    Exercises Based on Chapter 15 100

A doctor can bury his mistakes but an architect can only advise his client to plant vines.

Frank Lloyd Wright

This chapter is a cursory introduction to SOA with emphasis on the advancements made possible by the Decision Model.

This chapter is mostly nontechnical and, therefore, appropriate for all audiences. It describes SOA only to the point of introducing the role of the Decision Model in it. The content of this chapter is based on Chapter 15, contributed by a recognized expert on the subject, Mike Rosen. Readers who wish to obtain a more comprehensive technical treatment should refer to that chapter.

Because this chapter focuses on SOA in light of the Decision Model, it is short. It starts with a definition of SOA and explains its importance. From here, the chapter provides a definition of service, explaining the four layers in SOA and different service roles. The chapter concludes with insights into how the Decision Model is used in, and improves, current SOA practices.

From a business perspective, the Decision Model serves as the framework for business logic that can be initiated, validated, and managed by businesspeople. From a technical perspective, the Decision Model serves as the natural mechanism for separating decision services from other kinds of services in SOA.

By definition and by name, SOA is a kind of architecture. Therefore, as an architecture, SOA implies the construction of something that results from (or seems to result from) controlled thought, not a haphazard outcome or one left to chance. A complete architecture envisions the final constructed product from a broad perspective as well as the details necessary for every aspect of it.

What Is SOA?

SOA is an architecture that applies to the construction of automated systems. As an architecture that is service-oriented, SOA implies the construction of (automated) services in an orderly, not haphazard, manner. But what is a service?

What Is a Service?

Rosen defines a service as "a discrete unit of business functionality that is made available through a service contract. The service contract specifies all interaction between the service consumer and service provider. This includes the following:

- Service interface
- Interface documents
- Service policies
- Quality of service
- Performance."

The definition does not indicate how many services an enterprise needs or acknowledge that there are services playing different roles, having different sizes, and living in different layers of the architecture. Determining these aspects is what SOA is all about and for which Rosen provides useful guidance in Chapter 15.

However, in this chapter, the most important characteristics of SOA are its broad perspective (i.e., enterprisewide) and its details (i.e., inventory of organized services).

SOA's Broad Perspective and Details

In SOA, the broad perspective is an entire enterprise needing services. The details for every aspect of those services are defined in a service inventory, along with mechanisms for organizing and integrating them in a controlled and useful manner. The task of creating and delivering a service inventory is complex. This is especially true because most businesses currently operate with a plethora of legacy systems and technologies. These need to be leveraged in the SOA but have not been designed according to the service-oriented mindset.

Nevertheless, SOA is interesting because of its broad enterprise perspective. Creating a service inventory means transcending individual business processes, tasks, business decisions, use cases, and current application silos to envision and deliver an expansive enterprise view of services.

SOA as the Next Generation of Computer Systems Architecture

SOA is the current and next generation of architectural approaches for computer systems.

Rosen reveals three trends that support this contention. First, major software platforms are moving toward SOA. Second, major application vendors are reengineering products into discrete services. Third, there has been an increase in offerings as Software as a Service (SaaS). Rosen concludes that "the steady march toward SOA is almost inevitable."

Why Is SOA Important?

SOA's enterprise view is what makes it strategic today. Rosen states that SOA represents a better, more modular, flexible way to build enterprise solutions for business processes. Aimed at the enterprise level, Rosen explains that SOA has the potential to deliver significant business value. Specifically:

- Consistency: SOA enables a single, common entry point into a business process, task, or business decision.
- Commonality: SOA enables a single point of access to common information.
- Modularity and flexibility: SOA enables an excellent mechanism for implementing modules of business functions, business decision, and information.
- Decoupling: SOA enables a means for integrating business functions and information while minimizing dependencies among them.
- Manageability: SOA enables the management of the business by service level agreements at the modular level.

SOA as a Layered Architecture

SOA is a multilayered (i.e., n-tiered) architecture. Rosen's chapter defines four layers, as shown in Figure 5.1. These layers are Business Process, Business Services, Integration Services, and Operational Resources. One layer is pure business-oriented, the Business Process layer. Two layers are service-oriented, the Business Services and

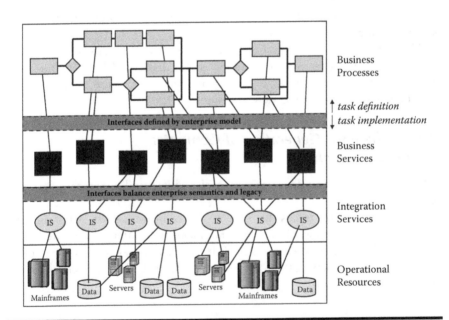

Figure 5.1 Layered SOA architecture. (Source: Rosen, M., Lublinsky, B., Smith, K. T., and Balcer, M. J. (2008). *Applied SOA: Service-Oriented Architecture and Design Strategies.* **New York: Wiley. Used with permission.)**

Integration Services layers. One layer, the Operational Resource layer, is resource-oriented, representing automated resources such as databases and applications.

Business people have an important role in the Business Processes and Business Services layers.

For the Business Process layer, as explained in Chapter 4, businesspeople define business process models consisting of process tasks, decision tasks, and Decision Models. For the Business Services layer, businesspeople assist in identifying which services will be useful in supporting the business process. Technical people design such services. So, the service inventory is based on business insight as well as technical insight. The Business Services layer is then populated with coarse-grained and fine-grained services, some of which implement the business logic of Decision Models. A fine-grained service provides a small amount of information to a task, for example, a loan applicant's information or a conclusion about a loan applicant's risk. A coarse-grained service is richer and larger in functionality, such as the approval of a loan.

SOA's Service Inventory

The basis of organization of SOA is its service inventory. Therefore, SOA's usefulness is related to how well that inventory is structured. Although there are no standards for doing so, there are useful ways in practice, such as those offered in Chapter 15. The one characteristic of a service that is most relevant to the Decision Model in SOA is its service role.

SOA Service Roles

Although there are many considerations that contribute to the identification of services (i.e., size, stewardship, etc.), a most important consideration is the separation of concerns.* Rosen presents three concerns deserving of separation and associates each with a service role. So, these are task services (for procedural action), decision services (for business logic), and entity services (for data access). Task services are about general business tasks (i.e., issuing a policy, entering an order), decision services are about declarative business logic (i.e., determining the policy renewal method), and entity services are about access and update of information sources (i.e., Customer create, read, update, or delete).

At a fine-grained level, there may be one service for each instance of these. That is, there may be one fine-grained service for each process task, one for each access to a specific information group, and one for each Decision Model.

At a more coarse-grained level, there may be one service that bundles several of these together into a composite service.

---

* The separation of concerns is discussed in Chapter 1, related to teasing out the big ball of mud of previous computer systems architecture and design.

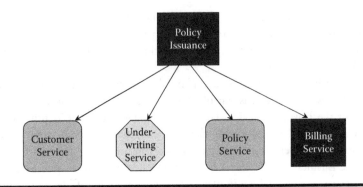

Figure 5.2 Insurance policy issuance example. (Source: Rosen, M., Lublinsky, B., Smith, K. T., and Balcer, M. J. (2008). *Applied SOA: Service-Oriented Architecture and Design Strategies.* New York: Wiley. Used with permission.)

Why Businesspeople Should Care about SOA Service Roles

Regardless of how these service roles are bundled together, most of the resulting composite services will have a business logic aspect. And, even when this aspect is bundled with other aspects, it should be defined and managed separately from the other aspects for all of the reasons given in Chapter 1. And its content should be defined and managed by the business experts. This means that the business logic should be visible to those who need to know it, changeable for those who need to change it, and shareable by those (processes) who need to use it. A good example of this is Figure 5.2, which illustrates a composite Policy Issuance service. This service is composed of four different discrete services, two of them entity services (e.g., Customer Service, Policy Service), one of them another task service (e.g., Billing Service), and the fourth a decision service (e.g., Underwriting Service).

What Everyone Needs to Know about SOA and the Decision Model

Obviously, a primary focus when developing an enterprise's SOA is the creation of the service inventory. It is also important for the service inventory to be useful for and understandable by both business people and information technology professionals. The Decision Model provides a starting point from which to create an inventory of services for business logic. That's because each Decision Model has a well-defined scope and can be measured not only for technical performance but for its impact on business performance.

Services can be at a very fine-grained or coarse-grained level. A Decision Model has granular pieces—from single instances in a Rule Family to a Rule Pattern to an

Table 5.1 A Simple Matrix Demonstrating Reuse of Business Decisions

Candidate Task Services	Business Decisions (Decision Models)				
	Claim Decisions			Policy Decisions	
	Decision Model 1	Decision Model 2	Decision Model 3	Decision Model 4	Decision Model 5
Service A	X	X	X		
Service B		X	X		
Service C	X	X	X		
Service D		X	X		X
Service E	X			X	X

entire Rule Family to partial or entire Decision Model. Because the unit of reuse in a Decision Model is essentially the Rule Family, a thoughtful design pattern casts it as the lowest granular component of a decision service—that is, that each Rule Family is potentially a stand-alone decision service. A composite decision service may be constructed by composing together the Rule Family services of the Rule Family dependencies that together make the particular decision service.

At the coarse level, multiple decision services can be used in a task service composed of many different services. For example, a task service, decision service, and corresponding entity service may be bundled into one composite service. Determination of the appropriate inventory of such composite services should be based on size, stewardship, volatility, and reusability of Decision Models as a starting point.*

Once there is a preliminary inventory of composite services, it can be cross-referenced to Decision Models to understand and confirm the enterprise need for decision services. That is, such a cross-reference reveals the opportunity for sharing decision services, thereby providing useful input to the identification of shared services. A simple concept of such a matrix is shown in Table 5.1. The input to a decision service developed from a Decision Model includes a set of values for all fact types in those Decision Models for which there are no inferential relationships to other Rule Families. Simply put, the only input a Decision Model needs is a set of values for all fact types whose values are not the conclusion from another

---

* This is much like the way enterprise data resources are identified using a CRUD (create, read, update, delete) matrix to better understand which data is shared and by whom across an enterprise.

Rule Family. The output from a Decision Model is the conclusion fact type of the Decision Rule Family. In other words, the interface to the potential decision service is rigorously defined by the Decision Model.

In Table 5.1, Decision Models 2 and 3 appear to be of interest to most of the candidate task services, whereas Decision Model 4 is relevant only to one. At the very least, this points out that the design and delivery of the decision services for Decision Models 2 and 3 need to consider their wide enterprise usage.

Regardless, most services (other than fine-grained task or entity services) are likely to contain a business logic aspect. It is important that business logic be separated in a manner enabling it to be defined and managed by the business. Therefore, services should always be built with the business logic organized into a Decision Model and separated into a separate service, even if the decision service is never used in a stand-alone mode.

How the Decision Model Makes SOA Even More Important

A subtle value of SOA is that, combined with the Decision Model, it allows the separation of business logic from other aspects in a manner that other architectures do not. This is a major differentiator because it solves an important business challenge and reconnects the business to the business logic automated in its technology. The separation of business logic into discrete services also delivers maximum agility.

It is extremely important to understand and promote the role of business people in creating and managing Decision Models, regardless of how those models are implemented as services in SOA. However, the concept of fine- and coarse-grained services connected to stewardship, reusability, and performance measurement delivers Decision Models in a valuable architecture.

The time has come to stop burying the business logic within the next generation of computer systems and to give the business experts visibility and proper stewardship to it.

Summary

SOA is the current and next generation of architectural style for computer systems. It is a layered architectural style built around automated services. A foundation of SOA is the service inventory, and the quality of the SOA depends on how well the inventory is organized. The services within the Business Services layer are business-oriented, whereas those in other layers are technically oriented. Business people have an important role in defining the services that are business-oriented. This means defining business process models, Decision Models, and corresponding services.

There are also service roles within SOA, and it is useful to think of a service role as representing a separation of concern. Most common service roles are task services and information or data services. Less common is the recognition of decision services, representing the important separation of business logic within SOA. Business decisions and the Decision Model provide a distinct way to respectfully separate business logic, perhaps at a granular level, which can be rolled up into appropriate decision services, based on all of the characteristics of a good-quality service.

The most important concepts in this chapter are the following:

- According to Rosen, a service is "a discrete unit of business functionality that is made available through a service contract."
- SOA's enterprise view is what makes it strategic.
- The Decision Model in the Business Processes Layer distinguishes between decision tasks and process tasks.
- The Decision Model in the Business Services Layer serves as the basis for defining decision services.
- Even when the Decision Model is bundled with other aspects into a service, it should be defined and managed separately from the other aspects for all of the reasons given in Chapter 1.
- SOA, combined with the Decision Model, allows the separation of business logic from other aspects in a manner that other architectures do not.

New Vocabulary Introduced in This Chapter

- SOA
- service
- service-oriented
- service inventory
- consistency
- commonality
- modularity and flexibility
- decoupling
- manageability
- service layer
- business processes layer
- business services layer
- fine-grained service
- coarse-grained service
- task service
- decision service
- entity service

And What about the Quote

The quote reminds us that an architect is a creator of constructed forms. The constructed forms are of many types, ranging from bridges to skyscrapers to computer systems. People live in, travel to, or operate within such forms. Therefore, the creations of the architect are detectable in one way or another. Defects in the design require workarounds. This means overriding broken system logic or planting vines to hide imperfections in buildings. A well-conceived architecture yields a well-constructed form. It requires a broad vision and careful attention to details. SOA is the emerging architecture for computer systems that embraces the broad vision and drives it to details. One of the most important details is the business logic. Whether visible or lost, correct or incorrect, it will be detectable one way or another.

Discussion Points and Exercises

Exercises Based on Chapter 5

1. Using the definition of a service, explain why a Decision Model is a good starting point as a candidate service in a service inventory.
2. Discuss reasons why sometimes an entire Decision Model is an appropriate service and why at other times a combination of business process tasks and their Decision Models is an appropriate service. (Hint: Consider reuse, change management, stewardship, proprietary nature of business logic).
3. Using the Determine Policy Renewal Method Decision Model in Chapter 2, Figure 2.1, discuss the various ways you may want to deliver it as services. If it were one service, what information would the service require as input and what information would it provide as output?
4. Create a services diagram (such as the example in Figure 5.2) for some of the services needed to support an airline traveler. (Refer to the description in Chapter 4 of a sample business process for this).

Exercises Based on Chapter 15

Chapter 5 is essentially a primer on SOA and the Decision Model. Those interested in delving in greater detail are invited to read Chapter 15. The following discussions and exercises are intended for those that who completed a reading of that chapter:

1. Consider a well-known e-business site—for convenience, select Amazon. com. Review the site, up to the shopping cart checkout stage (or, even better, to the completion of the checkout). Now construct a Service Inventory that you believe would be appropriate for that site, using the matrix provided in Chapter 15, Figure 15.7.

    1.1. Select a Decision Service from that inventory.
- Define the information likely to be passed at the service interface.
- Define the condition and conclusion fact types likely to be used in the Decision Rule Family for that Decision Service.
- Determine what scenarios may exist for a reuse of that Decision Service in the rest of the site, or in the enterprise.

    1.2. Select a composite service from that inventory, and define the services that make up that composite service.

2. Using the definition of a service and corresponding service contract from this chapter, explain why an entire Decision Model or parts of it are better suited as a service instead of another software construct.
3. Referring to Figure 15.2, (Chapter 15) create a diagram of the components of a generic decision service and suggest which parts of a Decision Model (e.g., conclusion fact types, condition fact types provided by consumer, condition fact types determined by the decision service, execution design of the decision service, persistent data accessed by the decision service, actual access paths used by the decision service) fit into service operations, semantic business data, internal functions, and internal data.
4. Explain how the fact types in a Decision Model relate to the information architecture layers explained in this chapter.
5. Propose a high-level design for a collection of services to support the business process model and decisions from the Food Stamp Eligibility example in Chapter 4, Figure 4.3. In particular, consider dividing the Decision Model into smaller reusable services, when doing so seems appropriate.
6. Using this service design, and referring to Chapter 15, Figures 15.4 and 15.5, discuss the service types and roles of the services that you have designed. What is the granularity of these services? Referring to Figure 15.2, what are the functional and informational concepts associated with each service?
7. Further elaborating on the service design, select a task, entity, and decision service and sketch out the interface. Remember the separation of interface and implementation. What aspects of the implementation have been encapsulated by the interfaces?
8. Discuss how the idea of external configuration mechanisms can lead to the design of flexible (hence, customizable) industry-specific decision services.

Chapter 6

How the Decision Model Improves Requirements, Business Analysis, and Testing

Contents

The Need for Better Requirements 105
What Are Requirements? 105
    Defining Requirements 106
    The Nature of Requirements 106
Ways of Expressing Requirements 107
    Textual Statements 107
    Business Use Cases 107
    Models 111
        Why Different Models and How Do They Connect? 112
        Different Models in Requirements 113
    Prototypes 113
    Program Code 114
Business Logic in Classical Functional Requirements 117
    Requirements Change but Business Logic Changes More Often, and
    Rapidly 118
    Current Methods of Capturing Business Rules as a Part of Requirements 118

The Decision Model as a Coequal Requirement Artifact 119
  Business Motivation Model (BMM) 119
  Business Process Model 122
  Business Use Case 122
  Semantic Models 127
  Connection Points and Shared Metadata 128
The Decision Model and Testing against the Functional Requirements 129
  Directly Testing the Decision Model 129
  Scenario Testing 133
Putting It All Together 134
What about Agile Development and the Decision Model? 136
Summary 136
New Vocabulary Introduced in This Chapter 137
And What about the Quote 138
Discussion Points and Exercises 138

You can't always get what you want and if you try sometime you just might find you get what you need.

M. Jagger/K. Richards, "You can't always get what you want"

This chapter traces the wide impact that the Decision Model has on requirements. The emergence of a stable, technology-independent model of business logic allows business analysts, for the first time, to accurately and completely define the logic within requirements. The relationship between the Decision Model and other artifacts of well-defined requirements is outlined. The chapter also examines the opportunities the Decision Model provides in establishing test cases to directly test the business logic. Finally, the chapter touches on whether the Decision Model fits into an Agile development methodology.

The Decision Model is a model that, properly used, dramatically improves the quality of requirements for projects that develop systems, and most specifically software systems, for business. The use of the Decision Model leads to more agile, higher-quality systems at lower cost, in shorter time cycles. It leads to a significant improvement in business analysis, because it provides a stable, normalized model for the business logic of a business process. Moreover, the Decision Model serves as the basis for developing test cases that directly test the decision logic in the systems.

These improvements occur in most phases of a project and accrue whether the projects use waterfall, iterative, or agile development methods. To understand the reason for this it is necessary to examine the state of requirements in projects today.

The Need for Better Requirements

The failure rate of software projects is legendary.* This is perhaps a reflection of the fact that software engineering is a much younger discipline than other branches of engineering. Sometimes, the failure results in total project collapse. However, frequently it takes a more subtle form, where projects overrun costs, time frames, or suffer a necessary reduction in scope. Even more frequently, a project is declared a success, but business users work around problems to compensate for a less than fully satisfactory solution. After many software projects are completed, efforts continue to correct and improve the system over time.

There are many reasons for this unsettling situation, but failure to define the expectations of the business users is usually one of the most important. A recent report states that "a hefty 40% of businesses experienced project failure between 2004 and 2006, according to consultant Avanade. Poor system specification was the largest cause of problems, contributing to 66% of cases" (Kelly, 2007). A frequently cited article on the failure of software projects ranks "badly defined system requirements" as chief among the reasons for projects failures (Charette, 2005).

What Are Requirements?

To fully understand the nature of requirements, it is important first to define what is meant by "requirements" in the context of business system projects. It is also important to understand where requirements end, where system design starts, and why this is an important distinction.

---

* However, the legendary number is difficult to pin down. A 1994 report by a U.S. consulting organization, Standish, famously announced that 70% of projects do not achieve their goals. This number is often attributed to other sources who were simply quoting the original report, and often with the erroneous claim that "70% of projects fail," a very different statistic ("not meeting their goals" and "failing" are not necessarily the same thing). This number is still quoted, even though the study is now almost 15 years old. In 2004, Standish shared statistics indicating their research into 50,000 projects worldwide showed that 29% of projects succeeded, 53% were "challenged," and 18% "failed," which they said was a significant improvement over the 1994 study (Jim Johnson, 2006).

Defining Requirements

The Institute of Electrical and Electronics Engineers (IEEE) provides the following definition:
"Requirement:

A. a condition or capability needed by a user to solve a problem or achieve an objective;
B. a condition or capability that must be met or possessed by a system or system component to satisfy a contract, standard, specification, or other formally imposed document;
C. a documented representation of a condition or capability as in definition (A) or (B)." (IEEE, (Std 610.12-1990))

This definition is usually made more concrete by classifying requirements for software project purposes into two broad categories:

1. **Functional requirements**—Requirements for functions that the system performs to directly execute the mission of the software. These include process steps, calculations, data manipulations, or reporting activities.
2. **Nonfunctional requirements**—Requirements for constraints on the system. These include constraints about system performance, reliability, maintainability or ease of use, cost, and other overall characteristics.

Functional requirements deliver business value and are the focus of this chapter. Consequently, wherever the word requirement is used, it means "functional requirement." These requirements are most easily misinterpreted and frequently implemented incorrectly or not at all. But before considering the ways that requirements may be expressed, it is important to understand the difference between requirements and design.

The Nature of Requirements

The nature of requirements varies among methodologies. In some methodologies, requirements are only the needs that business users describe at the highest level of abstraction. In others, the needs may be described at a greater level of detail, including many specific design elements that are elements of system design, such as screen design. For the purpose of this chapter, a very broad view is taken of the definition of requirements, regardless of where in the timeline of methodology they are gathered. So, requirements consist of those elements of the system over which the business user is expected to (or should) provide. Thus, models of business processes—both the "as-is" and the "to-be"—and elements such as user interface are requirements.

Ways of Expressing Requirements

Requirements are meaningful if expressed in ways that are clear to every audience. Consequently, different kinds of requirements are expressed in different ways, each aiming to communicate the requirement in the most understandable manner. These methods include textual statements, business use cases, a wide range of different models, prototypes, and in certain approaches, the program code itself.

Textual Statements

A series of textual statements has been long used as the principal means for expressing requirements. These have the form of "The system shall …" (for mandatory or obligatory requirements), or "The system should …" (for preferred requirements).

Effective textual statements are difficult to write because natural language is imprecise and does not represent rigorous communication. If textual statements are developed as the sole source of requirements, the risk of misunderstanding and rework is high.

The best use of textual statements is to serve contractual purposes. In other words, the software is to be assessed against them. Often, textual statements are written after other types of requirements are captured because sometimes the textual statements explain the nature of the other type of requirements.

A useful set of characteristics for a well-formulated textual requirement statement is in Table 6.1.

But even a well-formulated textual statement may not—indeed will probably not—communicate the full meaning of a requirement, especially when the requirement is best viewed within a particular context. This leads to other means of expressing requirements to show context, including business use cases, models, prototypes, and—according to some—the program code itself.

Business Use Cases

A business use case is a step-by-step narrative of a single business user ("Actor") interacting with the system, where the narrative yields a valuable result. An example of a business use case for an online banking system is "Prequalify a Loan Request." An extract of the steps for such a business use case are in Table 6.2. A complete business use case provides a basic course of action when all goes well, in addition to alternative paths when something goes wrong. There may be many alternative paths in a full business use case, in addition to several additional pre- and postconditions.

A typical system requires many business use cases to fully describe all interactions of all actors. Note that a business use case can include many individual requirements. A set of business use cases can be diagramed, as in Figure 6.1, to illustrate the association of business use cases with actors.

Table 6.1 The Characteristics of Good Functional Requirements

Characteristic	Explanation
Cohesive	The requirement addresses one and only one thing.
Complete	The requirement is fully stated in one place with no missing information.
Consistent	The requirement does not contradict any other requirement and is fully consistent with all authoritative external documentation.
Relevant	The requirement is related to a business rationale (or business motivation) that is relevant to the mission of the software.
Correct	The requirement meets all or part of a business need as authoritatively stated by stakeholders.
Current	The requirement has not been made obsolete by the passage of time.
Externally observable	The requirement specifies a characteristic of the product that is externally observable or experienced by the user. "Requirements" that specify internal architecture, design, implementation, or testing decisions are properly constraints, and should be clearly articulated in the Constraints section of the Requirements document.
Feasible	The requirement can be implemented within the constraints of the project.
Unambiguous	The requirement is concisely stated without recourse to technical jargon, acronyms (unless defined elsewhere in the Requirements document), or other esoteric verbiage. It expresses objective facts, not subjective opinions. It is subject to one and only one interpretation. Vague subjects, adjectives, prepositions, verbs, and subjective phrases are avoided. Negative statements and compound statements are prohibited.
Mandatory	The requirement represents a stakeholder-defined characteristic the absence of which will result in a deficiency that cannot be ameliorated.
Verifiable	The implementation of the requirement can be determined through one of four possible methods: inspection, analysis, demonstration, or test.

Source: Wikipedia, 2008 (amended by the authors).

Table 6.2   Steps from a Business Use Case Example

Business use case: "Pre-qualify a Loan Request"

Step 1: The use case begins when Applicant logs on

Step 2: Applicant selects loan type

Step 3: System determines if Applicant is known (alternative path 1)

Step 4: System presents loan-specific screen

Step 5: Applicant reviews/changes information

Step 6: System determines if Applicant's income is sufficient

Step 7: System determines Applicant's Probability of default

Step 8: System determines if Applicant prequalifies for the loan request (alternative path 2)

Step 9: System determines other terms for the loan request

Step 10: System presents terms to Applicant

Step 11: The use case ends when Applicant accepts loan terms

Business use cases help stakeholders better understand requirements within the context of an actor interaction. In some cases, textual requirements statements are actually developed from the business use case. The business use case in Table 6.2 may give rise to the following textual requirement:

■ The system shall have the ability to prequalify an online Loan Request (business use case "Prequalify a Loan Request," basic course of action)

Another requirement is also evident from the business use case, but will only be complete when the alternative path 2 is completed in it:

The system shall have the ability to provide options to customers whose online Loan Request fails to prequalify (business use case "Prequalify Loan Request," alternative path 2 will determine the option in the event the loan request is not accepted online)

The textual statements that relate to business use cases are cross-referenced to the business use cases that rely on them. This cross-referencing among requirements is called traceability, a very important concept. It enables verification and testing of requirements in the software, and facilitates changes to the system when requirements change after the system is deployed.

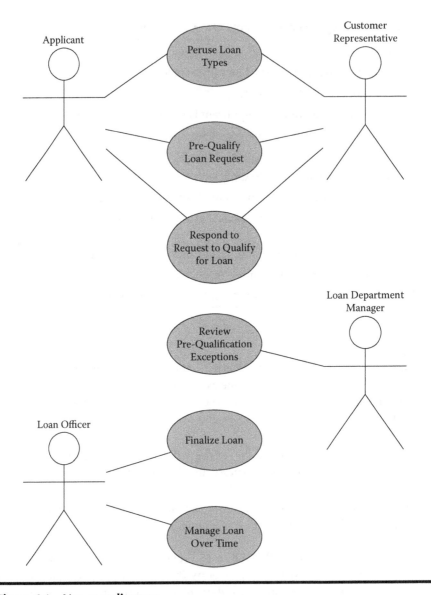

Figure 6.1   Use case diagram.

In several object-oriented development methodologies, including the unified process,* business use cases are the first step toward the development of detailed (or system) use cases and activity diagrams. System use cases and activity diagrams are detailed and are referenced by programmers for developing the program code

---

* The unified process is discussed at greater length in Chapter 16.

for the system. In some development environments, system use cases and activity diagrams are transformed automatically into program code. The system use cases are technical artifacts. The system use cases are cross-referenced to the business use cases. The system use cases are also cross-referenced to the program code that implements them.

Use cases, whether business use cases or system use cases, are often referred to as a special kind of model. However, there are many other models used in developing functional requirements.

Models

The dictionary defines a model as "a description or analogy used to help visualize something (as an atom) that cannot be directly observed" (Merriam-Webster Online Dictionary "model"). This means that models give rise to requirements because the models help visualize an aspect of the system to which the requirement applies.

An even better definition for model takes into account important characteristics that are appropriate to the modeling of systems:

> Modeling, in the broadest sense, is the *cost-effective* use of something in place of something else for some *cognitive* purpose. It allows us to use something that is *simpler*, safer or cheaper than reality instead of reality for some purpose. A model represents reality for the *given purpose*; the model is an abstraction of reality in the sense that it cannot represent all *aspects* of reality. This allows us to deal with the world in a simplified manner, avoiding the complexity, danger and irreversibility of reality. (Rothenberg, 1989) (Authors' italics)

Models are used to tease apart the "big ball of mud" (discussed in Chapter 1). Models represent different aspects of the real system (i.e., borrowing from the phrase in the aforementioned definition, "aspects of reality") so that each aspect may be addressed individually, in a simplified manner. For functional requirements, the aspects of primary concerns are reporting, data, presentation, workflow, and business logic. In addition, there are other aspects that may be external to the actual system, but which assist in understanding (because they have a direct bearing on) the requirements. Here are some examples of additional aspects that may be modeled:

■ **Motivation,** the "why" of the system, the rationale and motivation for the system and requirements. The motivation may reflect the organization's internal objectives, or those of external organizations such as regulatory agencies. The Business Motivation Model (BMM) is a model of the various considerations of motivation.

■ **Organization,** the people and roles that interact with the system.
■ **Location,** the physical locales of system hardware and software.

Models provide graphical and semantic representations of their target aspects in ways that are easier to view and understand than are textual statements or narratives. Because each model captures just one aspect of the system, several models, each orthogonal to the other, provide a sufficiently complete view of the proposed system.* So, like the business use case, models are used both for shared understanding and assistance in developing related textual requirement statements. In some approaches, a model may be used as input for the automatic generation of the system. When this is so, it is called Model-Driven Architecture (MDA) and is discussed further in Chapter 14.

Why Different Models and How Do They Connect?

There are at least three reasons for modeling each aspect with its own model. First, each model reduces complexity. Second, each model enables independent change of its aspect from other aspects. Third, it turns out that each aspect is best represented by a model specifically tailored to the characteristics of the modeled aspect. For example, data is best modeled in diagrams that show the relationship of each data entity to another, where icons represent the data entities and lines represent data relationships. On the other hand, process flow is best modeled in diagrams that represent flow of process tasks, where icons represent the process tasks and lines represent process sequence.

To understand how models connect to each other, consider the analogy of the many different maps that may be used for a given geographical area. There are the conventional road maps used for driving directions that are the most familiar. But beyond that there are topographical maps, flight maps, weather maps, demographic maps, geological maps, and many others.

Connection points allow the modeling of various aspects of the same reality with different models because the connection points enable the viewer to understand the perspective of each model in relation to the other. The accuracy of the connection points is dependent on the degree and accuracy to which the models share common metadata.

A map reader can readily use two different map types at the same time because the maps have many connection points. In the broadest sense, the shape of the

---

* The operative word is *sufficiently*; after all, if an exhaustively complete and comprehensive model of every aspect of the system is created, it would no longer be a model, but would be the system itself! Rather like Lewis Carroll's map in *Sylvie and Bruno Concluded*, where the mapmakers' "grandest" solution to absolute accuracy in their map of the country was to make it on a scale of a mile to the mile. Unfortunately, it could never be spread out without blotting out the sunlight, and the population had to resort to using the actual country as their map, discovering that it did nearly as well!

boundaries is an easy reference for the eye to orient one map to the other. Also a set of common landmarks—such as a city or feature name that is common on both maps—provides somewhat better connection points. But these are relatively rough connection points. For a really accurate match between any properly drawn terrestrial maps, they should display a set of latitude and longitude coordinates. These coordinates are based on a global system of measurements, universally accepted, that enables one map to be inherently connected to another, regardless of its scale and scope. The co-ordinates are important metadata that significantly enhance the quality of the connection points.

Different Models in Requirements

The analogy follows in the models used for requirements. There are a number of types of models, and each can be related to the other through common connection points and similar metadata. The Decision Model is the model of the business logic—an aspect of a system that has not previously been modeled in a universal way. The Decision Model shares metadata with, and has connection points to, the other models commonly used in requirements today, including the following:

- **Business planning models** (such as the BMM). These models represent strategic and operational plans for the business and are important drivers for systems. The drivers from these models are captured in and traceable to the rest of the requirements. The system's success, based on verifiable business metrics, can be monitored against the objectives set in the business plan.
- **Business process models** (and other sequential activity models). These models depict the required flow of activities that the system and the actors are to execute.
- **Semantic models such as data, object, and fact models.** These models contain the glossary of terms, the fact types, and logical data structures that are required for an accurate and shared set of semantics for the system.
- **Organization and location models.** These models contain the stakeholders and the relevant physical locations of the system and stakeholders.

Later in this chapter, the connection points and common metadata between the Decision Model and these model types (and business use cases) are explored in depth. First, there are other requirement types to understand.

Prototypes

Prototypes are a mock-up of the software solution that permits the business user to visualize the software by displaying the user interface of the proposed solution.

The interface is displayed either on a screen or in flat diagrams (called wireframes). Some screen-based prototypes emulate the software functionality for key program flows.

The value of prototyping is that it provides the business user with a more tangible idea of the software than even a model can provide. The business user can see, in a way that is not as abstract as a business use case or business process model, what the interface to the software will look like and how the system is likely to act in the case of different inputs.

The most valuable use of the prototype is for the business user to understand screen flow and layout. In fact, the prototype may be considered a model of the user interface. Like other models, the prototype may be used to derive or verify textual requirement statements.

In some development methodologies, such as Rapid Application Development (RAD), the prototype is actually evolved into a working prototype, and eventually into the software system itself. In this case, the business user validates each advance in the coding by testing the prototype until the software is deemed complete. RAD was a precursor to the Agile development approach, where the Program Code and functional requirements are one and the same thing.

Program Code

Proponents of the Agile development approach prefer a radically different approach to the classical method of gathering of requirements in advance of development. In fact, proponents of the Agile development approach refer somewhat disdainfully to the classical requirements approach as the Big Requirements Up Front (BRUF). The Agile development approach is a variation of an iterative approach, rather than the old waterfall (linear) approach, to software development. However, the Agilists go further than simply decomposing the development process into multiple iterations.

In fact, Agilists prefer to do away with the term requirements because it implies an artifact that is gathered and finalized early in the development lifecycle: "… it really isn't requirements which we are gathering, or eliciting, or whatever verb you prefer, but instead it is the stakeholder's intent which we are trying to understand" (Ambler, 2007b). In the Agile approach, business requirements fully emerge during an iterative process between developers and stakeholders as, or very shortly before, the program code is developed. This iterative process includes the development of many simple business use cases and models during discussions between the developer and the business user. These models are depicted informally, typically on a white board (Agilists refer to this as "Plain Old Whiteboard (POW)"), or index cards as shown in Figure 6.2.

The Agilists' goal is to deliver rapidly, based on what is known, and then to evolve quickly based on what is learned from each iteration. So, requirements,

Figure 6.2   Sketching artifacts on POW.

evolve through iterative deliverables. "The urge to write requirements documentation should be transformed into an urge to instead collaborate closely with your stakeholders and then create working software based on what they tell you" (Ambler, 2007a).

In other words, Agilists do not consider requirements to be an asset that is maintained in addition to and separate from the working system. Models and business use cases serve only as aids to shared understanding and guidance for developers and testers.

The philosophical underpinnings for this approach may be found in a series of three essays by Jack W. Reeves which assert that the actual software code is the design of the system. A key passage in these essays says:

> The final goal of any engineering activity is some type of documentation. When a design effort is complete, the design documentation is turned over to the manufacturing team. This is a completely different group with completely different skills from the design team. If the design documents truly represent a complete design, the manufacturing team can proceed to build the product. In fact, they can proceed to build lots of the product, all without any further intervention of the designers. After reviewing the software development life cycle as I understood it, I concluded that the only software documentation that actually seems to satisfy the criteria of an engineering design is the source code listings. (Reeves, 1992)

This idea changed decades of thinking. Before this, the software programmer was perceived as the builder. The software designers were thought to be the business (or solution) architects, business and system analysts, specialists in data, security, and so on. The design, in fact, was the detailed requirements (complete with models, use cases, prototypes, test cases). Instead, Reeves sees the programmers as being very much part of the design process, and source code as the final product design: "… everything is part of the design process. Coding is design, testing and debugging are part of design, and what we typically call software design is still part of design" (Reeves, 1992). The "build" part of software engineering is thus just the compiling and linking process. Thus, "software is very expensive to design, but incredibly inexpensive to build" (Reeves, 1992)—the cost being the time and effort that it takes to simply run the compiler and linker.

This philosophy changes the role of the programmer, who now assumes the designer's role. The programmer is the engineer, not the builder. It also gives rise to earlier development of program code to ensure that coding begins almost at the commencement of the development cycle. This is to reduce risk or deliver earlier, but also to allow the coder to participate, even lead, in the design. It also ensures that the test cycle occurs earlier, consistent with the idea that the programmers and testers are leaders in the design phase. The contrast between this approach and the classical approach is illustrated in Table 6.3.

The result is that the program code is perceived as part of the design, and thus is considered an artifact, in fact, the principle artifact, of requirements. In this paradigm, the artifacts that were classically considered as part of the requirements—textual statements, business use cases, models, prototypes—are simply helpful techniques in creating the design (which is the program code). Given this idea, it makes sense to sketch these artifacts using POW or handwritten

Table 6.3 Requirements in Classical versus Agile Theories

Classical Approach

	Requirements	*Design*	*Build & Test*
Role	Analyst, SME, user	Solution architect	Developer, tester
Work Product	Requirements (extensively documented)	Technical design	Source code, Test cases

Agile Approach

	Requirements, Design & Test	*Build*
Role	User, developer, SME, tester	Compiler
Work Product	Source code, test cases (Requirements may be included in documentation, done after the design is complete.)	Object code

index cards (Figure 6.2) and not to maintain them as formal documents. The Agile approach recognizes the importance of requirements as the means for documenting the system. So, textual statements and models serve as documentation for the system after completion of the system.

The next section introduces the role of business logic and the Decision Model within requirements. The section begins by recognizing business logic as an aspect worthy of its own model and how that recognition significantly improves the approach to classical functional requirements.

Business Logic in Classical Functional Requirements

Interestingly, a review of a representative sample of books about functional requirements reveals that a very small amount of the material (i.e., less than 5% in average page count) is devoted to business logic or business rules. Yet, business decisions and corresponding business logic are critical in implementing business policy, controlling business processes, and providing decision services on the Web. It is important today that the management of business logic becomes an essential component of the classical functional requirements approach.

Requirements Change but Business Logic Changes More Often, and Rapidly

Requirements for business systems change because of a wide range of circumstances. These include changes in regulations, business climate, business objectives, or other circumstances. Requirements often change before projects are complete, and certainly continue to change after completion.

However, business logic is the aspect that changes most frequently. Not only does it change more frequently than do other aspects, but the lead time for implementing the change can be very short. Competitive pressure in the world of global business is one driver. Once a need for change is identified, the business is often under pressure to implement change immediately. Today, more than ever before, when crude oil and other commodity prices can swing over 30% in a matter of days, when the business climate can change from a fair outlook to economic recession in a matter of weeks, and when government can introduce wide-ranging regulatory legislation within months, the cycle time for change is becoming very compressed.

So, the compressed change cycle demands that business logic emerges as a critical aspect of business requirements. More importantly, business logic needs to be implemented and managed in a way that assumes it will change at any time. Today and for the foreseeable future, business logic must be designed to change, by definition.

Current Methods of Capturing Business Rules as a Part of Requirements

In publications on requirements practices, there are references to business rules. However, little is said of their structure in any detail. The most common recommendation is to indicate simply, where in a business use case or business process model a business rule applies and to create a cross-reference from that point to the business rule number or name. In some cases, a business use case simply contains a list of business rules or their numbers at the bottom of the business use case description; they are not even attached to specific steps within it.

There is also a maintenance difficulty with connecting one business rule at a time to points in a business process model or business use case. Most often, groups of business rules are to be connected to a point in business process models and use cases. When the nature of that group changes (e.g., business rules are to be added, removed, or changed), the change needs to be made in many places because the concept of a well-defined group of business rules does not exist. In other words, the new business rules must be added to, removed from, or updated at every relevant connection point in business process models and business use cases.

There are a number of books on business rules. Unfortunately, most do not deal with methods of relating the business rules to functional requirements. A general assumption appears to be that the business rules are maintained as an indexed catalogue in a database or spreadsheet. How these business rules are to be organized within a particular business use case or business process model is not covered in many of these publications.

In short, until now there has been no model specifically for the representation of business rules or business logic. So, there is no concept of connecting a model of business rules or business logic to other requirements-oriented models. Again, without connection points and common metadata, it becomes difficult, if not impossible, to relate the business rules and business logic to the rest of the requirements. This means that developers, coders, testers, and ultimately the business users, will not be able trace the business rules and business logic to the models that reference them. This, to a large degree, explains why, despite good intentions, the business rules become "lost" in the system, even when a classical business rules approach is followed.

The Decision Model as a Coequal Requirement Artifact

The Decision Model fulfills the need for a technology-independent model of business logic with a well-defined connection point to all related models. The Decision Model has one clear connection point to, and shared metadata with, every other model used in requirements modeling. With this common connection point, any changes in the group of business rules within a Decision Model need to be made only once, in one place, in one Decision Model. The changed Decision Model is then automatically referenced by related models.

The next sections discuss some of the models that comprise classical functional requirements and how the Decision Model connects to them in a straightforward way.

Business Motivation Model (BMM)

The BMM is a model to support business planning and manage business motivations that drives projects and related systems.

The BMM, shown in Figure 6.3, is a model for managing means and ends. It captures courses of action that implement strategy and related tactics, to achieve a desired result driven by goals and objectives. Business policies and business rules are represented in the BMM as directives to govern the courses of action.

Table 6.4 provides examples of some of the elements of a business plan that are included in the BMM. Specifically, Table 6.4 contains examples for Vision, Goal, Objective, Mission, Strategy, Tactic, Business Policy, and Business Rule.

The sample business rule, or business logic statement, appears in the table as a directive that constrains business behavior and supports a business policy (or policies). A business rule is often formulated in response to an opportunity, threat, strength, or weakness. The business rule in the example prescribes business logic from an underwriter for coming to a conclusion about an applicant's likelihood

Table 6.4 Example of Elements of a Business Plan

End:	Vision:	Desired Result:
	To become the leading workers compensation underwriter in the 16 states that we are active	**Goal:** Achieve the number 1 or number 2 underwriting status in each of the 16 states, while continuing to maintain current margins
		Objective: By December 2012 achieve 95% retention of existing business and drive increase in new business by 15% for an overall growth of 10% per annum. [SMART Objective]
Means:	Mission: Significantly increase customer service by reducing underwriting and renewal turnaround	**Course of Action:** **Strategy:** Reduce renewal processing time
		Tactic: Increase automated underwriting of renewals
		Directive:
		Business Policy: A minimum of 80% of policies must be renewed automatically
		Business Rule: A Policy that is not flagged as manual renewal and that has a policy tier of greater than 2 and has a policy discount of less than 10% and has no other red flags such as change of major ownership or location must be automatically renewed: Also ....etc, etc.

of defaulting on a loan. The sample business policy governs a course of action in a general sense, whereas the sample business rule, supporting the business policy, governs a course of action in a specific sense. For any given business policy, there are likely to be many business rules. Note that the business rule in the example does not appear to directly implement the policy. It does belong to a group of business rules that together enable an automated renewal to be made under specific circumstances, in turn meeting the business objective. This is illustrative of the more direct connection between business decision and business policy than business rule and business policy. Also, a business policy may remain unchanged but its related business rules may change, still remaining faithful to the directive of the business policy.

Figure 6.3 contains the Decision Model on the left and the BMM on the right. It also shows one connection between them, suggesting that each business rule in the BMM connects to a single Rule Family row in the Decision Model. Not shown, however, is that there is metadata behind the Decision Model containing

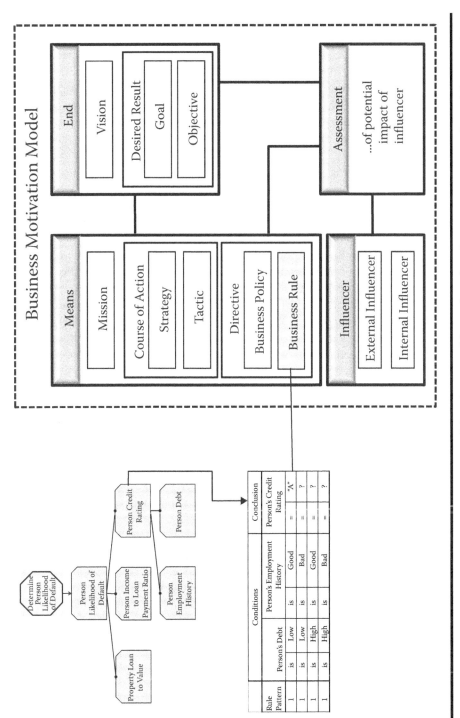

Figure 6.3 Connection between the Decision Model and BMM and BMM without changing the BMM. (Source: Adapted from Business Motivation Model (BMM) Specifications reprinted with permission. Object Management Group, Inc. © OMG. 2009.)

entities such as Business Policy, Business Objectives, and Business Tactics to further enhance the connection between the two kinds of models.

The connection of each business rule in a single Rule Family row in the Decision Model to the business rule directive sets up the prescribed association between the two models. However, in practice, the maintenance of this link becomes challenging, especially when there are a lot of business rules, as there invariably are. Therefore, it is more practical (without losing usefulness) to relate an entire Business Decision rather than a single business rule (or Rule Family row) to the Business Policy Directive. Treating a Business Decision as a Directive also better reflects business planning reality. Figure 6.4 illustrates this connection between models. The result of this adjustment can be seen by contrasting the business plan in Table 6.5 with that in Table 6.4. The Business Policy and Business Objective are now directly implemented by the single Business Decision. This is the mechanism of adaptive control and optimization that is described in Chapter 19.

This improvement also allows Business Decision to be represented as a Directive that governs a Course of Action connected to Objective. This is important, because the Objective should be "SMART" (**S**pecific, **M**easurable, **A**ttainable, **R**elevant, and **T**ime-based). The addition of Business Decision to the BMM enables the Business Decision to support the Objective, and, therefore, be measured and managed against criteria set in the business plan. The business logic in the Business Decision can be adjusted if necessary to improve the results when necessary.

Business Process Model

The relationship between the Decision Model and the business process model is discussed in detail in Chapter 4. The notation for integrating a Decision Model in BPMN is explored in Chapter 17. In summary, the business process model and the Decision Model are connected via the decision task (or business rule task) in the business process model, as illustrated in Figure 6.5. This connection is best strengthened by using the same naming conventions for the business decision and the decision task. Not shown is that the Decision Model and the business process model share the following common metadata: Business Policy, Business Objectives, and Business Tactics (which is also common to the BMM.)

The connection between the business process model and the Decision Model is extremely powerful in developing an agile business process. It also completes the connections among the business process model, Decision Model, and BMM. These connections create complete traceability from a single task in a business process model to a business decision in the Decision Model to a directive in the BMM.

Business Use Case

The connection between a business use case and the Decision Model occurs at those use case steps identified as decision steps. In practice, the use of decision-oriented

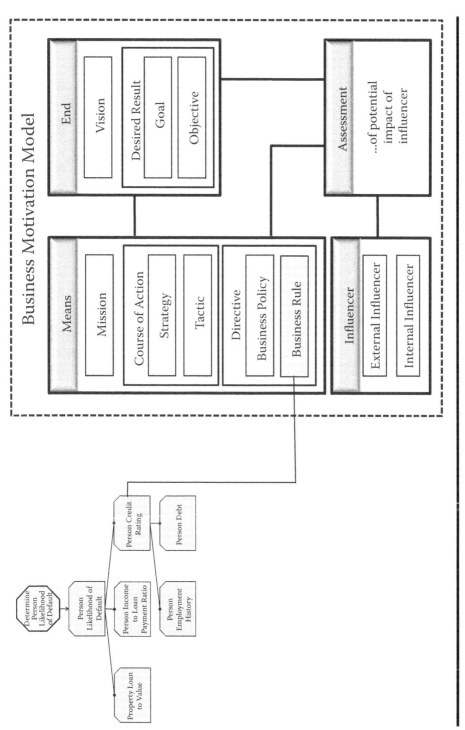

Figure 6.4   Better connection between the Decision Model and BMM with a simple change to the BMM. (Source: Adapted from Business Motivation Model (BMM) Specifications reprinted with permission. Object Management Group, Inc. © OMG. 2009.)

Table 6.5 Business Plan using Business Decisions

End:	Vision:	Desired Result:	
	To become the leading workers compensation underwriter in the 16 states that we are active	**Goal:** Achieve the number 1 or number 2 underwriting status in each of the 16 states, while continuing to maintain current margins	
		Objective: By December 2012 achieve 95% retention of existing business and drive increase in new business by 15% for an overall growth of 10% per annum. [SMART Objective]	
Means:	Mission: Significantly increase customer service by reducing underwriting and renewal turnaround	**Course of Action:**	
		Strategy: Reduce renewal processing time	
		Tactic: Implement a process to manage flow of policies to automated renewal system	
		Directive:	
		Business Policy: A minimum of 80% of policies must be renewed automatically	
		Decision: Determine Policy Renewal Method (D#1)	

words, such as determine, calculate, estimate, validate, and so on, are good clues that a business decision exists behind the step. In the case of Table 6.6, steps 6, 7, 8, and 9 are denoted as decision steps. Once the decision steps in a business use case are identified, a Decision Model is needed, if one is not already in existence. The use case step needs a unique identifier for each business decision noted in it, the connection point between the use case step and the Decision Model. In practice, the connection is strengthened by using the same naming convention for the business decision and the corresponding use case step.

Table 6.6 is the business use case from Table 6.2, but with some business decisions properly annotated, identified by a Decision Number. In this instance, the name of use case step 6 has been changed to match the name of the business decision. Note that step 3 has not been designated as a decision step because a business expert indicated that this step involves only a data lookup.

Decision steps in a business use case are similar to decision tasks in a business process model, and become the connecting points between the business use case and the Decision Model. Figure 6.6 illustrates this connection between a business use case and a corresponding Decision Model.

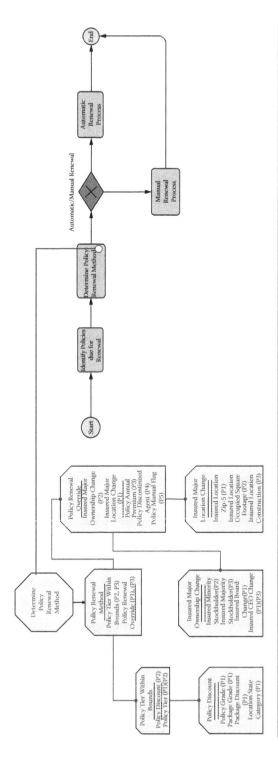

Figure 6.5 Connection between the Decision Model and the business process model.

Table 6.6 Steps from a Business Use Case Example Adding Decisions

Use case: "Prequalify loan request"

Step 1: The use case begins when applicant logs on

Step 2: Applicant selects loan type

Step 3: System determines if applicant is known (alt 1)

Step 4: System presents loan-specific screen

Step 5: Applicant reviews/changes information

Step 6: System determines if applicant's income is sufficient **for loan request**

    Decision #1067: Determine if applicant Income is sufficient for loan request

Step 7: System determines Applicant's probability of default

    Decision #1068: Determine applicant probability of default

Step 8: System determines if applicant prequalifies for the loan request (alt 2)

    Decision #1070: Determine if applicant prequalifies for loan request

Step 9: System determines other terms for the loan request

    Decision #1071: Determine other terms for loan request

Step 10: System presents terms to applicant

Step 11: The use case ends when applicant accepts loan terms

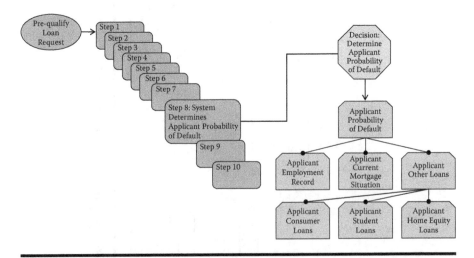

Figure 6.6 Connection between the Decision Model and Business Use Case.

Table 6.7   Business Use Case Example Simplified

Use case: "Prequalify loan request"
Step 1: The use case begins when applicant logs on
Step 2: Applicant selects loan type
Step 3: System determines if applicant is known (alt 1)
Step 4: System presents loan-specific screen
Step 5: Applicant reviews/changes information
Step 6: System determines if applicant prequalifies for the loan request (alt 2)
Decision #1070: Determine if applicant prequalifies for loan request
Step 7: System determines other terms for the loan request
Decision #1071: Determine other terms for loan request
Step 8: System presents terms to applicant
Step 9: The use case ends when applicant accepts loan terms.

Once decision steps are identified, it is worth examining a business use case to see if there is an opportunity for simplification* using the same principles that simplify business process models in Chapter 4. In this business use case, steps 6 through 8 need not be carried out sequentially. In other words, it really doesn't matter in what order the system makes the three business decisions. These steps may be combined into one single business decision, "Determine if Applicant prequalifies for loan request." The two Decision Models, #1067, #1068, will therefore become part of Decision #1070. Table 6.7 shows a simplified version of the original business use case, with clear traceability to its underlying business logic (i.e., the corresponding Decision Models). The business logic can now be changed independently of the business use case steps. Note that this business use case will still be connected to the same textual requirement as identified for Table 6.2.

Semantic Models

Simply speaking, a semantic model is a representation of the pieces of information referenced in a Decision Model, as conditions or conclusions. A range of semantic models are developed to serve as requirements artifacts; these are discussed at length in Chapter 16. They include the following:

- Glossary of fact types
- Fact model

---

* Essentially, a business use case can be simplified in much the same way a business process can be simplified, once the decision tasks and steps become apparent.

- Object model
- Logical data model

An example of a glossary of fact types is provided in Table 7.7 (Chapter 7). It is simply a list of the fact types used in the Decision Model with corresponding business definitions and, often, domain specifications. The fact types in the glossary should map to a fact model, object model, or logical data model, as appropriate.

Keep in mind that a glossary of fact types is required to support a Decision Model so that the model can be interpreted correctly. Because the Decision Model is to be understood by both business and technical audiences, the naming conventions used for fact types should result in fact type names that are meaningful to the business audience. In practice, the fact type names need not match exactly the names of corresponding pieces of information represented in a fact model,* logical data model, or object model. It is necessary that there be a link from each fact type in a Decision Model to its representation in those other models.

This separation and linkage is important for two reasons. The first is that a Decision Model can be created with a meaningful business glossary of fact types even without the preexistence of a fact model, logical data model, or object model. In some cases, such models are needed for clarity, but they need not exist at the very beginning of a Decision Model project. In fact, deciding which kind of semantic model to deliver is usually a factor of the intended usage of the Decision Model. If the model is to guide human behavior, a glossary of fact types or fact model may suffice. On the other hand, if the Decision Model is to be automated, most likely an object model, logical data model, physical data model, or all of these may be needed.

The second reason for the separation from and linkage of the glossary to related models is that the scope of a Decision Model is one business decision. This means that the glossary of fact types can name and define them as they need to be understood within the boundary of the target business decision. However, the glossary of fact types can be cross-referenced to broader models (i.e., an enterprise data model, enterprise object model, enterprise fact model). In other words, a glossary of fact types for one business decision can be cross-referenced to multiple models.

Connection Points and Shared Metadata

Table 6.8 summarizes the connection points and shared metadata between different models and the Decision Model.

---

* Most often, in practice, the fact type names in the glossary will be the same as those in a related fact model. In fact, such a fact model can replace the glossary of fact types.

Table 6.8   Connection Points between Models

Model	Model Connection Point	Equivalent Decision Model Connection Point	Shared Metadata
Business Motivation Model	Business Rule (or Decision)	Business Logic Statement (or Decision)	Business Policy, Business Objective, Business Tactic
Business Process Model	Decision Task, or Business Rule Task	Decision	Decision, Object Model, Data Model, Actor (Stakeholder)
Use Case	Decision Step	Decision	Decision, Actor (Stakeholder)
Logical Data Model	Entity or Attribute	Fact Type	Glossary Alias, Description
Object Model	Entity or Attribute	Fact Type	Glossary Alias, Description
Fact Model	Fact Type	Fact Type	Operator, Operand

Because the Decision Model is based on the inherent nature of business logic and because business logic is closely bound to the other models in requirements, it is natural that all models connect together, sharing metadata. These connections make possible the inclusion of the Decision Model into functional requirements as a universal model of business logic, and solve the problem of separating the business logic from the big ball of mud.

But that is only the beginning of the story. The Decision Model also plays an even more significant role in improving how systems are tested for conformance to the functional requirements.

The Decision Model and Testing against the Functional Requirements

Program testing in development projects traditionally takes place after a module has been programmed. The writing of test cases is vital and is considered to be an integral part of developing functional requirements. Test cases are designed to test the inputs and outputs of the module as a whole. Their purpose is to exercise the business logic within the program for the circumstances likely to occur.

However, there are two common problems in this conventional method of testing:

■ Because the tests are conducted after the module is completely programmed, test failures often result in significant rework.
■ Because the business logic is not separated from the rest of the code, test results don't necessarily measure the accuracy of the original business logic as errors in it may be shielded by program manipulations. This can lead to failure of the code in unanticipated circumstances,* or as a result of future maintenance.

Directly Testing the Decision Model

The Decision Model can shorten the testing and development cycle drastically. The rigor of the Decision Model offers opportunities for testing strategies that can be used to exhaustively test the business logic in the Decision Model, down to the granularity of each row within each Rule Family. Testers, based on the nature of the module, can determine at what level of granularity the Decision Model needs to be tested. Because Decision Models are designed for reuse, their test cases can be maintained as a part of the Decision Model. In this way, the test cases are available for reuse when the corresponding Decision Model is reused in other systems or updated.

The optimum approach for developing a test of a Rule Family is to consider the operands of each column as input to the test case for that Rule Family. Some examples of how the Rule Family may be used to build the test cases follow.

Assume the Rule Family in Table 6.9 is not dependent on any other Rule Family. That is, it obtains all of its input from persistent data or a Web page. A test case has two columns of fact types whose values would be tested as input: Policy Tier and Policy Discount. An inspection of the operands in the Policy Tier columns indicates that the values for this column can range from less than 1 to a value above 2.6. The tester determines whether to test every possible value in this range (unlikely, but under certain circumstances it may be practical and necessary), or just the boundary values. The boundary values are the values around each of the tier breaks (0.9, 1, 1.1, 1.4, 1.5, 1.6, and so on). For each of these values, the tester determines the Policy Discount values to test. Again, it may not be necessary to test every value possible (every point from 0% to 100%), if tests of the boundary values will suffice. The Rule Family's conclusion column, "Policy Tier within Bounds," contains the output value that the Rule Family should return (Yes or No) from those tests.

---

* Every experienced tester knows that it is difficult, if not impossible, to test every possible circumstance in even the simplest piece of software. In a program containing only five paths and a single loop there can be 10^{14} (100 trillion) different circumstances. It would take thousands, perhaps millions, even billion of years to write, let alone execute the test cases for this number of circumstances (Kamer, 1997).

Table 6.9 Rule Family "Policy Tier within Bounds"

	Conditions				Conclusion	
Pattern	*Policy Tier*		*Policy Discount*		*Policy Tier Within Bounds*	
1	≤	1			Is	No
2	Between	(1, 1.5)	≤	10%	Is	Yes
2	Between	(1,1. 5)	>	10%	Is	No
2	Between	(1.5, 2)	≤	12.5%	Is	Yes
2	Between	(1.5 ,2)	>	12.5%	Is	No
2	Between	(2, 2.6)	≤	20%	Is	Yes
2	Between	(2, 2.6)	>	20%	Is	No
2	>	2.6	≤	22%	Is	Yes
2	>	2.6	>	22%	Is	No

In very large Rule Families with a large number of columns, the tester, consistent with standard testing techniques, determines whether to test all possible values, boundary values, or a statistically meaningful sample of values. Table 6.10 contains a sample partial test case for Policy Tier within Bounds, testing the first two rows of business logic quite exhaustively, probably more than is likely to be tested in practice.

The Rule Family in Table 6.11 is a dependent Rule Family of the Rule Family in Table 6.9, because it has a condition column that uses the Fact Type Policy Tier within Bounds. An inspection of the columns for this fact type from Table 6.9 and Table 6.11 indicates that the only value that Policy Tier within Bounds can have is "No" and "Yes." Table 6.11 also shows that there is a row where the value of Policy Tier within Bounds does not matter. This means that the row in question should be tested with both values of Policy Tier within Bounds to ensure that they both return the correct value for Policy Renewal Method. For future uses of the test cases, the Rule Family will have to be examined to determine whether the values for either column require additional tests.

The test case for the Rule Family will therefore have the input of "Yes" and "No" for Policy Renewal Method and for each one of those values, will have a "Yes and "No" for Policy Tier within Bounds. For this Rule Family, the complete test case is in Table 6.12.

Of course, the tester may decide to test the Decision Model as a whole by combining these test cases and cascading the tests. This would have value, particularly

Table 6.10 Partial Test Case for Policy Tier within Bounds

Input		Output
Policy Tier	*Policy Discount (%)*	*Policy Tier within Bounds*
0	0	No
0	10	No
0	28	No
0	31	No
.9	0	No
.9	10	No
.9	28	No
.9	31	No
1	0	No
1	10	No
1	28	No
1	31	No
1.3	5	Yes
1.3	9	Yes
1.3	10	Yes
1.3	13	No
1.3	21	No
...	...	...

in unit and acceptance testing. The inputs for testing of the Decision Model as a whole will be based on the pool of the domain values for all the non-dependent fact types of all the Rule Families. It can readily be seen that a rigorously constructed Decision Model tool should be capable of automatically generating test cases.

Table 6.11 Rule Family "Policy Renewal Method"

Pattern	Conditions				Conclusion	
	Policy Manual Override		*Policy Tier within Bounds*		*Policy Renewal Method*	
1	Is	Yes			Is	Manual Renewal Process
2			Is	No	Is	Manual Renewal Process
3	Is	No	Is	Yes	Is	Automatic Renewal Process

Table 6.12 Test Case for Rule Family "Policy Renewal Method"

Inputs		Output
Policy Manual Override	Policy Tier within Bounds	Policy Renewal Method
Yes	Yes	Manual Renewal Process
Yes	No	Manual Renewal Process
No	Yes	Automatic Renewal Process
No	No	Manual Renewal Process

These simple examples illustrate the practicality of automatically generating test cases from the Rule Families themselves. Even if test cases are not automatically generated, the ability to provide direct testing of the business logic in a very early stage of development has a significant impact on the quality of the code and productivity of both the programmer and tester.

Scenario Testing

One effective way to test the business functionality of a system is scenario testing. Scenario testing does not test the business logic directly; it tests the whole implemented business process model for a given set of inputs. This approach to testing business logic was originally suggested by Michael Beck and Art Moore, and the examples below are based on their work (Beck and Moore, 2006).

Figure 6.7 contains a simplified business process model. A business scenario is described in Table 6.13.

The table is a simplified view of the scenario and associated fact type logical expressions. In practice, the scenario would include a selection of inputs, which

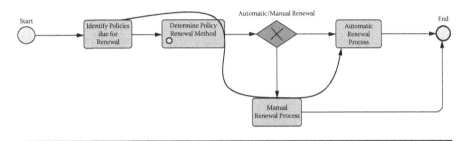

Figure 6.7 Path through the Process Model of a Single Business Scenario. (With Acknowledgment to Michael Beck and Art Moore of Clear System LLC.)

Table 6.13 Testing Business Scenarios

Scenario	Fact Types Evaluated
A Policy is submitted for renewal and is evaluated to determine whether it will be routed to the manual or automotive renewal method.	Fact types evaluated are: Policy Tier > 2.6 Policy Discount = 0% Policy Manual Override = No
The Policy Tier is within bounds.	
The conditions meet the requirements for automatic renewal; consequently, the policy should be submitted for automatic renewal.	

in this case means policies that exercise the range of relevant values for all fact types across the business process. These scenarios exercise the system as a complete business process model. In the words of Beck and Moore (their references to "business model" mean the business process model together with the relevant business rules):

> Our project experience has shown that the advantage of this approach, which is based on the information contained in the business model, is that we can develop the scenarios early in the development process (no later than logical design); giving the test team valuable input on the number and complexity of tests they will be required to perform. The second advantage is that the scenarios and subsequent test scripts based on the content of the business model are readily understood by the business users, which has the benefit of removing ambiguity from the testing and acceptance process. (Beck and Moore, 2006)

Putting It All Together

Figure 6.8 illustrates how classical requirements fit together, including the Decision Model. The central box labeled "Project Models" illustrates all of the models that comprise the project models, including the Decision Model. External to the models are relevant project textual statements representing requirements. A person can view one of these statements and discover related models, and also view a model and discover related textual requirement statements. The project requirements also trace, where appropriate, to enterprise models and enterprise textual statements. In addition, there is a relationship of test scripts to business decisions and to the business scenarios, as was discussed in the previous section.

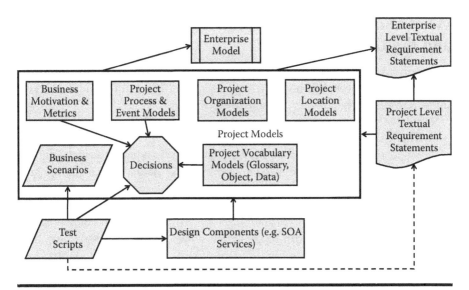

Figure 6.8 A diagrammatic view of functional requirements. (With acknowledgment to Michael Beck and Art Moore of Clear Systems LLC.)

Beck and Moore explain the success they experienced in integrating business rules into the models in a large government agency:

> … This … represents a validation of one final observation: Business rules were always there in our business and/or our system models and requirements statements. They may not have been separated out or completely stated, but they were there someplace, otherwise they would not, for the most part, have been implemented at all (a nod to rogue programming). It makes sense that if business rules do represent a specific, essential component of a holistic business model, then bringing more order and rigor to that component would further clarify and organize the rest of the model and its parts, and this is exactly what we have discovered to be the case. (Beck and Moore, 2006)

There is one element that has not been discussed in this chapter, and that is the Design Component. The Design Component refers to the manner in which business functions are grouped within a system. The business user has an interest in this grouping from a functional perspective. Today, the grouping of business functions within a system (or across systems) is related to how an organization wants to deliver services. A discussion about the organization of services from the perspective of a business user is in Chapter 5.

What about Agile Development and the Decision Model?

Agilists would not develop "up front" a complete set of business requirements as depicted in Figure 6.8. Yet, not only is the Decision Model still useful, it is ideally suited to Agile methodologies. Reasons are as follows:

■ The business logic modeled in the Decision Model fits into a very well-defined scope, the business decision. Because that scope is typically a single step in a business use case or task in the business process model, it is an appropriately bounded scope for the single increment that Agile development seeks for its iterations.

■ The Decision Model serves as an ideal mechanism by which domain experts share understanding with programmers about the business logic for a business function.

■ The Decision Model provides the business logic in a form that is compatible with its programmatic representation. This ease of transformation from the modeled business logic to program logic allows simpler, perhaps fewer and shorter, interactions between developer and business experts. An opportunity also exists for an Agile developer to maintain structures that are like Rule Families in the code such that the code truly mirrors and becomes a requirement that the user can easily understand.

■ The Decision Model can easily be drawn and detailed without technology, using POW, index cards, or spreadsheets.

Experience with the Decision Model indicates it is the ideal artifact for representing business logic in requirements. This is true whether those requirements are developed in a comprehensive formal process, or developed in an informal, iterative process designed to discover the true intent of the business expert. Astute developers will recognize the opportunity to use development patterns that correlate closely to the structure of logic in the Decision Model. These patterns may be employed whether BRMS, object orientation, or procedural coding methods are used. This approach will improve development productivity, the traceability between the Decision Model and the code, testing, and the long-term maintenance of the code.

Summary

This chapter presented the various ways in which the Decision Model improves requirements by relating the Decision Model into other models used in functional requirements. This significantly improves all requirements because, prior to the Decision Model, business logic was "lost": either missed, captured later, or spread throughout various kinds of requirements artifacts.

The most important concepts in this chapter are the following:

- Functional requirements are defined as "a condition or capability needed by a user to solve a problem or achieve an objective."
- Requirements for the purpose of the chapter consist of those elements of the system over which the business user is expected to (or should) provide.
- Poor or incomplete functional requirements have led to project failure or diminished value.
- Requirements are expressed in various ways:
  - Textual statements—Used primarily for contractual purposes
  - Business use cases—Used to describe interactions between actors and the system for a specific purpose
  - Prototypes—Used to help describe the user interfaces needed in the system
  - Models—Used for a variety of reasons to build a complete view of the proposed system
  - Code—The Agile method describes the code as the design of the system, and derives the requirements from the artifacts—models that are drawn on POW—after the code is complete.
- The Decision Model connects to other model types such as BMM, business use cases, business process models, and semantic models through common connection points and metadata. The Decision Model simplifies business use cases and business process models.
- The Decision Model provides a means for developing, very early and very completely, test cases of the business logic within the systems. It also provides a means for developing test cases for business scenarios of the business processes.
- The integration of all requirements-related models, including the Decision Model, together with textual requirement statements, and test cases, form a complete collection of requirements. This has proved to be an effective form of requirements.
- Finally, Agile methodologies also benefit from the Decision Model because it provides a technique for shared understanding of the business logic between business user and developer.

New Vocabulary Introduced in This Chapter

- requirements
- functional requirements
- nonfunctional requirements
- textual statements as requirements
- business use case
- system use case
- model

- prototype
- semantic model
- Agile methods
- BRUF—Big requirements upfront
- POW—Plain old whiteboard

And What about the Quote

The late 1960s classic Rolling Stones tune "You can't always get what you want" captures the essence of initial optimism followed by disillusionment and, finally, acceptance of an inevitable pragmatic conclusion to many software projects. The Decision Model is an artifact that helps project teams manage business logic and related requirements. In this way, the Decision Model helps deliver a system closer to what business users want, rather than what they merely need.

Discussion Points and Exercises

1. Express textual requirements for the business use case in Tables 6.6 and 6.7.
2. Develop a test case for the Rule Family in Table 7.6 (Chapter 7).
3. The text in the chapter does not consider the connection points that may exist between prototypes and Decision Models. Consider whether connection points may exist between these two artifacts, and if so, what impact this may have on the prototype model. Also, consider whether the prototype may have a utility in discovering the existence of business decisions.
4. Drawing upon a recent project that you participated in, describe the types of requirements developed by the project team and consider the completeness of the artifacts; consider the possible impact to the project of applying the Decision Model to the project and the possible effects of not doing so.

Chapter 7

Getting Started

Contents

The Decision Model in Practice Prior to This Book 140
The Fictional Project and Approach 140
Step 1: Respond to an Executive Management Mandate 141
Step 2: Assemble a Decision Model Project Team with New Skills 142
Step 3: Define a Reasonable Decision Model Scope 145
    Aspect #1: Scope of the Business Process Model 145
    Aspect #2: Scope of the Decisions 146
    Aspect #3: Subset of Business Transactions for Those Decisions 147
    Aspect #4: Fact Types 148
    Aspect #5: Business Performance Metrics 149
    Aspect #6: Decision Model Estimations 151
Step 4: Develop a Decision-Aware Business Process Model 153
Step 5: Develop the Decision Model Diagram 155
Step 6: Populate Rule Families 158
Steps 7–8: Test and Refine the Decision Model before Implementing It 161
Step 9: Automate the Decision Model 162
Step 10: Plan for SOA, BRMS, BPMS, and Governance 162
Summary 163
New Vocabulary Introduced in This Chapter 163
And What about the Quote 164
Discussion Points and Exercises 164

All glory comes from daring to begin.

Eugene F. Ware

This chapter is for readers who want to put the Decision Model into play for a particular business opportunity or challenge. The recommendation is to do so on a small project or pilot first. This provides insights into how best to leverage the Decision Model based on cultural readiness and leadership.

This chapter presents a fictional project with common characteristics borrowed from many real-world projects. It leads the reader through ten basic steps in the management and execution of a Decision Model project, including its challenges.

The Decision Model in Practice Prior to This Book

Prior to the writing of this book, the Decision Model had been applied with success at several corporations. The resulting Decision Models delivered business decisions in a tangible and manageable form. Even in skeletal form (i.e., Decision Model diagram without populated Rule Families), a Decision Model sets the stage for strategic business thinking, creativity, and distinction. It is significant that using the Decision Model and its principles has led to greater productivity. However, more importantly, in most cases, it has provided the opportunity to accomplish business objectives that remained elusive without it.

This chapter presents a fictional project that is typical of many Decision Model projects. In a realistic step-by-step manner, the chapter leads the reader through the initiation, planning, and completion of a Decision Model for the project.

The Fictional Project and Approach

The fictional project in this chapter provides sufficient detail for embarking on a first Decision Model project with confidence and minimal risk. Not only that, the fictional project has parallels in almost every industry.

Each part of the case study in this chapter is borrowed from actual Decision Model projects. The case study is not meant to represent the complexity of real-world business process models or Decision Models. Rather, it is meant to illustrate a reasonable and practical approach to building them.

The approach includes experience-based insights into the following:

■ Responding to an executive management directive
■ Assembling a project team with Decision Model skills
■ Defining a reasonable Decision Model scope

- Developing a decision-aware business process model
- Creating, testing, and refining a Decision Model before implementation
- Automating the Decision Model in current systems
- Planning for the Decision Model in future systems: System-Oriented Architecture (SOA), business rules management system (BRMS), business process management system (BPMS), and Decision Model governance.

Step 1: Respond to an Executive Management Mandate

A fictional insurance company specializing in commercial insurance is concerned about the viability of its commercial auto insurance business. Customers for commercial auto insurance include companies owning vehicles for employee usage and limousine companies, for example.

The company's commercial auto insurance business generates revenue through the issuance of new policies and renewal of expiring policies. These activities are currently supported by a set of legacy systems developed many decades ago.

Of immediate concern is that only a small percentage of new and renewed policies are completely handled by the automated systems. In fact, just 30% of new policies and 50% of renewed policies are handled completely through the automated systems. The systems route the rest of the policies to the appropriate region, where local regional experts determine whether each policy should be written or renewed. The good news is that the extensive human handling of most policies means that the company has been able to minimize its risk and maintain consistent profits on its policies. The bad news is that there are inconsistencies in how renewals have been handled by human experts, and the cost of extensive human handling has led to dissatisfaction among customers. Even more alarming is a disappointing decline in revenue despite projections by analysts that commercial auto insurance is a growth market. The executive management team is also painfully aware that recent competitors are able to process larger volumes of new and renewed policies in significantly shorter time frames. That's because competitors have invested in more sophisticated automated policy writing and renewal systems.

The executive management team decides to be aggressive in new and renewed commercial auto insurance policies over the next six months. They issue a mandate requiring 75% of both new and renewable policies to be handled completely through the current automated systems. At the same time, the executive management team requires that the risk associated with automatically approving these policies remain as low as it is today. Further, they want to see customer satisfaction increase in measurable ways. Most importantly, the company wishes to aggressively grow this revenue by 15%. As usual, the executive management team

Table 7.1 Executive Management Goals and Objectives

Executive Management Goal	Executive Management Measurable Objectives
Increase the percentage of automated new and renewed commercial auto insurance policies	New policy automation to increase from 30% to 75% Renewed policy automation to increase from 50% to 75%
Increase time spent by regional experts on other kinds of tasks	Free up regional experts' time by 20%
Increase the level of customer satisfaction regarding new and renewed commercial auto insurance policies	Retention of renewable policies to increase from 60% to 90% Number of new policies to increase by 15%
Maintain (do not increase) current risk level of new and renewed commercial auto insurance policies	Average profitability on new policies to be at least 12% Average profitability on renewed policies to be at least 15%
Increase the revenue from new and renewed commercial auto insurance policies	Revenue from new commercial auto policies to increase by 15% Revenue from renewed commercial auto policies to increase by 15%

imposes a strict time frame and fixed budget on finding and implementing the solution. No new software or technology can be purchased. Table 7.1 summarizes the executive management team's mandate, including its general goals and measurable objectives.

Step 2: Assemble a Decision Model Project Team with New Skills

After the executive management team publishes the mandate, they select a project manager who has a background in the auto insurance business and information technology (IT). The project manager decides that a Decision Model is at the core of the solution because the mandate involves rethinking the business logic that distinguishes between policies appropriate for automated versus human processing and consistent application of that business logic. The new Decision Model's content is to be tested and tuned until the objectives in Table 7.1 are measured and met. The project manager decides that the project team will first address the Decision Model for policy renewals. That's because crafting new business logic for the renewal of existing policies is less risky than doing so for the issuance of new policies for new customers. Also, the company maintains statistics on how well its renewed policies have done over the years. These statistics will provide a means for measuring the impact of the Decision Model.

A very short time frame (e.g., a few weeks) and minimal budget are established for scoping the policy renewal Decision Model. A project team of in-house staff is assembled. The core project members will need new skills, such as business process modeling, decision modeling, and the managing of fact type definitions.

The core team consists of the following roles:

- One overall project manager (full-time resource) reports either directly to the president of the company or to an executive steering committee due to the strategic nature of the project. This role ensures that the project remains on-time, within budget, and focused on business objectives at all times.
- One business governance manager (full- or part-time resource) works side-by-side with the overall project manager and ensures that the appropriate business expertise is available to the project team and that all the business stakeholders are heard in resolving any conflicting views as to the business logic. The business governance manager will refer any unresolved conflicts to a business governance council for resolution and will implement decisions of the council. The role will continue after the completion of the project in order to maintain governance over the business decisions.
- A business governance council (part-time resources) is a committee of key representatives of the business stakeholders whose role is to resolve any conflicts about business decisions and their business logic. It is convened by the business governance manager to provide final determinations when disputes arise that cannot be resolved among the stakeholders. The council will continue after completion of the project to maintain governance over the business decisions.
- One facilitator (part-time resource) leads the business experts through interactive, iterative sessions on business process modeling and Decision Modeling.
- Three kinds of business analysts (full-time resources) are responsible for guiding and documenting the models. These include a business process modeler, a decision modeler, and someone to manage the fact type definitions.*
  - The business process modeler (full-time resource) defines and refines high-level and detailed business process models or use case models, identifies business decisions within these models, supports business experts in investigating related business issues, and works with the Decision

---

* In some organizations, the person responsible for managing fact type definitions may be called an *ontology developer*.

Modelers to revise the relationship between the business process model and the Decision Models.

- The Decision Modeler (full-time resource) leads the effort to identify business decisions, prioritize them, create the Decision Model diagram, and populate Rule Families; seeks validation of business logic among stakeholders; and investigates critical test scenarios. One of the Decision Modelers serves as the integrator who will integrate various Decision Models into one, where appropriate.

- The person in charge of fact type definitions (full-time resource), called a glossary administrator, maintains them, enforces consistency of usage, integrates fact types from various sources, and works with modelers (e.g., such as fact modelers, data modelers, business object or class modelers) to correlate fact types to those models.

■ One librarian or knowledge manager (part-time resource) collects input materials, publishes all deliverables, and provides standard reports. This role also includes training the other members in, supporting, and managing the repository of business process models, Decision Models, and ensuring that the repository integrates into the IT environment.

■ One or more business experts (part-time resources) provide input to the modeling effort and are empowered to make decisions about the business process and business logic. These people provide business context, information, and expertise and act as the bridge between their business unit and the project. This role also assists in resolving inconsistencies, incompleteness, and overlaps in the Decision Model content and develops appropriate Decision Model test scenarios. This role may include representatives from each region such as regional managers, sales leaders, or agents. The role may also include representatives who span regions, such as global or corporate experts from a centralized underwriting group or legal function.

■ Two to four kinds of IT professionals (part-time resources) provide knowledge of legacy systems. One professional is a system support person who researches the business logic currently executing in the systems. Another is a business intelligence analyst who runs reports against a data warehouse and transaction data to test the business logic in the Decision Model as it evolves. Another professional may be a representative of an enterprise data management function who assists in defining fact types and correlating them to available data sources. Other IT professionals may modify logical data models or physical database technology to accommodate new fact types. Another may create an object model if one is needed to automate the new business logic.

The project team organization is shown in Figure 7.1.

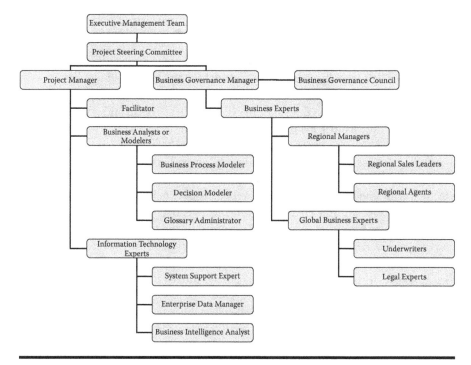

Figure 7.1   Project team organization chart.

Step 3: Define a Reasonable Decision Model Scope

In many ways, defining the scope of a Decision Model project is much like other projects. As such, the scope includes a list of business objectives, stakeholders, risks, risk mitigations, human and technology resources, deliverables, timeline, and budget. There are, however, at least six unique aspects to scoping a Decision Model.

Aspect #1: Scope of the Business Process Model

The first unique aspect is the development or review of a high-level business process model for which the target business decision is to provide guidance. In this case study, as is typically the case, there is no existing high-level business process model to review. So, the team develops the high-level business process model shown in Figure 7.2, which depicts a simplified full life cycle of a commercial auto insurance

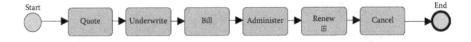

Figure 7.2 High-level business process model for the lifetime of a policy.

policy.* This simple process flow indicates how a policy is born, critical states it goes through, and how its lifetime might come to an end.

The start shape represents a request from a customer, prospect, or internal or external insurance agent. Based on information gathered for the policy, an initial quote is defined and offered. If accepted, the policy is approved and officially executed with underwriter support, as needed. The customer is billed for the policy, and the policy is administered throughout its effective dates. It is considered for renewal prior to expiration date, and may eventually be cancelled.

The + in the Renew task shape indicates that the project team has created an additional level of detail for this task because this is where the Decision Model is to provide guidance. If this were a full business process model, it would contain additional levels behind the other tasks. However, this business process model is needed only to assist in scoping the target Decision Model. The other tasks are not relevant to the executive mandate and, therefore, their details are not defined by this project team.

Aspect #2: Scope of the Decisions

The next aspect of scoping is the gathering of information about the target business decisions. This information includes a list of desirable participants, documentation, operative context, economic value, and business logic complexity.

As for a list of desirable participants, the target business decision requires business experts from each region. These would be the regional managers, underwriters, lead sales persons, or agents.

As for documentation, the team identifies and the librarian gathers available documentation. These include procedure manuals from the regions as well as legacy systems documentation. The librarian also assesses the quality of each piece of documentation, indicating whether it is out of date, nonexistent, or not clearly written. The librarian also assesses the accessibility of additional knowledge. Is it in peoples' heads? Are those people available? Is it in program code, technical documentation, or technical models? Are people available who use the system and understand its hidden business logic? These considerations allow the team to assign time frames to the development of various parts of the target Decision Models.

---

* Naturally, such business process models in real case studies are more complex and may be divided into swim lanes showing organizational roles that drive each task. Typically, the business decisions may not be visible from a high-level business process model. Most high-level business process models need to be decomposed into more detail to locate the target business decisions that are within scope for the immediate project.

Table 7.2 Scoping Considerations for the Decision Model

Scoping Consideration	Assessment
Participants	Regional managers, lead salespeople, underwriters, legal experts, information technology specialists
Documentation	Regional procedure manuals: medium clarity, up to date, people available
	Technical documentation: out of date or nonexistent, people unavailable
	Database models: up to date, people available
Operative context	Simple to complicated
	Fact types unknown
Economic value	High
Business logic complexity	Medium
Proprietary nature	Extremely proprietary

As for operative context, the team decides that the business decision operates in the simple domain as it guides a business process. However, it also has characteristics of the complicated domain because the new fact types and fact values are yet to be determined.

As for the economic value, the project team decides that the volume-based economic impact of this business decision is high. Specifically, this is a business decision that is carried out for every commercial auto insurance policy and has a high economic impact due to the value of each renewed policy.

As for business logic complexity, because the future fact types and values are not yet known, the project team decides that the expected complexity of the business logic will be medium. That is, it won't be as complex as the business logic for underwriting decisions, but will be more complex than renewal logic is today. The business logic will, however, be considered extremely proprietary to the company and perhaps should not even be disclosed to everyone in the company.

The scoping considerations for the Decision Model are summarized in Table 7.2.

Aspect #3: Subset of Business Transactions for Those Decisions

The third step is to prioritize the business transactions that rely on the target business decision. The goal is to narrow the focus to those business transactions with

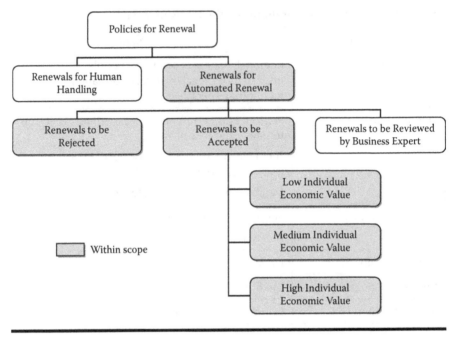

Figure 7.3 Creating target subsets of transactions for the Decision Model.

the most impact on the business objectives. This is where the economic impact of the target business decisions becomes even more important.

For this case study, the set of commercial auto insurance policy renewals that today are handled by humans are divided into three groups: those whose renewal should be rejected by the automated system, those whose renewal should be accepted and completed by the automated system, and those whose renewal should be evaluated by a business expert. The group whose renewal should be accepted by the system is further divided into smaller groups based on individual economic value and risk. This breakdown is illustrated in Figure 7.3.

Aspect #4: Fact Types

The fourth consideration is to propose a preliminary list of fact types for the target Decision Model. This is particularly challenging if the Decision Model is to contain new business logic.

In this case study, the project team relies on the IT system support person to research the legacy system documentation and program code to discover the fact types in its underlying business logic. This research indicates that very few basic fact types are tested to distinguish between automated and manual policy renewals. This was expected because the systems are only processing a small percentage of renewals. Therefore, the systems must be testing only a few fact types against very conservative business logic expressions.

The IT expert points out that any policy that had been renewed fewer than three times (i.e., the company has only administered the policy for fewer than three years) is routed to manual policy review and renewal. For those that had been renewed more than three times (i.e., have been administered by the company for more than three years), the system then checked for average premium value over its years, average claim payout amount over its years, and the annual increase in fleet size over those years. Nothing else was checked by the systems.

The project team determined that the new Decision Model may well contain these fact types, but the tests against them need allow more renewals to be processed automatically by the system. And, there will be new fact types to consider. From a scoping perspective, a quick facilitated session is conducted to explore the nature and estimated quantity of additional fact types that might be relevant to pushing a transaction through complete automation at reasonable risk.

In that session, sample additional fact types might be fact types about the insured company: the executive ownership, location changes. Additional fact types might be those that assess the value and risk of policies by assigning them to tiers. The team agreed that there was a need for forcing a manual renewal without giving a reason.

Discussions ensued about different geographical locations and differing demographics of customers. Finally, the project team determined that there would be a common set of fact types across all regions along with region-specific fact types.

Aspect #5: Business Performance Metrics

The fifth aspect in scoping a Decision Model project is the establishment of metrics by which the Decision Model can be measured against target business objectives.

It is important to identify these metrics before the project is completed because some ungathered metrics may need to be gathered to get the before and after picture. It is also important to determine how often the metrics will be captured and analyzed.

Table 7.3 summarizes goals, objectives, and specific metrics to be captured as they relate to the renewal of commercial insurance auto policies. Apparently,

Table 7.3 Executive Management Goals, Objectives, and Metrics for the Immediate Project

Executive Management Goal	Executive Management Measurable Objectives	Business Performance Metrics: Evaluated Every 90 days
Increase the percentage of automated renewed commercial auto insurance policies	Renewed policies automation to increase from 50% to 75%	Total quantity of policies targeted for renewal by region Total quantity and percentage of policies completed through automated renewal by region Total quantity and percentage of policies completed through human renewal by region
Increase time spent by regional experts on other kinds of tasks	Free up regional experts' time by 20%	Quantity of nonrenewal task hours from employee timesheets by region Evaluate subjective survey from regional experts themselves on how they perceive their time is used
Increase the level of customer satisfaction regarding renewed commercial auto insurance policies	Retention of renewable policies to increase from 60% to 90%	Total quantity and percentage of renewed policies per region
Maintain (do not increase) current risk level of renewed commercial auto insurance policies	Average profitability on new policies to be at least 20%	Average profitability of manually renewed policies per region Average profitability of automated renewed policies per region
Increase the revenue from renewed commercial auto insurance policies	Revenue from renewed commercial auto policies to increase by 15%	Total revenue from renewed auto policies per region

the metrics will be evaluated every 90 days after the new Decision Model is put into place. This allows the team to see incremental changes in performance of the policy renewal process and to make adjustments to the Decision Model, if appropriate. It also allows for comparing performance of different regions against the original mandate, which may lead to region-specific business logic changes.

Aspect #6: Decision Model Estimations

The sixth step is to establish estimation metrics for developing the corresponding Decision Models based on the number of sources, number of stakeholders, anticipated complexity of the business logic, quantity of fact types, and so on.

Table 7.4 indicates that there is only one target business decision for the project, and it is called Determine Policy Renewal Method. The project team has decided that the quantity of Rule Families will be between 5 and 10, not expecting a first Decision Model to consist of a large number of Rule Families. The estimated quantity of fact types is 20 compared to the quantity in current systems, which is fewer than 5. The quantity of rows per Rule Family may be as few as 20, but is permitted to increase to 100 to allow for region-specific business logic. The sources are the business experts, system documentation, and regional policies and procedures manuals. Based on the availability of appropriate experts and the librarian's assessment of other documentation, the sources are of medium quality and accessibility. The business logic complexity is expected to be simple due to small quantities of Rule Families, Rule Family rows, and fact types. However, the project plan needs to allow more time than is typically needed for other simple Decision Models. This is because this case study requires creative and analytical business thinking and testing to discover the most appropriate business logic. Also, the project team expects important and heated discussions about region-specific business logic versus business logic that should apply to all regions. Periodic consultations with global experts will be needed to resolve conflicting opinions.

With such a worksheet for the target business decision, the project manager applies resource and time estimates to each aspect of building the Decision Model. These estimates will vary from project to project and will be impacted by organizational culture.

Once the project manager determines such estimates, the estimates are incorporated into a project plan. A skeletal list of tasks for such a project plan is shown in Table 7.5.

Once the project plan is approved by the steering committee, the project team revisits or continues developing the corresponding business process model.

Table 7.4 Sample Worksheet for Estimating Decision Model Effort

Target Decision	Estimated Quantity of Rule Families	Estimated Quantity of Fact Types	Estimated Quantity of Rows per Rule Family	Estimated Quantity of Reference Sources (people, documents, code)	Assessment of Accessibility of Sources	Assessment of Quality of Sources	Assessment of Business Logic Complexity
Determine Policy Renewal Method	5–10	20	20–100	50	Medium	Medium	Simple, but fact types are unknown and regional versus global issues are important

Table 7.5   Sample Project Tasks

Task				
Present Management Overview				
Facilitate session to confirm scope				
Develop and revise business process model to business decision				
Develop and revise Decision Model Diagram as a whole group				
Populate and revise Rule Families as a whole group				
Run reports against real data with new business logic				
Populate and revise Rule Families as regional groups				
Run reports against real data with new business logic per region				
Integrate regional results into one Decision Model				
Confer with global business experts				
Analyze Decision Model for integrity				
Present Decision Model to steering committee				
Present deliverables to Information Technology Group				
Update system				
Test updates				
Put changes into production				
Collect performance metrics				
Evaluate performance metrics				

Step 4: Develop a Decision-Aware Business Process Model

As indicated earlier, the project team, through sessions with the facilitator, has developed initial business process model diagrams during scoping. If the team had spent sufficient time on a business process model for new and renewed policies, the team may have realized that these two business processes are similar enough to combine into a more generic business process that handles new and renewed policies. In fact, it is possible that the two processes can be combined into one business process only up to a certain point. Then, one of the two different business decisions for automatic versus manual processing can be called into play depending on whether the transaction was a new or renewable policy.

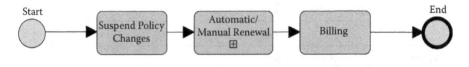

Figure 7.4   More detailed business process model for renew task.

For now, the project team is focused only on the policy renewal process. Therefore, Figure 7.4 shows the next level of detail behind the Renew task.

The + in the Automatic/Manual Renewal task indicates that the project team deems it necessary to develop yet another level of detail before arriving at the point where the target Decision Model provides guidance.

The next level of detail created by the project team is shown in Figure 7.5.

In Figure 7.5, the second task, Determine Policy Renewal Method, is a decision task, not a process task. So, it is depicted as containing the octagon shape. There is no further process detail behind this task as it now relies on the declarative Decision Model.*

Too often, in practice, project teams fail to see the value of creating a business process model in conjunction with developing a Decision Model. The assumption is either that everyone understands the business process well enough or that it isn't worth the time to create one. Operating without a business process model has always turned out to be a mistake. In fact, experience proves that creating a quick business process model not only solidifies the Decision Model scope, it also crystallizes for the participants the distinction between procedural process and declarative business logic. The business process model also saves a lot of time throughout the life of the project, and it can even lead to creative business improvements. More often than not, when project teams create or analyze decision-aware business process models, opportunities to significantly simplify the business process models, or even combine them, turn up. The creation of a business process model can also lead to the realization that several current business processes can be combined into one common business process, differentiated simply by different Decision Models. These realizations simplify the project plan and streamline a solution. But such realizations do not become apparent until a high-level decision-aware business process model is created. It is best when these advantages show up early, as in scoping.

---

* In most Decision Model projects, the decisions fit into second- or third-level process details. Also, most business process models are far more complex than this example and usually contain tasks that operate in different swim lanes. Each swim lane represents a different role (people or system) responsible for carrying out the tasks in the swim lane, providing insight into stakeholders in the entire business process.

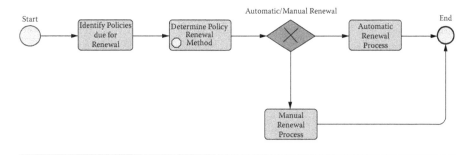

Figure 7.5   Third level of detail in the business process model.

Step 5: Develop the Decision Model Diagram

Once the project team comes to an agreement on the business process model, the team confirms the stakeholders who will benefit from the target Decision Model and how they will benefit. Stakeholders in this case study include customers, agents, salespeople, and regional managers. Such insights may influence the content of the Decision Model.

At this point, the project team starts to develop the Decision Model Diagram. This is the diagram of Rule Family structures, condition fact types, and inferential relationships among Rule Families, but does not include Rule Family content. It is best that the project members agree ahead of time to follow certain standards for development of Decision Models. These standards include naming conventions for business decisions and fact types and an acceptable set of valid operators to use in Rule Families.*

Through facilitated sessions, the project team explores the following:

- Which of the fact types used in current systems should be in the future Decision Model?
- For each of the business objectives and performance metrics, what other kinds of fact types might be of interest?
- For each stakeholder, what fact types might be of interest?
- Should there be a mechanism by which a business expert can override the automatic versus manual renewal decision of the Decision Model?
- Are there region-specific considerations?
- Is the data for the newly proposed fact types available at this point in the business process?

---

* The authors have developed such standards based on experience in developing Decision Models. More information on these can be found at www.TheDecisionModel.com.

These facilitated sessions take place for a few hours each day. At the end of each session, questions and issues are assigned to participants and a revised skeletal Decision Model diagram is produced. IT representatives check on the definition of proposed fact types and the availability of the data behind them. Business regional representatives discuss issues with other representatives from their region. Occasionally, questions are routed to an underwriter or legal expert. In some cases, questions are routed to the steering committee, which may send them to the Executive Management Team.

At the beginning of each subsequent session, the scope is revisited in case the new fact types imply a change in scope. The business process model is revisited for possible changes. For example, if the information behind some of the proposed fact types is not available at the noted point in the business process, additional tasks (e.g., for obtaining that information) may be needed in the business process model. From here, the proposed fact types are revisited and discussions continue until there is agreement on the first-cut Decision Model diagram.

The project team decides on fact types that should apply to all regions, but they decide to allow each region some level of control over certain aspects of the business logic.

The first-cut Decision Model diagram is shown in Figure 7.6, although initially it is not likely to denote the Rule Patterns. Note that this Decision Model is very similar to the one used in Chapter 2, Figure 2.1, to illustrate the Decision Model. However, the model for this fictional project includes the consideration of Insured Region as a fact type to allow for region-specific business logic.

At this point, the business process model and the Decision Model diagram are reviewed with the steering committee.

The Decision Model diagram represents critical and creative thinking by the team as follows:

- A policy will be assigned to a tier based on the perceived value of the policy to the company.
- The business logic for assigning a policy to a tier is not part of this Decision Model. Therefore, there is no Rule Family for it in this Decision Model, although the Policy Tier is used as a condition fact type.
- The Policy Renewal Method is based on whether a Policy Tier is Within Bounds unless overridden by a Policy Manual Override.
- A Policy Discount is determined by Policy Grade (e.g., whose value is determined outside the scope of this Decision Model), Package Grade and Package Discount (e.g., values also determined outside this scope), and Location State Category. Location State category is a way to rate different states in desirability.

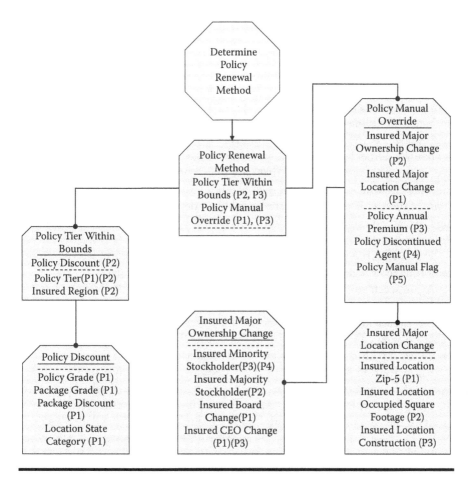

Figure 7.6   First-cut Decision Model diagram.

▪ The Policy Manual Override is determined based on evaluating the Insured for Major Ownership Change or Major Location Change, a test of the Policy Annual Premium, Policy Discontinued Agent, or Policy Manual Flag. The Decision Model indicates that any one test of these fact types is needed for a conclusion because each is in its own Rule Pattern in the Rule Family for Policy Manual Override.

Regions have the ability to control the conditions for which the Policy Tier is within bounds. This is evident because the fact type of Insured Region is included in the Rule Family for Policy Tier Within Bounds. This means that each region can decide whether a Policy Tier is within bounds.

Step 6: Populate Rule Families

The next step is for the project team to populate the Rule Families. The project team can do so in a facilitated session. Alternatively, they can separate into groups, with each group presenting its recommendations to the entire team. The sessions with the entire team can span many days, with questions assigned and the IT professionals providing support. For example, a useful report is one indicating how many policies currently due for renewal fall into the different policy tiers and different bounds. Other helpful reports are those indicating how many policies currently due for renewal are for Insured's that have undergone significant business changes; these policies will be routed for human handling based on the new Decision Model. Some of these policies can be previewed by underwriters or other experts, allowing the team to experiment with different logical expressions in the corresponding Rule Families.

Eventually, the project team divides into regional groups, and those groups determine their region-specific contributions to the Rule Families.

Again, each team session starts by reviewing the scope, the business process model, and the Decision Model diagram before delving into the Rule Family populations. Eventually, agreement is reached for a first-cut populated Decision Model. Table 7.6 shows a simple first-cut populated Rule Family. It determines whether a policy tier is within bounds for allowing automatic renewal.

An interesting point to note is that Table 7.6 contains only a single specified region, the Southeast. This is the only region with a current need to vary from the cross-regional business logic. Apart from this region, the other rows have "*" listed for the region. This is a form of shorthand to depict that the Policy Tier and Policy Discount values represent all regions other than those specifically noted in the Rule Family. An alternative representation is to populate the Rule Family with a row for all other regions, each with the complete set of duplicate policy tiers.

Table 7.7 contains a glossary of fact type names and definitions used in the Rule Families. For fact types that are conclusion fact types, the definitions specifically do not include reference to the condition fact types that determine their values because the condition fact types belong in the Decision Model where they may change. The definition of a fact type should not need to change when the Decision Model changes. Readers should keep in mind that development of a Decision Model is not considered complete until it is compliant with all Decision Model principles. Such compliance ensures that a Decision Model exhibits optimum semantic and business integrity, as discussed further in Chapters 8 through 10. The principles can be applied either during or after populating all Rule Families.

Table 7.6 Sample Populated Rule Family

		Conditions				Conclusion	
Pattern	Insured Region	Policy Tier		Policy Discount		Policy Tier Within Bounds	
1	*	Is Less Than or Equal to	1	Is Less Than or Equal to	10%	Is	No
2	*	Is Between	{1, 1.5}	Is Greater Than	10%	Is	No
2	*	Is Between	{1, 1.5}	Is Less Than or Equal to	12.5%	Is	No
2	*	Is Between	{1.5, 2}	Is Greater Than	12.5%	Is	No
2	*	Is Between	{1.5, 2}	Is Less Than or Equal to	20%	Is	Yes
2	*	Is Between	{2, 2.6}	Is Greater Than	20%	Is	Yes
2	*	Is Between	{2, 2.6}	Is Less Than or Equal to	22%	Is	Yes
2	*	Is Greater Than	2.6	Is Greater Than	22%	Is	Yes
2	*	Is Greater Than	2.6			Is	No
1	Is Southeast	Is Less Than or Equal to	1			Is	No
2	Is Southeast	Between	{1, 1.5}	Is Less Than or Equal to	12%	Is	No
2	Is Southeast	Between	{1, 1.5}	Is Greater Than	12%	Is	No
2	Is Southeast	Between	{1.5, 2}	Is Less Than or Equal to	14%	Is	No
2	Is Southeast	Between	{1.5, 2}	Is Greater Than	14%	Is	Yes
2	Is Southeast	Between	{2, 2.6}	Is Less Than or Equal to	25%	Is	Yes
2	Is Southeast	Between	{2, 2.6}	Is Greater Than	25%	Is	Yes
2	Is Southeast	Is Greater Than	2.6	Is Less Than or Equal to	27%	Is	Yes
2	Is Southeast	Is Greater Than	2.6	Is Greater Than	27%	Is	No

Table 7.7   Fact Type Glossary

Fact Type	Definition
Insured Board Change	An indicator for a named Insured to denote a change in the board of directors of the named Insured that may contribute to determining risk. Such changes may include the resignation or addition of one or more board members.
Insured CEO Change	An indicator for a named Insured denoting a change in the CEO that may contribute to determining risk.
Insured Location Construction	An indicator for a named Insured Location that assesses the type of construction of the premise of the named Insured, if any.
Insured Location Occupied Square Footage	The total square footage occupied by named Insured at a Location.
Insured Location Zip-5	The five-digit zip code of the Location of the Insured as assigned by the U.S. Post Office.
Insured Major Location Change	An indicator for a named Insured to denote a major location change for the named Insured that may contribute to determining risk. Such changes may include a physical move to another location, a change in size of occupied space, and construction activities at the location, or others, for example.
Insured Major Ownership Change	An indicator for an Insured whose purpose is to denote that a significant change has occurred in the ownership of the Insured that may contribute to determining risk.
Insured Majority Stockholder	A stockholder of an Insured who has greater than 50% of the ownership of the Insured.
Insured Minority Stockholder	A stockholder of an Insured who has less than or equal to 50% of the ownership of the Insured.
Insured Region	A geographic grouping of corporate operations in which a named Insured resides.
Location State Category	The category assigned to the state in which the Insured Location Zip-5 is based to indicate the desirability of doing business in specific states.
Package Discount	The credit or debit amount applied to the premium for a group of policies for a named Insured.

Table 7.7   Fact Type Glossary (Continued)

Fact Type	Definition
Package Grade	A code assigned to a whole package of policies owned by a named Insured to indicate the Package's financial value, usually based on loss ratios over a certain number of years.
Policy Annual Premium	The annual amount to be paid on behalf of a named Insured for a Policy.
Policy Discontinued Agent	An indicator for a Policy that the Agent for the Insured is no longer an active agent.
Policy Discount	The credit or debit amount applied to the rated premium resulting in the Policy Premium.
Policy Grade	A code assigned to a Policy to indicate the Policy's financial value, usually based on its loss ratios over time.
Policy Manual Flag	An indicator for a Policy indicating that the Policy must undergo manual renewal process regardless of other factors. This indicator is usually controlled by an underwriter or administrator.
Policy Manual Override	An indicator that forces a manual renewal process regardless of other factors.
Policy Renewal Method	The type of process by which Policy can be renewed (e.g., manual, automatic).
Policy Tier	The assignment of a policy to a group to indicate the policy's perceived value to the company.
Policy Tier Within Bounds	An indicator (Y or N) to denote whether a Policy is within a specific range by which the Policy can be renewed through the automatic method.

Steps 7–8: Test and Refine the Decision Model before Implementing It

When new fact types are developed, IT representatives can often run reports against real transaction data, in a test environment, to ascertain how current transactions would have been treated by the Decision Model. Doing so provides insight into how the business logic will perform even before the Decision Model is implemented in program code.

Step 9: Automate the Decision Model

When the Decision Model and its Rule Families reach an acceptable state, the team presents them, along with the glossary of fact types, to the IT Group. The project team also develops test cases to test the business logic in any implementation of the Decision Model, as discussed in Chapter 6.

This group then determines where in the legacy systems to make the corresponding changes, the businesspeople test the changes, and the changes are put into production.

Step 10: Plan for SOA, BRMS, BPMS, and Governance

If this is the first Decision Model project, it usually spurs interest in the relevance of the Decision Model to SOA, BRMS, BPMS, and governance over the business logic.

The IT group can use the Decision Model diagrams to assess the applicability of a BRMS so that the business logic is separated from other business and technical concerns.

The IT group can also use the business process model to assess the usefulness of BPMS technology to manage the workflow of transactions through the procedural part of the business process (not the declarative part). The declarative component is a candidate for a Web service, called a decision service, discussed in Chapter 5. This decision service may be a service in its own right or a component in a larger, composite service.

For this case study, the IT team decides to design a single Web service of the Automatic/Manual Renewal subprocess illustrated by Figure 7.5. The Decision Model to Determine Policy Renewal Method becomes a decision service within the larger composite task service called Automatic/Manual Policy Renewal. As the new systems and Decision Models become an integral part of the business, there is a desire to become more advanced in Business Decision Management. In this case study, IT begins to explore sophisticated decision analytics. That is, IT implements an automated means of optimizing the business logic in the Decision Model by deploying sophisticated BDM (or EDM) analysis techniques as described in Chapter 19.

Finally, business governance over the business logic becomes important because the business participants in the Decision Model project want to continue to measure its effectiveness and be proactive in making changes. Governance implies stewarding the business logic on behalf of and for the good of the entire business. The governance organization is anchored by the business governance manager, who is assisted by the business governance council in this ongoing responsibility.

Summary

Early practice of the Decision Model has confirmed its value by demonstrating considerable improvements in productivity, quality, and actual business performance. Early practitioners have had positive experiences, and many have delivered additional Decision Models on additional projects.

This chapter covered ten realistic steps in the life of a Decision Model project. The chapter pointed out the following:

- It is important to identify first a Decision Model project's general goals and measurable objectives.
- Project team members need training in business process modeling, decision modeling, and managing fact type definitions.
- It is important to prioritize Decision Models, if there is more than one in a project.
- The project team should comprise business and technical people. Three kinds of business analyst roles are needed: business process modeler, decision modeler, and the person responsible for the fact type glossary.
- The scope of a Decision Model project should address six aspects unique to Decision Models.
- Business process models are critical for all aspects of a Decision Model project.
- Rule Family population happens iteratively.
- Decision Models can often be tested through reporting.
- Automation of Decision Models can be to legacy systems or new technology.
- Selection of future technology should happen after a Decision Model is defined to better understand corresponding technology requirements.

Hopefully, this chapter will assist interested readers in getting a head start on a Decision Model project. Experience with a real project will reinforce the ideas in this book. In fact, as Tehyi Hsieh says, "Activity will remove the doubts that theory cannot solve."

New Vocabulary Introduced in This Chapter

- business governance manager
- business governance council
- facilitator
- librarian or knowledge manager

And What about the Quote

This chapter ends with a review of the quote at its beginning. It implies that the road to reward and success has a beginning but that the beginning originates in courage. This chapter aims to help readers begin the Decision Model experience with confidence.

Discussion Points and Exercises

1. Discuss how a Decision Model might lead to greater productivity from a business perspective and from a technical perspective.
2. Discuss how a Decision Model might provide the opportunity to accomplish business objectives that remained elusive without it.
3. Describe a business challenge in a different industry that is similar to the fictional project. Explain similarities, differences, and how a Decision Model can be part of the solution.
4. If you could only have three full-time staff on a Decision Model project team, what roles would you suggest they play? (Consider combining roles into one person, as needed.)
5. Explain how the scoping considerations in Table 7.4 affect project plan and estimates.
6. Make a list of tasks on a Decision Model project for which IT people are needed. Make a list of tasks on a Decision Model project for which business experts are needed. Discuss the role of business analysts on a Decision Model project.

THE DECISION MODEL IN DETAIL

Intended for the advanced reader (e.g., an experienced business or technical analyst), this section presents the details of the Decision Model. It is appropriate for readers interested in the Decision Model principles or needing to reference a particular issue encountered in practice.

Each of the first three chapters of the section addresses one group of the 15 principles of the Decision Model. Chapter 8 covers the seven structural principles that define the look and feel of the Decision Model. Chapter 9 covers the declarative principles that give the Decision Model its technology-independent character. Chapter 10 covers the integrity principles that ensure the structural, logical, and business-oriented integrity of the Decision Model.

Throughout these chapters, each principle is defined, given a purpose, and supported with examples. Each chapter ends with insights into methodology that a reader can follow when applying the principles in practice.

Chapter 11 examines the similarities and differences between the Relational Model for data and the Decision Model for business logic. This analysis may prove intriguing to readers wishing to evolve the definition and practice of the Decision Model.

Chapter 12, the final chapter in the section, is a full definition of the Decision Model along with the terms used to describe it, serving as a convenient reference. Readers can find more information on the Decision Model at www.TheDecisionModel.com.

Chapter 8

The Structural Principles

Contents

Why Does a Decision Model Need a Structure? 170
  Difficult to Manage 170
  Different Ways of Grouping Business Logic 170
  Seeking a Common and Uniform Decision Model Structure 170
The Goal of the Structural Principles 171
Principle 1: The Tabular Principle 171
  Principle 1 Description 172
  How Principle 1 Addresses the Simplicity of the Decision Model 172
  Applying Principle 1 in Practice 173
Principle 2: The Heading Principle 173
  Principle 2 Description 173
    What Is a Fact? 173
    What Is a Fact Type? 174
  How Principle 2 Addresses the Simplicity of the Decision Model 176
  Applying Principle 2 in Practice 176
The Body Principles: Principles 3–6 178
Principle 3: The Cell Principle 178
  Principle 3 Description 178
    Cell Content Conforming to the Heading 180
  How Principle 3 Addresses the Simplicity of the Decision Model 180
  Applying Principle 3 in Practice 180
Principle 4: The Row Principle 181

Principle 4 Description 181
   Can All Business Logic Be Recast as Inferential Logic? 183
   Example #1: Constraints without Conditions 183
   Example #2: Computations without Conditions 184
How Principle 4 Addresses the Simplicity of the Decision Model 185
Applying Principle 4 in Practice 186
   Normalization and First Normal Form 186
Principle 5: The Conclusion Principle 187
Principle 5 Description 188
How Principle 5 Addresses the Simplicity of the Decision Model 190
Applying Principle 5 in Practice 190
Principle 6: The Conditions Principle 191
Principle 6 Description 192
   Principle 6a: Rule Family Minimal Rule Patterns Principle 193
   Principle 6b: Rule Pattern Fully Empty Condition
   Key Principle 193
   Principle 6c: Rule Pattern Partially Empty Condition
   Key Principle 194
   Principle 6d: Rule Pattern Partial Condition Key
   Dependency Principle 195
How Principle 6 Addresses the Simplicity of the Decision Model 197
Applying Principle 6 in Practice 197
Principle 7: The Connection Principle 199
Principle 7 Description and Subprinciples 199
   Principle 7a: Rule Family Empty Conclusion Cell Principle 199
   Principle 7b: Rule Pattern Empty Conclusion Cell Principle 201
   Inferential Relationship and Unconditional Computations 201
   Making the Inferential Relationship a "Key" in the Decision Model 201
How Principle 7 Addresses the Simplicity of the Decision Model 202
   Applying Principle 7 in Practice 202
Important Terminology for Describing the Decision Model Structure 202
Insights into Methodology 204
Summary 205
New Vocabulary from This Chapter 208
And What about the Quote? 209
Discussion Points and Exercises 209

Simplicity is the ultimate sophistication.

Leonardo da Vinci

This chapter is the first of three chapters that examine the rigor of the Decision Model. Specifically, it introduces the Decision Model principles that address its structural simplicity.

As a model of business logic, the Decision Model is a model of conclusions derived from facts that the business is interested in managing. In other words, the Decision Model is a model of conclusions in the real-world about which the business is interested in storing business logic. These conclusions include assessments, classifications, determinations, and evaluations of business concern. The business logic behind these conclusions includes constraints, computations, and conditional statements. So, business logic is all about testing detailed facts, such as a Person's Annual Income and a Person's Credit Rating, and coming to conclusions about other facts, such as a Person's Likelihood of Defaulting on a Loan. These facts are nothing more than pieces of data. A business may have no control over some pieces of data, such as a Person's Credit Rating. Yet, using business logic, a business defines prescriptions for exactly how it comes to conclusions about a person having a specific credit rating value. Thus, the Decision Model contains the business logic as the business needs or wants it to be.

As Chapter 2 points out, a Decision Model is an intellectual template for perceiving, organizing, and managing the business logic behind a business decision. As such, the Decision Model does not prescribe specific technical approaches for storing or automating that business logic. Instead, the transformation of a Decision Model into a particular technology environment is the subject of design methodologies, not the Decision Model itself.

Nevertheless, the Decision Model must conform to a certain level of rigor if it is to serve as a starting point for all target technologies. That rigor is defined by the Decision Model's set of principles, as set forth in this section of the book. The principles address the three most important qualities of a Decision Model:

■ Structural simplicity
■ Declarative nature
■ Optimal integrity

Therefore, the principles are organized into three groups, where each group addresses one of these qualities. This chapter is about the first group and consists of seven principles aiming for structural simplicity. However, this chapter starts with the most obvious question.

Why Does a Decision Model Need a Structure?

Why is a structure necessary? Why not simply create a list of business logic statements (or business rules) in much the same way as is done with a list of business or system requirements? For small projects, this list may include hundreds of business logic statements. For large projects, the list will likely include thousands of them. Such a list of business logic statements can be attached to business process documentation or included as part of traditional business requirements.

Difficult to Manage

Regardless of size, however, experience proves that a one-dimensional list of anything becomes difficult to manage. This is especially true as the list grows in size over time or needs to accommodate change.

To enable growth and change, a list is better divided into smaller, more manageable groups. However, without rigor for doing so, different people will divide the same list into different kinds of groups. As a result, there is no standard way to perceive, organize, or manage the list.

Different Ways of Grouping Business Logic

For example, process modelers are likely to group together business logic statements that are executed in the same process task. Not surprisingly, data, object, and fact modelers are likely to group together business logic statements that pertain to the same data entity or database table, object class, or a subset of a fact model. No doubt, technical developers are likely to group together business logic statements in a way that works best for a target technology. As a result, without specific rigor, the way that business logic statements are organized is based on the biases, needs, and knowledge of the person who is capturing them. There is no universal grouping or resulting structural representation.

Seeking a Common and Uniform Decision Model Structure

A mechanism for organizing business logic into a common and uniform structural representation must be useful for both human perception and logical design of decision-aware systems. It must serve the interests of all parties and be devoid of unnecessary distracting biases. To be free of unnecessary biases, the structural representation must be one that is specifically suitable for representing only business logic. That means its structural representation must be independent of (i.e., not unnecessarily influenced by) process tasks that use it, data or other models that inform it, or technology that executes it.

For business logic to have a structural representation independent of other considerations, business logic itself must possess unique properties and integrity. Its unique properties and integrity must be unrelated to the properties and integrity of other assets that have their own model, such as processes, data, objects, and facts. It is these unique properties and integrity issues that give rise to the unique structure set forth in the Decision Model.

The Goal of the Structural Principles

The first seven principles support the common goal of structural simplicity. Therefore, these principles enable creation of a Decision Model that is easy and intuitive to understand, comprises uncombined (i.e., reusable) atomic pieces, and is free from confusion because it has only one interpretation. So, the goal is to minimize complexity and maximize comprehension of the Decision Model structure. Each of these principles does this by providing rigor to one specific structural aspect of the Decision Model as follows:

- Principle 1: Tabular Shape
- Principle 2: Heading
- Principle 3: Cells
- Principle 4: Rows
- Principle 5: Conclusions
- Principle 6: Conditions
- Principle 7: Connections

An equally important goal of the structural principles is to impose discipline on Decision Model structure so that an entire Decision Model is always represented and interpreted in one and only one way. Principles 1–4 define the basic structure, and Principles 5–6 impose the required discipline. Principle 7 addresses the connections in the Decision Model.

The rest of this chapter defines each of these seven principles, provides insights into how to apply each one in practice, and explains how each contributes to the simplicity of the Decision Model. The sequence of principles is deliberate because each builds on the rigor of those before it.

Principle 1: The Tabular Principle

Principle 1 places rigor on the general shape of the Decision Model's basic structural element. The tabular shape refers to the image or basic look-and-feel of the Decision Model's structure.

Table 8.1   Two-Dimensional Structures Showing Heading across the Columns

Heading 1	Heading 2	Heading 3	Heading 4

Principle 1: The fundamental structure of a Decision Model is called a Rule Family and has two dimensions: one dimension is the heading and the other dimension is the body. (Or, informally, the basic element in a Decision Model resembles a two-dimensional table.)

Principle 1 Description

Principle 1 sets the stage for simplicity by prescribing that a Decision Model is a set of special two-dimensional structures, called Rule Families. A Rule Family, as an intellectual template, has no specific visual or physical representation. However, the easiest way to represent it visually is as a two-dimensional table of rows and columns. For this reason, Principle 1 is called the Tabular Principle.

Tables 8.1 and 8.2 present the same two-dimensional structure in two different ways. In Table 8.1, the heading is shown as a set of labels across the columns, and the body is shown as a set of empty rows awaiting population. In Table 8.2, the heading is shown as a set of labels down the rows, and the body is shown as a set of empty columns awaiting population. As intellectual templates, both representations suffice. However, in most cases, as will become evident, the body will have more entries than will the labels. Therefore, the most practical representation (and the one used throughout this book) is that shown in Table 8.1.

How Principle 1 Addresses the Simplicity of the Decision Model

Principle 1 leads to Decision Model structures that are intuitive and familiar to most people. After all, two-dimensional look-up tables and decision tables are common in automated systems and procedure manuals.

Table 8.2   Two-Dimensional Structures Showing Heading down the Rows

Heading 1		
Heading 2		
Heading 3		
Heading 4		

Applying Principle 1 in Practice

For the sake of illustration, the Decision Model principles are applied one at a time to build a Decision Model. Starting with Principle 1, statements are gathered from conversations, documents, or program code that allude to business logic. Based on Chapter 2, these are statements hinting at computational formulas, conditional judgments, and constraints.

In this regard, the following statements are gathered from a business meeting and highlighted as ones that allude to business logic:

- A Person is assigned an "A" credit rating and a "low" likelihood of defaulting on a loan if he or she has a good employment history and low debt.
- A person is assigned an "A" credit rating if his or her employment history is good and debt is low or if the employment history is excellent.
- A person is assigned an "F" credit rating if his or her employment history is poor and debt is high.
- A person is assigned a "C" credit rating if his or her employment history is poor and debt is low.

Principle 1 implies that these statements should be converted into two-dimensional structures with a heading and a body. However, to understand what constitutes the heading versus the body, Principle 2 is needed.

Principle 2: The Heading Principle

Principle 2 places rigor on the heading of a Rule Family. The heading of a Rule Family is the set of labels governing the body.

> Principle 2: The heading of a Rule Family is a set of fact types. (Or, informally, the column labels represent different kinds of information.)

Principle 2 Description

Principle 2 prescribes that each label in the heading is a fact type. Table 8.3 shows three Rule Families with fact types in their headings. So, what is a fact type? What is a fact?

What Is a Fact?

A common definition of a fact is "a piece of information, e.g., statistic or a statement of truth" (Encarta "fact"). Therefore, the statement that "Person named John

Doe has five years at his current employer" is a fact. Not only that, it is a fact of a particular type (i.e., fact type). So, what then, is a fact type?

What Is a Fact Type?

A fact type is simply the general classification of a fact (or piece of information), not the piece of information itself. In the example about John Doe, the general classification, or fact type, is "Person's Years at Current Employer" while the actual fact (or fact value or piece of information of the fact type) is five. So, a fact type of Person's Years at Current Employer gives context to a fact value of five. Another fact type of Person's Age gives a different context to a fact value of five. These fact values are the same value (i.e., five) but represent different fact types such that the meaning of the value of five is different.

Principle 2 states that the heading of a Rule Family is a set of fact types. So, the heading of the top Rule Family in Table 8.3 is a set of the three fact types shown as its labels. There are no fact values in the heading.

Table 8.3   A Set of Rule Families with Fact Types across Columns

Person Years at Current Employer	Person Number of Jobs in Past Five Years	Person Employment History

Person Student Loans	Person Business Loans	Person Miscellaneous Loans

Person Employment History	Person Mortgage Situation	Person Miscellaneous Loans	Person Likelihood of Defaulting on a Loan

Sometimes, it is useful to add a bit more rigor to the definition of fact type. So, a more rigorous definition is that a fact type is a predefined relationship among business terms (i.e., nouns or noun phrases with definitions) where that relationship makes business sense and where instances of that relationship (i.e., fact type values, or simply, facts) are referenced in a Decision Model.* Examples of fact types where the relationship among business terms is made obvious follow:

- Fact Type 1: Person's Eye Color (a predefined relationship between the noun, Person, and the noun phrase, Eye Color)
- Fact Type 2: Person's Date of Birth (a predefined relationship between the noun, Person, and the noun phrase, Date of Birth)
- Fact Type 3: Healthcare Policy's Effective Date (a predefined relationship between the noun phrases Healthcare Policy and Effective Date)
- Fact Type 4: First Name on a Claim of a Dependent of a Member covered by a Plan (a predefined set of relationships among the nouns Claim, Dependent, Member, Plan, and noun phrase First Name)
- Fact Type 5: Person's Credit Rating (a predefined relationship between the noun, Person, and noun phrase, Credit Rating)

Simple and Complex Fact Types

As the examples illustrate, the fact type in a label of a Rule Family can be simple, such as Person's Eye Color, or complex, such as First Name on a Claim of Dependent of Member covered by a Plan. For the most part, it makes no difference whether the fact type is simple or complex. It is important that the fact type be well defined from a business perspective, including the definitions of its business terms and the relationships among them. It is also important that the constraints on a fact type's values (called its domain) also be defined. In this way, people can interpret the fact type correctly when it is used in a Decision Model.†

Table 8.3 contains a total of eight different fact types about a person as shown as column headings in its Rule Family structures: Person Years at Current Employer, Person Number of Jobs in Past Five Years, Person Employment History, Person Student Loans, Person Business Loans, Person Miscellaneous Loans, Person Mortgage Situation, and Person Likelihood of Defaulting on a Loan.

---

* Readers who are more comfortable using the word *term* to mean what this book calls *fact* can feel free to do so without losing the essence of the Decision Model principles.

† It is common practice to create a formal structural model of fact types either as a fact model, data model, or business object model. Such models, of course, represent the fact types by themselves, unbiased by processes, decisions, and technology. Each of these models is a separate deliverable that can accompany a Decision Model providing clarity for the fact types. Fact models are discussed in greater detail in Chapter 16.

At first glance, the meaning and domain of some of these fact types may seem obvious, such as Person Years at Current Employer. However, it is never appropriate to assume that the meanings of fact types are understood without formally defining them. In this case, are the years are to include fractions, rounded up, down, or how are they counted if the Person worked for the Current Employer in noncontiguous time frames? Even less obvious is the meaning and domain of the fact type Person Mortgage Situation. Is this a judgment, such as good, bad, or terrible? Or, is this a dollar amount, such as $100K, $500K? Or is this yet something else? So, the definitions and domains of the fact types are crucial to delivering a high-quality, understandable Decision Model.

In applying Principle 2, it is important that each label in the heading of a Rule Family represent one and only one fact type. This prevents use of the same column, for example, to reference both a Person's Number of Jobs in Past Five Years and Person's Age. Instead, these two fact types require two labels in the Rule Family. It is inappropriate to mix fact types within one column because there can be no ambiguity as to what is meant by a value of 16. Is 16 the Person's Number of Jobs in Past Five Years or is 16 the Person's Age?

How Principle 2 Addresses the Simplicity of the Decision Model

Principle 2 results in Rule Family headings that are free from confusion because each label represents one fact type whose business terms, relationship, definition, and domain are well defined.

Applying Principle 2 in Practice

Principle 2 is applied to the creation of a Decision Model by identifying the fact types referenced in the business logic statements.

From the business logic statements uncovered under Principle 1, the following business terms (or nouns and noun phrases) are identified:

■ Person
■ Credit Rating
■ Likelihood of Defaulting on a Loan
■ Employment History
■ Debt

A standard naming convention is recommended for fact types. This book assigns names to fact types as follows:

■ Business context (e.g., form, screen, Web page, business object, data entity, business concept)

Table 8.4 Fact Types in a Potential Rule Family

Person Credit Rating	Person Employment History	Person Debt	Person Likelihood of Defaulting on a Loan

- Descriptive words (e.g., role—like patient, state—like approved, or adjective - like first, current, previous)
- Nature of data indicating the type of the values (e.g., date, indicator, name, description, code)

Using the business context as the first part of a fact type name allows for easy viewing in alphabetical order of those fact types belonging to the same context. For example, this groups together all fact types about a Claim.

So, turning the aforementioned terms into fact types as predefined relationships among business terms results in the following:

- Person Credit Rating
- Person Employment History
- Person Debt
- Person Likelihood of Defaulting on a Loan*

Fact values in the gathered statements can also be identified as follows:

- Person Credit Rating of "A," "F," "C"
- Person Employment History of "good," "poor," "excellent"
- Person Likelihood of Defaulting on a Loan of "low"
- Person Debt of "low," "high"

These fact values provide insights into the fact type domains and raise questions. What other values are possible for Person Credit Rating? Are there other values for Person Likelihood of Defaulting on a Loan? And so it goes before the full domain for each fact type is understood.

Once identified, named, and defined, the fact types can be organized into the Rule Family in Table 8.4.

At this point, the next four principles address the body of the Rule Family.

---

* Of course, each of these fact types is documented along with its meaning and domain.

The Body Principles: Principles 3–6

The body of a Rule Family is simply its content. As a structure containing business logic, its content is a set of business logic expressions organized into instances (or rows) because those expressions belong together as a unit according to the Body Principles.

There are four Body Principles, each one governing a different aspect of a Rule Family body: its cells, its rows, its conclusion, and its conditions. Principles 3 and 4 define the content of a Rule Family cell and row. Principles 5 and 6 place restrictions on the conclusion and conditions in a Rule Family. Although the following sections discuss the Body Principles separately and consecutively, the principles are usually applied at the same time to create the initial Rule Family content.

Principle 3: The Cell Principle

Principle 3 places rigor on the cell of a Rule Family. The cell of a Rule Family is the intersection of a row and column.

> Principle 3: The content of each cell of a Rule Family is an atomic logical expression conforming to the heading. (Or, informally, each cell is a logical expression, with operators and operands.)

Principle 3 Description

The phrase "atomic logical expression" is an expression of the form operand 1 + operator + operand 2. Principle 3 states that the cell of a Rule Family is populated with such an expression. This means that the content of a cell is the heading label (i.e., the fact type in the heading serves as operand 1) plus the body for that label and results in a phrase of the form:

Heading (fact type) + Body (operator + operand 2)

Principle 3 simply requires that the cell for a fact type consist of an operator that makes sense for the fact type followed by an operand that also makes sense for the operator plus the fact type.

The operand can be another fact type, a literal or value, a set, or a computational formula.

As an example, in Table 8.5, the column beneath each heading is shown as two subcells: one is for the operator and the other for the operand. Note that the

Table 8.5   Potential Rule Family, Showing Operators and Values in Rows

Person Years at Current Employer		Person Number of Jobs in Past Five Years		Person Employment History	
Is Less Than	1	Is Less Than	3	Is	Good
Is Less Than	1	Is Greater Than	8	Is	Poor

column for Person Years at Current Employer contains "Is Less Than" as the operator (in the first subcell) of the first populated row and "1" as the operand (in the second subcell) of the first populated row. The full interpretation of this expression combines the heading with the body to become "Person Years at Current Employer Is Less Than 1." In this case, the operator "Is Less Than" makes sense with respect to a Person Years at Current Employer.*

Principle 3 requires that the content of a cell be atomic and that it conform to the heading.

In Table 8.5, the operators are straightforward. They are "Is Less Than," "Is Greater Than," and "Is." With such operators, the operand is usually a single value, as shown in Table 8.5 as "1," "3," "8," "Good," and "Poor."

Some operators are more complex. One of these is the Is In operator, which is defined as a "function word to indicate inclusion, location, or position within limits" (Merriam-Webster Online Dictionary "in") and has an n-member set as an operand. When a Rule Family contains an Is In operator, the operand is a set of values. The operand is still considered to be atomic (i.e., nondecomposable) because it is one set. An example of using the Is In operator:

> "Person First Name Is In {John, Larry, Mitchell}."†

Another more complex operator is the Is Between operator, which is defined as "in common to," (Merriam-Webster Online Dictionary "between") The operand of Is Between is a set containing two members delineating the full range of the Is Between operator. An example of using the Is Between operator:

> "Person Age Is Between {25, 27}," which means
> Person Age is between 25 and 27 and includes 25 and 27.

---

* From this point on, the term *cell* is used to include subcells, for simplicity.
† It is also acceptable to name the set as in "Person's First Name IN {American male names}." The domain of the set must also be specified somewhere.

Cell Content Conforming to the Heading

The cell content must conform to the constraints implied by the fact type's domain. So, if a cell tests a Person Date of Birth, the Person Date of Birth must be tested against valid values for a date. If a cell derives a Person Credit Rating, the Person Credit Rating must be within the range of acceptable credit rating values. In this way, the domain for a fact type places real-world restrictions on how to populate the body of the Rule Family so that its logic makes sense.

Look at Table 8.5, at the expression for Person Number of Jobs in Past Five Years. The operands "3" and "8" make sense as applied to the operators "Is Less Than" and "Is Greater Than" for this fact type because a Person Number of Jobs in Past Five Years can be less than 3 or greater than 8. On the other hand, populating the operand with the value "−2" does not make sense because the domain for the fact type of Person Number of Jobs in Past Five Years, in the real world, is usually not compared to a negative number. That is, a negative number does not make business sense.

So, the fact type in the heading imposes rigor on the cell for that heading.

How Principle 3 Addresses the Simplicity of the Decision Model

Principle 3 results in a Rule Family cell that is easy to understand because the content of each cell matches the heading and has a specific interpretation.

Applying Principle 3 in Practice

Principle 3 is put into practice by creating Rule Family cell content for each logical expression in the statements gathered in Principle 1, using the fact types identified in Principle 2. This means converting each such expression into the following form:

Fact type + operator + operand

The statements gathered under Principle 1 are repeated in the following list, each one followed by a translation of the logical expressions in it:

- A Person is assigned an "A" credit rating and a "low" likelihood of defaulting on a loan only if he or she has a good employment history and low debt.
  - Person Credit Rating Is A
  - Person Likelihood of Defaulting on a Loan Is Low
  - Person Employment History Is Good
  - Person Debt Is Low
- A person is assigned an "A" credit rating if his or her employment history is good and his or her debt is low or if employment history is excellent.
  - Person Credit Rating Is A
  - Person Employment History Is Good

- – Person Debt Is Low
- – Person Employment History Is Excellent
■ A person is assigned an "F" credit rating if his or her employment history is poor and debt is high.
  - – Person Credit Rating Is F
  - – Person Employment History Is Poor
  - – Person Debt Is High
■ A person is assigned a "C" credit rating if his or her employment history is poor and debt is low.
  - – Person Credit Rating Is C
  - – Person Employment History Is Poor
  - – Person Debt Is Low

Principle 3 ensures that populated cells make sense with respect to the corresponding heading. When applying Principle 3, it is a good idea to have discussions as to whether all possible values for the heading need to be covered in the Rule Family. For example, if a Person's Credit Rating can be any of the values of A, B, C, D, E, or F, discussions ought to address whether there is a need for logical expressions covering all of these values or if only a subset of them is important at this time.

Regardless, to arrange the cells of logical expressions into Rule Family row, Principle 4 is needed. So, whereas Principle 3 specifies how to interpret and populate individual Rule Family cells, Principle 4 specifies how to pull them together into a Rule Family row.

Principle 4: The Row Principle

Principle 4 places rigor on the row of a Rule Family. The row in a Rule Family is the correlation of condition to conclusion fact types (i.e., a row).

> Principle 4: The populated cells playing the role of conditions infer the corresponding populated cells playing the role of a conclusion. (Or, informally, each row represents conditions leading to conclusions the way business leaders want or need it to be).

Principle 4 Description

Principle 4 defines the rigor that ties together the cells within a Rule Family row based on the general concept of functional dependency. Functional dependency means that the values of one cell or a set of cells uniquely determine the value of another cell in the same Rule Family. Because a Rule Family represents business logic, this functional dependency is nothing more than an inference. Inference is the operation of reasoning, of making a judgment based on applying thinking and arguments to evidence or facts. In the Decision Model, the whole point of populating a Rule Family is to create expressions of conditions inferring (i.e., leading to, providing reasons for) conclusions that the business wishes to enforce.

Highly relevant to the Decision Model is that inference (i.e., reasoning) is defined at the level of fact types in a Rule Family but that the act of reasoning is actually carried out during real-world interactions at the level of fact type values that populate the Rule Family (Schreiber et al., 2001). So, the Rule Family heading represents reasoning at the level of fact types, but the body represents reasoning that occurs during real-world interactions by inspecting fact type values.

This is important because often the Rule Family heading remains unchanged over time, whereas the population in the cells changes. Heading changes and cell changes represent two different kinds of business logic changes. Heading changes are more significant changes than cell changes, in terms of the impact on Decision Model structure.

Therefore, Principle 4 means that each fact type in the heading plays a role in a condition or a conclusion.

If a fact type in a heading is being tested, it plays a role in a condition and is called a condition fact type. If its value is being concluded, it plays a role in a conclusion and is called a conclusion fact type.* Therefore, Principle 3 requires that a Rule Family structure distinguish between the condition and conclusion fact types. This means the full context of the label for each fact type consists of the following:

■ Fact Type (indicating which fact type is governing the population of the cell)
■ Fact Type Role (indicating whether the fact type is serving as a condition or a conclusion)

The remainder of the book doesn't use such formal labels. Instead, when showing Rule Family tables, the label above the columns indicates whether the fact type of a column is playing the role of condition or conclusion, as shown in Table 8.6.†

Principle 4 is called the Row Principle because it enforces the inference connection among cells within each row of one Rule Family.‡

---

* For simplicity, this book uses the terms *condition fact* and *condition fact type* interchangeably when the meaning is clear. It does the same with the terms *conclusion fact* and *conclusion fact type*.

† The diagramming notation in this book for the Decision Model deliberately avoids the issue of grammar for expressing the business logic represented in a Rule Family. In other words, each row in a Rule Family table can be stated using "If/Then" or "When" or other syntax. It makes no difference to the *structure* of the Decision Model because the structure needs only to differentiate conditions from conclusions; it does not need to enforce grammar. In other words, the Decision Model does not impose syntax on translations of the Rule Family body (e.g., in a business-friendly or other standard manner) nor does it need to.

‡ Later, Principle 6 discloses the inference relationships that are *not* in the same Rule Family.

Table 8.6   Fact Types Designated as Condition or Conclusion Fact Types

Conditions			Conclusion
Person Credit Rating	Person Employment History	Person Debt	Person Likelihood of Defaulting on a Loan

As an example, Table 8.7 contains a Rule Family with two condition fact types and one conclusion fact type. It has been populated with two business logic statements based on how the business wants to come to a conclusion about a Person's Employment History.

Can All Business Logic Be Recast as Inferential Logic?

Sometimes a business statement doesn't seem to represent reasoning or inference. In other words, it might not seem to be made up of condition fact types leading to conclusion fact types. Two examples come to mind.

Example #1: Constraints without Conditions

Suppose a business expert proclaims that "Every Loan Application Must Be a Secured Loan." This sounds like an unconditional constraint, meaning that there is no inference, no reasoning. In the context of a Decision Model, it seems that there are no condition fact types that lead to the conclusion. The conclusion appears to be mandatory under all conditions and circumstances. However, this means one should look deeper into the meaning of the business expert's words.

Quite often, when viewed in the context of a business decision (which is the scope of a Decision Model), such statements evolve into a structure that fits quite appropriately into condition fact types leading to conclusion fact types. In other

Table 8.7   Two Condition Fact Types and One Conclusion Fact Type Populated with Business-Specific Inference

Conditions				Conclusion	
Person Years at Current Employer		Person Number of Jobs in Past Five Years		Person Employment History	
Is Less Than	1	Is Less Than	3	Is	Good
Is Less Than	1	Is Greater Than	8	Is	Poor

Table 8.8 Translating a Constraint into Decision Model Logic

Conditions				Conclusion	
Person Requested Loan Amount		Person Secured Amount		Person Loan Request Recommendation	
Is Less Than	$100,000			Is	Accepted
Is Greater Than	$100,000	=	0	Is	Rejected

words, when such statements are viewed within the context of a business decision, the operational intent of the statement is revealed as an inference. An example is useful.

It is highly probable that, during the course of a regular operational transaction, the business does not really want to unconditionally reject a Loan Application that is not secured. Instead, the business wants such Loan Applications simply to take a different route through the Loan Approval Process. That is, instead of being a candidate for automatic approval, such Loan Applications are to undergo further analysis (or judgments) before making a final decision. If this is the case, the original statement, appearing to be unconditional, evolves into a series of inference statements. That is, the original statement is a valid policy, but not sufficient as an operational piece of business logic.

On the other hand, sometimes such a statement turns out to be truly unconditional in the course of operational transactions. If so, the correct interpretation is that "under no circumstances are such Loan Applications to be processed further." In such cases, the statement can be translated into those condition fact types leading to an "accept" conclusion value and those condition fact types leading to a "reject" conclusion value, as shown in Table 8.8. Note that only Requested Loan Amounts Is Greater Than $100,000 without a secured amount are rejected. This Rule Family is incomplete as there are likely additional rows indicating which Person's Requested Loan Amounts require which Person's Secured Amounts.

Example #2: Computations without Conditions

Computations are business logic statements that involve a mathematical formula. Some computations are conditional, meaning that under some conditions one formula is used but under other conditions another formula is used. Consider the very simple example in Table 8.9. The conclusion fact type is Person Annual Bonus Amount, and the value of this conclusion fact type is determined by executing a formula. The table contains two formulas for determining the Person Annual Bonus Amount. One formula (i.e., in the first populated row) sets the value to 5% of the Person Salary Amount, whereas another formula (i.e., in the second populated row) sets the value to 10%. There are two condition fact types (i.e., Person Salary Grade

Table 8.9 Conditional Computation Logic

Conditions				Conclusion	
Person Salary Grade		*Person Years at Company*		*Person Annual Bonus Amount*	
Is Less Than	5	Is Less Than	3	Is Computed As	(Person Salary Amount) multiplied by 0.05
Is Greater Than	5	Is Greater Than	2	Is Computed As	(Person Salary Amount) multiplied by 0.10

and Person Years at Company) that determine which formula to use. This Rule Family is not meant to be complete. Some business logic is obviously missing.

However, sometimes computational logic is unconditional, which means that the same computational formula is to be used under all circumstances.

For the purpose of illustration, assume there is one—and only one—specific formula for calculating Person's Credit Rating.* At the risk of oversimplifying, the formula calculates a Person Credit Rating by adding the Person Total Income Over the Past Five Years to the Person Anticipated Total Income Over the Next Five Years and dividing this result by a Proprietary Number that is unique to the company. The use of the Proprietary Number allows the company to influence the result in a way that is unique to the company and is, in fact, one way in which the company distinguishes itself from competitors. There are two points to understand when dealing with such unconditional computational logic.

The first point is to make sure that this truly is an unconditional computation, that the same formula is always used. There are no conditions under which a different formula applies. If so, it is represented as shown in Table 8.10.

The second point is that the conclusion fact type of an unconditional computation can serve as a condition fact type in another Rule Family. The Rule Family in Table 8.11 is one in which Person Credit Rating plays the role of condition.†

How Principle 4 Addresses the Simplicity of the Decision Model

Principle 4 contributes to the simplicity of the Decision Model by prescribing Rule Families in which condition cells are distinct from conclusion cells, but are together in one structural representation: a row in a Rule Family.

---

* Typically, the business logic for computing a person's credit rating is quite complex.
† Table 8.11 is illustrative only, showing two rows of many.

Table 8.10   Unconditional Computation

Conditions			Conclusion
			Person Credit Rating
		Is Computed As	(Person Total Income Over Past Five Years + Person Anticipated Total Income Over Next Five Years) divided by Proprietary Number

Applying Principle 4 in Practice

Applying Principle 4 means revisiting the statements from Principle 1, the condition and conclusion fact types from Principle 2, and the atomic logical expressions from Principle 3. The fact types in the heading are noted as conditions or conclusions.

So far, Principles 1–4 provide the basic structure for the Rule Family; two-dimensional, fact types as heading, logical expressions as cells, and the correlation of conditions leading to conclusions as the prescription for the rows.

However, these principles alone do not lead to a Rule Family representation that is always represented in one—and only one—way. Principles 5 and 6 are needed for this because together they deliver Rule Families in first normal form.

Normalization and First Normal Form

Normalization in the Decision Model is a body of theory addressing analysis and decomposition of business logic structures into a new set of structures that exhibit more desirable properties.

The Decision Model is introduced in this book with three basic normal forms (first, second, and third). Higher normal forms are likely to exist. The higher the normal form, the more desirable the Decision Model structure and content.

Although higher normal forms are more desirable, first normal form is required for minimal structural integrity. The purpose of first normal form is to constrain

Table 8.11   Conclusion Fact Type of an Unconditional Computation Serving as a Condition Fact Type

Conditions				Conclusion	
Person Employment History		*Person Credit Rating*		*Person Likelihood of Defaulting on a Loan*	
Is	Poor	Is Less Than or Equal to	500K	Is	High
Is	Good	Is Greater Than	501K	Is	Low

Table 8.12   Condition Fact Types Tied Through Inference to Conclusion Fact Type

Conditions				Conclusions	
Person Employment History		*Person Debt*		*Person Credit Rating*	*Person Likelihood of Defaulting on a Loan*

Rule Family content so that a Rule Family (and an entire Decision Model) is always represented and interpreted in one and only one way. This is a strategic property of the Decision Model. First normal form leads to simplicity in interpreting, predictability in creating and changing, and ease of manipulating each model.

So far, Principles 1–4 have led to a Rule Family instance as a collection of logical expressions that together convey a conclusion. With this in mind, first normal form means that, in terms of the tabular picture of a Rule Family, each Rule Family row cannot be decomposed into more than one row reaching the conclusion. If a row can be decomposed into more than one row reaching a conclusion (without losing the intent of the original row), the original row is not in first normal form and should be recast as multiple conclusions down the rows and not across columns. This delivers the most atomic pieces of business logic, which is what the Decision Model is all about.

Although this sounds confusing, in practice it is very simple. It means applying Principles 5 and 6 to each row in a Rule Family. Principle 5 puts a restriction on the conclusion, whereas Principle 6 puts a restriction on the conditions. These restrictions result in a Rule Family structure that does not contain any nested conclusions, and hence leads to one and only one Rule Family structure for any given set of business logic.

Principle 5: The Conclusion Principle

Principle 5 places rigor on the conclusion fact type of a Rule Family. The conclusion fact type is the fact type about which the Rule Family delivers its conclusions.

> Principle 5: A Rule Family has only one conclusion fact type. (Or, informally, there is only one conclusion column)

Principle 5 Description

The meaning of Principle 5 is very clear because it ensures that every row in a Rule Family represents a conclusion about a single fact type. However, more subtly and even more importantly, Principle 5 eliminates rows nested within another row. That is, a two-dimensional business logic structure with more than one conclusion fact type can always be decomposed, without losing its intent, into a set of structures, each having only one conclusion fact type. That's because a row with more than one conclusion fact type actually contains more than one row nested inside. It is not atomic and can be reduced to its atomic judgments. By separating it into two Rule Families, each with its own conclusion fact type, the set of conditions for one Rule Family can be changed independently of the conditions for the other Rule Family. That is, one Rule Family for each conclusion fact type allows for each Rule Family to evolve, if necessary, such that they no longer contain the same conditions.

As an example, Table 8.13 contains three conditions that, if true, lead to two conclusions. More than one conclusion fact type in a Rule Family is undesirable because it leads to many different ways of representing the business logic in that Rule Family. Imagine that one person creates a separate Rule Family for each of the conclusion fact types while another person creates one Rule Family that contains both conclusion fact types. Both representations would be correct without Principle 5. If there were three or more possible conclusion fact types, how many different representations are possible without Principle 5? But there is another important reason for Principle 5. Principle 7 will point out that the conclusion fact type in the Decision Model is the glue that holds Rule Families together. The restriction on a Rule Family of having only one conclusion fact type is critical if there is to be one and only one Decision Model representation that is also the simplest.

Reducing Table 8.13 to comply with Principle 5 simply means creating a separate Rule Family for each of these conclusion fact types, as shown in Table 8.14. The same three conditions appear in two Rule Families, but each Rule Family reaches a conclusion about a single conclusion fact type. Together, these Rule Families are semantically equivalent to the previous Rule Family, but are now in full compliance with Principle 5. This simplifies the representation and management of the business logic because all business logic coming to a conclusion about a Person Likelihood

Table 8.13 Two Conclusion Fact Types

Conditions			Conclusions	
Person Credit Rating from Outside Credit Bureau	*Person Credit Card Balance*	*Person Education Loan Balance*	*Person Likelihood of Defaulting on a Loan*	*Person Risk Rating*
Is	X	Is Greater Than	Y	Is Greater Than	Z	Is	High	Is	High

Table 8.14   One Conclusion Fact Type per Rule Family

Conditions						Conclusion	
Person Credit Rating from Outside Credit Bureau		*Person Credit Card Balance*		*Person Education Loan Balance*		*Person Likelihood of Defaulting on a Loan*	
Is	X	Is Greater Than	Y	Is Greater Than	Z	Is	High

Conditions						Conclusion	
Person Credit Rating from Outside Credit Bureau		*Person Credit Card Balance*		*Person Education Loan Balance*		*Person Risk Rating*	
Is	X	Is Greater Than	Y	Is Greater Than	Z	Is	High

of Defaulting on a Loan belongs in one Rule Family, whereas all business logic coming to a conclusion about a Person Risk Rating belongs in another. Although these Rule Families appear to have the same three conditions in common at this point in time, this may not be true in the future. Separating them into different Rule Families does not lose any of the business logic and allows each to evolve independently of each other.

Usually, decomposing a Rule Family having multiple conclusion fact types into a set of Rule Families each with one conclusion fact type raises questions about the business logic itself. For example, is it really true that evaluating these three condition fact types determines both the Person Likelihood of Defaulting on a Loan and the Person Risk Rating? Perhaps the truth is that whenever a "Person Likelihood of Defaulting on a Loan is evaluated as "High," the Person Risk Rating is also evaluated as "High." If that is the case, the structure in Table 8.14 needs to change so that its condition fact type is Person Likelihood of Defaulting on a Loan, as is now shown in Table 8.15.

Table 8.15 is actually more concise than Table 8.14. For example, there may be many rows in the first structure in Table 8.15, leading to a conclusion of Person Likelihood of Defaulting on a Loan of "High." Even so, only one row is needed in the second structure. Regardless, applying Principle 5 results in as many two-dimensional structures as there are conclusion fact types.

Table 8.15   Second Revision to One Conclusion Fact Type per Rule Family

Conditions						Conclusion	
Person Credit Rating from Outside Credit Bureau		Person Credit Card Balance		Person Education Loan Balance		Person Likelihood of Defaulting on a Loan	
Is	X	Is Greater Than	Y	Is Greater Than	Z	Is	High

Conditions		Conclusion	
Person Likelihood of Defaulting on a Loan		Person Risk Rating	
Is	High	Is	High

How Principle 5 Addresses the Simplicity of the Decision Model

By restricting a Rule Family to only one conclusion fact type, the Decision Model will comprise more Rule Families than without that restriction. At first glance, a Decision Model containing more Rule Families seems more complex, not simpler. However, simplicity is not a measure of how many structures there are. Rather, the most important measure of simplicity is that there is one and only one way to represent and interpret the business logic. Likewise, a related measure of simplicity is how easy it is to make changes, such as there being one—and only one—place in which to make any change. A Decision Model with one structure for each conclusion fact type provides that kind of simplicity.

And so the inherent relationship of condition fact types leading to one—and only one—conclusion fact type is crucial to the Decision Model. The inferential dependency leading to only one conclusion fact type exposes the self-defining structure of the Decision Model because all statements with the same conclusion fact type, by definition, fall into a self-defining group.

Applying Principle 5 in Practice

Applying Principle 5 in practice means making sure that each conclusion fact type has its own Rule Family.

Table 8.16 Creating Rule Families with Only One Conclusion Fact Type

Conditions		Conclusion
Person Employment History	*Person Debt*	*Person Credit Rating*

Conditions		Conclusion
Person Credit Rating	*Person Credit Rating from Outside Agency*	*Person Likelihood of Defaulting on a Loan*

Continuing with the example from the other principles, the two-dimensional structure from Table 8.12 has two conclusion fact types. After confirming with a business expert, the two condition fact types (i.e., Person Employment History and Person Debt) lead to a conclusion about Person Credit Rating. The conclusion about Person Likelihood of Defaulting on a Loan is inferred from the condition fact types of Person Credit Rating and Person Credit Rating from an Outside Agency. So, Principle 5 leads to Table 8.16.

Even at this point, a Rule Family is not necessarily in a form that represents one—and only one—way to represent and interpret it. It needs also to conform to Principle 6.

Principle 6: The Conditions Principle

Principle 6 places rigor on condition fact types of a Rule Family. The condition fact types in a Rule Family are the fact types governing the conditions that lead to the conclusions.

> Principle 6: All populated condition cells must be true for the conclusion cells to be true. (Or, informally, the populated conditions are ANDed together to reach the conclusion; No ORs are permitted among populated conditions.)

Table 8.17 Conditions with ORs

	Conditions							Conclusion	
Rule Pattern	Person Credit Rating from Outside Agency		AND Person Credit Card Balance)		OR Person Education Loan Balance		Person Likelihood of Defaulting on a Loan		
1	Is	X	Is Greater Than	Y	Is Greater Than	Z	Is		High

Principle 6 Description

Like Principle 5, Principle 6 also eliminates rows nested within another row. That is, a two-dimensional business logic structure in which the condition cells are processed with an OR can always be decomposed, without losing meaning, into a set of rows, each having only the mandatory conditions. What this means is that a Rule Family row comprising conditions to be ORed together represents more than one row nested inside. This is a situation that violates first normal form.

Consider the following example of a business logic statement:

If (a Person's Credit Rating from the Outside Credit Bureau is X and the Person's Credit Card Balance is greater than Y) or the Person's Education Loan Balance is greater than Z, then the Person's Likelihood of Defaulting on a Loan is High.

This business logic statement is represented in Table 8.17 and requires parentheses for correct interpretation. Without the parentheses, interpretation is ambiguous as the conclusion will be different depending on sequence of evaluation. Adding parentheses removes the ambiguity but imposes a sequence on how the conditions are to be processed. Ambiguity and sequence* have no place in the Decision Model.

Business logic in which conditions are connected with ORs can always be decomposed without ORs and without loss of meaning. Table 8.18 decomposes the original business logic with ORs into two rows in the Rule Family, neither of which involves an OR in its interpretation. In this way, every populated condition in a Rule Family row must be true for the corresponding condition to be true. That is, every row is interpreted and processed in exactly the same simple manner.

Principle 6 is so important to the structure of the Decision Model that there is a special name, Rule Pattern, for the rows in a Rule Family with a common set of condition cells that are populated.

Note that the body of the Rule Family in Table 8.18 contains two different kinds of rows: one testing two condition fact types (i.e., Person Credit Rating from Outside Agency and Person Credit Card Balance) and another testing the fact type

---

* Recall that if sequence is required for proper execution of business logic, the sequence is depicted in a process model, not in a Decision Model. In this case, the process flow enforces the sequence, and the business logic behind the tasks of that flow does not imply sequence. This is covered in more detail in the Declarative Principles in Chapter 9.

Table 8.18   Conditions without ORs

	Conditions			Conclusion	
Rule Pattern	Person Credit Rating from Outside Agency		Person Credit Card Balance		Person Education Loan Balance		Person Likelihood of Defaulting on a Loan	
1	Is	X	Is Greater Than	Y			Is	High
2					Is Greater Than	Z	Is	High

Person Education Loan Balance. In each row, all of its populated condition cells must evaluate to true for the corresponding conclusion cells to be true. In other words, in the first populated row, both conditions must evaluate to true for the Person Likelihood of Defaulting on a Loan to be High.

The two different kinds of rows in Table 8.18 represent two different Rule Patterns, labeled 1 and 2. A Rule Pattern is defined as a set of Rule Family rows with a common set of condition cells that are populated. The remainder of this section presents additional subprinciples pertaining to Rule Patterns. Some may be obvious. Others may not be obvious. They are most useful when applying Principle 6 in practice, as a reference.

Principle 6a: Rule Family Minimal Rule Patterns Principle

Principle 6a: A Rule Family must have at least one Rule Pattern.

This subprinciple requires that there be at least one set of populated condition cells that logically infer the corresponding conclusion cells (which includes a Rule Pattern with an empty set of condition cells, as a later subprinciple states). This means that there must be at least one row leading to a conclusion value. That's because the conclusion fact type is how Rule Families are related to each other (per Principle 7). The requirement for at least one Rule Pattern means at least one conclusion value ensures that the corresponding Rule Family can connect via its conclusion fact type to other Rule Families.

Often, Rule Patterns are not discovered until a Rule Family is populated. Therefore, this subprinciple prompts corrections to a Decision Model containing a Rule family without any populated rows.

Principle 6b: Rule Pattern Fully Empty Condition Key Principle

Principle 6b: The whole condition key of a Rule Pattern can be empty if there is only one Rule Pattern in the Rule Family.

A condition key is the set of fact types in a Rule Pattern governing the populated condition cells. Thus, in Table 8.18, the condition key of the Rule Pattern 1 consists of two condition fact types: Person Credit Rating from Outside Agency and Person Credit Card Balance. Likewise, the condition key of the Rule Pattern 2 consists of one condition fact type: Person Education Loan Balance.

The term empty is used rather than null to refer to a set of cells in a Rule Family that appear unpopulated. Thus, in Table 8.18, the condition for fact type Person Education Loan Balance in the first populated row is empty. Unfortunately, an empty cell can be interpreted in at least two ways: the value is not known or the value is irrelevant to the rest of the row.

If the condition key of a Rule Pattern is wholly empty, the conclusion is unconditional. It follows then that a Rule Family with more than one Rule Pattern cannot have one Rule Pattern whose conclusion is always true and another Rule Pattern whose conclusion is sometimes true. So, if a Rule Family has more than one Rule Pattern, none of these Rule Patterns can be unconditional, and hence none of their condition keys can be wholly empty.

However, by the same logic, the condition key of a Rule Pattern where the pattern is the only one in the Rule Family may be totally empty if the conclusion is unconditional (i.e., always true).

Principle 6c: Rule Pattern Partially Empty Condition Key Principle

Principle 6c: The condition key of a Rule Pattern cannot be partially empty unless the whole condition key is empty. (Therefore, there is only one Rule Pattern in the Rule Family.)

This subprinciple states that, in the absence of an unconditional Rule Pattern in a Rule Family, the situation of a partially empty condition key is inappropriate. That is, either the entire condition key is empty (unconditional) or the entire condition key is populated. An example is useful.

Refer to Table 8.19. It suggests the existence of two Rule Patterns, labeled 1 and 2. However, in the second row of Rule Pattern 1, the cell for the condition fact type Person Credit Card Balance is empty, meaning that this expression is either

Table 8.19   Rule Pattern with Condition Key Partially Empty

	Conditions						Conclusion	
Rule Pattern	Person Credit Rating from Outside Agency		Person Credit Card Balance		Person Education Loan Balance		Person Likelihood of Defaulting on a Loan	
1	Is	X	Is Greater Than	Y			Is	High
1	Is	X					Is	Low
2					Is Greater Than	Z	Is	High

irrelevant to the conclusion or the appropriate condition test is not known. Either situation puts the business logic in jeopardy.

If the emptiness implies that the appropriate condition test is not known, then there is no way of knowing if the test in the cell will turn out to be Greater Than Y which is the same as the test for the cell in the first row. In other words, this row may represent a potential duplicate. If the appropriate condition test is not known, then there is no way of knowing whether we will have a logical anomaly in Rule Pattern 1 such that its rows are in conflict or overlap with each other. For example, if the second row tested Person Credit Rating from Outside Agency Is X and Person Credit Card Balance Is In {Y, Z}, with a conclusion of Person Likelihood of Defaulting on a Loan as Low, there is a conflict. So, in summary, if the appropriate condition test is not known, the row is incomplete. It must be completed before proceeding further.

On the other hand, if the empty cell means that the condition test is irrelevant to the conclusion, then this row does not represent an instance of Rule Pattern 1, but instead represents yet another Rule Pattern. It is called Rule Pattern 3, having one relevant condition fact type of a Person Credit Rating from Outside Agency. If so, there is still a logical anomaly in this Rule Family.

There is another important consideration in representing high-quality Rule Families, and that is second normal form.

Second Normal Form

As indicated earlier, functional dependency means that the values of one cell or a set of cells uniquely determines the value of another cell in the same Rule Family via an inferential dependency from conditions to conclusions. The purpose of second normal form is to eliminate functional dependencies involving only part of the condition key of a Rule Pattern. That's because such partial dependencies result in duplicate representation of business logic, leading to complexity and errors in managing change.

Principle 6d: Rule Pattern Partial Condition Key Dependency Principle

Principle 6d: A conclusion in a Rule Pattern should not depend on a partial condition key.

Principle 6d addresses second normal form for the Decision Model and implies that each conclusion in a Rule Pattern is fully functionally dependent on the entire condition key. This subprinciple addresses the case where all condition cells are populated (i.e., none are empty), but the population of one or more of them has no influence on the conclusion cells. In other words, one or more of the populated condition cells is irrelevant to the determination of the conclusion cells.

An example of a violation of second normal form in a Rule Pattern is seen in Table 8.20. It contains a condition key comprising two fact types: Person Age and Person Annual Income.

Table 8.20 Rule Pattern Whose Conclusion Depends on a Partial Condition Key

Rule Pattern	Conditions				Conclusion	
					*Person Marketing Desirability*	
	Person Age		*Person Annual Income*			
1	Is Greater Than	18	Is Greater Than	$50K	Is	High
1	Is Greater Than	18	Is Less Than or Equal to	$50K	Is	Medium
1	Is Greater Than or Equal to	18	Is Greater Than	$50K	Is	High
1	Is Greater Than or Equal to	18	Is Greater Than or Equal to	$50K	Is	Medium

However, upon close examination, it seems that whenever Person Annual Income Is Greater Than $50K, the conclusion is that the person is desirable from a marketing perspective, no matter what his or her age is. A person appears to be of medium desirability from a marketing perspective if the Person Annual Income Is Less Than $50K, regardless of age. When this is brought to the attention of businesspeople and they confirm that this is always the case, then Person Age is irrelevant to the conclusion. In other words, the conclusion is dependent on only part of the condition key.

The violation causes logic to be duplicated because the conclusion is not dependent on the entire condition key. Specifically, the conditional test against Person Annual Income is repeated for each test of Person Age because the latter is irrelevant. The duplicate logic also causes execution of unnecessary conditions because the results of those conditions are irrelevant to the conclusion.

Removing partial dependencies from a condition key to the conclusion results in a Rule Pattern that is compliant with second normal form for the Decision Model. Therefore, the solution is to remove Person Age from the condition key as shown in Table 8.21.

The difference between Principles 6c and 6d is that the former deals with empty cells in a condition key whereas the latter deals with populated cells that make no difference to the conclusion.

Table 8.21 Rule Pattern Where Conclusion Depends on Entire Condition Key

Rule Pattern	Conditions		Conclusion	
			*Person Marketing Desirability*	
	Person Annual Income			
1	Is Greater Than	$50K	Is	Yes
1	Is Greater Than or Equal to	$50K	Is	No

Rule Patterns usually become evident, not from examination of condition headings, but mostly from populating sample instances (or rows) in the Rule Family and noticing that some condition columns are not needed for some rows. It is then that Rule Patterns start to emerge.

Suffice it to say that, where a Rule Family has only one Rule Pattern, the Rule Family and the Rule Pattern are the same, and the Rule Family is compliant with Principle 6. Also, a Rule Family with zero or only one populated condition cells is automatically compliant with Principle 6 because there are no condition cells whose populated expression need not evaluate to true for the corresponding conclusion value to be true.

How Principle 6 Addresses the Simplicity of the Decision Model

Principle 6 eliminates confusion because all populated condition cells in a Rule Pattern are processed in the same manner. That is, each populated condition cell is evaluated, and the truth values are all relevant to determining whether the corresponding conclusion expression can be reached. It is as simple as that. There is no need to clear up ambiguity or worry about parentheses or any implications in the sequence of processing conditions.

Applying Principle 6 in Practice

Applying Principle 6 means populating the Rule Family with appropriate rows in Rule Patterns by decomposing ORed conditions into two Rule Family rows, and hence, different Rule Patterns. Applying Principle 6 also means making sure Rule Patterns are in second normal form and compliant with the additional Principle 6 principles.

Consider the following business logic statements:

A person is assigned an "F" credit rating if his or her employment history is poor and debt is high.
A person is assigned a "C" credit rating if his or her employment history is poor and debt is low.
A person is assigned an "A" credit rating if his or her employment history is good and debt is low or if the employment history is excellent.

The first and second statements express inferential dependencies among condition expressions that must all evaluate to true for the conclusion expression to be true. So the first two rows are populated as shown in Table 8.22. The third statement, however, references condition fact types (i.e., Person Employment History and Person Debt) but the OR indicates a situation where a test of only a subset of the condition fact types needs to evaluate to true for the conclusion expression to be

Table 8.22 Rule Family Populated with Two Rule Patterns

Rule Pattern	Conditions				Conclusion	
	Person Employment History		*Person Debt*		*Person Credit Rating*	
1	Is	Poor	Is	High	Is	F
1	Is	Poor	Is	Low	Is	C
1	Is	Good	Is	Low	Is	A
2	Is	Excellent			Is	A

Rule Pattern	Conditions		Conclusion
	Person Credit Rating	*Person Outside Credit Rating*	*Person Likelihood of Defaulting on a Loan*

true. Therefore, this statement cannot be represented as one instance (e.g., row) in the Rule Family. After clarifying the parentheses implied by the OR, it is represented as two instances (e.g., rows) in the Rule Family, as shown in the third and fourth populated rows in Table 8.22. Specifically, the statement has been translated from an OR into two rows in the Rule Family so that all conditions in all rows are processed simply by ANDing their truth values together.

Essentially, after applying Principle 6, there emerges a set of two-dimensional structures called Rule Families, comprising of the ultimate atomic populated pieces of business logic called Rule Patterns, such that there is no loss of intent of the original business logic statement (no matter how complex the original statement was). Decomposition into ultimate atomic pieces is what makes the Decision Model structure simple, whereby a change applies to one and only one self-defining place in the model.

Each Rule Family has one and only one conclusion fact type. Each populated condition cell in a row is ANDed to each other to reach the corresponding conclusion value. (Note: The rows in a Rule Family can be ORed together to create one whole (nonatomic) logical expression representing the entire Rule Family).

At this point, the Decision Model consists of a set of Rule Families that are islands because they are not connected to one another. For those connections, Principle 7 is needed.

Principle 7: The Connection Principle

Principle 7 places rigor on the connections among Rule Families. The connection among Rule Families is a logical link relating the conclusion of one Rule Family to a condition in another.

> Principle 7: A Rule Family has an inferential relationship with another Rule Family when the conclusion fact type of the latter serves as a condition fact type in the former. (Or, informally, the conclusion of one Rule Family may serve as a condition in another Rule Family.)

Principle 7 Description and Subprinciples

Until this point, the principles focused on creating high-quality Rule Family structures in first and second normal form, such that each by itself is simple and predictably created. That is, each Rule Family is easy to understand, comprises atomic pieces, and is free from ambiguity. Principle 7 deals with how these Rule Families connect to each other, creating an entire model of business logic that continues to reflect the property of structural simplicity.

Essentially, Principle 7 reveals that some Rule Families are related to others because a conclusion fact type in one is a condition fact type in another. This is simply an inferential relationship whose integrity must be protected. (It is a logical connection, not requiring physical pointers, hashing, indexes, or any other specific implementation in automated solutions.)

This is the self-defining glue, the inferential relationship that binds together the Rule Families. By following Principles 1–6, the web of Rule Families begins to weave itself. As long as the business logic statements are correctly translated into Rule Families, Principle 7 confirms the structure of the entire web of related Rule Families. Thus emerges the self-defining web of business logic behind a business decision.

There are two subprinciples of Principle 7 that should be obvious. They are stated here for completeness and to reinforce the nature of the full structure of the Decision Model as prescribed by Principle 7.

Principle 7a: Rule Family Empty Conclusion Cell Principle

Principle 7a: A Rule Family cannot have an empty conclusion cell.

A Rule Family cannot have an empty conclusion cell because the conclusion fact type is the glue that ties together inferentially related Rule Families. An empty conclusion cell implies that the corresponding row either is not inferentially related to any row in another Rule Family or is related to some or every row. An example makes this point.

Table 8.23 Exploring the Consequences of a Null Conclusion Cell

Rule Pattern	Conditions				Conclusion	
	Person Employment History		Person Debt		Person Credit Rating	
1	Is	Poor	Is	High		
1	Is	Poor	Is	Low	Is	C
1	Is	Good	Is	Low	Is	A
2	Is	Excellent			Is	A

Rule Pattern	Conditions		Conclusion
	Person Credit Rating	Person Outside Credit Rating	Person Likelihood of Defaulting on a Loan

Refer to Table 8.23, where the conclusion cell for the first row is empty. This means either that these values are unknown or these values are irrelevant. Neither situation is acceptable. At the very least, without values for the conclusion cells, there is no way of knowing whether the values in its condition cells will lead to a conclusion value that is covered by the second Rule Family in Table 8.23. In other words, a situation where a Person Employment History is Poor and Person Debt is High leads to an unspecified value for the Person Credit Rating; hence, which row in the second Rule Family will subsequently lead to a Person Likelihood of Defaulting on a Loan in this situation? Perhaps none of the rows in the second Rule Family is meant to cover an unspecified conclusion. Or, perhaps some or all of the rows in the second Rule Family are meant to cover it. So, the first Rule Family is incomplete in its business logic.

Obviously, this subprinciple disallows empty conclusion cells because the presence of empty conclusion cells breaks the Decision Model. Its business logic cannot be guaranteed to execute to successful completion. Such a Decision Model falls apart.

Because all Rule Patterns within a Rule Family have the same conclusion fact type, the Rule Family (rather than the Rule Pattern) remains the fundamental structure in the Decision Model because it is the conclusion fact type that links the pieces of the model together.

Principle 7b: Rule Pattern Empty Conclusion Cell Principle

Principle 7b: A Rule Pattern cannot have empty conclusion cells.

The previous subprinciple required that no conclusion cells in a Rule Family be empty. Therefore, it follows that no conclusion cells in a Rule Pattern can be empty. Otherwise, its Rule Family would contain empty conclusion cells. When there are empty conclusion cells in a Rule Pattern or Rule Family, some Rule Pattern's population is incomplete.

Inferential Relationship and Unconditional Computations

There is a need to revisit unconditional computations one more time. It is often the case that the values of the fact types (or parameters) used in such a formula may themselves be determined by Rule Families. Consider the example where earlier Person Credit Rating involved a formula using fact types of Person Total Income Over the Past Five Years, Person Anticipated Total Income Over the Next Five Years, as well as the Proprietary Number. Each of these fact types may be a conclusion fact type in another Rule Family. In other words, their values may be determined by executing a set of business logic statements represented in a different Rule Family. In fact, for this example, it is highly likely that the person's past and anticipated income is obtained by executing business logic.

However, even when the parameters in an unconditional computation are determined by other Rule Families, there is no inferential relationship in the Decision Model to connect those Rule Families to the one representing the unconditional computation. The reason is that the relationship among these values does not represent inferential logic; there is merely a computational dependency. So, the Rule Families for determining the values of the parameters would need to be executed in a process before executing the Rule Family for the unconditional computations. In other words, the sequential relationship between the Rule Families is part of the process model, not the Decision Model.*

Making the Inferential Relationship a "Key" in the Decision Model

Given the importance of the inferential relationship that emerges among some Rule Families, an inferential key is defined as a condition fact type in one Rule Family that serves as a conclusion fact type in another Rule Family. The integrity of the inferential key comes into play in Chapter 10, when an Integrity Principle will seek full coverage of inferential key values in Rule Families, as appropriate.

---

* Remember that, when sequence matters, it becomes part of a process model. When sequence is immaterial, it becomes part of the Decision Model. This is revisited in Chapter 9.

How Principle 7 Addresses the Simplicity of the Decision Model

Principle 7 results in an integrated Decision Model structure because Rule Families connect to one another based on a conclusion fact type in one Rule Family serving as a condition fact type in another. It is as simple as that. In fact, a Decision Model diagram can be generated automatically from the headings of Rule Families based only on the headings and their roles as conditions and conclusions. (There is no opportunity for errors in the connections if the business logic is represented correctly in the Rule Family content.)*

Applying Principle 7 in Practice

Applying Principle 7 in practice means seeking the natural inferential relationships among Rule Families. So far, after applying Principles 1–6, the Decision Model contains the two Rule Families shown in Table 8.22. Using Principle 7 to study these Rule Families, we see there is an inferential relationship between them. The "inferential key" is Person Credit Rating because it serves as a condition fact type in one Rule Family and as a conclusion fact type in the other Rule Family.

To best illustrate this relationship of Rule Families, a Decision Model diagram is useful. It allows for viewing only the overall structure of Rule Families and their connections. The diagram is in Figure 8.1, where the inferential relationships between two Rule Families are shown as lines that connect those two Rule Families to each other

Important Terminology for Describing the Decision Model Structure

Figure 8.1 illustrates the graphical representation of the important concepts: Decision Model, business decision, decision, and Decision Rule Family.

The Rule Families and their connections in Figure 8.1 comprise one Decision Model. The scope of the Decision Model is all of the business logic that leads to a conclusion for a business decision. The business decision in Figure 8.1 is a conclusion about a person's likelihood of defaulting on a loan. The business logic in the Decision Model is based on all the fact types contained in all the Rule Families in the figure.

The Rule Family that connects directly to the business decision is called a Decision Rule Family. A Decision Rule Family may have other Rule Families

---

* In the case where the operand 2 in a cell is another fact type, the Decision Model diagram cannot be generated completely from the Rule Family headings, knowledge of cell content is needed to discover another connection among Fact Types in the Decision Model.

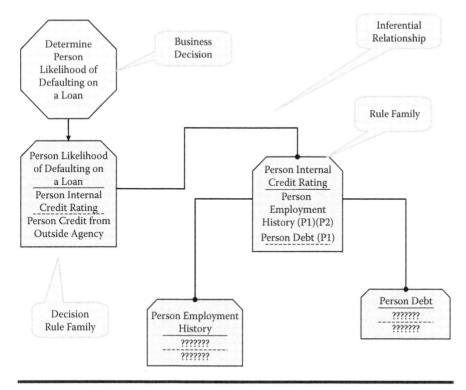

Figure 8.1 Important terminology in a Decision Model.

related to it directly or indirectly within the same Decision Model, as shown in the figure.

Finally, the Decision Model from a structural perspective is a group of well-formed Rule Families that, taken together, come to a conclusion about a particular fact type.

The definitions of the structures in Figure 8.1 are described by the Decision Model principles. The structural principles render the structure as simple as possible, without unnecessary distractions and without losing the intent of the business logic itself.

Note the following notation conventions:

■ The business decision shape (octagon) represents the entire Business Decision.
■ The name of the business decision appears in the Business Decision shape.
■ Each Rule Family shape (tombstone) represents an entire Rule Family.
■ The name of each Rule Family appears at the top of each Rule Family shape and is the name of the conclusion fact type for that Rule Family.

- The names of the condition fact types for each Rule Family appear within the Rule Family shape underneath the name of the conclusion fact type.*
- The names of the condition fact types below the solid line indicate that these condition fact types serve as "inferential keys," in that they are a conclusion fact type in an inferentially related Rule Family.
- The names of the condition fact types below the dotted line indicate that these condition fact types do not serve as "inferential keys," in that they are not conclusion fact types in another Rule Family (as far as has been determined); hence, the values of these condition fact types are simply supplied as raw data.
- The lines connecting one Rule Family shape to another represent the inferential relationships among the Rule Families.
- The P's within the Rule Family shapes indicate that the corresponding condition fact type belongs to a particular Rule Pattern. As the process of discovering all the conditions is not yet completed, some of the Rule Families do not yet contain full Rule Pattern notation at the point of the recording of this model.
- Rule Family shapes with "????" represent those Rule Families whose conclusion fact types serve as a condition fact type in another Rule Family, but about which enough information is not yet available to confirm the details.

So, Figure 8.1 delivers a Decision Model using the notation introduced in Chapter 2. This entire Decision Model links to a task in a business process model or to a step in a use case or to several of each, becoming an important component in a comprehensive modeling environment. This ensures that the business logic is modeled separately from the business process. The Decision Model can link to other business model components, as discussed in Chapter 6.

Insights into Methodology

Steps 1–6 in the following list correlate to the application of the seven structural principles directly. The steps need not be carried out in this sequence. The remaining steps are covered in Chapters 9 and 10, and relate to additional principles:

> Step 1: Gather business logic statements from people, documents, and program code in preparation for translating them from textual form to tabular form (Principle 1).

---

* Sometimes a condition will contain two fact types, specifically when operand 2 is a fact type rather than a value. In this case, the Decision Model diagram includes a notation indicating the second fact type in parentheses. More information on this diagramming convention is in Chapter 12.

Step 2: Identify fact types and logical expressions (fact type + operator + operand) that are relevant to the scope of the Decision Model (Principles 2 and 3).

Step 3: Distinguish between condition fact types and conclusion fact types and which ones inferentially lead to the other (Principle 4).

Step 4: Create two-dimensional structures for each conclusion fact type (the decision's conclusion fact type plus other interim conclusion fact types) (Principle 5).

Step 5: Reduce to Rule Patterns (Principle 6).

Step 6: Connect Rule Families based on integrity relationships among them (Principle 7).

Summary

This chapter is the first of three chapters addressing the principles of the Decision Model. The concept of first normal form is adapted for the Decision Model to deliver the one—and only one—way of interpreting and manipulating business logic behind business decisions in a Decision Model. This leads to one extremely simple kind of structure that can be executed in any way by any technology to arrive at the correct result.

Normalization plays a critical role in delivering such a Decision Model structure. First normal form imposes a discipline on the content so that the model is represented and interpreted in one and only one way. First normal form leads to simplicity in interpreting, predictability in creating and changing, and ease of manipulating each model.

In the Decision Model, first normal form means that, in terms of the tabular picture of a Rule Family, each Rule Family row cannot be decomposed into more than one row reaching the conclusion. In practice, this means decomposing a row when it includes an OR between conditions or more than one conclusion column. In both cases, this means recasting these kinds of logic as business logic statements down rows rather than across columns.

Second normal form means making sure that the entire condition key is needed to determine the conclusion cells. In the Decision Model, this means conclusion values that depend only on part of the condition key are noted as belonging to a separate Rule Pattern along with that part of the condition key.

The important detailed points in this chapter are the following:

■ The first seven principles aim to simplify the Decision Model structure.
■ Simplicity is not a measure of how many structures a Decision Model has, but of how easy it is to make changes and how certain it is that only one structure is correct.

- The Decision Model structure does not enforce a particular grammar for business logic statements or business rules, nor does it need to.
- A simple Decision Model structure is one that is easy to understand, comprises simple atomic uncombined pieces, and free from confusion such that it can only be interpreted in one straightforward way.
- A Decision Model comprises Rule Families that are two-dimensional structures, with a heading and a body.
- The heading is a set of fact types, and the body is a set of logical expressions that conform to the fact types in the heading.
- Principles 5 and 6 deliver Rule Families in first normal form by eliminating nested rows in two different ways.
- Principle 6 delivers Rule Patterns in second normal form by eliminating condition cells that are irrelevant to the conclusion cell.
- The inferential dependency leading to only one conclusion fact type exposes a self-defining structure to the Decision Model because all statements with the same conclusion fact type, by definition, fall into a self-defining group.
- The Decision Model comprises several types of atomic pieces:
  - Atomic fact types governing the heading of Rule Families
  - Atomic logical expressions in the cells of Rule Families
  - Atomic (only one) conclusion fact type in a Rule Family
  - Atomic (only relevant) logical expressions in a Rule Pattern.
- Most often, Rule Patterns are not evident until the Rule Family is partially or wholly populated.
- One Rule Family has an inferential relationship with another if a conclusion fact type of the former Rule Family serves as the conclusion fact type of the latter.
- The Decision Model is held together as a self-defining web of business logic because of two factors: the inferential dependency within a Rule Family and the inferential relationships across Rule Families.
- These seven principles can be applied in their numerical sequence to construct a first-cut Decision Model exhibiting the simplicity reflected in these seven principles. In reality, many of these principles will be applied together at the same time, whereas others will come into play when we sense that something seems not quite right with the simplicity of the resulting Decision Model.
- Although the Decision Model is logical and atomic, design methodologies might advocate physical designs that deviate from the Decision Model structure to meet performance or functionality requirements.

Table 8.24 summarizes the seven structural principles.

Table 8.24 Summary of Principles 1–7

Principle	Principle Name	Purpose	Principle
1	The Tabular Principle	Place rigor on the shape of a Rule Family.	The fundamental structure of a Decision Model is called a Rule Family and has two dimensions: one dimension is the heading, and the other dimension is the body.
2	The Heading Principle	Place rigor on the heading of a Rule Family.	The heading of a Rule Family is a set of fact types.
3	The Cell Principle	Place rigor on the cell of a Rule Family.	The content of each cell of a Rule Family is an atomic logical expression conforming to the heading.
4	The Row Principle	Place rigor on the row of a Rule Family.	The populated cells playing the role of conditions infer the corresponding populated cells playing the role of a conclusion.
5	The Conclusion Principle	Place rigor on the conclusion fact type of a Rule Family.	A Rule Family has only one conclusion fact type.
6	The Conditions Principle	Place rigor on condition fact types of a Rule Family.	All populated condition cells must be true for the conclusion cell to be true. - A Rule Family must have at least one Rule Pattern. - The whole condition key of a Rule Pattern can be empty if there is only one Rule Pattern in the Rule Family. - The condition key of a Rule Pattern cannot be partially empty unless the whole condition key is empty. - A conclusion in a Rule Pattern should not depend on a partial condition key.

Table 8.24 Summary of Principles 1–7 (Continued)

Principle	Principle Name	Purpose	Principle
7	The Connection Principle	Place rigor on the connections among Rule Families.	A Rule Family has an inferential relationship with another Rule Family when the conclusion fact type of the latter serves as a condition fact type in the former. - A Rule Family cannot have an empty conclusion cell. - A Rule Pattern cannot have empty conclusion cells.

New Vocabulary from This Chapter

- Rule Family
- heading
- body
- fact type
- fact
- business term
- domain
- cell
- atomic logical expression (fact type + operator + operand)
- Is In
- Is Between
- Inference
- condition fact type
- conclusion fact type
- fact type role
- row
- functional dependency
- normalization
- Decision Model first normal form
- Decision Model second normal form
- Rule Pattern
- condition key
- inferential relationship
- inferential key
- inferential dependency
- Rule Pattern integrity
- Decision Rule Family

And What about the Quote?

The quote at the beginning of this chapter reminds us that unnecessary complexity adds little value. The principles in this chapter minimize complexity, thereby maximizing sophistication, because a simple Decision Model is easy to understand and maintain. As such, it is likely to endure as a stable foundational element of business decision management, BPM, and SOA automation.

Discussion Points and Exercises

1. Describe some structural differences among data models, business object models, business process models, and decision models.
2. Create a list of fact types from the information on your driver's license. Give them names, definitions, and domains.
3. Create a list of fact types you might use as conditions to decide whether to hire a person. Decide on what the conclusion fact type would be. Provide names, definitions, and domains for your condition and conclusion fact types. For extra credit: attempt to put them into a Decision Model structure of several Rule Families that are related.
4. Define what the following means in terms of a Decision Model structure:
   a. Atomic heading
   b. Atomic row
   c. Atomic cell
5. Discuss why it is so important for a Rule Family to have only one conclusion fact type.
6. Review the following statement from a loan officer of a bank. Create a Rule Family table from it and a list of questions you want to ask:

We always set a high default probability even if the applicant has no mortgage and does not have an X outside credit rating, but does have another kind of loan and has a credit card balance. Oh, and an education loan balance.

Chapter 9

The Declarative Principles

Contents

Why Should a Decision Model Structure Be Declarative?..................................213
    What Does "Declarative" Mean?..213
    What Does "Procedural" Mean? 214
    Everyday Example of a Procedural and Declarative Approaches 214
    Seeking the Declarative Nature of the Decision Model 215
The Goal of the Declarative Principles..216
Principle 8: Declarative Heading Principle 217
    Principle 8 Description 217
    How Principle 8 Addresses the Declarative Nature
    of the Decision Model..218
    Applying Principle 8 in Practice..219
        Hidden Condition Sequences...219
        Unnecessary Condition Sequences 221
Principle 9: Declarative Body Principle 221
    Principle 9 Description 222
    How Principle 9 Addresses the Declarative Nature
    of the Decision Model..222
    Applying Principle 9 in Practice..223
Principle 10: Declarative Inferential Relationship Principle 223
    Principle 10 Description 224
        Forward-Chaining through a Decision Model (Option 1)......................225
        Backward-Chaining through a Decision Model (Option 2)....................225
        Which Is Better: Forward or Backward? 226

How Principle 10 Addresses the Declarative Nature
of the Decision Model...226
Applying Principle 10 in Practice..227
One More Time, Doesn't the Decision Model Really Require
a Procedural Approach to Arrive at Its Conclusion? 227
Insights into Methodology 227
Summary.. 228
New Vocabulary Introduced in This Chapter...229
And What about the Quote? 229
Discussion Points and Exercises...230

> Overall, the relational model is declarative and not procedural in nature; that is, we favor declarative solutions over procedural ones, whenever such solutions are feasible. The reason is obvious; declarative means the system does the work, procedural means the user does the work.
>
> **C. J. Date in *Database in Depth: Relational Theory for Practitioners***

This chapter is the second part (of three) addressing the rigor of the Decision Model. Specifically, it explains the Decision Model Principles that render it declarative in nature, and hence logically independent of other considerations or limitations.

Readers are reminded that the populated Rule Family structures in this chapter are not necessarily meant to be fully populated. This means that readers ought not to be concerned that the Rule Families are not complete. They are simply populated with instances that illustrate a particular point about Rule Families.

In Chapter 8, Principles 1–7 simplified the Decision Model structure so that a person can visualize it and know how to interpret its content in an unambiguous manner. The ability to visualize and interpret a Decision Model is a good beginning. But the Decision Model structure also must be declarative so that it is logically independent of other considerations. Specifically, the Decision Model structure must represent an unbiased understanding of how its business logic is used in the business—without concern for processing patterns or technology limitations. This unbiased characteristic of the Decision Model is not obvious from the look and feel of its structure or from its first seven principles.

Therefore, the next three principles pertain to the declarative nature of the Decision Model's structure. This chapter presumes these principles are being applied to Decision Model structures that already conform to Principles 1–7. Therefore, the next three principles are now applied to a Decision Model consisting of Rule Families, comprising Rule Patterns, and connected via inferential relationships. The goal is to deliver a Decision Model that is declarative in structure and logically independent of unnecessary and distracting biases. But again, this chapter starts with the obvious question of why the Decision Model should be declarative.

Why Should a Decision Model Structure Be Declarative?

A Decision Model must be declarative for it to be logically independent of technology and other considerations. A Decision Model that is logically independent of other considerations provides maximum stability and flexibility in the design and management of its business logic.

A stable Decision Model is one that is "steady in purpose" (Merriam-Webster Online Dictionary "stable"). Therefore, it will remain faithful to its intended purpose regardless of the environment in which it is referenced or deployed. That's because it comprises pure business logic and nothing else.

A flexible Decision Model is one that is "characterized by a ready capacity to adapt to new, different, or changing requirements" (Merriam-Webster Online Dictionary "flexible"), so it will not favor some requirements over others. In this way, all changes in business logic will require similar effort.

A stable and flexible Decision Model serves as a common foundation across technology platforms. It should be tailored to specific technology challenges while still retaining a faithful representation of the pure business perspective.

For a Decision Model to be logically independent of limitations imposed by technology and processes, its structure must be declarative and not procedural in nature. But what does this mean? Let's explore the important difference.

What Does "Declarative" Mean?

A declarative solution is distinct from a procedural one in that a declarative solution is all about what needs to be done; a procedural solution is all about how something is done. "HOW means saying how, step by step, the work is to be done; WHAT just means saying what the work to be done is" (Date, 2000).

In the case of a Decision Model, the work to be done is simply determining the conclusion of a business decision. That's all. It follows then, that a declarative structure for a Decision Model specifies only what needs to be done to determine the conclusion of a business decision. In other words, the declarative structure represents only what the business logic is that is needed for determining the result of a business decision but not how it is to be executed. Such a declarative structure for a Decision Model must depict an arrangement of conditions and conclusions that are agnostic to how they are executed.

What Does "Procedural" Mean?

On the other hand, a procedural structure for a Decision Model would specify how, in a step-by-step manner, the business logic is to be executed in determining the conclusion of a business decision. So, a procedural Decision Model would depict the same conditions and conclusions as in the declarative structure, but arranged in a deliberate execution sequence.

So, in general, a procedural approach to achieving a goal is a step-by-step progression for reaching it. A declarative approach to achieving a goal is independent of such a step-by-step progression because the steps are irrelevant to reaching the goal. In fact, different step-by-step progressions can lead to the same goal. When this is so, a declarative solution enjoys a high level of processing and technology independence.

Some goals require a procedural approach. Others do not. This difference is important to understand.

Let's look at two common examples from everyday life that clarify the difference between procedural and declarative approaches to a goal.

Everyday Example of a Procedural and Declarative Approaches

Consider the task of giving someone directions to someone's house. Most people start by defining a starting point followed by a sequential set of road navigations leading to the correct home address as the destination:

1. Head south on a certain highway for a specific distance.
2. Exit at a specific exit.
3. Bear left.
4. Make first right turn.
5. Travel so many miles.
6. At the third light turn left, and so forth.

Obviously, when providing such driving directions, sequence is of utmost importance, especially if the driver hopes to arrive at the correct destination in a reasonable time frame and with minimal frustration. These steps of road navigations are a procedural solution to a request for driving directions.

In fact, even the description of the example—the task of giving someone directions to a house—is expressed in a procedural manner. For starters, it was presented as a task of doing something rather than a set of decisions for doing so. Second, the implication was that the solution is a set of directions, which also implies a step-by-step procedural approach. However, with experience in teasing out the declarative versus procedural nature of problems, the example could have been framed with nonprocedural terminology. For example, if the example had been described simply as the arrival from a starting point to an ending point, a declarative solution may have come to mind. A declarative solution would consist of not step-by-step road navigations, but very simply a map, with the designated starting and ending positions. Given the map and the goal, the navigation is unconstrained; the driver is free to choose among many step-by-step (i.e., procedural) mechanisms for navigating the map and achieving the desired goal. In fact, different drivers may choose different sets of driving instructions, but all should (eventually) arrive at the designated destination.

In seeking a declarative solution, there is no specific reason to constrain a driver to one pathway through it. Obviously, some routes will be faster, slower, more expensive, less expensive, more scenic, and so forth. But there are many possible step-by-step solutions that work. So, when teasing out declarative business logic from a procedural background, it is most valuable to look for goals that could be of a declarative nature, if possible, rather than assuming from the start that it is strictly procedural. That is, there is more creativity and freedom in providing an endpoint and a map than in providing turn-by-turn driving directions.

This has profound implications for the relationship between business process modeling and the Decision Model. Chapter 4 demonstrates how to distinguish between the procedural business process and declarative business logic.

Seeking the Declarative Nature of the Decision Model

Even with an understanding of the declarative approach, it is often a challenge to uncover the declarative structure for a particular Decision Model because business experts must also understand it. History can (and probably will) stand in the way to some extent. For example, business experts may be very familiar with the current business logic behind a business decision. Perhaps they know how to carry it out step by step in manual processes every day. Or, perhaps business experts know how the supporting systems carry out the business logic in a step-by-step implementation. So, teasing out the declarative nature of a Decision Model, even when working with people who know the current business logic, is often an iterative learning activity. The activity aims to transcend current procedural thinking. It becomes an exercise in rethinking the business. It should uncover opportunities for better business logic. This exercise can be enlightening and, sometimes, politically challenging.

Regardless, when creating or reviewing a Decision Model, it is important to seek out hidden and unnecessary sequence. For this reason, pay attention if someone describes parts of the model with words such as "first I do this," or "after the system does that," or "before I know that." When words suggest a prescribed sequence, determine whether that sequence is required to achieve the goal or whether it is superfluous. If it is required, it becomes part of the related business process model, which is procedural by definition, not part of the Decision Model. If the sequence is not required, the business logic is cast into a Decision Model and the Declarative Principles are applied to render it a declarative structure, devoid of pointless sequence.

Keep in mind that humans, by nature or by historical experience, usually think and act procedurally. But the good news is that the ability to transcend procedural thinking can lead to business creativity and, correspondingly, valuable Decision Models.*

The Goal of the Declarative Principles

The three principles in this chapter support the common goal of a declarative nature, which delivers logical independence. This is business logic independence. A Decision Model supporting business logic independence means that it enables changes in the way the business logic is physically stored, accessed, and executed without having to make related changes in the way the business logic is perceived by the (nontechnical) audience.

The Decision Model brings this distinction to the forefront, and practitioners will deliver two separate models: a procedural business process model and a declarative Decision Model.

Therefore, the principles in this chapter enable creation of a Decision Model whose entire structure of Rule Families and their inferential relationships is declarative and not procedural.

A declarative Decision Model works well regardless of who or what system processes it and in which sequence the processing is done. A Decision Model structure adhering to the Declarative Principles does not rely on a specific processing sequence of its content. Any method of processing of the content results in the correct conclusion. When this is so, the model is reusable and is the starting point for many kinds of technology, even as technology matures over time. Applying the Declarative Principles means eliminating unnecessary constraints from Decision

---

* Recognition of the Decision Model's declarative nature is much like the historical recognition of the Relational Data Model's declarative nature, where the latter implied separation of a data model from its surrounding process models. It took decades for practitioners to fully understand that distinction well enough to deliver two separate models. Today, the challenge in Decision Modeling is recognizing that the differentiation between pure *process* and pure *decision* is not widely understood. Therefore, this differentiation is not well practiced today.

Model structures because they impose a pointless sequence. It means delivering a Decision Model free from sequential limitations where none need exist. To do this, the principles in this chapter address the declarative nature of the following aspects of a Decision Model:

- Principle 8: Its declarative heading
- Principle 9: Its declarative body
- Principle 10: Its declarative relationships

The rest of this chapter defines each of the three principles, explains how each one contributes to the declarative nature of the Decision Model structure, and provides insights into how to apply each in practice. Perhaps it is only fitting that, unlike the Structural Principles, the sequence of Principles 8–10 is not significant. That is, each does not necessarily build on the one before it. These principles can certainly be applied to Decision Models in any sequence.

Principle 8: Declarative Heading Principle

Principle 8 removes unnecessary procedural constraints from the heading of a Rule Family.

> Principle 8: The fact types in the heading of a Rule Family are unordered. (Or, informally, there is no implied sequence to columns of a Rule Family.)

Principle 8 Description

Principle 8 prescribes that there must be no implied order in the sequence of fact types in the heading of a Rule Family. That is, the columns need not be evaluated or interpreted in the sequence shown. Most importantly, this means there is no hidden meaning behind the sequence of the columns in a Rule Family.

As an example, Table 9.1 shows a Rule Family table with two populated condition columns.

Table 9.1   Rule Family Diagram: Sequence of Conditions Is Irrelevant

	Conditions				Conclusion	
Rule Pattern	Person Years at Current Employer		Person Number of Jobs in Past Five Years		Person Employment History	
1	Is Less Than	1	Is Less Than	3	Is	Good
1	Is Less Than	1	Is Greater Than	8	Is	Poor

Principle 8 informs us that Table 9.1 is not meant to imply that the leftmost condition column needs to be evaluated before the next condition column is evaluated. In fact, the correct conclusion is reached regardless of whether a system or a person evaluates the Person Years at Current Employer before or after evaluating the Person Number of Jobs in Past Five Years. Table 9.1 could just as easily have shown the two condition columns in the other sequence. But what about the conclusion column and the relevance of sequence?

At first glance, it may seem that Table 9.1 implies some sequence because the conclusion column is shown as the rightmost column, suggesting that the position of the conclusion column is relevant. In fact, the rightmost column is always the conclusion column in Rule Family tables in this book. However, depicting the conclusion column as the rightmost column is merely a convention, a convenient way of viewing the Rule Family. The Decision Model does not require that the conclusion column appear as the last column in a Rule Family. The conclusion column can appear as the first, last, or even somewhere in the middle of the columns and the correct conclusion would still be reached. Why is this so?

The structural principles already differentiate condition from conclusion fact types in a way that does not depend on column sequence. The differentiation is achieved by giving each column a unique name, where its role as condition or conclusion is part of its name, as described under Principle 3. As a reminder, Principle 3 stated that the full context of a column label is Fact Type plus Fact Type Role. Fact Type Role depicts the fact type as playing a role in a condition or conclusion. With such contextual information as the unique name of a column label, the sequence of the columns makes no difference because a person or a system can simply determine, by full name, which ones are conditions and which are conclusions. The sequence of the columns is irrelevant to knowing how to "process" them, and hence is irrelevant to a particular process for arriving at the correct conclusion.

How Principle 8 Addresses the Declarative Nature of the Decision Model

Principle 8 results in structures with declarative columns, meaning that the sequence of columns has no meaning—the column sequence is unconstrained. Hence, the sequence in which columns are evaluated or interpreted makes no difference. In fact, columns are uniquely identified, not by position in a Rule Family but by a name; Fact Type and Fact Type Role.

Therefore, Principle 8 delivers Rule Families that can be implemented with more than one technology, even if one technology processes columns in one sequence, another technology processes columns in another sequence, and yet another technology dynamically determines sequence. That's because, logically, the sequence of column evaluation makes no difference at all.

From a performance or user preference perspective, certain column sequences may be preferable. For example, availability, volumes, and values of data related to

Table 9.2   Rule Family and Implied Condition Sequence

Rule Pattern	Conditions				Conclusion	
	Previous Order		*Previous Order Payment Status*		*Order Discount Amount (%)*	
1	Is	Found	Is not	Paid	Is	0
1	Is	Found	Is	Paid	Is	10
2	Is	Not found			Is	0

specific transactions may favor execution of some Rule Patterns before others. This would mean that certain subsets of condition columns are more interesting than others, given specific input values and volumes. Even specific technology may be better suited for one sequence over the other. Not only that, but, under the covers (i.e., not visible to humans), Rule Family columns can be tailored and tuned with technology options (e.g., pointers, arrays, indexes, fast scans and prefetches of data, and sophisticated intelligent algorithms*). Although such options may be critical to design approaches, they are irrelevant to the Decision Model itself, precisely because it is logically independent of them.

Applying Principle 8 in Practice

At first glance, applying Principle 8 in practice seems trivial. It means studying each condition column to be sure that there is no required sequence among them. In fact, there is no need to check for sequence among conclusion columns, because each Rule Family, adhering to Principle 5, has only one conclusion column.

Yet there are two common types of situations that may lead to Rule Families that are not compliant with Principle 8: (1) failing to recognize hidden condition sequences and (2) adding unnecessary sequences. Let's explore these further.

Hidden Condition Sequences

Hidden condition sequences usually arise when sequential steps become buried inadvertently into the columns of a Rule Family. Consider the Rule Family in Table 9.2. It contains two condition columns and one conclusion column. It also seems to contain two Rule Patterns,. The first two rows belong to one Rule Pattern, and the third row belongs to another Rule Pattern. So far, it looks fine.

---

* One kind of intelligent algorithm is the Rete algorithm, used as a special way of narrowing a set of possible executable rules into a smaller set that is actually relevant to a set of facts known to be true (Stuart and Norviq, 2003).

Looking closely, the first populated condition column seems to test for a Previous Order. A subtle observation is that the first column does not represent pure business logic. It actually alludes to the invisible task of attempting to retrieve a possible Previous Order. The second condition column then applies a logical expression to a fact type related to the Previous Order. So, the second populated condition column seems to be irrelevant if the first column determines that there is no Previous Order to access.

Is there a hidden sequence to the columns? In other words, does sequence really matter? Must it first be determined if a Previous Order exists before determining if there is an amount due on it? It seems so.

So, there is a hidden sequence because, first, a task must attempt to find such an order and then the second column may or may not be relevant. Because sequence is important to how the condition columns execute, this Rule Family is not compliant with Principle 8. The sequence must be removed; the Rule Family structure must be changed.*

This kind of example is common. Creating a Rule Family in which a specific sequence of interpreting conditions is required results in a Rule Family that mixes elements of "process" (i.e., a sequential task) with elements of pure business logic (i.e., declarative conclusions). The implied sequence in Table 9.2 can be removed from the Rule Family if a business process model is created that contains two tasks, and a Rule Family that guides the second task in a declarative manner, as shown in Figure 9.1.

The first task obtains corresponding Customer Order records. It does not contain declarative business logic, although it may contain declarative data access logic. The second task, "Determine Order Discount Amount," is a Decision Task, as indicated by the decision shape incorporated within the task shape. As such, it is guided by declarative business logic for evaluating a Customer's Previous Order to determine the Order's Discount Amount. The Decision Model for this business logic is represented by the decision shape, which would lead to a structural representation of Rule Families. Figure 9.1, for completeness, shows both a Decision Model diagram and the single Rule Family behind this declarative decision.†

---

* Recall that the Decision Model is an intellectual template and not a physical design. In many implementations, the task of retrieving data and of testing its values may, in fact, be bundled together. However, this book deals with the logical separation of procedural tasks from declarative business logic, by which the result (i.e., the Decision Model) can serve as the starting point for various kinds of technology solutions.

† In particular, if a BRMS is the target technology, sometimes it is better for the BRMS to retrieve data and sometimes data is better retrieved outside of the BRMS. Regardless, this is a *design* decision. Data access is *never* part of the business logic in a Decision Model. Data access code is not business logic!

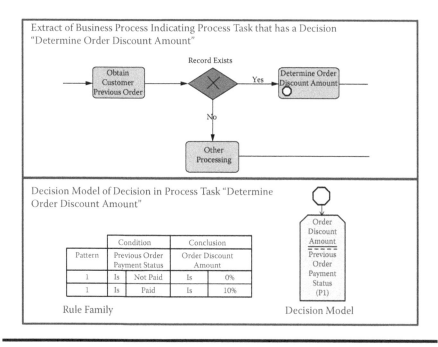

Figure 9.1 Separating procedural process from declarative decisions.

Unnecessary Condition Sequences

Sometimes, the opposite situation happens. Declarative logic is buried inadvertently in procedural representations. In other words, the conditional logic is modeled as tasks in a business process model or as steps in a use case instead of in a Decision Model. In Chapter 4, detailed examples are given of situations of this nature. In addition, Chapter 17 contains a discussion on the implementation of the Decision Model in BPMN, an emerging standard in business process modeling notation.

Now that Principle 8 has provided an understanding of the declarative nature of a Rule Family's headings,* Principle 9 moves on to the declarative nature of a Rule Family body.

Principle 9: Declarative Body Principle

Principle 9 removes unnecessary procedural constraints from the body of a Rule Family.

---

* Principle 8 essentially addresses the declarative nature of a single business logic statement or business rule. That is, Principle 8, addresses the declarative nature of columns as they are interpreted for each row.

Principle 9: Entries in the body of a Rule Family are unordered. (Or, informally, there is no implied sequence to rows of a Rule Family.)

Principle 9 Description

Principle 9 prescribes that there can be no implied order or hidden meaning behind the sequence of the rows in a Rule Family. The rows need not be evaluated or interpreted in the sequence shown. There is no hidden meaning behind the sequence of rows.

As an example, the Rule Family in Table 9.1 shows two rows in a particular sequence where the first row is at the top and the second row is at the bottom.

Principle 9 cautions that Table 9.1 is not meant to imply that the topmost row must be evaluated before the next row is evaluated. In fact, it makes no difference whether a system or a person evaluates the top, the second, or the third row first, and so forth. The table could just as easily have shown the rows in any other sequence.

Because Principle 9 states that the sequence of rows does not matter, the Decision Model must have a way to differentiate each row from another that does not depend on row sequence so that updates can occur to specific rows, for example. This differentiation is possible by the values in the set of conditions in each Rule Pattern. Simply put, the populated condition columns in a Rule Pattern uniquely determine a specific row (assuming that duplicate rows and contradicting rows are not allowed). In fact, the populated condition columns in a Rule Pattern are referred to as its condition key. Indirectly, Principle 9 disallows duplicate and contradictory rows in a Rule Family.

Duplicate rows in a Rule Pattern represent the same set of populated condition evaluations leading to the same conclusion value. Duplicate rows do not add new business logic because duplicate rows are totally redundant. Even worse, duplicate rows create the opportunity for update anomalies. For example, suppose there were two duplicate rows in a Rule Pattern and the business experts wanted to change one of the populated conditions. There would be an error if the updater failed to recognize the need to change both such rows. Even more errors are likely if, for example, there were four or five or six duplicate copies of a row. Not only that, but duplicate rows do not add any new business logic to the Decision Model and can be avoided without any loss.

How Principle 9 Addresses the Declarative Nature of the Decision Model

Principle 9 results in structures with declarative rows, meaning that the sequence of rows has no meaning: the row sequence is unconstrained. In fact, a row is uniquely identified, not by its position in the Rule Family but by its condition keys. Further, duplicate rows are not allowed.

Therefore, Principle 9 delivers Rule Families that can be implemented in more than one technology, even if one technology executes the rows in one sequence, another technology executes them in another sequence, and yet another technology dynamically determines the row sequence. That's because, logically, the sequence of row evaluation makes no difference at all.

Again, from a performance or user perspective, certain row sequences may be preferable. Again, availability, volumes, and values of data related to specific transactions may favor certain row sequences. And specific technology may be better suited for one row sequence than another. Not only that, but, under the covers (i.e., not visible to humans), Rule Family rows can be tailored and tuned with technology options (e.g., pointers, arrays, indexes, fast scans and prefetches of data, and sophisticated intelligent algorithms). Such options may be critical to design approaches, but are irrelevant to the Decision Model itself, again because it is logically independent of them.

Applying Principle 9 in Practice

Applying Principle 9 in practice is usually simple. It is not often that people populate two-dimensional tables with a specific row sequence in mind. People might be accustomed to scanning such tables from top down or bottom up. In fact, for convenience, it may be useful to view the rows in a specific sequence, such as grouping all rows for a Rule Pattern together. However, such a sequence is merely a convenience and does not imply a hidden sequential processing requirement.

Now, with an understanding of the declarative nature of a Rule Family body,* the next section moves on to the declarative nature of the connections among Rule Families.

Principle 10: Declarative Inferential Relationship Principle

Principle 10 removes unnecessary procedural constraints from the Rule Family inferential relationships.

> Principle 10: There is no implied sequence in the path among Rule Families related through inferential relationships. (Or, informally, there is no implied sequence among Rule Families.)

---

* Principle 9 essentially addresses the declarative nature of a *set* of business logic statements or business rules. Specifically, Principle 9 addresses the declarative nature of the set of rows taken collectively. Another way to state Principle 9: Each set of such business logic must be expressed in a way devoid of sequence of execution. The set can be executed from first to last row, from last to first row, or in any other sequence as long as all relevant rows are executed.

Principle 10 Description

Principle 10 prescribes that there can be no hidden meaning behind the sequence, left to right or top to bottom, as to how inferentially related Rule Families are depicted in a Decision Model diagram. Further, the Rule Families need not be applied or executed in the order in which they appear in the diagram.

As an example, Table 9.3 contains a set of Rule Families to determine a Person's Car Rental Discount Amount. It contains two Rule Families that are related through an inferential relationship. The conclusion column of Rule Family 1 serves as a condition column in Rule Family 2. Although Rule Family 1 is labeled as "Rule Family 1," appears at the top of the diagram, and also has a conclusion that seems to be input to Rule Family 2, this diagram does not imply a particular processing sequence. That is, this diagram does not imply that Rule Family 1 needs to be evaluated before Rule Family 2. It makes no difference whether a system or a person evaluates Rule Family 1 first or Rule Family 2 first. Table 9.3 could just as easily have shown the Rule Families in different locations on the diagram. Regardless, the inferential relationship in any diagram will always involve Person's Credit Rating.

At first glance, it may seem that the only sequence in which to process these Rule Families is to process Rule Family 1 first, followed by Rule Family 2. But this is not the only sequence possible. Let's look at this more closely.

Table 9.3 Rule Families Showing Inferential Relationships

Rule Family 1						
	Conditions				Conclusion	
Pattern	Person Employment History		Person Debt		Person Credit Rating	
1	Is	Good	Is	Low	Is	A
1	Is	Good	Is	Medium	Is	B
1	Is	Bad	Is	Low	Is	F

Rule Family 2						
	Conditions				Conclusion	
Pattern	Person Credit Rating		Person Driving Record		Person Car Rental Discount Amount (%)	
1	Is	A	Is	Excellent	Is	20
1	Is	B	Is	Excellent	Is	10
1	Is	F	Is	Poor	Is	0

Forward-Chaining through a Decision Model (Option 1)

No doubt, the most natural way to think of executing the business logic in Table 9.3 is to start by interpreting Rule Family 1 to determine a Person's Credit Rating. From here, knowing a Person's Credit Rating, it is possible to interpret Rule Family 2 to determine the Person's Car Rental Discount Amount.

This is similar to how some business rule engines or business rules management systems (BRMSs) would execute these Rule Families and is roughly what is known as forward-chaining, or data-driven reasoning. Forward-chaining begins with facts that are true and assesses conditions about those facts, thus leading to the corresponding conclusions that are true. Each true conclusion is added to a virtual list of true facts. This process continues until no further true facts lead to a conclusion (Stuart and Norviq, 2003). In the Decision Model, this is the same as executing first those Rule Families whose facts are simply raw input data. The conclusions of these Rule Families are then used in evaluating the Rule Families that are dependent upon those conclusions; this process continues until the Decision Rule Family is evaluated, reaching a conclusion. However, logically, there is nothing that requires this execution sequence. Another sequence that suffices is described in Option 2.

Backward-Chaining through a Decision Model (Option 2)

A less intuitive approach is to select one possible Person's Car Rental Discount Amount from Rule Family 2, such as 10%. Then select, from Rule Family 1, the rows where the conclusion value for Person Credit Rating matches the related condition value in Rule Family 2. If there is none, another Person Car Rental Discount Amount can be selected from Rule Family 2 and the process started again until a match is found for a selected Person Rental Car Discount Amount. In our example, the conclusion value of 10% for Person Car Discount Amount in Rule Family 2 has a related condition value for Person Credit Rating of "B." Finding a row in Rule Family 1 that has "B" as the value of its conclusion column for Person Credit Rating, it is obvious that a Person Employment History must be Good and a Person Debt must be Medium for this to be true. If these two conditions, which are based on raw data, are true, then a 10% Order Amount Discount is a correct conclusion.

This is similar to how some BRMSs would execute these Rule Families and is roughly what is known as backward-chaining, or goal-directed reasoning. Backward-chaining starts with a conclusion value and finds those conditions that lead to the conclusion value. Backward-chaining continues by starting again with these condition values as conclusions and finds the next set of condition values that lead to the conclusion values. This process continues until a set of condition values is found that is true based on known facts, in which case, the original conclusion value is now known to be true (Stuart and Norviq, 2003). If none of the final condition values is true, the entire process begins again by starting with another conclusion value and tracing it backward to conditions, and so forth. In the Decision Model, this is the same as selecting a conclusion from the Decision Rule Family, finding those conditions that lead to that conclusion evaluating to true, and then finding the Rule Families in which those conditions are conclusions, finding the conditions that lead to those conclusions being true, and so forth.

Which Is Better: Forward or Backward?

Which sequence is optimum: forward or backward? Essentially, it depends on the nature of the logic and of the target problem. For the purposes of a Decision Model, however, there is no difference. Naturally, performance requirements or user preferences may favor one over the other. Specific technology may be better suited for one over the other. Does this sound familiar? These are considerations for design methodologies, not the Decision Model itself.*

Note two important points regarding Principle 10. First, in a rigorous (and declarative) Decision Model, the inferential dependencies among Rule Families are inherent (and important) to the nature of the Decision Model. Nevertheless, the sequence of execution of those Rule Families is not constrained by these dependencies, although it is obviously guided by them in a meaningful way.

Second, Principle 10 reinforces that the inferential relationships among Rule Families is a logical connection. Not only is the inferential relationship self-defining based on the structure of the logic itself, but it does not imply a particular physical implementation to support that connection (e.g., pointers, indexing, storing in matched sequence). In this way, the declarative nature of the inferential relationship permits variations in implementation while preserving the original logical structure and intent.

How Principle 10 Addresses the Declarative Nature of the Decision Model

Principle 10 results in inferentially related Rule Families whose inferential relationships are declarative. The Rule Family relationships need not be traversed in the sequence shown, top to bottom or left to right. This means that the sequence in which Rule Families are evaluated has no meaning: the sequence is unconstrained. Declarative Rule Family inferential relationships are important because it means that the entire web of the Decision Model structure can be evaluated in any sequence.

---

* Where more than one conclusion is possible, backward chaining requires checking all possible conclusions and working backward to determine which ones apply. That is, the backward chaining is not finished when it finds one conclusion that works.

Applying Principle 10 in Practice

Applying Principle 10 in practice is usually simple once there is a good understanding that the Decision Model does not really have a prescribed beginning or even a prescribed end. It has a goal that is the conclusion of a business decision. As a declarative structure, it represents what (i.e., which business logic) is needed to reach such a goal, but not how (i.e., where to start and in what sequence to proceed).

One More Time, Doesn't the Decision Model Really Require a Procedural Approach to Arrive at Its Conclusion?

The desired goal of a Decision Model is the conclusion of a business decision. In reality, it must be reached by following some steps in some sequence. The point of the Declarative Principles is that these steps and their sequence should be invisible and irrelevant when creating and understanding the pure business logic of a Decision Model. The steps and their sequence, if truly invisible, can be changed without changing the functionality of the Decision Model. The Decision Model will always produce the result of a business decision based on business criteria as specified by business experts.

Of course, a specific set of steps for navigating through a Decision Model structure and their sequence may have tremendous implications for performance. But performance is related to technology and to specific data and transaction volumes. The Decision Model itself should not be constrained by technology, data volumes, transaction volumes, or to one way of processing. If it remains unconstrained, it will endure through maturing technology as well as growth in business volumes and directions.

Insights into Methodology

Steps 7–9 in the following list correlate to the application of the three principles directly. The steps need not be carried out in this sequence.

> Step 7: Ensure that condition columns in each Rule Family need not be evaluated in a particular sequence (Principle 8).
> - Resolve hidden sequence in Rule Family conditions by moving them to a procedural process model.
> - Remove unnecessary sequence in procedural process models by incorporating them into the appropriate Rule Family.

Step 8: Ensure that rows in each Rule Family need not be evaluated in a particular sequence (Principle 9).
  – Remove duplicate rows.
Step 9: Ensure that Rule Families related through inferential relationships need not be evaluated in a particular sequence (Principle 10).

Summary

This chapter is the second of three chapters introducing the principles of the Decision Model. The principles in this chapter establish the declarative nature of the Decision Model. The important points covered in this chapter are the following:

- A Decision Model supporting business logic independence means that it enables changes in the way the business logic is physically stored, accessed, and executed without having to make related changes in the way the business logic is perceived by the (nontechnical) audience.
- A declarative Decision Model works well regardless of who or what system processes it and in what sequence they do so.
- Principles 8–10 ensure that the Decision Model is logically independent of processing patterns and technology limitations by requiring declarative rows, columns, and relationships.
- Principle 8 prescribes that labels in a Rule Family have no implied sequence. It is equivalent to saying that each business logic or rule statement is declarative by itself.
- Principle 8 relies on Principle 5 for a means of distinguishing one column from another in a Rule Family using Fact Type plus Fact Type Role.
- Principle 9 prescribes that rows in a Rule Family have no implied sequence. It is equivalent to saying that an entire set of business logic or rule statements is declarative by itself.
- Principle 9 implies that there are no duplicate rows in a Rule Family.
- Principle 10 prescribes that inferential integrity relationships among Rule Families have no implied sequence. It is equivalent to saying that an entire web of sets of business logic statements is declarative.
- A Decision Model that is declarative in all three senses, and hence free from pointless sequences, is one that will transcend current and future technologies. It will serve as a foundation by which different and future technologies can support the same business view of the Decision Model.
- Today, the differentiation between pure process and pure decision is not widely understood. The Decision Model brings this distinction to the forefront, and practitioners who fully understand it will deliver two separate models (i.e., a process model and a Decision Model).

Table 9.4   Summary of Declarative Principles

Principle	Principle Name	Purpose of Principle	Principle
8	Declarative Heading Principle	Remove unnecessary procedural constraints from the heading of a Rule Family.	The fact types in the heading of a Rule Family are unordered.
9	Declarative Body Principle	Remove unnecessary procedural constraints from the body of a Rule Family.	The entries in the body of a Rule Family are unordered. (Duplicate rows in a Rule Family are not allowed.)
10	Declarative Inferential Relationship Principle	Remove unnecessary procedural constraints from the Rule Family inferential relationships.	There is no implied sequence in the path among Rule Families related through inferential relationships.

Table 9.4 summarizes the three principles from this chapter.

New Vocabulary Introduced in This Chapter

- declarative
- procedural
- business logic independence
- forward chaining
- backward chaining

And What about the Quote?

The quote at the beginning of the chapter indicates that a declarative solution is one that shifts responsibility for work from the observer to the system, automated or otherwise. Principles 8–10 require work on the part of the person creating the Decision Model so that, from then on, interpretation and maintenance of the Decision Model will require little work.

Discussion Points and Exercises

1. Consider a game of American baseball. What parts of the game are procedural and what parts are declarative? What is the role of the official rule book?

2. Discuss how Principle 9 allows more than one person to update a Rule Family without fear of duplicating another person's work?

3. Even though there is no implied sequence among columns in a Rule Family, explain why the conclusion fact type is shown as the top fact type in a Decision Model diagram.

4. Assume you are interviewing candidates for a particular employment position. Also assume that you have the qualifications required of candidates. Explain how you would evaluate a candidate using forward chaining through the qualifications. Also explain how you would evaluate a candidate using backward chaining through the qualifications. Which approach seems more convenient to you and why?

Chapter 10

The Integrity Principles

Contents

What Is Meant by Decision Model Integrity? 233
    In What Ways Does a Decision Model's Content Make Sense? 234
The Goal of the Integrity Principles.. 234
Principle 11: Rule Pattern Transitive Conditions Principle 235
    Third Normal Form 235
    Principle 11 Description 236
    How Principle 11 Addresses the Optimal Integrity of a Decision Model.......236
    Applying Principle 11 in Practice..236
    How Does Principle 11 Reduce Redundancy?..240
Principle 12a: Rule Pattern Maximum Conclusion Values Principle 241
    Principle 12 Description 241
        In General, a Rule Pattern Should Result in at Most One Conclusion
        Value for Any Set of Valid Input Values for the Condition Fact Types 241
        Principle 12b: Rule Pattern condition Key Coverage Principle 243
        Principle 12c: Rule Pattern Overlapping Condition Key
        Coverage Principle 244
        Principle 12d: Rule Family Overlapping Condition Key
        Coverage Principle 244
        Principle 12e: Rule Family Minimum Conclusion Values Principle......... 246
        Principle 12f: Rule Family Maximum Conclusion Values Principle 247
        Principle 12g: Rule Family Condition Key Coverage Principle 248
    How Principle 12 Addresses the Optimal Integrity of a Decision
    Model..248
    Applying Principle 12 in Practice...248

Principle 13: Rule Family Transitive Conditions Principle 249
  Principle 13 Description 249
  How Principle 13 Addresses the Optimal Integrity
  of a Decision Model 250
  Applying Principle 13 in Practice..250
  How Does Principle 13 Reduce Redundancy?..254
Principle 14: Inferential Integrity Principle..256
  Principle 14 Description 256
  How Principle 14 Addresses the Optimal Integrity
  of a Decision Model 256
  Applying Principle 14 in Practice..256
Integrating Decision Models 259
Principle 15: Business Alignment Principle...261
  Principle 15 Description 261
  How Principle 15 Addresses the Optimal Integrity
  of a Decision Model 262
  Applying Principle 15 in Practice..262
Insights into Methodology 265
Summary...266
  Integrity Related to Decision Model Conclusions.....................................267
    Correct Conclusions...267
    Minimally Redundant Conclusions..267
    Consistent Conclusions..267
    Complete Conclusions 267
  Integrity Related to Decision Model Conditions.......................................267
    Correct Conditions 268
    Complete Conditions..268
    Minimally Redundant Conditions 268
    Consistent Conditions 268
New Vocabulary from This Chapter 268
And What about the Quote? 270
Discussion Points and Exercises..270

"It is easy. You just chip away the stone that doesn't look like David."

—reported response from Michelangelo when asked how he sculpted his statue of David

This chapter is the third of three chapters disclosing the rigor of the Decision Model. Specifically, it introduces the Decision Model Principles that address additional aspects of its integrity to ensure its business logic makes sense.

Readers are reminded that the populated Rule Family structures in this chapter are not necessarily meant to be fully populated. This means that readers ought not to be concerned that the Rule Families are not complete. They are simply populated with instances that illustrate a particular point about Rule Families.

The Structural Principles simplify the structure of a Decision Model whereas the Declarative Principles render it declarative, and hence, logically independent of processing and technology concerns. However, there is still room for important improvement. Specifically, a Decision Model ought to be optimal in that its business logic should be as free from logical and business anomalies as possible. The integrity of a Decision Model may not be optimal from its initial structural representation (compliant with the Structural Principles) nor from its logical independence (compliant with the Declarative Principles).

Therefore, the principles in this chapter pertain to additional Decision Model integrity. This chapter assumes these principles are applied to a Decision Model that already conforms to the Structural and Declarative Principles. Therefore, the Integrity Principles are applied to a Decision Model consisting of Rule Families, comprising Rule Patterns, connected via inferential relationships, and in which the sequence of the heading, body, and inferential relationships is insignificant. The goal now is to revise such a Decision Model until its business logic exhibits optimal integrity. Again, this chapter starts with an obvious question.

What Is Meant by Decision Model Integrity?

Is it possible to improve a Decision Model that is already simple and unbiased by processing and technology concerns? The Structural and Declarative Principles provided rigor for the Decision Model's heading, its body, and its inferential relationships. Applying them results in a Decision Model that looks roughly the same regardless of who created it. However, the previous principles do not prescribe adequate rigor for its fully populated content. Without such rigor, the content may be irrational and illogical and it may make no sense. So, Decision Model integrity is defined as the property that measures whether its content fully makes sense.

In What Ways Does a Decision Model's Content Make Sense?

There are three ways in which a Decision Model's content should make sense: structurally, logically, and businesswise. A Decision Model's content makes sense structurally if its structure is minimally redundant. A Decision Model makes sense logically if its business logic is consistent and complete. A Decision Model's content makes sense from a business perspective if it influences business performance in the intended ways. That is, it is correct with respect to business directions. These are critical qualities: minimally redundant, consistent, complete, and correct. After all, the whole point in building and managing a Decision Model is to deliver a valuable business asset.

The Goal of the Integrity Principles

The five principles in this chapter support the common goal of optimal integrity by governing the content. Therefore, these principles refine the content of a Decision Model until it is consistent structurally, logically, and businesswise. So, the goal is to minimize business logic anomalies in Decision Model content. Each principle adds rigor to the content of a Decision Model by addressing one specific aspect of its integrity:

- ■ Principle 11: Minimal redundancy (Rule Pattern level)
- ■ Principle 12: Consistency
- ■ Principle 13: Minimal redundancy (Rule Family level)
- ■ Principle 14: Completeness
- ■ Principle 15: Correctness

The rest of this chapter defines each of these five principles, explains how each contributes to the optimal integrity of the Decision Model, and provides insights into how to apply each in practice.

Keep in mind that this chapter deals with the discovery of complex logical errors. Therefore, the subject matter is complex, and the chapter is not necessarily meant to be read from start to finish. The chapter is more useful as a reference when the reader is actually creating or reviewing a Decision Model. In that case, the principles in this chapter can be applied to the target Decision Model.

Table 10.1 summarizes the aspects of Decision Model integrity covered by the principles in this chapter.

As indicated earlier in this book, normalization is critical to the Decision Model. Normalization in the Decision Model is a body of theory addressing analysis and decomposition of business logic structures into a new set of structures that exhibit more desirable properties. First and second normal forms were introduced as part of the Structural Principles. It is appropriate that the Integrity Principles begin with a principle addressing third normal form.

Table 10.1   Three Aspects of Decision Model Content Integrity

Aspect of Integrity	Characteristic of the Aspect	Description
Structural integrity	Minimally redundant content	Decision Model content is represented in one and only one place in the model and in the right place.
Logical integrity	Consistent content	Decision Model content does not contradict itself logically.
	Complete content	Decision Model content is not missing any logic.
Business integrity	Correct content	Decision Model content is correct with respect to business directions related to it.

Principle 11: Rule Pattern Transitive Conditions Principle

Principle 11 removes redundancies in a Rule Pattern by eliminating functional dependencies among its conditions, thereby reducing a Rule Pattern in second normal form to one in third normal form.

> Principle 11: There are no inferential dependencies within a Rule Pattern condition key. (Or, more informally, the conditions in a Rule Pattern are independent of each other in reaching the conclusion.)*

Principle 11 actually addresses Decision Model third normal form.

Third Normal Form

The purpose of third normal form is to eliminate functional dependencies (i.e., inferential dependencies) among conditions. In terms of the tabular structure of a Rule Pattern, third normal form means that at every row, there are no conditions leading to a conclusion about another condition. In other words, the Rule Pattern

---

* It is possible to discover inferential dependencies within a Rule Pattern condition key by careful inspection of the Rule Pattern *structure* alone, without populated *content*. And so Principle 11 is as much about structure as it is about content. Yet, on the practical side, inferential dependencies within a condition key are most often discovered during population of the Rule Pattern when something about the content does not "feel" quite right. Therefore, Principle 11 is part of the Integrity Principles, most closely associated with examining Rule Pattern content.

conditions do not contain a conclusion nested within them. That means that the conditions in a Rule Pattern in third normal form cannot be decomposed into more than one conclusion. If they can, the original Rule Pattern row is not in third normal form and should be recast as a different set of more atomic Rule Patterns. Again, this reduces the original Rule Pattern structure into more atomic pieces of conclusions, which is what the Decision Model is all about.

Explaining third normal form is more difficult than applying it. Applying it means applying Principle 11 to each Rule Pattern.

Principle 11 Description

Principle 11 prescribes that there can be no subset of a Rule Pattern condition key that leads to a conclusion about (i.e., value of) a subset of its condition key. When part of a condition key logically determines (i.e., infers a conclusion about or value of) another part, the conclusion is not directly determined from the latter subset. In fact, the populated Rule Pattern will contain redundant business logic. So, Principle 11 ensures that the conditions in a condition key are truly independent of each other in coming to conclusions.

A Rule Pattern with a functional dependency among conditions can always be decomposed, without losing its intent, into a set of Rule Patterns, each one having no functional dependencies among conditions. An example is provided in the section on Applying Principle 11 in practice.

Therefore, Principle 11 leads to decomposing such a Rule Pattern into multiple Rule Patterns by removing redundancy, and does not lose the intent of the original structure.

How Principle 11 Addresses the Optimal Integrity of a Decision Model

Principle 11 minimizes redundancies by uncovering Rule Families hidden within Rule Patterns.* This removal of redundancies simplifies maintenance and minimizes opportunity for the inadvertent introduction of business logic errors.

Applying Principle 11 in Practice

Applying Principle 11 means seeking inferential dependencies within a condition key. This can be done in five steps.

Suppose someone has created the Decision Model diagram in Figure 10.1, which addresses the business decision to Determine the Driver Insurance Premium

---

* Principle 6 in the chapter on Structural Principles uncovers Rule Patterns within a Rule Family. Principle 11 in this chapter uncovers Rule Families hidden with a Rule Family.

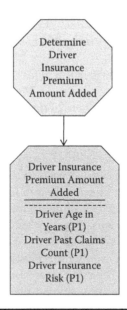

Figure 10.1   Sample Decision Model diagram.

Amount Added. The Decision Model, so far, consists of one Rule Family that comprises one Rule Pattern (designated by P(1)). That Rule Pattern has a condition key consisting of three fact types: Driver Age in Years, Driver Past Claims Count, and Driver Insurance Risk. Table 10.2 presents the Rule Family table.

Table 10.2   Sample Rule Family Table

	Conditions							Conclusion	
Rule Pattern	*Driver Age in Years*		*Driver Past Claims Count*		*Driver Insurance Risk*			*Driver Insurance Premium Amount Added (%)*	
1	Is Greater Than	24	Is Between	{2,4}	Is	Medium	=	10	
1	Is Greater Than	24	Is Greater Than	4	Is	High	=	20	
1	Is Less Than	24	Is Between	{2,4}	Is	Medium	=	20	

At first glance, this Rule Pattern does not seem to have any obvious integrity problems. In particular, the Rule Pattern does not seem to contain redundant business logic.

However, Principle 11 encourages a search for a possible inferential dependency within the condition key.

Even a careful review of the definitions of the condition fact types will not expose such a dependency. That's because the definitions provide a business description of the fact types, but not necessarily how they may be logically related to one another.* Instead, analysis is required of the content in the Rule Pattern. Does the content suggest that one condition actually infers (i.e., comes to a conclusion about) another condition?

So, the first step in applying Principle 11 is to look closely at each combination of conditions in search of a dependency lurking among them.

Consider the first two conditions. Does the content suggest an inferential dependency between Driver Age in Years and Driver Past Claims Count? Table 10.2 shows two rows with the same condition expression for the first condition (i.e., Driver Age in Years Is Greater Than 24), where each of those rows has a different condition expression for the second condition (i.e., Driver Past Claims Count Is Between {2, 4} versus Is Greater Than 4). So, there is no evidence of an inferential dependency between these conditions. One does not determine the other.

Next, move on to the first and third conditions. Does the content suggest an inferential dependency between Driver Age in Years and Driver Insurance Risk? Again, these seem to be independent of each other because the same condition expression in one condition (i.e., Driver Age in Years Is Greater Than 24) is associated with a different condition expression for the third condition (i.e., Driver Insurance Risk Is Medium versus High).

Finally, consider the second and third conditions. Does the content suggest an inferential dependency between a Driver Past Claims Count and Driver Insurance Risk? Perhaps.

Table 10.2 shows two rows with the same condition expression for the second condition (i.e., Driver Past Claims Count Is Between {2,4}, and each of those rows has the same condition expression for the third condition (i.e., Driver Insurance Risk Is Medium). Is this merely a coincidence? Or is there a true inferential dependency at work?

To determine if this is a coincidence, the business experts are asked if it would ever make business sense for a future row to test for "Driver Past Claims Count Is Between {2, 4}" and "Driver Insurance Risk As Low or High." If the answer is yes,

---

* Sometimes, someone who is very knowledgeable in how the business currently comes to a conclusion in a Rule Pattern *might* be suspicious of a hidden inferential dependency simply by knowing the condition fact types. But this is not usually the case. Most often, the inferential dependencies are not very obvious simply by looking at the condition fact types. Inferential dependencies most often become apparent only when viewing the content and noticing a potential inference correlation among condition cells.

Table 10.3   Rule Pattern with Transitive Dependencies Removed

	Conditions					Conclusion
Rule Pattern	Driver Age in Years		Driver Insurance Risk			Driver Insurance Premium Amount Added (%)
1	Is Greater Than	24	Is	Medium	=	10
1	Is Greater Than	24	Is	High	=	20
1	Is Less Than	24	Is	Medium	=	20

these conditions are independent of each other. This means the suspicion based on the content of Table 10.2 is simply a coincidence, and the Rule Pattern, as it exists, is compliant with Principle 11.

If the answer is no, these conditions are not independent of each other. This means a test for a Driver Past Claims Count Is Between {2, 4} is always associated with a test of Driver Insurance Risk Is Medium. And a check for a Driver Past Claims Count Is Greater Than 4 is always associated with a test of Driver Insurance Risk Is High. And so on. This would mean there is an inferential dependency between these two conditions. One condition expression determines the other. There is an inferential dependency within the condition key. They are not independent of each other.

The second step for applying Principle 11 is to reveal these findings to business experts.

Assume, in the example, that the business leaders confirm that the Driver Past Claims Count indeed determines the Driver Insurance Risk Level. There truly is a hidden inferential dependency in the condition key.

So, the third step is to remove this inferential dependency from the original Rule Pattern, resulting in a revised Rule Pattern. Therefore, Table 10.3 shows the revised Rule Pattern, which no longer contains a condition fact type for Driver Past Claims Count.

In the fourth step, a new Rule Pattern is created for the removed inferential dependency, as shown in Table 10.4. Here, a condition fact type for Driver Past

Table 10.4   New Rule Family Containing New Rule Pattern

	Conditions		Conclusion	
Rule Pattern	Driver Past Claims Count		Driver Insurance Risk	
1	Is Between	{2, 4}	Is	Medium
1	Is Greater Than	4	Is	High

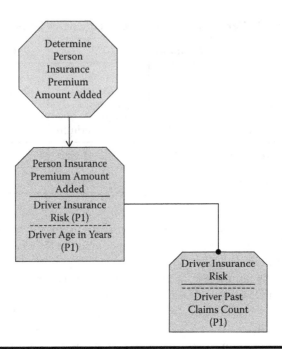

Figure 10.2   Revised Decision Model compliant with Principle 11.

Claims Count results in a conclusion for Driver Insurance Risk. This is a new Rule Family because the conclusion fact type of the Rule Pattern differs from the conclusion fact type of the previous Rule Pattern.

For the fifth step, in the Decision Model diagram, the Rule Families are connected, containing the new Rule Patterns with the appropriate inferential relationship as shown in Figure 10.2.

How Does Principle 11 Reduce Redundancy?

Recall that the goal of Principle 11 is to reduce redundancies. So, how does Figure 10.2 represent less redundancy than Figure 10.1?

If Table 10.2 contains a hidden inferential dependency between Driver Past Claims Count and Driver Insurance Risk, this dependency is actually represented three times: once in each row. In particular, the dependency between "Driver Past Claims Count Is Between {2, 4}" and "Driver Insurance Risk Is Medium" appears twice: in the first and third rows (redundantly).* Principle 11 leads to the creation of another Rule Pattern in which the dependency is represented in only one row, never more. What is the problem with representing it in more than one row? The

---

* Table 10.2 contains only three rows. However, as the population of the table grows, this inferential dependency would be represented redundantly, in many more rows, all unnecessarily so.

answer lies in the need for later changes that are likely to introduce inadvertent business logic anomalies. An example illustrates this.

Suppose the business later decides that a Driver Past Claims Count Is Between {2, 4} leads to a Driver Risk Level of Low, not Medium. Making this change to Table 10.2 means changing every row in this Rule Pattern in which that dependency exists, which at the moment, require changes to two rows. But, if by mistake the change is made to only one of the rows, the Rule Pattern will contain business logic errors. Recall that a goal of the Decision Model is to deliver a model in which a change is made in one and only one place. In that way, the risk of error is reduced.

So, making the same change to Table 10.4 means changing only one row, leaving no room for inadvertently introducing business logic errors. So, the difference between a Rule Pattern in second normal form and its decomposition into two Rule Patterns in third normal form is the ability to make changes in only one place, making errors less likely.

It may be of interest that a Rule Pattern with zero or only one condition column can have no transitive inferential dependencies among its conditions. Hence, it is automatically compliant with Principle 11.

Principle 12: Rule Family and Role Pattern Consistency Principle

Principle 12 removes inconsistencies within a Rule Pattern and among overlapping Rule Patterns.

> Principle 12: A Rule Family should be free of inconsistencies within each Rule Pattern and among Rule Patterns.

Principle 12 Description

Essentially, Principle 12 prescribes that the business logic within a Rule Pattern and Rule Family cannot contain inadvertent logical errors. This is a very complicated subject. In fact, the search for logical inconsistencies in complex business logic benefits greatly from use of sophisticated software. Principle 12 presents seven subprinciples that have been applied and proved helpful in the absence of such software.

Principle 12a: In General, a Rule Pattern Should Result in at Most One Conclusion Value for Any Set of Valid Input Values for the Condition Fact Types

This subprinciple states that generally the execution of a Rule Pattern should result in one conclusion or no conclusion; it should not result in multiple conclusions.

Table 10.5 Rule Pattern That May Result in No Conclusion Value for Certain Condition Values

Rule Pattern	Conditions				Conclusion	
	Person Salary		Person Highest Education Level		Person Credit Rating	
1	Is Between	{$25K,$34K}	Is	Master	Is	C
1	Is Between	{$35K,$50K}	Is	Master	Is	B
1	Is Greater Than	$50K	Is	Doctorate	Is	A

It is possible for a Rule Pattern to result in no conclusion if a set of valid input values does not evaluate to true for any rows in the Rule Pattern. Consider Table 10.5, which contains a Rule Pattern for concluding a Person Credit Rating based on Person Salary and Person Highest Education Level.

The Rule Family will not reach a conclusion for a person whose highest education level is high school. However, another Rule Pattern in the Rule Family may reach a conclusion about such persons, such as the Rule Pattern in Table 10.6. This Rule Pattern concludes a value for a Person Credit Rating if the Person Highest Education Level is high school, based on how many years such a person has been at the current employer.

So, this subprinciple simply states that a particular Rule Pattern in a Rule Family need not result in a conclusion value for the valid input values, because another Rule Pattern may do so (and will be required to do so as discussed later).

This subprinciple also states that generally the execution of a Rule Pattern should not result in more than one conclusion for any set of valid input values.

Consider the Rule Pattern in Table 10.7, which will result in more than one credit rating (i.e., B and C) for a person with a salary between $25K and $35K and a highest education level of a master's degree. The possibility of more than one conclusion leads to the question of whether the business logic is correct. Looking at

Table 10.6 Another Rule Pattern That May Result in a Conclusion Value for Condition Values Not in Table 10.5

Rule Pattern	Conditions				Conclusion	
	Person Highest Education Level		Person Years at Current Employer		Person Credit Rating	
2	Is	High School	Is Greater Than	5	Is	B
2	Is	High School	Is Between	{0,5}	Is	C

Table 10.7 Rule Pattern That Results in More than One Conclusion Value for Certain Condition Values

Rule Pattern	Conditions				Conclusion	
	Person Salary		Person Highest Education Level		Person Credit Rating	
1	Is Between	{$25K,$35K}	Is	Masters	Is	C
1	Is Between	{$25K,$35K}	Is	Masters	Is	B
1	Is Greater Than	$5K	Is	Doctorate	Is	A

Table 10.7, there is an inconsistency in that exactly the same condition values lead to two different conclusion values. In most cases, this is not what was originally intended, and so there is an inconsistency in the logic.

This subprinciple also refers to the phrase "valid input values for the condition fact types." The next subprinciple explains what is meant by valid input values for a Rule Pattern.

Principle 12b: Rule Pattern Condition Key Coverage Principle

Principle 12b: The conditions of a Rule Pattern need cover only the subset of the condition fact type domains that are within scope.

This subprinciple states that, while the conditions in a Rule Pattern need to represent tests that are consistent with the underlying fact type, the conditions need not test for all possible domain values for any of the underlying condition fact types. Instead, a Rule Pattern may have a scope that is limited to a subset of the fact type domains and so it need only cover that subset.

For example, consider Table 10.4 again, which contains tests for Driver Past Claims Count of greater than or equal to 2. It does not contain tests for Driver Past Claims Count of fewer than 2. If the scope of the Rule Pattern is bounded by Driver Past Claims Count of greater than or equal to 2, then these tests suffice. In other words, the only valid input values expected at this time for this Rule Pattern are those greater than or equal to 2.

A common example of limiting the coverage of a condition in a Rule Pattern is when dealing with geographical areas. For example, while a Rule Pattern may contain a condition fact type of State of Residence, at any point in time the Rule Pattern may be designed to address only a subset of those states. When the scope of the Rule Pattern is extended, maybe one state at a time, the valid input values for the Rule Pattern are extended.

In summary, this subprinciple simply states that the conditions of a Rule Pattern need to address only the input values for the conditions that the Rule Pattern is expected to process.

Table 10.8 Rule Pattern with Overlapping Condition Key Coverage

	Conditions				Conclusion
Rule Pattern	Person State of Residence	Person Salary		Person Highest Education Level	Person Allowed Discount Amount (%)
1	Is NC	Is Less Than	$50K	Is Masters	= 10
1	Is NC	Is Between	{$30K,$80K}	Is Masters	= 20

Principle 12c: Rule Pattern Overlapping Condition Key Coverage Principle

Principle 12c: Within one Rule Pattern, an overlapping condition key coverage means inconsistency exists in the Rule Pattern.

This subprinciple addresses a situation that leads to a single Rule Pattern resulting in more than one conclusion. Refer to Table 10.8 as an example.

Table 10.8 suggests that the Rule Family has only one Rule Pattern, labeled 1. This Rule Pattern's condition key consists of three condition fact types. However, inspection of the content of those condition columns discloses that there is an overlap in condition key coverage. An overlap in condition key coverage either can be the presence of exactly the same expression or the presence of expressions that partly coincide in more than one instance of a condition fact type.

Consider the content of each condition fact type in the condition key in Table 10.8. First, the condition for the fact type of Person State of Residence contains exactly the same expression in both rows—specifically "Person State of Residence Is NC." The same is true for the condition for the fact type of Person Highest Education Level—specifically "Person Highest Education Level Is Masters." Second, the condition for the fact type of Person Salary contains expressions that partly coincide in both rows. In this case, a salary between $30K and $49K is covered by the expressions in both rows. As a result of the overlapping condition key coverage, a person whose state of residence is North Carolina who earns a salary of $35K and has achieved a highest education level of a master's degree will, in fact, qualify for two allowed discount amounts: 10% and 20%.

This subprinciple suggests that such overlaps be corrected so that only one conclusion is reached. Business experts need to be consulted for changes so that only one conclusion is reached. One possible correction is shown in Table 10.9.

Principle 12d: Rule Family Overlapping Condition Key Coverage Principle

Principle 12d: Across two Rule Patterns in the same Rule Family, an overlapping condition key coverage often means inconsistency exists in the Rule Family.

Table 10.9   Rule Pattern with Possible Correction for Overlapping Coverage in the Condition Key

	Conditions					Conclusion
Rule Pattern	Person State of Residence		Person Salary		Person Highest Education Level	Person Allowed Discount Amount (%)
1	Is	NC	Is Less Than	$50K	Is Masters	= 10
1	Is	NC	Between	{$50K,$80K}	Is Masters	= 20

This subprinciple addresses the situation whereby Rule Patterns within a Rule Family have overlapping condition key coverage. Consider Table 10.10, which is a Rule Family consisting of two Rule Patterns. The condition key of Rule Pattern 1 consists of two fact types: Person State of Residence and Person Salary. The condition key of Rule Pattern 2 consists of two fact types: Person State of Residence and Person Highest Level of Education. Even without looking at the content, it is obvious that these two Rule Patterns have a condition fact type in common: Person State of Residence. This subprinciple prompts an inspection of the populated columns for this condition fact type to see if the coverage overlaps.

Consider the content of this common condition fact type in Table 10.10. The expression for this condition fact type in the first row (i.e., Rule Pattern 1) partly coincides with that in the third row (i.e., Rule Pattern 2). As a result, a person whose state of residence is NC who earns a salary less than $30k and with a highest education level of a master's degree would indeed qualify for the condition in both Rule Patterns and would qualify for two Person Allowed Discount Amounts (i.e., 10% and 25%).

In most cases, when more than one conclusion value is possible from execution of Rule Patterns having overlapping condition key coverage, there is a logical

Table 10.10   Overlapping Condition Key Coverage across Rule Patterns

	Conditions					Conclusion
Rule Pattern	Person State of Residence		Person Salary		Person Highest Education Level	Person Allowed Discount Amount (%)
1	Is	{NC,NY}	Is Less Than	$30K		= 10
1	Is	NJ	Is Less Than	$30K		= 15
2	Is	NC			Is Masters	= 25

inconsistency in the Rule Family. That is, the business intention was for one conclusion to be reached, but the business logic has been incorrectly specified.

Table 10.10 actually illustrates the common example of a geographic criteria being a condition fact type in different Rule Patterns. It is often the case that reaching a conclusion is based on different criteria (condition fact types), depending on which state or region a customer hails from. This subprinciple ensures that the conditions in the common condition fact type differentiate each possible geographical location and associate each with its proper set of condition fact types.

Principle 12e: Rule Family Minimum Conclusion Values Principle

Principle 12e: A Rule Family must result in at least one conclusion value for any set of valid input values for the condition fact types.

In Chapter 8, Principle 7 states that a Rule Family cannot have empty conclusion cells, because the conclusion cell provides the glue that connects inferentially related Rule Families together. If a conclusion cell is empty, the connection is unknown and the Decision Model is broken.

The same is true if a Rule Family does not have any empty conclusion cells, but its conditions are such that no condition key evaluates to true for a valid set of input values. When that is the case, a conclusion is not reached. This has the same effect as having an empty conclusion. The glue that connects inferentially related Rule Families together is broken.

The Rule Pattern in Table 10.5 will not come to a conclusion for someone with a highest education level of high school. The Rule Pattern in Table 10.6 will not come to a conclusion for someone with a highest education level of master's or doctorate. Combining them, as shown in Table 10.11, will make it possible to arrive at a

Table 10.11   Combining Tables 10.5 and 10.6 into One Rule Family

	Conditions							Conclusion	
Rule Pattern	Person Salary		Person Highest Education Level		Person Years at Current Employer			Person Credit Rating	
1	Is Between	{$25K,$35K}	Is	Masters				Is	C
1	Is Between	{$35K,$50K}	Is	Masters				Is	B
1	Is Greater Than	$50K	Is	Doctorate				Is	A
2			Is	High School	Is Greater Than	5		Is	B
2			Is	High School	Is Between	{0,5}		Is	C

conclusion for a larger universe of input values, although it does not address persons whose highest education level is an undergraduate degree. It also will not reach a conclusion for all possible valid input values (e.g., Person Salary Is Less Than $25K and Person Highest Education Level Is Masters).

So, although a previous subprinciple indicated that a Rule Pattern can result in no conclusion, it is incorrect for all Rule Patterns in a Rule Family to result in no conclusion for any set of input values. That is, at least one Rule Pattern must reach a conclusion for any set of valid input values.

Principle 12f: Rule Family Maximum Conclusion Values Principle

Principle 12f: A Rule Family can result in more than one conclusion value for any set of valid input values for condition fact types.

This subprinciple states that a Rule Family, unlike a Rule Pattern, may result in more than one conclusion value. Consider Table 10.12, which contains two Rule Patterns within one Rule Family where the Rule Patterns do not contain common condition fact types.

Obviously, a person whose credit rating is Excellent and whose driving record is Excellent qualifies in both Rule Patterns, resulting in two conclusions for Person Car Rental Discount Amount (i.e., 20% and 10%). What should be a person discount if this is the case? Should a Rule Family be restricted to having only one conclusion value for any set of valid input values?

The answer is no, because the desired number of Rule Family conclusions depends on the nature of the business decision itself. For example, suppose the business decides that it is permissible for a person to qualify for more than one discount because each Rule Pattern leads to a discount based on a different set of business criteria. This might be a perfectly legitimate business decision. If so, it is appropriate for a Rule Family to yield more than one discount. When this is the case, the business must prescribe how multiple conclusion values are to be treated. Options include selecting the highest discount or the lowest or adding them together or averaging them together.

If, however, the nature of the business decision is such that only one conclusion value is appropriate, the Rule Family (in addition to each Rule Pattern and

Table 10.12 Rule Patterns in a Rule Family with No Common Condition Fact Types

Rule Pattern	Conditions				Conclusion	
	Person Credit Rating		Person Driving Record		Person Car Rental Discount Amount (%)	
1	Is	Excellent			=	20
2			Is	Excellent	=	10

overlapping Rule Patterns) should arrive at a maximum of one conclusion value. In this case, the Rule Family needs to contain all possible combinations of condition expressions to make that possible.

Principle 12g: Rule Family Conclusion Key Coverage Principle

Principle 12g: The conclusions in a Rule Family need cover only the subset of the conclusion fact type's domain that is within scope.

In Chapter 8, Principle 3 states that each cell in a Rule Family conforms to the fact type in the heading. This includes the conclusion cell. However, the conclusions in the Rule Family need not result in values covering all possible domain values for the underlying conclusion fact type. Instead, a Rule Family may have a scope that is limited to a subset of the fact type domains and so it need only to cover that subset.

For example, consider Table 10.3 again, which comes to conclusions about Amount Added to Driver Insurance Premium. The Rule Family results in amounts of 10% and 20%. It does not contain conclusions for amounts other than 10% and 20%. It is possible that the complete domain for such amounts can range from 0 to 100% but that the company is only adding amounts of 10% and 20% at this time. If the scope of the Rule Family is bounded by Amount Added to Driver Premium of 10% and 20%, then these conclusions suffice. In other words, the only valid conclusion values for this Rule Family are 10% and 20%.

In summary, this subprinciple simply states that the conclusions of a Rule Family need to address only the values for the conclusions that it is expected to arrive at.

How Principle 12 Addresses the Optimal Integrity of a Decision Model

Principle 12 removes inconsistencies in Decision Model content by describing situations within a Decision Model in which business logic inconsistencies may be lurking, but they may not be obvious. By uncovering such situations, Principle 12 helps identify places in the Decision Model where conclusions may not be as expected. For example, the subprinciples point out specific characteristics in business logic that can lead to pure logical inconsistencies, such as overlapping coverage of values in conditions. The subprinciples also ensure that the correct number of conclusion values is reached in Rule Patterns and Rule Families to protect the connections among Rule Families. The subprinciples also ensure that domains behind conditions and conclusions are consistent with the scope of the Decision Model.

Applying Principle 12 in Practice

The goal of Principle 12 is to find inconsistencies in business logic during the Decision Modeling process, long before the Decision Model is implemented in software and testing. In reality, Principle 12 is not often applied sequentially. Usually, business people and business analysts conduct a formal review of a Decision Model structure and then of the Decision Model content, seeking business logic that doesn't look quite right. Then, the business people and business analysts refer to the subprinciples to discover why and how to fix the business logic.

However, a sequential approach for applying Principle 12 can be carried out in six steps. The first step is to identify the range of domain values for each fact type of the Decision Model that is in scope. The second step is to make sure that each Rule Pattern results in a maximum of one conclusion value for that range of condition fact type values. The third step is to make sure that at least one Rule Pattern in each Rule Family comes to one conclusion value for that range of condition fact type values. The fourth step is to seek overlaps in condition key coverage within Rule Patterns and within a Rule Family. The fifth step is to present violations from the second through fourth step to business experts, because most of the time such violations are invalid from a business perspective. The sixth step is to make related changes and start all over again with the second step.

Principle 13: Rule Family Transitive Conditions Principle

Principle 13 removes redundancies among Rule Families in much the same way that Principle 11 removes redundancies among Rule Pattern conditions. That is, Principle 11 and Principle 13 both resolve transitive inferential dependencies.

> Principle 13: There are no inferential dependencies among inferentially related Rule Families. (Or, informally, there are no transitive dependencies among Rule Families in a Decision Model.)

Principle 13 Description

Principle 13 prescribes that there can be no transitive dependencies among Rule Families. A transitive dependency is one where a conclusion fact type in one Rule Family serves as a condition fact type in two other Rule Families; also, the conclusion fact type in one of the latter Rule Families serves as a condition fact type in the other. This sounds complicated, but is easy to see in practice. Transitive dependencies among Rule Families usually become obvious in a Decision Model diagram. Figure 10.3 is a simple Decision Model with such a dependency.

In Figure 10.3, the transitive dependency among Rule Families is evident because the Rule Family called Car Insurance Policy Desirability is inferentially dependent on the conclusion of the Rule Family called Insured Geography Tier and also on the Rule Family called Insured Vehicle Tier. This, by itself, is fine. However, the Rule Family called Insured Vehicle Tier is also inferentially dependent on the conclusion of the Insured Geography Tier. Thus, a circle of logic is formed that is visible in the diagram. When there is such a transitive dependency among Rule Families, one of the dependencies is redundant. Principle 13 resolves

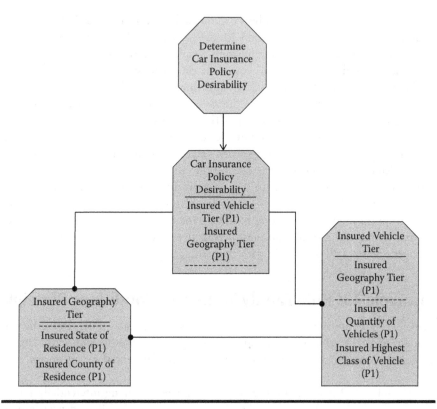

Figure 10.3 Transitive dependency among Rule Families.

this by removing the unnecessary inferential dependency without losing the intent of the original business logic. This becomes clearer when applied in practice, as described in the following text.

How Principle 13 Addresses the Optimal Integrity of a Decision Model

Principle 13 removes redundancies by uncovering inferential dependencies hidden across Rule Families. As in Principle 11, the removal of these redundancies simplifies maintenance and reduces the risk of business logic errors.

Applying Principle 13 in Practice

Principle 13 can be applied in five steps. Suppose Figure 10.3 is a Decision Model created for a Car Insurer Company. What does the Decision Model represent?

For starters, the Decision Model seeks a conclusion about a Car Insurance Policy Desirability. Presumably, this is a conclusion that rates the desire to issue a particular car insurance policy. The Decision Rule Family has one Rule Pattern [marked P(1)], which has two condition fact types. One condition tests the Insured Vehicle Tier, and the other tests the Insured Geography Tier. In this way, the Decision Model reaches a conclusion about the desirability of a policy based on conclusions about geography and vehicles. Each of these condition fact types is the conclusion fact type of its own Rule Family.

The Rule Family that determines the Insured Geography Tier comprises one Rule Pattern [marked P(1)], which has two condition fact types. These condition fact types are the Insured State of Residence and Insured County of Residence. Input to these conditions seems to be raw data because neither serves as a conclusion fact type in another Rule Family.

The Rule Family that determines the Insured Vehicle Tier comprises one Rule Pattern [marked P(1)], which has three condition fact types. These are Insured Geography Tier, Insured Quantity of Vehicles, and Insured Highest Class of Vehicle. Again, input to the latter two conditions is raw data, but input to the first condition is supplied by the Rule Family called Insured Geography Tier.

The first step in applying Principle 13 is to study the Rule Families, seeking evidence of (transitive) dependencies among Rule Families. Hopefully, the circular nature of these dependencies will appear as prominent features in the Decision Model diagram. In the worst case, the Decision Model is so complex that it may be difficult to spot the transitive dependencies among the Rule Families. If so, there is a need to dissect the complex Decision Model into smaller pieces and look for circular paths within those pieces. In either case, transitive dependencies among Rule Families become obvious when Rule Family relationships resemble those in Figure 10.4, where the circles are visible.

It is quite common to find transitive dependencies among Rule Families within Decision Models that establish marketing tiers. Examples include establishing tiers of customers based on demographics, such as location, financial status, and so on. The business logic for creating such tiers often needs to balance reasonable risk with desirable potential for profit. When creating a Decision Model to establish such tiers, it is a common error to specify a particular fact type, such as State of Residence, as a condition in multiple Rule Families, with the result that transitive dependencies among Rule Families result unintentionally.

The second step is to present these suspected transitive dependencies among Rule Families to business experts in order to tease out the true dependencies.

In the example, such discussions reveal that the Decision Model is based on two different organizational perspectives regarding Car Insurance Policy Desirability. One group is responsible for Insured Vehicle Tier, and another group is responsible for Insured Geography Tier. Investigation involves learning more about these two groups of people.

The business experts responsible for analyzing Insured Geography Tier do so based on financial health and differences in cost of car repairs. On the other hand, the business experts responsible for Insured Vehicle Tier are specialists in

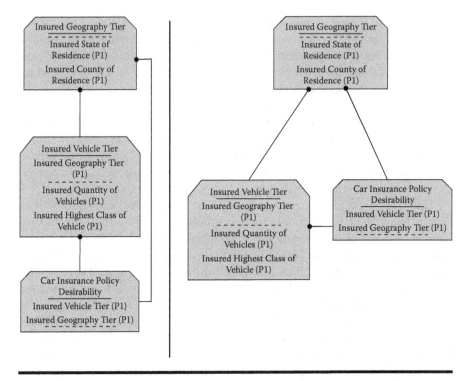

Figure 10.4   Various ways in which transitive dependencies among Rule Families show up in Decision Models.

the relative repair costs of different classes of vehicles, severity of injuries in different classes of vehicles, and likelihood of profit and loss among individuals with multiple vehicles.

Most often, when business logic is specified by different organizations or roles, the chance for transitive dependencies among Rule Families is great because neither party is usually concerned about the other party's business criteria. In fact, the creation of a Decision Model may be the first time that consistency is sought across such groups.

Looking back at the example, there is suspicion that Insured Geographic Tier ought not to be a condition both in the Insured Vehicle Tier and in the Car Insurance Policy Desirability. In other words, if the Geography Tier is a condition in the Insured Vehicle Tier and it is tested also in the Car Insurance Policy Desirability, there is a risk of business logic errors occurring.

During a conversation about the Rule Family called Insured Vehicle Tier, the following question emerged: why does it also include a condition about Geography Tier? Initial information was that the Geography Tier conclusion indicates those geographical locations where the business wants to offer policies. Initial information

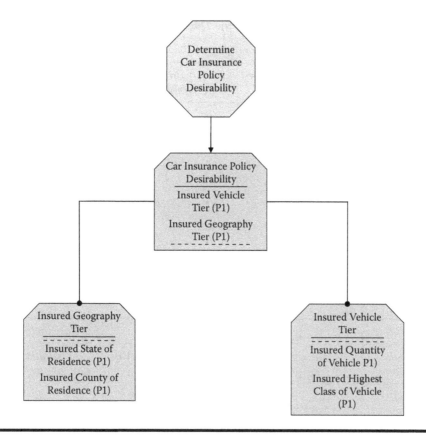

Figure 10.5 Decision Model without transitive dependencies among Rule Families.

also was that the Insured Vehicle Tier conclusion indicates the characteristics of vehicle ownership for which the business wants to offer policies. If the latter Rule Family also considers Geography, this would mean that it comes to a conclusion for certain vehicles only in certain geographical locations. If so, then why also test for Geography Tier in the Decision Rule Family when the Vehicle Tier conclusion already considers the influence of geography? After much discussion and some debate, the business experts confirm that Geographical Tier should only be examined once and ought not to be in the Insured Vehicle Tier Rule Family.

Therefore, the third step is to remove the redundant inferential relationship, followed by the fourth step, which creates a Rule Family for this transitive dependency. In the example, there is no need to create a new Rule Family, because the business logic rightfully belongs in the existing Rule Family for the Insured Geography Tier. The revised Decision Model View diagram is shown in Figure 10.5. It no longer contains a visually obvious circle of business logic.

Table 10.13 Rule Families behind the Decision Model in Figure 10.5

Rule Pattern	Conditions				Conclusion	
	Insured's Vehicle Tier		*Insured's Geography Tier*		*Car Insurance Policy's Desirability*	
1	Is	Excellent	Is	Excellent	Is	High
1	Is	Excellent	Is	Poor	Is	Low

Rule Pattern	Conditions				Conclusion	
	Insured's Quantity of Vehicles		*Insured's Highest Class of Vehicles*		*Insured's Vehicle Tier*	
1	Is Greater Than	3	Is	Luxury	Is	Excellent
1	Is Between	{2,3}	Is	Midsize	Is	Very Good
1	=	1	Is	Economy	Is	Good

Rule Pattern	Conditions				Conclusion	
	Insured's State of Residence		*Insured's County of Residence*		*Insured's Geography Tier*	
1	Is	Mogagog	Is	A	Is	Excellent
1	Is	Mogagog	Is	B	Is	Poor

How Does Principle 13 Reduce Redundancy?

Recall that the goal of Principle 13 is to reduce redundancies. How does Figure 10.5 represent less redundancy than Figure 10.3?

Table 10.13 contains three Rule Families corresponding to the Decision Model in Figure 10.5.

The second row in the top Rule Family indicates that if Insured Vehicle Tier is Excellent but the Insured Geography Tier is Poor, then the Car Insurance Policy Desirability is Low. Presumably, the business doesn't want to insure expensive cars in poorly ranked locations. The top row in the second Rule Family indicates that owning more than three cars, one of which is a Luxury class car, is an Excellent set of vehicles to insure. The rows in the third Rule Family indicate that one county in the state of Mogagog is ranked as an Excellent location, whereas the other county is ranked as a Poor location.* After careful study, there does not appear to be redundant logic in this set of Rule Families.

---

* The state of Mogagog is a fictitious state in the novel *Accursed* by Chris von Halle.

Table 10.14   Rule Families behind the Decision Model in Figure 10.3

	Conditions				Conclusion	
Rule Pattern	Insured's Vehicle Tier		Insured's Geography Tier		Car Insurance Policy's Desirability	
1	Is	Excellent	Is	Excellent	Is	High
1	Is	Excellent	Is	Poor	Is	Low

	Conditions						Conclusion	
Rule Pattern	Insured's Quantity of Vehicles		Insured's Highest Class of Vehicles		Insured's Geography Tier		Insured's Vehicle Tier	
1	Is Greater Than	3	Is	Luxury	Is	Excellent	Is	Excellent
1	Is Greater Than	3	Is	Luxury	Is	Poor	Is	Excellent
1	Is Between	{2,3}	Is	Midsize	Is	Excellent	Is	Very Good
1	Is Between	{2,3}	Is	Midsize	Is	Poor	Is	Very Good
1	=	1	Is	Economy	Is	Excellent	Is	Good
1	=	1	Is	Economy	Is	Poor	Is	Good

	Conditions				Conclusion	
Rule Pattern	Insured's State of Residence		Insured's County of Residence		Insured's Geography Tier	
1	Is	Mogagog	Is	A	Is	Excellent
1	Is	Mogagog	Is	B	Is	Poor

Now turn to Table 10.14, which contains three Rule Families corresponding to the Decision Model in Figure 10.3. There are no differences in the first and third Rule Families from those in Table 10.13. However, the difference in the second Rule Family becomes apparent. First of all, it has more rows. Second, there is redundancy in these rows. Let's explore that redundancy.

In the second Rule Family, the business experts want to state that an ownership of more than three cars, one of which is a Luxury class car, is an excellent set of cars to insure. However, by adding the Geography Tier as a condition fact type, there is a need also to populate this Rule Family with the Geography Tier in which such ownership is desirable. So, for all rows in the second Rule Family, there is a need to add rows that also consider the (irrelevant) Geography Tier. That is, the second Rule Family needs to consider both Poor and Excellent Geography Tiers, even though they are irrelevant. Doing so duplicates the business logic in the third Rule Family, and also allows updates to one Rule Family without making the same updates to the other, thereby introducing business logic errors.

Principle 14: Inferential Integrity Principle

Principle 14 ensures completeness of inferential relationships among Rule Families.

> Principle 14: There are no conclusions in a supporting Rule Family that are not covered by the corresponding dependent Rule Family. (Or, informally, there mustn't be any uncovered inferential keys.)

Principle 14 Description

A supporting Rule Family is a Rule Family whose conclusion fact type is a condition fact type in another Rule Family. In Figure 10.2, the Rule Family "Driver Insurance Risk" is a supporting Rule Family.

A dependent Rule Family is a Rule Family with a condition fact type that is a conclusion fact type in another Rule Family. In Figure 10.2, the Rule Family "Person Insurance Premium Amount Added" is a dependent Rule Family.

Principle 14 prescribes that every value in a conclusion of a supporting Rule Family should be covered by the corresponding condition in the dependent Rule Families. If a Decision Model is not in compliance with Principle 14, it contains at least one supporting Rule Family that comes to a conclusion not tested in a corresponding dependent Rule Family. Hence, either the supporting Rule Family is incorrect in reaching such a conclusion, or, more commonly, the dependent Rule Family is incomplete in testing those conclusions as conditions. This becomes clear in the example in the following section, "Applying Principle 14 in Practice."

How Principle 14 Addresses the Optimal Integrity of a Decision Model

Principle 14 ensures that all inferential relationships in a Decision Model are complete. Thus, Principle 14 leads to content that is complete from a logical perspective and is not obviously missing any logic.

Applying Principle 14 in Practice

Principle 14 can be applied in five steps. The first step is to study inferential relationships, seeking evidence of conclusions in the supporting Rule Family not covered in the condition of the dependent Rule Family. To illustrate this principle, consider the Decision Model in Figure 10.6.

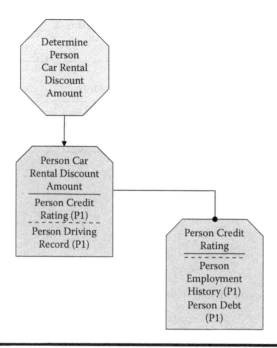

Figure 10.6 Sample rental car Decision Model.

First, there is one inferential relationship in Figure 10.6. Second, the supporting Rule Family in this relationship is the Rule Family for Person Credit Rating. The Rule Family is shown in Table 10.15.*

This Rule Family results in three conclusion values for Person Credit Rating. These values are 10, 15, and 30.

Third, consider the inspection of the dependent Rule Family. The dependent Rule Family is the Rule Family for Person Car Rental Discount Amount. This Rule Family is shown in Table 10.16. The goal is to look for the related condition to cover the values of 10, 15, and 30.

This Rule Family does not cover the value of 30 for a Person Credit Rating. This means that the Decision Model may come to a conclusion of 30 for a Person Credit Rating and then come to a stop, not able to continue the inferential relationship.

Therefore, the fourth step is to review this incompleteness with business experts, seeking a correction. The business experts discuss, debate, and escalate their differences up the management ladder. They finally provide a correction which, in the fifth step, is incorporated into the Rule Family as shown in Table 10.17.

---

* It is important to note that applying Principle 14 requires that both the supporting and dependent Rule Families be fully populated. Principle 14 either confirms that the population is complete or points out where such population is missing.

Table 10.15 Supporting Rule Family in Figure 10.6

	Conditions				*Conclusion*	
Rule Pattern	*Person Employment History*		*Person Debt*		*Person Credit Rating*	
1	Is	Good	Is	Low	=	30
1	Is	Good	Is	Medium	=	15
1	Is	Bad	Is	Low	=	10

Table 10.16 Dependent Rule Family

	Conditions				*Conclusion*	
Rule Pattern	*Person Credit Rating*		*Person Driving Record*		*Person Car Rental Discount Amount (%)*	
1	Is Between	{9,16}	Is	Poor	=	0
1	Is Between	{20,29}	Is	Excellent	=	10
1	Is Greater Than	30	Is	Excellent	=	20

Table 10.17 Dependent Rule Family with Corrected Coverage

	Conditions				*Conclusion*	
Rule Pattern	*Person Credit Rating*		*Person Driving Record*		*Person Car Rental Discount Amount (%)*	
1	Is Between	{9,16}	Is	Poor	=	0
1	Is Between	{20, 29}	Is	Excellent	=	10
1	Is Greater Than	29	Is	Excellent	=	20

Integrating Decision Models

Throughout this book so far, the assumption has been that given a business decision, its entire Decision Model is created. In reality, development of a Decision Model may be done in pieces. The selection of the pieces usually depends on the availability, importance, or controversial nature of different Rule Families.

So, separate Decision Models or pieces of them may be delivered, based on project priorities, resource availability, or even political issues. At some point, the Decision Models will need to be integrated together.

The good news is that the first step in integrating separate Decision Models is straightforward because the Rule Family automatically unites together those pieces having a common conclusion fact type.

However, once Rule Families are combined, the challenge of Decision Model integration begins. It involves refining the integrity of the combined result so that the content of the integrated Decision Model makes sense structurally, logically, and businesswise. That's why this chapter includes the integration of Decision Models. Because the original Decision Models by themselves conformed to all principles, their preliminary integrated version will conform to most of the Structural and Declarative Principles automatically. The refining of integrity issues introduced by the integration usually boils down to the application of the Integrity Principles, because integrity may have been jeopardized in the integration process.

It is also important to remember that the Integrity Principles address three types of integrity within the new integrated Decision Model: structural, logical, and business. If there are business directions in conflict among the original Decision Models, these business directions will result in business logic contradictions, needing correction. An example is helpful.

Figure 10.7 is a Decision Model developed by one set of modelers based on input from the Vehicle Tier experts.

Figure 10.8 is a Decision Model developed by another set of modelers based on input from the Geography Tier experts.

How to integrate them? Start by seeking a common Rule Family. In this example, both have the Decision Rule Family in common. So these can be combined into one Rule Family. Now, the first Decision Model integrity challenge arises. There is one common condition fact type between these two Rule Families (i.e., Insured Vehicle Tier), but an extra condition fact type in the one in Figure 10.8 (i.e., Insured Geography Tier), Both condition fact types can be included in the new Integrated Rule Family. If so, the second Decision Model integrity challenge arises. This one pertains to Rule Patterns.

The Decision Rule Family from Figure 10.8 has one Rule Pattern with two conditions, but the Decision Rule Family from Figure 10.7 has one Rule Pattern with only one of those conditions. What is the relevance of the second condition on Rule Patterns in the newly combined Decision Rule Family? Are these Rule Patterns that share a condition fact in common? Or are they one Rule Pattern needing values

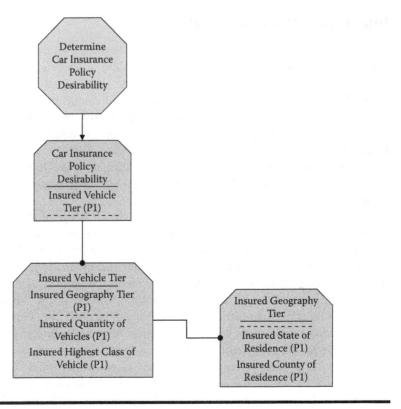

Figure 10.7   An independent Decision Model from vehicle tier experts.

filled in for the additional condition for the new Rule Pattern? Further analysis is needed.

For now, note that Figure 10.7 also has an additional Rule Family (i.e., Insured Vehicle Tier) not found in Figure 10.8. This Rule Family can be added to the Integrated Decision Model.

At this point, the third Decision Model integrity challenge arises. Both Figure 10.7 and Figure 10.8 contain a Rule Family for Insured Geography Tier. But now the challenge pertains to inferential relationships. In Figure 10.7, this Rule Family is inferentially related to the Rule Family for Insured Vehicle Tier. In Figure 10.8, it is inferentially related to the Rule Family for Car Insurance Policy Desirability. Simply adding both relationships to the Integrated Decision Model results in transitive dependencies among Rule Families shown in Figure 10.3. So, transitive dependencies among Rule Families may emerge when integrating Decision Models representing different business points of view.

Thankfully, the business experts from both groups get together, have heated arguments, and then provide a solution that is represented by Figure 10.5.

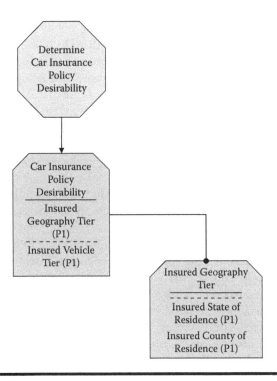

Figure 10.8   An independent Decision Model from geography tier experts.

Principle 15: Business Alignment Principle

Principle 15 attaches responsibility and metrics for tangible business results to a Decision Model.

> Principle 15: A Decision Model directly aligns with business directions and metrics for measuring progress. (Or, informally, a Decision Model aims for business results and is managed against business metrics.)

Principle 15 Description

Principle 15 prescribes that a Decision Model, as a cohesive deliverable, should be utilized as a business lever, serving as a means for achieving desired ends.

Principle 15 is perhaps the most important principle of all. Principle 15 reveals the relative importance of each Decision Model. So, development and maintenance of Decision Models can be prioritized, and appropriate technology can be selected based on the anticipated business value.

Each business decision (and its corresponding Decision Model) has reasons for its importance and metrics for measuring its effectiveness. Information about related importance and metrics can be captured for each Decision Model, providing a direct means for governing the impact of that Decision Model on the business's performance. In fact, the motivational aspects of a Decision Model can, and should, be investigated and understood even before constructing its corresponding Decision Model structure.

In general practice, an entire Decision Model is traced to specific business directions. These may be high-level strategies, intermediate tactics, or specific measurable objectives. Each of these business directions, especially measurable objectives, should be supported with metrics. Metrics may include measurements of actual business performance or size of work queues, for example. From these metrics, business experts can ascertain if the Decision Model is performing as expected. If not, business experts can make appropriate changes in business logic within the Decision Model, as needed.

It is also appropriate for an individual Rule Family or a Rule Family instance (i.e., row) to trace to business directions and metrics in addition to those that apply to the entire Decision Model. That's because a Rule Family and a Rule Family instance lead to one conclusion fact type or value. Conclusions are closely related to business direction and objectives.

Some readers may be adopting the OMG's Business Motivation Model, which addresses items of business direction. Within the context of the Business Motivation Model, the Decision (and its Decision Model) becomes important "elements of guidance." Therefore, while the Business Motivation Model lacks a link to Decision, the way to connect a Decision Model to the Business Motivation Model is to connect it to objectives and tactics.*

How Principle 15 Addresses the Optimal Integrity of a Decision Model

Principle 15 ensures that a Decision Model denotes business logic that is expected to bring about desired business performance. Business directions and metrics justify a Decision Model and continue to guide, not only its initial development, but its changes over time.

Without Principle 15 to align a Decision Model with the business, any Decision Model will suffice, even none at all.

Applying Principle 15 in Practice

In practice, Principle 15 is applied in many steps during the life of a project. The first step is the recognition of a business initiative, business opportunity,

---

* More details on the OMG's Business Motivation Model and connections to the Decision Model are found in Chapter 16.

or challenge whose solution partially lies with delivery and management of a Decision Model.

Assume, for example, a financial institution has identified opportunities and challenges. To keep it simple for illustrative purposes, the example provides only very simple and general business requirements. The point is not to be detailed and complete (or even real-world*). Rather, the goal is to provide insight into how connections are made in spirit from business direction to business metrics to Decision Models. So consider the following input from executives at this financial institution:

- The financial institution needs to increase revenue and increase its customer base.
- A proposal is under consideration to introduce an Internet-based Web-Loan process whereby a person can determine if his or her loan request is likely to be acceptable to the institution with terms acceptable to the customer.
- The Web-Loan process is to provide feedback to the person as to whether his or her loan will be accepted
- The Web-Loan process will suggest areas in which the person can improve the terms of the desired loan.
- Once satisfied with the terms and chance of approval, the person can request that a loan officer approve the loan. Then the loan officer will finalize the loan.
- If the loan is not prequalified, the loan department manager reviews any exceptions. The data warehouse receives information about both loan requests that are prequalified and those that are not prequalified.
- The loan will be managed over time by the loan officer.
- Auditors need closer management of compliance issues with respect to approving loans.
- A disturbing organizational issue is that the processing of loan requests often differs depending on who the loan officer is. Different loan officers use different criteria, for example, in deciding the default probability for an applicant. The financial institution needs to be consistent here so as to process such requests quickly and consistently and to only require immediate handling by a person for exceptional cases.
- Another disturbing issue is that the number of defaults on loans over the past six months has significantly increased.

From this description, Table 10.18 contains several general motivations or business directions derived from the input from executives.

The second step is to identify specific metrics for measuring the aforementioned business directions. Table 10.19 has some suggestions for one direction.

---

* A real-world example in almost any industry would likely be complex enough that the general approach would be lost in the details.

Table 10.18 Sample Business Motivations and Decision Model Value

Business Motivation
Consistency in Loan Approval
Decrease in Loan Defaults
Increase Revenue from Loans
Increase Customer Base
Human Review of Exceptions Only
Compliance

There are many additional steps, including development of business process models and identification of where business decisions execute within those models. From here, the business directions and metrics are refined and associated with each Decision Model. Each Decision Model is crafted so that the criteria in the metrics appear appropriately in its business logic content.

For an example, simplified for this illustration, assume there is a business decision to Determine a Person Likelihood of Defaulting on a Loan. From Table 10.19, there is a need to decrease these and include the referenced metrics in the Decision Model. A preliminary Decision Model is shown in Figure 10.9. Not enough is known. There may be many other supporting Rule Families whose conclusion fact types appear as condition fact types. But, for now, the model represents condition

Table 10.19 Preliminary Metrics

Business Direction	Preliminary Metrics
Decrease Loan Defaults	Quantity of Loans Defaulted by Persons with Large Student Loans
	Quantity of Loans Defaulted by Persons with Large Home Equity Loans
	Quantity of Loans Defaulted by Persons without Adequate Employment
	Quantity of Loans Defaulted From Persons with Large Mortgages
	Quantity of Loans Defaulted by Persons with Miscellaneous Loans

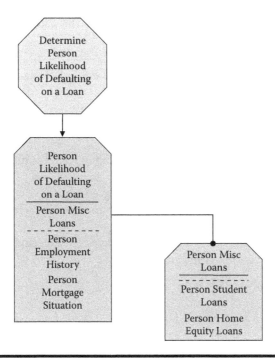

Figure 10.9   Preliminary Decision Model to determine person likelihood of defaulting on a loan

fact types correlating to anticipated metrics. For example, Rule Families contain fact types for student loans, home equity loans, employment history, mortgage situations, and miscellaneous loans because these are fact types involved in the metrics of Table 10.19. When one of these metrics suggests a need for a business logic change, the Decision Model will be the template for analyzing that change. Keeping track of business governance for Rule Families and individual instances provides guidance as to who to involve in analyzing that logic.

Insights into Methodology

The five principles in this chapter are not typically carried out sequentially. Instead, when something in the content of a Decision Model does not look quite right, these principles serve as guidance. This set of principles assists in identifying exactly what is not right about Decision Model content and, as important, how to correct it.

Nevertheless, applying these principles sequentially means performing the following steps:

Step 1: Remove inferential dependencies among Rule Pattern conditions into a separate Rule Family (Principle 11).

Step 2: Remove inconsistencies within a Rule Pattern, and consider doing so across overlapping Rule Patterns by forcing one conclusion for any set of input values (Principle 12).

Step 3: Remove inferential relationships among Rule Families, creating a new Rule Family if needed (Principle 13).

Step 4: Ensure complete coverage among conclusions in one Rule Family and corresponding conditions in an inferentially related Rule Family (Principle 14).

Step 5: Attach business responsibility and metrics to a Decision Model and measure its effectiveness (Principle 15).

Summary

This is a good place to summarize important integrity qualities of business logic made possible by the Decision Model.

Normalization is critical to the Decision Model. Normalization in the Decision Model is a body of theory addressing analysis and decomposition of business logic structures into a new set of structures that exhibit more desirable properties. It is appropriate that the Integrity Principles begin with a principle addressing third normal form.

In terms of the tabular structure of a Rule Pattern, third normal form means that at every row, there are no conditions leading to a conclusion about another condition. In other words, the Rule Pattern conditions do not contain a conclusion nested within them. If there are such nested conclusions within conditions, they should be recast as a different set of more atomic Rule Patterns. Again, this reduces the original Rule Pattern structure into more atomic pieces of conclusions, which is what the Decision Model is all about.

The other principles in this chapter address other kinds of business logic integrity, yet all of the Decision Model principles contribute to its integrity. It is the delivery of this integrity that renders the Decision Model the highest quality deliverable for important business logic. It is important to appreciate the significance of Decision Model integrity. In fact, without the Decision Model, business logic is often represented in decision trees or buried in business process models. It would be quite difficult, if not impossible, to determine if the business logic is normalized or if it contained internal logic errors.

The section below divides the Decision Model integrity into two parts: integrity related to conclusions and integrity related to conditions. That's because the essence of business logic is the way its conditions lead to correct conclusions.

Integrity Related to Decision Model Conclusions

Optimal integrity for Decision Model conclusions means that all connections in a Decision Model among its Rule Families are intact. For all such connections to be intact, the values in the connecting columns must be correct, minimally redundant, consistent, and complete. The Decision Model facilitates these properties for conclusions in the following ways.

Correct Conclusions

- A Rule Family has one and only one conclusion fact type (Principle 5).
- A Rule Family cannot have empty conclusion cells (Principle 7).
- A Decision Model directly aligns with business directions and metrics for measuring progress (Principle 15).

Minimally Redundant Conclusions

- There are no inferential dependencies among inferentially related Rule Families (Principle 13).

Consistent Conclusions

- A Rule Pattern results in at most one conclusion value for any set of valid input values for the condition fact types (Principle 12).
- A Rule Family must have at least one Rule Pattern (Principle 6).
- A Rule Family must result in at least one or more conclusions values for any set of valid input values for condition fact types (Principle 12).
- A Rule Family can result in more than one conclusion value for any set of valid input values for condition fact types (Principle 12).

Complete Conclusions

- The conclusion values in a Rule Family need cover only the subset of the conclusion fact type's domain that is within scope (Principle 12).

Integrity Related to Decision Model Conditions

Optimal integrity for Decision Model conditions means that all connections in a Decision Model within each Rule Family are intact. For all such connections to be intact, the values in the condition columns must be correct, complete, minimally redundant, and consistent. The Decision Model facilitates these characteristics for conditions in the following ways.

Correct Conditions

- The conditions of a Rule Pattern need cover only the subset of the condition fact type's domain that are within scope (Principle 12).
- A Decision Model directly aligns with business directions and metrics for measuring progress (Principle 15).

Complete Conditions

- There are no conclusions in a supporting Rule Family that are not covered by the corresponding dependent Rule Family (Principle 14).

Minimally Redundant Conditions

- There are no inferential dependencies within a Rule Pattern condition key (Property 11).
- A conclusion in a Rule Pattern can never be dependent on a partial condition key (Principle 6).
- The condition key of a Rule Pattern cannot be partially empty (Principle 6).

Consistent Conditions

- The whole condition key of a Rule Pattern can be empty if there is only one Rule Pattern in a Rule Family (Principle 6).
- The whole condition key of a Rule Pattern must not be empty if there is more than one Rule Pattern in the Rule Family (Principle 6).

The Integrity Principles are summarized in Table 10.20.

New Vocabulary from This Chapter

- Decision Model integrity
- structural integrity
- logical integrity
- business integrity
- Decision Model third normal form
- overlap in condition key coverage
- transitive inferential relationship
- supporting Rule Family
- dependent Rule Family

Table 10.20   A Summary of the Integrity Principles

Number	Principle Name	Purpose of Principle	Principle
11	Rule Pattern Transitive Conditions Principle	Remove redundancies among Rule Pattern conditions.	There are no inferential dependencies within a Rule Pattern condition key.
12	Rule Family and Rule Pattern Consistency Principle	Remove inconsistencies within Rule Patterns and among overlapping Rule Patterns.	A Rule Family should be free of inconsistencies within each Rule Pattern and among Rule Patterns. • In general, a Rule Pattern should result in at most one conclusion value for any set of valid input values for the condition fact types. • The conditions of a Rule Pattern need cover only the subset of the condition fact type domains that are within scope. • Within one Rule Pattern, an overlapping condition key coverage means inconsistency exists in the Rule Pattern. • Across two Rule Patterns in the same Rule Family, an overlapping condition key coverage often means that inconsistency exists in the Rule Family. • A Rule Family must result in at least one conclusion value for any set of valid input values for condition fact types. • A Rule Family can result in more than one conclusion value for any set of valid input values for condition fact types. • The conclusion values in a Rule Family need cover only the subset of the conclusion fact type's domain that is within scope.

(Continued)

Table 10.20   A Summary of the Integrity Principles (Continued)

Number	Principle Name	Purpose of Principle	Principle
13	Rule Family Transitive Conditions Principle	Remove redundancies among Rule Families.	There are no inferential dependencies among inferentially related Rule Families.
14	Inferential Integrity Principle	Ensure completeness of inferential relationships among Rule Families.	There are no conclusions in a supporting Rule Family that are not covered by the corresponding dependent Rule Family.
15	Business Alignment Principle	Attach responsibility and metrics for tangible business results to a Decision Model.	A Decision Model directly aligns with business directions and metrics for measuring progress.

And What about the Quote?

The quote advocates that a finished product is obtained by removing pieces that it started with but which contribute little value and actually detract from value. The Integrity Principles remove redundancy and inconsistencies because these contribute no value and, even worse, detract from value because they allow for introduction of dangerous integrity problems.

Discussion Points and Exercises

1. How would you add the logic statement that "Driver Past Claims Count Is Less Than 2" results in a "Driver Insurance Risk Is low" in Tables 10.2 and 10.4?
2. What questions would you ask if someone wanted to add a condition of "Person Highest Education Level Is Bachelors" to Table 10.11?
3. If someone added to Table 10.12 a row for "Person Credit Rating Is Excellent and Person Driving Record Is Good therefore Person Car Rental Discount Amount = 5%," what questions would you ask?
4. Suppose you are to create a Decision Model to determine whether to hire an applicant. The business wants to increase the number of new employees who have demonstrated long-term discipline through GPA, are likely to be long-term employees, and are likely to be promoted in a short time frame. Discuss the kinds of objectives and metrics to capture. Recommend some condition fact types that would seem of value.

Chapter 11

At a Glance
The Decision Model and the Relational Model

Contents

The Purpose of This Analysis 273
    Why This Analysis Is Interesting 274
    Ten Characteristics to Examine 274
The Relational Model and Its Impact 275
    The World of Data before the Relational Model 275
    Why the Relational Model Has Endured 276
    How the Relational Model Changed Everything 276
    Adoption of the Relational Model 276
The Two Models at a Glance 277
    The Most Obvious Difference 277
        A Model of Data 277
        A Model of Business Logic 277
        Different Assets 278
    The Most Obvious Similarity 278
The Two Models in More Depth 278
    Characteristic #1: Structural Foundation 278
        Differences in Structural Foundation 278
    Characteristic #2: Declarative Nature 279
        Declarative Nature in the Relational Model 279
        Declarative Nature in the Decision Model 279

Differences in Declarative Nature...280
Characteristic #3: Content...280
Content in the Relational Model...280
Content in the Decision Model..280
Characteristic #4: Primary Organizing Factor 280
Normalization in the Relational Model 280
Normalization in the Decision Model 281
Characteristic #5: First Normal Form 281
First Normal Form in the Relational Model 281
First Normal Form Applied to a Simple Attribute 282
First Normal Form Applied to a Decomposable Attribute 282
First Normal Form Applied to a Set Attribute 283
First Normal Form Applied to a Repeating Group Attribute 284
Why First Normal Form Is Important in the Relational Model 285
First Normal Form in the Decision Model 285
Applying First Normal Form to Business Logic with More than One
Conclusion Column..286
Applying First Normal Form to Conditions That Are ORed 288
Why First Normal Form Is Important in the Decision Model 288
Differences in First Normal Form...288
Characteristic #6: Functional Dependency 289
Functional Dependency in the Relational Model 289
Functional Dependency in the Decision Model 289
Characteristic #7: Identifiers 289
Identifiers in the Relational Model 290
Identifiers in the Decision Model 290
Differences in Identifiers 291
Characteristic #8: Connections..291
Connections in the Relational Model...291
Connections in the Decision Model...291
Differences in the Connections 293
Characteristic #9: Second Normal Form 293
Second Normal Form in the Relational Model...................................293
Second Normal Form in the Decision Model 294
Differences in Second Normal Form 294
Characteristic #10: Third Normal Form...294
Third Normal Form in the Relational Model......................................295
Third Normal Form in the Decision Model...296
Differences in Third Normal Form..296
Quick Summary of Normal Forms in Practice 296
First Normal Form 296

First Normal Form in the Relational Model 296
First Normal Form in the Decision Model 297
Second Normal Form...297
Second Normal Form in the Relational Model 297
Second Normal Form in the Decision Model 297
Third Normal Form 297
Third Normal Form in the Relational Model.......................................297
Third Normal Form in the Decision Model..298
Conclusion from These Ten Characteristics 298
Summary..298
New Vocabulary from This Chapter 299
And What about the Quote...300
Discussion Points and Exercises..300

At the time, Nixon was normalizing relations with China. I figured
that if he could normalize relations, then so could I.

Reportedly, Dr. E. F. Codd on the word normalization

This chapter is a cursory examination of the Relational Model (for data) and
the Decision Model (for business logic), covering high-level similarities and
very important differences.

Readers are reminded that the populated Rule Family structures in this
chapter are not necessarily meant to be fully populated. This means that
readers ought not to be concerned that the Rule Families are not complete.
They are simply populated with instances that illustrate a particular point
about Rule Families.

The Purpose of This Analysis

It is an intriguing intellectual exercise to scrutinize the similarities and differences
between the Decision Model and the Relational Model. Some readers will find this
exercise interesting, perhaps inspiring. Some may find it irrelevant. However, the
purpose for doing so is to inspire discussions that may lead to further evolution of
the Decision Model.

Why This Analysis Is Interesting

At a glance, there are six observations that make such an analysis interesting. These observations are as follows:

1. Each model defines a technology-independent way of organizing an important, somewhat intangible business intellectual asset (i.e., data versus business logic).
2. Each model, despite being independent of technology, is implementable in technology. This means that each transcends current and future technology products. Neither model is a language or grammar. Languages and grammar can be built on the Decision Model in much the same way that SQL was built on the Relational Model.
3. Each model is a solution to an important unsolved problem of its day (i.e., ineffective management of data versus ineffective management of business logic).
4. Each model adheres to three significant features of technology-independent models. These features are a simple structure, declarative nature, and optimal integrity.
5. Each model represents an intellectual template as a basis for technology solutions.
6. Each model is similar to the other, but the differences are even more interesting.

Ten Characteristics to Examine

These similarities and differences relate to ten characteristics that make each model unique. The ten characteristics addressed in this chapter are the following:

- Characteristic #1: Structural foundation
- Characteristic #2: Declarative nature
- Characteristic #3: Content
- Characteristic #4: Primary Organizing Principle
- Characteristic #5: First normal form
- Characteristic #6: Functional dependency
- Characteristic #7: Identifiers
- Characteristic #8: Connections
- Characteristic #9: Second normal form
- Characteristic #10: Third normal form

This chapter begins by reviewing the impact of the Relational Model. It explains the most obvious similarities and differences between the Relational Model and the

Decision Model. From here, it provides a detailed analysis of the ten characteristics. The summary outlines the similarities and differences.

For ease of understanding, the discussions on the Relational Model use informal versus formal terminology. For the purpose of this chapter, the strict terms and related discussions are not needed.*

The Relational Model and Its Impact

In his seminal paper, Dr. E. F. Codd wrote of a theory that changed forever the way automated information systems are built (Codd, 1970).[†] As such, the Relational Model is one of the most significant advances in the field of computer science. The paper defined a Relational Model for data, known today by most people simply as the Relational Model.

The World of Data before the Relational Model

Before the Relational Model, data for automated systems was stored mostly in sequential file technology (e.g., VSAM) or database technology. Database technology usually supported hierarchical or network data structures. There were also products based on inverted file structures. Each technology was proprietary, favored specific ways of accessing the data, and was incompatible with others.

The goal of database designs was to maximize the target technology (e.g., using pointers, hashing algorithms, and indexing) and minimize storage space (e.g., introducing shorter "codes" to represent the real data). However, eventually, the need became evident for a logical data organization. A logical data organization is one based only on the meaning of the data, independent of, and transcending, technologies. Such a logical data organization would unify the various database design approaches across incompatible technologies.

In the 1970s and 1980s, there were several important inventors and inventions addressing a way to unify the then incompatible ways of organizing computer-stored data. Most notable approaches include the Entity-Relationship Model, IDEF1x, and Information Engineering.

---

* Formal treatment of the Relational Model can be found in Date, 2005.
† Codd's first relational paper was published as an IBM Research Report and was called "Derivability, Redundancy, and Consistency of Relations Stored in Large Data Banks." The paper he is best known for is "The Relational Model of Data for Large Shared Data Banks," *Communications of the ACM*, 1970.

Why the Relational Model Has Endured

Although these innovations were important, the Relational Model was distinct in a very important way. It united the database field with a particular kind of science, allowing problems of the day to be approached from a different perspective. The science behind the Relational Model includes mathematical set theory, relational calculus and algebra, and the concept of normalization. Dr. Codd is credited with the definitions of the first three forms of normalization.

Some say his Relational Model was ahead of computer power at that time. Regardless, his Relational Model spurred innovations in technology and endures today.

How the Relational Model Changed Everything

The Relational Model changed the way the world perceives data.* Every person who, in the past 30 years, has ever ordered something, paid for something, or received a paycheck for doing something has been touched by systems influenced by the Relational Model. Some relational database products have come and gone. Others continue to thrive successfully. Most importantly, nonrelational databases have disappeared or are not in the mainstream.

Adoption of the Relational Model

The Relational Model is a comprehensive body of theory about relations, functional dependency, normalization, domains, primary keys, foreign keys, entity integrity, and referential integrity, not to mention manipulative operations based on set theory. It opened the door to innovative options in technology advances. It certainly spurred many debates and had its share of resistors.

Nevertheless, its rigor and predictability, backed by viable technology solutions, yielded a foundation that has endured. The Relational Model and related technology made people rethink the way to structure, organize, access, design, protect, value, and leverage data as a business asset.

In fact, the relational way of thinking about data led to additional trends, such as enterprise data modeling, data warehousing, data marts, business intelligence, data administration, data stewardship, and data quality.

The Relational Model's brilliance, simplicity, and far-reaching implications eventually took hold. Not only was a new generation of software born, but a whole new age emerged, called the information age.

---

* This chapter uses the term *data* interchangeably with *information* (despite the fact that *data* typically means a raw value and *information* refers to a raw value with a definitional context).

The Two Models at a Glance

It is important to note that the Relational Model and the Decision Model are not the same. In fact, no one needs to know anything about the Relational Model to understand the Decision Model.* Nevertheless, for many readers, especially those who are experienced with the Relational Model, the similarities and differences are worth noting.

The Most Obvious Difference

This may seem trivial, but the most obvious distinction between the Relational Model and the Decision Model is that each is a model of a different resource. The Relational Model is a model of data. The Decision Model is a model of business logic.

A Model of Data

As a model of data, the Relational Model is a model of things in the real world about which the business is interested in storing data. Things in the real world include persons, places, and objects of business concern.† Data about real-world things includes detailed facts, such as a person's first name, last name, and birth date. Today, relational databases store data about products, orders, customers, suppliers, and so forth.

So, the Relational Model is a model of data about things that exist in the real world. Some of this data exists outside the control of the business: a person has a first name no matter what, for example. Some of the data, however, is created by the business because the business makes it so: an order has a scheduled ship date because the business wants to schedule delivery.

A Model of Business Logic

As a model of business logic, the Decision Model is a model of conclusions in the real world about which the business is interested in storing business logic. Conclusions in the real world include assessments, classifications, determinations, and evaluations of business concern. Business logic about real-world conclusions includes constraints, computations, and conditional statements. Business logic includes testing detailed facts, such as Person Annual Income and Person Credit Rating, and coming to conclusions about other facts, such as Person Likelihood of Defaulting on a Loan. These facts are nothing more than pieces of data. A business may have no control over some pieces of data, such as Person Credit Rating. Yet, using business logic, a business defines prescriptions for exactly how it comes to a

---

* And vice versa, of course.
† These things of interest can be tangible, intangible, static, shared, long-lived, or short-lived.

conclusion about a person having a specific credit rating value. Thus, the Decision Model contains the business logic as the business needs or wants it to be.

Different Assets

The two modeled assets, data and business logic, are not the same asset. They are fundamentally different, serving different purposes and having different characteristics. It stands to reason that their models exhibit different native structures and different guiding principles.

The Most Obvious Similarity

The most important similarity between the Relational Model and the Decision Model is that each model is an intellectual template for logically and rigorously organizing a seemingly intangible asset. Both aim to do so with simplicity in mind. Both also aim to do so with a declarative nature unbiased by other considerations, especially technology and usage constraints. Both also aim for optimal integrity by minimizing update anomalies in their content and easily accommodating change.

Each model represents a unique way of thinking because each focuses on the inherent properties of the modeled asset (i.e., data and business logic).

Other similarities and differences relate to the ten characteristics.

The Two Models in More Depth

Characteristic #1: Structural Foundation

Each model comprises a fundamental structure that is simple to interpret and maintain, and is two dimensional.* In each model, fundamental structures are connected to each other by logical connections. In each model, elements within its fundamental structure are grouped together based on functional dependencies.

Differences in Structural Foundation

The functional dependencies in the Relational Model are data dependencies; in the Decision Model, they are business logic dependencies.

---

* Date points out that a relation is not really two dimensional but is *n*-dimensional, where *n* represents the quantity of its attributes. The same is true for a Rule Family, in that it can be considered an *n*-dimensional structure, where *n* is the number of condition cells plus conclusion cells.

Characteristic #2: Declarative Nature

Each model is declarative in nature, which makes it logically independent of technology and other considerations. Each therefore provides maximum stability and flexibility in the design and management of its content.

As a declarative model, neither relies on a specific processing sequence of its content. Any method of processing the content results in the correct conclusion. Thus, each model is reusable and serves as the optimum starting point for transformation into many kinds of technology, even as technology matures over time. The full declarative nature of each model means that it is free from sequential limitations in the heading, body, and relationships.

Declarative Nature in the Relational Model

The attributes in a relation can be in any sequence. It is possible to think of a relation as having the primary key attributes in the first, last, or middle position, and they need not even be necessarily adjacent to each other. The instances (i.e., rows) in a relation also can be in any sequence. So, it is also possible to think of a relation having any instance in the first, middle, or last position. Instances are differentiated by the value of their primary key attributes.* There are no duplicate instances. The relationships among relations can be in any sequence. That is, it is possible to think of accessing one relation first and then match its primary key to foreign keys in another relation or vice versa.

The declarative nature of the Relational Model leads to data independence. Data independence in the Relational Model "means we have the freedom to change the way the data is physically stored and accessed without having to make corresponding changes in the way the data is perceived by the user" (Date, 2005).

Declarative Nature in the Decision Model

The fact types in the heading of a Rule Family can be in any sequence. It is possible to think of a Rule Family as having the fact types of the condition headings as the first, last, or middle position and not even necessarily adjacent to each other. The instances (i.e., rows) in a Rule Family can also be in any sequence. It is possible to think of a Rule Family as having any instance in the first, middle, or last position. Instances are differentiated by the value of their condition key. There are no duplicate instances. The inferential relationships among Rule Families can be traversed in any sequence.

The declarative nature of the Decision Model leads to business logic independence. Business logic independence in the Decision Model means we have the

---

* This chapter ignores the concept of candidate versus primary keys for simplicity.

freedom to change the way the business logic is stored and executed without having to make corresponding changes in the way it is perceived by the user.

Differences in Declarative Nature

In the Relational Model, the declarative nature means that the way the data is perceived by the user need not change when the physical storage of the data changes.

In the Decision Model, the declarative nature means that the way the business logic is perceived by the user need not change when the sequence of execution of the business logic changes.

Characteristic #3: Content

The content in the Relational Model is data and in the Decision Model is business logic.

Content in the Relational Model

The data content in the Relational Model is simply a set of attributes (i.e., data elements) organized according to the dictates of the Relational Model. Informally stated, each instance of a relation represents an instance of one data record. One data record consists of individual attributes that belong together as a unit because the Relational Model dictates it.

Content in the Decision Model

Business logic content in the Decision Model is simply a set of business logic expressions organized according to the dictates of the Decision Model. It is appropriate to say that each instance of a Rule Family is an instance of one business logic record (i.e., a single business logic statement leading to a single conclusion about one fact type). One business logic record consists of individual logical expressions that belong together as a unit because the Decision Model dictates it.

Characteristic #4: Primary Organizing Factor

The primary organizing factor for content in each model is first normal form. A relation and a Rule Family are both in first normal form by definition.

The concept of normalization was introduced by Dr. Codd as it pertained to the Relational Model. This book applies it, in concept with adjustments, to the Decision Model.

Normalization in the Relational Model

Normalization in the Relational Model is "a body of theory addressing analysis and decomposition of data structures into a new set of relations (flat data structures) that exhibit more desirable properties" (Fleming and von Halle, 1989). As such, normalization promotes a desirable refinement of an initial data model that was crafted based on intuitive guidelines, but without normalization rigor. "Of importance is that a normalized data structure exhibits internal consistency, maximum stability, and is based solely on the meaning of the data and not on processing needs" (Fleming and von Halle, 1989).

The Relational Model was introduced with three basic normal forms (first, second, and third) and subsequently embellished with higher levels. The higher the normal form, the more desirable the Relational Model structure and content.

Normalization in the Decision Model

Normalization in the Decision Model also addresses analysis and decomposition, but of business logic structures into a new set of structures that exhibit more desirable properties.

The Decision Model is introduced in this book with three basic normal forms (first, second, and third). Higher normal forms are likely to exist. The higher the normal form, the more desirable the Decision Model structure and content.

Characteristic #5: First Normal Form

In each model, although higher normal forms are more desirable, first normal form is required for minimal structural integrity. First normal form in each model imposes a discipline on the content so that the model is represented and interpreted in one and only one way. This is a strategic property of both models. First normal form leads to simplicity in interpreting, predictability in creating and changing, and ease of manipulating each model.

First Normal Form in the Relational Model

Although first normal form in the Relational Model is a requirement, it is also the normal form least understood. Using Date as the authoritative expert: "Informally, this [first normal form] means that, in terms of the tabular picture of a relation, at every row-and-column intersection we always see just a single value. More formally, it means that every tuple in every relation contains just a single value, of the appropriate type, in every attribute position" (Date, 2005).*

---

* Date goes on to explain this with respect to values at row-and-column intersections being atomic. He states that the meaning of *atomic* is essentially in the eye of the beholder, that what you need or want to do with the data determines how much decomposition is necessary before it is "atomic."

Many practitioners describe a relation in first normal form as one in which attributes are atomic and which does not contain repeating groups. This description is very valuable in practice.

It is most important to understand why first normal form is required and that it serves as the starting point for higher levels of normalization. First normal form is the rigor that results in a Relational Model representation of data in one and only one way. First normal form is achieved by the preceding definition from Date to row-and-column intersections in a relation. Four different kinds of examples illustrate this: a simple attribute, a decomposable attribute, a set attribute, and a repeating group attribute.

First Normal Form Applied to a Simple Attribute

An example of a simple attribute is Person First Name. This attribute contains a single value in a row-and-column intersection, and that value will be drawn from a named set of acceptable first names, as shown in Table 11.1.

First Normal Form Applied to a Decomposable Attribute

Consider next an attribute for Person Telephone Number. Represented as one attribute, it will also contain a single value, and the value will be drawn from a named set of acceptable telephone numbers, as also shown in Table 11.1.

However, if parts of the telephone number—such as the country code, area code, exchange digits, or other digits—are of interest by themselves, a single attribute for Person Telephone Number doesn't really contain a single value. Rather, it contains a collection of different kinds of values—one for each part of the telephone number that is of interest. Representing it as one attribute hides the individual pieces from the user. First normal form disallows the hiding of individual pieces of data if those individual pieces are of interest.

So, if the individual pieces are of interest by themselves, a relation in first normal form needs to depict an attribute type for each of these pieces because each piece has an existence and a set of acceptable values that are different from each other. In this way, each part can be referenced individually by name (of course, never by sequence!), as shown in Table 11.2.

Table 11.1   Telephone Number as a Single Attribute

Person First Name	Person Last Name	Person Telephone Number
Fred	Smith	019087756
Louise	Jones	017250987
Kari	Nicholas	012015437

Table 11.2 Telephone Number as Three Attributes

Person First Name	Person Last Name	Person Telephone Number Country Code	Person Telephone Number Exchange Digits	Person Telephone Number Other Telephone Digits
Fred	Smith	01	908	7756
Louise	Jones	01	725	0987
Kari	Nicholas	01	201	5437

First Normal Form Applied to a Set Attribute

Next, consider an attribute representing the names of a person's children. If it is important only to know that a person has a set of children with names, but not to know anything about individual children's names, a relation in first normal form can depict this set of names as one attribute for Person Set of Children Names whose single value is a set of names. Table 11.3 illustrates this. No matter how many children a person has, from zero to unlimited, the value for the attribute for Person Set of Children Names is always one set. Not only that, adding a child's name means simply replacing an existing set with a new set containing the new child's name. So, regardless of the number of children's names, this relation will always only have three attributes, and making changes in the children is always a replace (or update operation) of one attribute.

Although the row representing Fred Smith contains three names for children, these names belong to one set, which implies that the set has a name and must be manipulated as a set. It cannot be decomposed or manipulated as its individual members.

However, if individual children's names—such as Mary, Ellen, Sam, and Tommy—are of interest by themselves, the relation in Table 11.3 will not suffice and is not in first normal form.

If individual children are of interest, a relation in first normal form must depict each child's name as its own attribute value. If every person has exactly three

Table 11.3 Attribute Whose Single Value Is a Set

Person First Name	Person Last Name	Person Set of Children Names
Fred	Smith	{Mary, Ellen, Sam}
Louise	Jones	{Tommy}
Kari	Nicholas	{}

Table 11.4   Separate Attributes for Child's Name

Person First Name	Person Last Name	Person First Child Name	Person Second Child Name	Person Third Child Name
Fred	Smith	Mary	Ellen	Sam

children, a first normal for relation can depict these as three attributes, such as first child name, second child name, and third child name. This is illustrated in Table 11.4.

But what if every person doesn't always have exactly three children? Table 11.5 shows an attempt at capturing all of these children's names using the data structure in Table 11.4.

Although Table 11.5 may appear to do the job, it is actually a bit disconcerting because it adds unnecessary complexity. For starters, what if someone wants to add a child? Sometimes this addition is accommodated by updating one of the child name columns. However, if that person already has three children, then what? Is this accommodated by adding a column, adding a row? It helps to recall that the purpose of first normal form is to ensure that the content is represented in only one way with simple manipulation. Table 11.5 requires more complex manipulation than is necessary to simply add a child.

This situation is representative of repeating groups, where practitioners aim for first normal form by removing such repeating groups as explained later.

First Normal Form Applied to a Repeating Group Attribute

Table 11.6 is a solution allowing for a variable quantity of children where each child name can be manipulated independently of the others. This relation allows for zero to unlimited children. Adding a child is always accomplished simply by adding a row. If birth order is important, an attribute for birth order will suffice (never sequence of rows!), as shown in Table 11.7.

Table 11.5   Variable Number of Children

Person First Name	Person Last Name	Person First Child Name	Person Second Child Name	Person Third Child Name
Fred	Smith	Mary	Ellen	Sam
Louise	Jones	Tommy		
Kari	Nicholas			

Table 11.6   Children Names as Rows

Person First Name	Person Last Name	Person Child Name
Fred	Smith	Mary
Fred	Smith	Ellen
Fred	Smith	Sam
Louise	Jones	Tommy

Table 11.7   Children Names and Birth Orders as Rows

Person First Name	Person Last Name	Person Child Name	Person Child Birth Order
Fred	Smith	Mary	1
Fred	Smith	Ellen	2
Fred	Smith	Sam	3
Louise	Jones	Tommy	1

Why First Normal Form Is Important in the Relational Model

First normal form is a way of supporting Codd's Information Principle which, according to Date, had been explained by Codd as follows:

> "An overriding principle is the information principle: The entire content of the database (at any given time) is represented in one—and only one—way; namely as explicit values in attribute positions in tuples (instances) in relations." (Date, 2005)

The Information Principle together with first normal form delivers the only way to interpret and manipulate data. Together, they lead to one extremely simple kind of structure that needs only one complete set of manipulation operators.

First Normal Form in the Decision Model

First normal form in the Decision Model is also a requirement of a Rule Family and serves as the starting point for higher levels of normalization. However, first normal form in the Decision Model has a different meaning than it does in the Relational Model, but a similar purpose.

Naturally, its purpose is to deliver the only way of representing and interpreting business logic. Its different meaning is related to the distinction between a relational data record and a Decision Model business logic record. A relational data record is a collection of individual attributes that together convey information. On the other hand, a Decision Model business logic record is a collection of logical expressions that together infer a conclusion.

With this in mind, first normal form in the Decision Model means that, in terms of the tabular picture of a Rule Family, each row cannot be decomposed into more than one row reaching the conclusion. If a row can be decomposed into more than one row reaching the conclusion (without losing the intent of the original row), the original row is not in first normal form and should be recast as multiple conclusions down the rows and not across columns.

Although this sounds confusing, in practice it is very simple. It means applying the definition of first normal form to each row in a Rule Family (i.e., every Rule Family row cannot be decomposed into more than one row reaching the conclusion). Two different kinds of examples of this are (1) business logic with more than one conclusion column and (2) business logic conditions that are ORed together.

Applying First Normal Form to Business Logic with More than One Conclusion Column

A two-dimensional business logic structure leading to more than one conclusion fact type can always be decomposed, without loss of meaning, into a set of structures, each having only one conclusion fact type. The example from Chapter 8, Table 8.13 is repeated here for convenience.

Table 11.8 contains three conditions that, if true, lead to two conclusions. This is a flagrant violation of first normal form because this row can be decomposed into two rows without loss of meaning. Again, it helps to recall the purpose of first normal form: to impose rigor so that content is represented and interpreted in only one way with simple manipulation. If more than one conclusion fact type were

Table 11.8 Two Conclusions

Conditions						Conclusions			
Person Credit Rating from Outside Credit Bureau		Person Credit Card Balance		Person Education Loan Balance		Person Likelihood of Defaulting on a Loan		Person Risk Rating	
Is	X	Is Greater Than	Y	Is Greater Than	Z	Is	High	Is	High

permitted, one person may create a Rule Family for each of the conclusion fact types and another person may create one Rule Family with both conclusion fact types. Without restricting a Rule Family to one conclusion fact type, there can be many ways, perhaps, to represent a Rule Family that, at one point in time, appears to result in multiple conclusion fact types. Further, because the conclusion fact type in the Decision Model is the glue that holds Rule Families together, this restriction is even more important in creating the one—and only one—Decision Model representation that is also the simplest.

Reducing Table 11.8 to first normal simply means creating a separate Rule Family for each of these conclusions, as shown in Table 11.9. The three conditions appear in two Rule Families, but each Rule Family reaches a conclusion about a single conclusion fact type. Together, these Rule Families are semantically equivalent to the previous Rule Family, but are now in first normal form. This simplifies the representation and management of the business logic because all business logic coming to a conclusion about Person Likelihood of Defaulting on a Loan belongs in one Rule Family. All business logic coming to a conclusion about a Person Risk Rating belongs in another. Although these Rule Families appear to have these three conditions in common at this point in time, they can evolve independently of each other.

Table 11.9   One Conclusion

Conditions						Conclusion	
Person Credit Rating from Outside Credit Bureau		*Person Credit Card Balance*		*Person Education Loan Balance*		*Person Likelihood of Defaulting on a Loan*	
Is	X	Is Greater Than	Y	Is Greater Than	Z	Is	High

Conditions						Conclusion	
Person Credit Rating from Outside Credit Bureau		*Person Credit Card Balance*		*Person Education Loan Balance*		*Person Risk Rating*	
Is	X	Is Greater Than	Y	Is Greater Than	Z	Is	High

Applying First Normal Form to Conditions That Are ORed

Consider the following example of a business logic statement from Chapter 8:

> If (Person Credit Rating from the Outside Credit Bureau is X and Person Credit Card Balance is greater than Y) or Person Education Loan Balance is greater than Z, then Person Likelihood of Defaulting on a Loan is High.

This business logic statement is represented in Table 8.17 (Chapter 8) and requires parentheses for correct interpretation. Without the parentheses, interpretation is ambiguous as the conclusion will be different depending on sequence of evaluation. Adding parentheses removes the ambiguity but imposes a sequence on how the conditions are to be processed. Ambiguity and sequence have no place in the Decision Model.

Business logic in which conditions are connected with ORs can always be decomposed without ORs and without losing the original intent. Table 8.18 decomposes the original business logic with ORs into two rows in the Rule Family, neither of which involves an OR in its interpretation. In this way, every populated condition in a Rule Family row must be true for the corresponding condition to be true. That is, every row is interpreted and processed in exactly the same simple manner.

Why First Normal Form Is Important in the Decision Model

First normal form in the Decision Model supports a business logic principle as follows:

> Business Logic Principle: The entire content of a decision base* is represented in one—and only one—way, namely, as explicit logical expressions in conditions leading to a conclusion about one fact type within instances in Rule Families.

Such a Business Logic Principle and Decision Model first normal form deliver the only way to interpret and manipulate business logic behind a business decision in a Decision Model. Together, they lead to an extremely simple kind of structure that, even in the absence of specific manipulation operators, can be executed in any way by any technology to arrive at the correct result.

Differences in First Normal Form

In the Relational Model, first normal form means that every cell in a relation contains a single value of interest, where that value cannot be decomposed without losing meaning.

---

* A decision base is simply the fully populated content of a Decision Model at any point in time.

Table 11.10 Functional Dependency

Person Identification Number	Person First Name
10	Susan
5	Michael
65	Margaret

In the Decision Model, first normal form means that every row in a Rule Family cannot be decomposed into more than one row reaching the conclusion.

In each case, informally, if a relational instance or a Rule Family instance can be decomposed, that instance is usually recast in a form with more rows and fewer columns.

Characteristic #6: Functional Dependency

Functional dependency is the rigor that ties together attributes within a relation and logical expressions within a Rule Family.

Functional Dependency in the Relational Model

In the Relational Model, functional dependency means that the value of one or a set of attributes in a relation uniquely determines the value of another attribute in the same relation. This is easier to see than to explain. Refer to Table 11.10, where the person whose Identification Number is 10 has a First Name of "Susan." In this case, the value of the attribute Person Identification Number uniquely determines the value of the attribute Person First Name in the same relation.

Functional Dependency in the Decision Model

In the Decision Model, functional dependency also means that the value of a one or a set of condition columns uniquely determines the value of another cell, specifically the conclusion column, in the same Rule Family. Specifically, the value of the conditions uniquely determines the value of the conclusion.

Characteristic #7: Identifiers

In each model, an identifier is a logical means of distinguishing a specific instance in the fundamental structure. But there is one difference.

Table 11.11   Relation with Two Candidate Keys

Course Catalog Number (CK1)	Department Number (CK2)	Department Course Number (CK2)	Course Name	Course Credits
101	10	1	Calculus	4

Identifiers in the Relational Model

In the Relational Model, an identifier is an attribute or set of attributes that uniquely identifies an instance of a relation. It is important that, if there are two such identifiers for a relation, they lead to the same instance of the relation.

For example, Table 11.11 has two possible identifiers (labeled CK1 and CK2 for candidate key 1 and candidate key 2) that uniquely identify a particular course. One candidate key (CK1) is the Catalog Course Number, which is a unique number given to each course across the college. Another candidate key (CK2) is a combination of the Department Number and a Course Number provided by each department.

With CK1, a Course Catalog Number of 101 uniquely identifies the Calculus course. With CK2, a Department Number of 10 and a Department Course Number of 1 also uniquely identifies the Calculus course.

In the Relational Model, a candidate key cannot have any null values.

Identifiers in the Decision Model

Condition keys in the Decision Model function like candidate keys because they uniquely identify an instance in a Rule Family. However, a Rule Family may comprise more than one Rule Pattern; hence, different condition keys in a Rule Family do not necessarily identify the same instance of the Rule Family. Consider Table 11.12, in which there are two condition keys for coming to a conclusion about a Person Likelihood of Defaulting on a Loan. One condition key (CK1) is the combination of Person Credit Rating and Person Salary, and the other (CK2) is simply the Person Employment History.

Table 11.12   Rule Family with Two Condition Keys

Rule Pattern	Conditions						Conclusion	
	Person Credit Rating (CK1)		Person Salary (CK1)		Person Employment History (CK2)		Person Likelihood of Defaulting on a Loan	
1	Is	X	Is	X			Is	High
2					Is	X	Is	Low

For a given person, the evaluation of Credit Rating and Salary may lead to a conclusion in a different row than for the evaluation of Person Employment History. Not only that, the two rows may have different conclusion values for that same person. What this means is that the Decision Model allows a Rule Family to have more than one condition key (i.e., one per Rule Pattern) and that different condition keys may lead to different conclusions for the same input. But there is one condition key for each Rule Pattern within a Rule Family.

Differences in Identifiers

In the Relational Model, an identifier is called a candidate key. A relation may have more than one candidate key that uniquely identifies an instance of a relation. A candidate key cannot contain null values.

In the Decision Model, an identifier is called a condition key. A Rule Family may have more than one condition key but there may only be one condition key per Rule Pattern. A condition key may be wholly empty (or null) if there is only one Rule Pattern in the Rule Family, meaning that its conclusion is unconditional.

Characteristic #8: Connections

In each model, a connection is a logical link that connects related fundamental structures together. But there are differences in how they do so.

Connections in the Relational Model

In the Relational Model, such a connection is called a foreign key. In a relation, the primary key attributes (i.e., a candidate key selected to serve as the primary way of identifying a unique instance) in one relation serve as the foreign key (i.e., the glue) connecting that relation to related ones. The connection from a primary key in one relation to a foreign key in another relation is how data structures are connected to each other, as shown in Table 11.13.

Person Identification Number is the primary key in the first table. Rows in the second table with the same value for Person Identification Number as a row in the first table are logically related to each other. So, the person with Person Identification Number of "10" has a First Name of "George," a Last Name of "Jones," and two week's worth of Hours Worked.

Connections in the Decision Model

In the Decision Model, a connection among fundamental structures is called an inferential key. In a Rule Family, the nonidentifying conclusion column serves as the inferential key (i.e., the glue) connecting that Rule Family to related ones. The connection from inferential key in one Rule Family to a condition key in another

Table 11.13 Connection from One Relation to Another

Person Identification Number (pk)	Person First Name	Person Last Name
10	George	Jones
5	Janet	Smith

Person Identification Number (pk) (fk)	Week-Ending Date (pk)	Person Hours Worked
5	1-1-2008	40
10	1-1-2008	30
10	2-1-2008	40

Rule Family is how business logic structures are connected to each other, as shown in Table 11.14.

Rows in the first table with Person Likelihood of Defaulting on a Loan of "High" are related to a row in the second table with the same value for the same logical expression. So, a person with a Credit Rating from an Outside Credit Bureau of

Table 11.14 Connection from One Rule Family to Another Is from Inferential Key to Condition Key

Conditions						Conclusion	
Person Credit Rating from Outside Credit Bureau		Person Credit Card Balance		Person Education Loan Balance		Person Likelihood of Defaulting on a Loan	
Is	X	Is Greater Than	Y	Is Greater Than	Z	Is	High

Conditions		Conclusion	
Person Likelihood of Defaulting on a Loan (IK)		Person Risk Rating	
Is	High	Is	High

X and a Credit Card Balance Is Greater Than Y and an Education Loan Balance Is Greater Than Z has a Likelihood of Defaulting on a Loan of High and a Risk Rating of "High."

Differences in the Connections

The difference in connections between the models is that data in a Relational Model is connected by identifiers, whereas business logic in the Decision Model is connected by nonidentifying conclusions.

Characteristic #9: Second Normal Form

Second normal form in both models eliminates the representation of functional dependencies that involve only part of the identifier. Simply stated, second normal form as defined for the Relational Model deals with a primary key attribute that is irrelevant to determining the value of another nonidentifying attribute in the relation. In the Decision Model, second normal form deals with a condition key logical expression that is irrelevant to determining the value of the conclusion in the Rule Family.

Second Normal Form in the Relational Model

Second normal form in the Relational Model implies that each nonkey attribute in a (first normal form) relation is fully functionally dependent on the entire primary key (the latter may be a set of attributes). By definition, a primary key (a candidate key chosen to be a primary key) is the set of attributes that uniquely identifies an instance in a relation.

Suppose the relation representing orders placed by customers is shown in Table 11.15. The primary key of this relation is Customer Number plus Order Number, because every customer starts with an Order Number of 1, as shown.

There is a problem in Table 11.15 because it is only necessary to know Customer Number (i.e., not necessary to know Order Number) to know the Customer Name. That is, Customer Name is functionally dependent on Customer Number but not on the combination of Customer Number plus Order Number. The result is duplication of information because the Customer Name, in this case ABC Corporation,

Table 11.15   Customer Orders

Customer Number (pk)	Order Number (pk)	Order Date Placed	Order Scheduled Ship Date	Customer Name
10	1	1/1/2008	2/1/2008	ABC Corporation
10	2	1/2/2008	2/2/2008	ABC Corporation

Table 11.16 Second Normal Form Solution

Customer Number (pk)	Customer Name
10	ABC Corporation

Customer Number (pk)	Order Number (pk)	Order Date Placed	Orders Scheduled Ship Date
10	1	1/1/2008	2/1/2008
10	2	2/1/2008	2/2/2008

is repeated for every Order placed by Customer Number 10. In other words, the Order Number is irrelevant in determining the Customer Name.

Correcting the violation of second normal form and hence, removing the redundancy, results in Table 11.16.

Second Normal Form in the Decision Model

Second normal form for the Decision Model implies that each conclusion in a Rule Pattern is fully functionally dependent on the entire condition key.

An example of a violation of second normal form in the Decision Model is in Chapter 8, Table 8.20. The violation causes logic to be duplicated because the conclusion is not dependent on the entire condition key. It also causes execution of unnecessary conditions because the results of those conditions are irrelevant to the conclusion.

Removing partial dependencies from a condition key to the conclusion results in a Rule Pattern that is compliant with second normal form for the Decision Model. An example of such a solution is in Chapter 8, Table 8.21.

Differences in Second Normal Form

In the Relational Model, second normal form results in a relation in which all nonidentifying attributes are fully functionally dependent on the entire primary key (the latter may be a set of attributes).

In the Decision Model, second normal form results in identification of a Rule Pattern within a Rule Family in which the conclusion is fully functionally dependent on the entire condition key.

Characteristic #10: Third Normal Form

Third normal form addresses the elimination of transitive dependencies among nonkey attributes in the Relational Model and among conditions in the Decision Model.

Table 11.17 Relation with Transitive Dependency among Nonkey Attributes

Customer Number (pk)	Order Number (pk)	Line Item Number (pk)	Product Number	Product Name	Product Quantity Ordered
10	1	1	64	Decision Model Book	100
10	1	2	03	SOA Book	5
10	2	1	64	Decision Model Book	1000

Third Normal Form in the Relational Model

Third normal form in the Relational Model means eliminating functional dependencies among nonkey attributes (other than alternate keys). Consider the example in Table 11.17.

This relation contains information about line items for an order. The primary key comprises three columns: the Customer Number, the Order Number (because every customer's first order is 1), and Line Item Number (because every order's first line item is 1).

However, there is a transitive dependency involving nonkey columns. Specifically, the primary key functionally determines the product number (i.e., the line item identifies the product ordered), but the product number by itself determines the product name.

This transitive dependency results in duplicate data because for every line item in every order for product 64, the product name of Decision Model book repeats.

The correction to the transitive dependency and resulting duplicate data is to remove the dependency, as shown in Table 11.18.

Table 11.18 Third Normal Form Solution

Customer Number (pk)	Order Number (pk)	Line Item Number (pk)	Product Number	Product Quantity Ordered
10	1	1	64	100
10	1	2	03	5
10	2	1	64	1000

Product Number (pk)	Product Name
03	SOA Book
64	Decision Model Book

Third Normal Form in the Decision Model

Third normal form in the Decision Model means eliminating functional dependencies among conditions within a Rule Pattern. A Rule Pattern is reduced to third normal form by removing from it all conditions that lead to other conditions; that is, putting them into a different Rule Family structure.

An example of a violation of Decision Model third normal form is Table 10.2 (Chapter 10). There is a dependency between condition Driver Past Claims Count and Driver Insurance Risk. That is, every specific logical expression for the former is associated in the Rule Pattern with a specific logical expression for the latter.

Violations of third normal form result in duplicate business logic, which adds complexity to making updates. It also allows for potential anomalies as a result of updates if the same change is not made to all copies of the duplicate business logic, as explained under Principle #11 in Chapter 10.

The solution is to remove these hidden dependencies within a condition key, as shown in Tables 10.3 and 10.4. In this way, there is only one place in the resulting structures for each different kind of business logic.

In both models, third normal form deals with transitive dependencies among columns. In both models, the presence of such transitive dependencies results in duplication (i.e., of data or business logic).

Differences in Third Normal Form

In the Relational Model, third normal form addresses transitive dependencies among nonkey attributes in a relation.

In the Decision Model, a Rule Pattern only has one nonkey column, and that column is its conclusion column. Therefore, third normal form in the Decision Model addresses transitive dependencies among condition (or key) columns.

Quick Summary of Normal Forms in Practice

This is a good place to summarize the three normal forms in each model, emphasizing how to apply them in practice.

First Normal Form

Ironically, first normal form tends to be the one most difficult to understand.

First Normal Form in the Relational Model

In the Relational Model, first normal form means single data attribute values in each cell. In practice, this means decomposing an attribute when it is a set into its individual members or when parts of an attribute have their own meaning, such as decomposing an address field into street number, street name, city name, state name, zip code, and country code. Also, if an attribute seems like a repeating group, such as children's names or monthly amounts, first normal form means decomposing those repetitions as data values down rows rather than across columns.

First Normal Form in the Decision Model

In the Decision Model, first normal form means single, nondecomposable rows coming to the conclusion. In practice, this means decomposing a row when it includes an OR between conditions or more than one conclusion column. In both cases, this means recasting these kinds of logic as business logic statements down rows rather than across columns.

Second Normal Form

In both models, second normal form means making sure that the entire identifying key is needed to determine the value of the other cells.

Second Normal Form in the Relational Model

In the Relational Model, this means making sure that all nonkey attribute values are dependent on the whole value of the primary or candidate keys. In practice, this means nonkey attributes that depend only on part of the primary or candidate key for its value are moved into a separate relation along with that part of the primary or candidate key.

Second Normal Form in the Decision Model

In the Decision Model, this means making sure that the nonkey conclusion values are dependent on the entire value of the condition key. In practice, this means conclusion values that depend only on part of the condition key are noted as belonging to a separate Rule Pattern along with that part of the condition key.

Third Normal Form

In both models, third normal form means making sure that there are no hidden transitive dependencies.

Third Normal Form in the Relational Model

In the Relational Model, this means making sure that there are no nonkey attribute values that are dependent on the values of other nonkey attribute values. In practice, this means creating a separate relation for that dependency.

Third Normal Form in the Decision Model

In the Decision Model, this means making sure that there are no condition key values that are dependent on the values of other condition key values. In practice, this means creating a separate Rule Family for that dependency.

Conclusion from These Ten Characteristics

If business logic is an asset worth harnessing, which is what data has become, it needs a model, like the Relational Model, that will stand the test of time. Therefore, a model for business logic should embrace long-lasting concepts such as atomic pieces, normalization principles, and declarative nature. In particular, it should embrace the ten characteristics in this chapter in ways similar to how the Relational Model incorporated these principles. However, it should also do so in some ways that are deliberately different, because the inherent nature of business logic is different from that of data.

Summary

This chapter compares some aspects of the Relational Model to those of the Decision Model. The similarities between the two models are the following:

- Both are intellectual templates for an intellectual business asset.
- Both aim for simplicity, declarative nature, and optimal integrity.
- Both represent a new way of thinking based on the inherent properties of the asset being modeled.
- The fundamental structure in each is simple, two dimensional, and linked together by logical connections.
- Both are governed by the notion of functional dependency.
- Higher normal forms in both represent more desirable structures and content.
- Both require structures to be in first normal form.
- First normal form is the rigor by which each model represents its asset in the one—and only one—way that makes manipulation of the structure simple.
- Second normal form in both deals with elimination of functional dependencies involving only part of the identifier.
- Third normal form in both deals with transitive dependencies.

The differences between the models are the following:

- The Relational Model is a model of data. The Decision Model is a model of business logic.
- A Relational Model data record conveys information. A Decision Model business logic record conveys conclusions.

- Functional dependency in the Relational Model is based on data dependencies. In the Decision Model, it is based on business logic dependencies.
- An identifier in the Relational Model is called a candidate key. A relation may have more than one candidate key, which identifies an instance of a relation and cannot contain null values. An identifier in the Decision Model is called a condition key. A Rule Family may have more than one condition key but only one per Rule Pattern, and each condition key identifies a different instance of the Rule Family. A condition key can be wholly null, where null means "unconditionally" if there is only one Rule Pattern in the Rule Family.
- A connection among relations in the Relational Model is called a foreign key and represents a primary key in one relation connecting to the foreign key in another. A connection among Rule Families in the Decision Model is called an inferential key and represents a nonidentifying conclusion in one Rule Family connecting to part of the condition key in another.
- First normal form in the Relational Model means that every cell in a relation contains a single value of interest and that value cannot be decomposed without loss of meaning. First normal form in the Decision Model means that every row in a Rule Family cannot be decomposed into more than one row reaching the conclusion.
- Second normal form in the Relational Model means that each nonkey attribute is fully functionally dependent on the entire identifier. Second normal form in the Decision Model means that the Rule Family has been reduced to Rule Patterns in which the conclusion is fully functionally dependent on the entire condition key.
- Third normal form in the Relational Model means eliminating functional dependencies among nonkey attributes (other than alternate keys). Third normal form in the Decision Model means eliminating transitive dependencies among condition key columns.

New Vocabulary from This Chapter

The following is a list of terms introduced in this chapter, in the sequence in which they appear in the text:

- model of data
- model of business logic
- data dependency
- business logic dependency
- data record
- business logic record
- first normal form in the Relational Model
- information principle

- business logic principle
- decision base
- Relational Model functional dependency
- candidate key in the Relational Model
- foreign key in the Relational Model
- second normal form in the Relational Model
- third normal form in the Relational Model

And What about the Quote

The quote is reportedly about Codd's explanation for selecting the word normalization to mean the disciplined organization of data in the Relational Model. Whatever word is used for it, the concept of normalization has led to standard and optimum ways of designing and automating data stored in databases.

The Decision Model was not designed to embody the rigor of mathematical set theory as is the Relational Model. However, as a humble beginning, it embraces some of the most important qualities introduced by Dr. Codd, but aimed at business logic.

Discussion Points and Exercises

1. Refer to a healthcare insurance card carried by a member in a healthcare insurance plan. (Or, use another example.) Identify some pieces of data on it that would be represented in a Relational Model. Also, identify potential conclusions to be reached through business logic that might be part of a Decision Model using that data when processing a claim.
2. Discuss why data and business logic are referred to in this chapter as "seemingly intangible assets." Specifically, why would they seem intangible? How do they become tangible? What are the benefits of making them tangible?
3. Give examples of instances of data records conforming to the Relational Model and of business logic records conforming to the Decision Model.
4. Explain why first normal form in both models disallows the hiding of pieces (i.e., pieces of data and pieces of business logic).
5. For all fact types in the Decision Model diagram in Figure 2.1 (Chapter 2), create a candidate set of relational tables. Discuss the benefits of delivering a third normal form Decision Model structure with a corresponding third normal form relational data structure. Also discuss how creating the two models together assists in understanding fact types and in giving them appropriate names.

Chapter 12

The Decision Model Formally Defined

Contents

Decision Model Definitions 302
The Principles of the Decision Model 302
Normal Forms in the Decision Model 302
Decision Model Notation..302
    The Decision Model Diagram...309
        The Business Decision Shape...309
    The Business Decision Connector 309
        The Rule Family Shape..310
        The Inferential Relationship Line 311
        Integrating the Shapes into a Diagram 312
    The Rule Family Table 312
    Rule Pattern Representation..313
Summary..315

This chapter is for the reader in search of a formal but terse definition of all aspects of the Decision Model. It can be read after reading the foundational material in Chapters 1 and 2, or after the detailed principles in Chapters 8, 9, and 10. Either way, it can be used as a succinct reference for the Decision Model and its notation.

This chapter does not explain how or why the definitions in it were conceived or justified. Such explanations are in the detailed chapters on the principles. A first-time reader is encouraged to read Chapter 2 before reading this chapter.

The Decision Model is a representation of fact-based business logic within the scope of a single business decision. The Decision Model uses a business vocabulary to represent that logic in structures that are based on the inherent nature of the logic itself. The detailed content of these structures can be viewed through one kind of representation, whereas the structures may be abstracted (i.e., devoid of content) to a high-level diagram to be seen as a whole.

Decision Model Definitions

The terms used in the Decision Model principles and their explanations are defined in Table 12.1.

The Principles of the Decision Model

The rigor of the Decision Model is embodied in 15 principles, divided into structural, declarative, and integrity principles. These principles are in Table 12.2.

Normal Forms in the Decision Model

Decision Model normal forms represent refinements of a Rule Family in which Rule Families in higher normal forms exhibit more desirable properties with respect to the level of integrity in structure and content. This book defines three normal forms in Table 12.3.

Decision Model Notation

The principles of the Decision Model do not prescribe any standard forms of depiction or shapes for diagramming it. There are two important points to make about any notation to represent a Decision Model. First, the notation must be distinct

Table 12.1 Definition of Terms

Term	Definition
Atomic business logic statement	A business logic statement that cannot be decomposed (into smaller business logic statements) without loss of meaning.
Business decision	A conclusion that the business arrives at through business logic and which the business is interested in managing.
Business logic	The means by which the business derives a conclusion from facts.
Business logic statement	An expression of conditions evaluating facts leading to a conclusion of a new fact.
Condition Key	Set of condition fact types in a Rule Pattern.
Decision Model	An intellectual template for perceiving, organizing, and managing business logic behind a business decision (specifically, a representation of business logic statements that together lead to a single business decision, and which ideally complies with the 15 Decision Model principles).
Decision Model declarative nature	The property of a Decision Model making it logically independent of other considerations, unbiased by processing patterns or technology (specifically, the declarative nature of the Decision Model is enforced by the three declarative principles in Table 12.2).
Decision Model integrity	The property that measures whether a Decision Model's content makes sense structurally, logically, and from a business perspective (specifically, these areas of integrity are enforced by the seven Decision Model integrity principles in Table 12.2).
Decision Model normal form	The degree of vulnerability to logical inconsistencies and anomalies of the content of a Decision Model. The higher the normal form, the less vulnerable to inconsistencies and anomalies. There are three levels of Decision Model Normal Form currently defined: first, second, and third Decision Model Normal Form. See Table 12.3.

(Continued)

Table 12.1   Definition of Terms (Continued)

Term	Definition
Decision Model structure	A representation of business logic independent of other considerations and based on the unique properties and integrity inherent in business logic itself (specifically, the Decision Model is a set of connected two-dimensional table-like structures called Rule Families that emerge from the five structural principles. See Table 12.2).
Decision Rule Family	A Rule Family that connects directly to a business decision without any intervening dependent Rule Family.
Dependent Rule Family	A Rule Family having a condition fact type that is the same as the conclusion fact type of a supporting Rule Family.
Fact (or fact value)	A piece of information (i.e., a piece of data within a context): • Example: "The Person Named John Doe has been employed 5 years at his current employer" • The piece of information is the value "5" in the context of years at current employer for John Doe.
Fact type	A general classification of a fact, not the piece of information itself: • Example: Person Years at Current Employer • There are many pieces of information for the preceding fact type because one person may be at current employer for 5 years, another for 2 years, and yet another for 35 years.
Fact type domain	The type and range of values that make business sense for a given fact type.
Inferential dependency	A functional dependency whereby the value of a cell or set of cells (conditions) uniquely determines through inference the value of another cell (conclusion) (specifically, an inferential dependency exists between the conditions in one row, and the conclusion in the same row of the Rule Family.
Inferential key	A condition fact type in one Rule Family that serves as a conclusion fact type in another Rule Family.

Table 12.1   Definition of Terms (Continued)

Term	Definition
Inferential relationship	Circumstance where a conclusion fact type in one Rule Family (called the supporting Rule Family) serves as a condition fact type in another Rule Family (called the dependent Rule Family; specifically, inferential dependency is an inference relationship within a Rule Family, and inferential relationship is an inference relationship among Rule Families).
Rule Family	A two-dimensional representation of business logic conforming to Decision Model first normal form (specifically, most often represented as a two-dimensional structure comprising columns and rows; each row represents one business logic statements; all business logic statements in a Rule Family reach a conclusion about a common conclusion fact type).
Rule Family body	Content of a Rule Family as a set of business logic expressions organized into instances or rows (specifically, a set of cells, each populated with an operator and operand conforming to the fact type in the heading, where some serve as conditions leading to another serving as conclusion).
Rule Family heading	Set of fact types, each serving as a condition or conclusion (specifically, comprising zero to many condition fact types and one conclusion fact type).
Rule Pattern	Set of Rule Family rows with a common set of condition cells that are populated (specifically, a set of rows that are grouped by common populated fact types in their condition columns; a Rule Pattern is said to be complete when all the populated conditional values required to know the conclusion are present in the Rule Family).
Supporting Rule Family	A Rule Family whose conclusion fact type serves as a condition fact type in another (dependent) Rule Family. The dependent Rule Family is inferentially dependent on the supporting Rule Family.

Table 12.2 The Decision Model Principles

#	Principle Name	Purpose	Principle
The Structural Principles			
1	The Tabular Principle	Place rigor on the shape of a Rule Family.	The fundamental structure of a Decision Model is called a Rule Family and has two dimensions: one dimension is the heading and the other dimension is the body.
2	The Heading Principle	Place rigor on the heading of a Rule Family.	The heading of a Rule Family is a set of fact types.
3	The Cell Principle	Place rigor on the cell of a Rule Family.	The content of each cell of a Rule Family is an atomic logical expression conforming to the heading.
4	The Row Principle	Place rigor on the row of a Rule Family.	The populated cells playing the role of conditions infer the corresponding populated cells playing the role of a conclusion.
5	The Conclusion Principle	Place rigor on the conclusion fact type of a Rule Family.	A Rule Family has only one conclusion fact type.
6	The Conditions Principle	Place rigor on condition fact types of a Rule Family.	All populated condition cells must be true for the conclusion cell to be true. A Rule Family must have at least one Rule Pattern. The whole condition key of a Rule Pattern can be empty if there is only one Rule Pattern in the Rule Family. The condition key of a Rule Pattern cannot be partially empty unless the whole condition key is empty. A conclusion in a Rule Pattern should not depend on a partial condition key.
7	The Connection Principle	Place rigor on the connections among Rule Families.	A Rule Family has an inferential relationship with another Rule Family when the conclusion fact type of the latter serves as a condition fact type in the former.

Table 12.2 The Decision Model Principles (Continued)

#	Principle Name	Purpose	Principle
The Declarative Principles			
8	Declarative Heading Principle	Remove unnecessary procedural constraints from the heading of a Rule Family.	The fact types in the heading of a Rule Family are unordered.
9	Declarative Body Principle	Remove unnecessary procedural constraints from the body of a Rule Family.	The entries in the body of a Rule Family are unordered. (Duplicate rows in a Rule Family are not allowed.)
10	Declarative Inferential Relationship Principle	Remove unnecessary procedural constraints from the Rule Family inferential relationships.	There is no implied sequence in the path among Rule Families related through inferential relationships.
The Integrity Principles			
11	Rule Pattern Transitive Conditions Principle	Remove redundancies among Rule Pattern conditions.	There are no inferential dependencies within a Rule Pattern condition key.
12	Rule Family and Rule Pattern Consistency Principle	Remove inconsistencies within a Rule Pattern and among overlapping Rule Patterns.	A Rule Family should be free of inconsistencies within each Rule Pattern and among Rule Patterns: • In general, a Rule Pattern should result in at most one conclusion value for any set of valid input values for the condition fact types. • The conditions of a Rule Pattern need cover only the subset of the condition fact type domains that are within scope.

(*Continued*)

Table 12.2 The Decision Model Principles (Continued)

#	Principle Name	Purpose	Principle
			• Within one Rule Pattern, an overlapping condition key coverage means inconsistency exists in the Rule Pattern.
			• Across two Rule Patterns in the same Rule Family, an overlapping condition key coverage often means inconsistency exists in the Rule Family.
			• A Rule Family must result in at least one conclusion value for any set of valid input values for condition fact types.
			• A Rule Family can result in more than one conclusion value for any set of valid input values for condition fact types.
			• The conclusions in a Rule Family need cover only the subset of the conclusion fact type's domain that is within scope.
13	Rule Family Transitive Conditions Principle	Remove redundancies among Rule Families.	There are no inferential dependencies among inferentially related Rule Families.
14	Inferential Integrity Principle	Ensure completeness of inferential relationships among Rule Families.	There are no conclusions in a supporting Rule Family that are not covered by the corresponding dependent Rule Family.
15	Business Alignment Principle	Attach responsibility and metrics for tangible business results to a Decision Model.	A Decision Model directly aligns with business directions and metrics for measuring progress.

Table 12.3 Normal Form in the Decision Model

Form	Description
First Normal Decision Model Form	A Rule Family is in first normal form if, in terms of its tabular picture, each Rule Family row cannot be decomposed into more than one row reaching the conclusion.
Second Normal Decision Model Form	A Rule Pattern is in second normal form if the conclusion is fully functionally dependent (i.e., inferentially dependent) on the entire condition key.
Third Normal Decision Model Form	A Rule Pattern is in third normal form if none of the conditions in a second normal form Rule Pattern are transitively functionally dependent (i.e. inferentially dependent) on other conditions.

from the notation for other kinds of models. Second, the notation must make visible the inherent properties of the Decision Model as described in its principles.

This section presents a notation that has been easy to use by all practitioners. There are two kinds of diagrams in this notation: a Decision Model diagram and a Rule Family table.

The Decision Model Diagram

The Decision Model diagram is composed of four shapes (or symbols), based on the major components of the Decision Model. These are the business decision shape, the business decision connector shape, the Rule Family shape, and the inferential relationship line.

The Business Decision Shape

The business decision shape is an octagon, displaying a label with the name of the business decision in text form, as displayed in Figure 12.1.

The Business Decision Connector

The business decision connector connects the business decision shape to the Decision Rule Family shape. The business decision connector is shown in Figure 12.2. The business decision connector has no label. The business decision connector has no terminator shape on the end that connects to the business decision, but has an arrow on the end that connects to the Decision Rule Family.

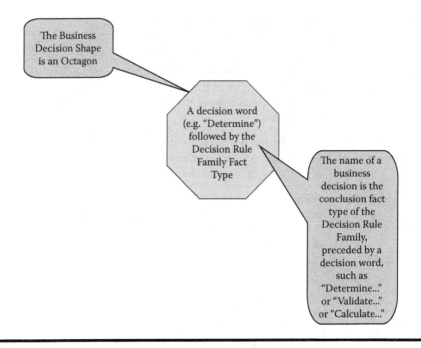

Figure 12.1 The business decision shape.

The Rule Family Shape

The Rule Family shape represents each Rule Family in a Decision Model and is shown in Figure 12.3. The Rule Family conclusion fact type is the name of the Rule Family, and this is the label at the top of the Rule Family shape. Below the Rule Family name is a solid line dividing the conclusion fact type from a list of condition fact types. The fact types comprising the inferential keys of all the Rule Patterns in the Rule Family (that is, all the fact types that have dependencies on other Rule Families) are listed first, followed by a further dividing line, this one being a broken, or dashed line. Below the dashed line appears a list of condition fact types that do not have dependencies on any other Rule Family, representing fact types of known fact values. These are the fact values that may be found in persistent

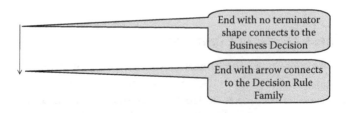

Figure 12.2 The business decision connector.

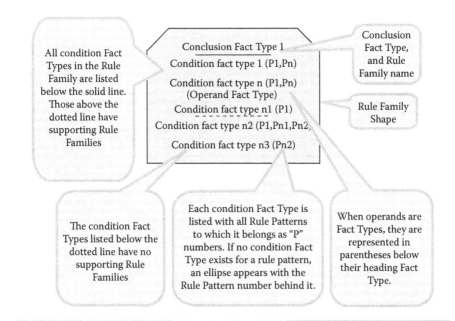

Figure 12.3   The Rule Family shape.

data, user inputs, or another source of known values. Each condition fact type has appended, in parentheses, the Rule Pattern numbers to which it belongs. If there is no condition fact type present in a Rule Family, an ellipse is shown in the place of the fact type, with the Rule Pattern number appended in parentheses. When the operand in a condition or a conclusion cell happens to be a fact type (as opposed to a fact value), then that fact type is noted in parentheses directly below the header fact type. If the operand is a formula, then each and every fact type in the formula is listed in parentheses below the fact type in the header.

The Inferential Relationship Line

The inferential relationships among Rule Families are shown in the Decision Model diagram by the inferential relationship line, as shown in Figure 12.4. This line does

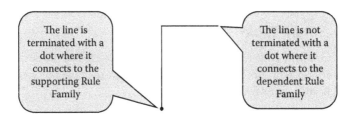

Figure 12.4   Inferential relationship line.

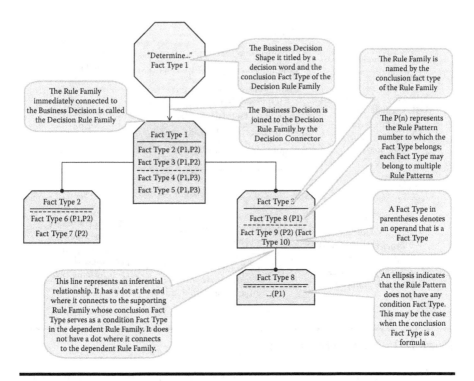

Figure 12.5   The Decision Model Diagram.

not require a label. There is no terminator of the line where it connects to the dependent Rule Family. However, the line is terminated with a dot where it connects to the supporting Rule Family.

Integrating the Shapes into a Diagram

The Decision Model Diagram depicts the structure of all Rule Families in a Decision Model, the business decision, and all the inferential relationships. This is illustrated in Figure 12.5.

The Rule Family Table

Table 12.4 contains a Rule Family table. A Rule Family table is the detailed view of the Rule Family, a two-dimensional populated structure made up of columns and rows with a heading for each column.

- ■ The heading of a column is Fact Type.
- ■ There may be zero to many condition columns.

Table 12.4   Rule Family Table

> There is a single conclusion column with a single fact type in the heading

	Conditions		Conclusion
Rule Pattern	Fact Type 1	Fact Type n	Fact Type
1	Operator | Operand: Fact Value, Fact Type, or formula	Operator | Operand: Fact Value or Fast Type	Operator | Operand: Fact Value, Fact Type, or formula
n	Operator | Operand: Fact Value, Fact Type, or formula		Operator | Operand: Fac Value, Fast T e, or formula

> A column in the Rule Family table consists of assertions about the column heading's fact type. Each cell contains an operator and operand appropriate to the fact type in the heading.

> A row in the Rule Family table is a business logic statement.

- There must be exactly one conclusion column.
- The body of a column represents an operator and operand of the fact type in the heading of the column; it is an assertion about the fact type in the heading.
- The operator is one that makes business sense for the fact type, and the operand is a value taken from the domain for each fact type or another fact type or a computational formula.
- The interpretation of a row is that the truth values of the assertions in its condition columns lead to the truth value of the assertion in its conclusion column.
- The condition assertions are joined by an implied AND.
- Ideally, the Rule Family conforms to the 15 principles of the Decision Model.

Rule Pattern Representation

A Rule Pattern is a set of Rule Family rows with a common set of condition cells that are populated. Stated another way, it is a set of rows that have common populated fact types in their condition columns. Table 12.5 illustrates four Rule Patterns. A Rule Pattern is said to be complete when all the condition values required to know the conclusion are present in the Rule Family.

Table 12.5 Rule Patterns

Rule Pattern	Conditions — Fact Type 1 (Operator)	Conditions — Fact Type 1	Conditions — Fact Type n (Operator)	Conditions — Fact Type n	Conditions — Fact Type n.. (Operator)	Conditions — Fact Type n..	Conclusion — Fact Type (Operator)	Conclusion — Fact Type
1	Operator	Fact type, value, or formula					Operator	Fact type, value, or formula
1	Operator	Fact type, value, or formula					Operator	Fact type, value, or formula
1	Operator	Fact type, value, or formula					Operator	Fact type, value, or formula
3	Operator	Fact type, value, or formula			Operator	Fact type, value, or formula	Operator	Fact type, value, or formula
2			Operator	Fact type, value, or formula	Operator	Fact type, value, or formula	Operator	Fact type, value, or formula
2			Operator	Fact type, value, or formula	Operator	Fact type, value, or formula	Operator	Fact type, value, or formula
2			Operator	Fact type, value, or formula	Operator	Fact type, value, or formula	Operator	Fact type, value, or formula
4			Operator	Fact type, value, or formula			Operator	Fact type, value, or formula
3	Operator	Fact type, value, or formula			Operator	Fact type, value, or formula	Operator	Fact type, value, or formula

Summary

The definition of the Decision Model in this chapter serves as a quick reference to the Decision Model. However, the 15 principles in the second section constitute the definitive rigor of the model. Alternative forms of notation, terms, and definition of terms may represent the Decision Model, provided they comply with its principles.

COMMENTARIES

This section is a collection of supplementary material. The chapters cover technical topics, topics of general business interest, and topics related to practice. Therefore, the section is divided naturally into three subsections: Technology Topics, General Business Topics, and Practitioner Insight Topics.

Some of the chapters are provided by recognized leaders in their areas who have given thought to the impact of the Decision Model.

Technology Topics

Chapter 13, "Enterprise Architecture: Managing Complexity and Change," by John Zachman.

This chapter explains the ideas behind the Framework for Enterprise Architecture. It walks the reader through the framework which is a background for understanding the opportunities that the Decision Model provides to Enterprise Architects (covered in Chapter 14).

Chapter 14, "Opportunities in Enterprise Architecture," by Larry Goldberg and Barbara von Halle. This chapter explores the role of the Decision Model in Enterprise Architecture, starting with the Zachman Framework and addressing other frameworks.

Chapter 15, "Service Oriented Architectures," by Mike Rosen. This chapter significantly expands on Chapter 5 by delving into SOA details, along with ideas for the use of the Decision Model in SOA.

Chapter 16, "Specifications, Standards, Practices and the Decision Model," by Larry Goldberg and Barbara von Halle. This chapter covers questions that arise when considering the Decision Model. How does it fit into current and emerging specifications, standards, and practices? While not exhaustive, this chapter deals with several of these and considers the fit of the Decision Model. The chapter considers business planning, business process modeling, business logic and business rule modeling, information modeling, system development methodologies, and system transformation.

Chapter 17, "Integrating the Decision Model with BPMN," by Bruce Silver. This chapter provides a clear understanding of the appropriate way by which the Decision Model should be integrated into BPMN.

Chapter 18, "The Case for the Physical Decision Mode," by Daniel Worden. Many Decision Models will be implemented in one technology or another or in several. This chapter explores considerations for the technologists who will be responsible for such a deployment.

General Business Topics

Chapter 19, "Enterprise Decision Management and the Decision Model," by James Taylor. This chapter builds on the ideas introduced in Chapter 4. It presents a comprehensive background of Enterprise Decision Management and reviews the role of Decision Model in EDM.

Chapter 20, "Introducing the Business Decision Maturity Model," by Barbara von Halle and Larry Goldberg. This chapter provides an overview of the original Rule Maturity Model as the means by which organizations assessed current and target states of maturity for business rule management. The chapter provides a new, more appropriate measure of maturity, the Business Decision Maturity Model, and sets out the means of assessing that maturity.

Chapter 21, "The Decision Model and Enterprise 2.0 – Enabling Collaboration," by Brian Stucky.

The chapter explores the impact on the evolving enterprise of the Decision Model in the light of Web 2.0 and other advances in collaboration.

Practitioner Insight Topics

Chapter 22, "A Management Perspective," by David Haslett and Tracy Matthias. This chapter covers the introduction of the Decision Model into the enterprise, and the impact of that introduction.

Chapter 23, "Better! Cheaper! Faster!" byDavid Pedersen. This chapter is a case study of the introduction of the Decision Model into a project. It discloses the positive impact of changing from the classic business rules approach to the Decision Model approach. Readers can find more information on the Decision Model at www.TheDecisionModel.com.

Chapter 13

Enterprise Architecture
Managing Complexity and Change

John Zachman*

The Zachman Framework is the seed, the original kernel from which grew the discipline of Enterprise Architecture. In this chapter, John Zachman traces the process that led him to the discovery of the framework and sets out its general principles. He then considers the role of Business Rules in the Enterprise Architecture, based on the framework. This chapter provides the theoretical foundation for the discussion about the role of the Decision Model in Enterprise Architecture that is found in Chapter 14.

It is my perception that Enterprise Architecture presently is a grossly misunderstood concept among management professionals, probably for several reasons, the principal one likely being that Enterprise Architecture is seen to be an information technology, or systems issue, not a management issue. Enterprise Architecture tends to surface in the enterprise through the information systems community, and the information systems people seem to have some skills to do Enterprise Architecture if any Enterprise Architecture is being done or is to be done in the enterprise.

However, the origins of the concept come from Robert Anthony's *Planning and Control Systems: A Framework for Analysis* (Anthony, 1965); Jay Forrester's *Industrial Dynamics* (Forrester, 1961); Eric Helfert's *Techniques of Financial Analysis* (Helfert, 1962); Peter Drucker's *The Practice of Management* (Drucker, 1954); George Steiner's *Comprehensive Managerial Planning* (Steiner, 1972); and more recently, Peter Senge's *The Fifth Discipline* (Senge, 1990), to name but a few. These works have nothing to do with information technology or information-related issues per se. The basic concept of Enterprise Architecture is that it is important to understand the enterprise before attempting to overlay infrastructure investments required to support the enterprise and to facilitate its ongoing change, because unless engineered correctly, infrastructure (including information systems) tends to be extremely costly and resistant to change.

Reviewing Alvin Toffler's books about change, first, "knowledge is change ... and the ever-increasing body of knowledge feeding the great engine of technology creates ever increasing change" (Toffler, 1970). The rate of change is increasing dramatically and putting extreme pressure on reducing time to market to accommodate the rapid change. Second, the Industrial Age was different from the Agricultural Age, and the Information Age is different from the Industrial Age (Toffler, 1970). The implication of this is, the game has changed—dramatically. Third, if you give everyone access to the same information at the same time, the power will shift outboard in the enterprise (Toffler, 1990). No longer will power be concentrated in two or three people at the top who know everything, decide everything, control everything. In fact, if the customer (or recipient of the product or service) of the enterprise has access to the same information that the enterprise has access to, the power will shift into the customer environment. It will become "market driven."

The practical implications of these observations are, first, the complexity of the enterprise will continue to escalate. The moment you say, "customer relationship management," or "one-on-one marketing," or "a market of one," etc., you are signing up for orders-of-magnitude increases in complexity. That is, the day you have to treat each customer as an individual (rather than as a group or a segment or a type), you are talking about major increases in complexity.

This is a fundamental change in the Industrial Age concept of the enterprise. In the Industrial Age, the basic idea was to get a good product or service and then find a lot of customers to sell it to. That is, from the perspective of the enterprise, the individual customers were undifferentiated within the market. By default, the customer had to deal with the complexity of "integration" of the enterprise products or services. In contrast, the basic idea of the Information Age is to find a good customer and then identify and provide whatever products or services are required to keep that customer a good customer. That is, from the perspective of the customer, the enterprise products have to be integrated. In the case of services, it is the enterprise itself that has to be integrated. In the Information Age case, it is the enterprise that has to deal with the complexity of integration. If the "Powershift" (Toffler, 1990) takes place (which I am sure will take place if you want to stay in the new, Information Age game), the burden of integration will transfer to the supplier. The customer wants to see the enterprise products or the enterprise itself customized to the interest of the customer.

Another practicality of the changing game is reduced time to market. That is, there will be less and less time from the moment the enterprise receives an order until it fulfills the order for a product or service customized for the customer. As the rate of change continues to escalate (Toffler, 1970), the time to market for whatever the enterprise produces will tend to shrink. In fact, if the rate of change goes to infinity, the time to market will go to zero. This is the case where the customer is unable to define the characteristics of the product or service they have to take delivery on until the point in time that they have to take delivery.

From an information technology perspective, the practical implication of extreme complexity and extremely high rates of change is that the enterprise will be unable to define the characteristics of the implementation they need to take delivery on until the point in time they need to take delivery. The requirement will be for enterprisewide, integrated implementations for immediate delivery.

The business-significant characteristics of the Information Age are dramatic escalation of complexity and dramatic escalation of the rate of change. The management question is, how do you intend to deal with orders-of-magnitude increases in complexity and orders-of-magnitude increases in the rate of change? If you review the 7000 years of known history, the only device humanity has come up with so far to deal with complexity and change is *architecture*.

First, regarding complexity, if it (whatever "it" is) gets so complex, you can't remember everything about it at one time, you have to learn how to describe it before you can create it. If somebody hadn't figured out how to describe buildings, we would still be living in log cabins. If somebody hadn't figured out how to describe automobiles, we'd still be riding around on horses. If somebody hadn't figured out how to describe airplanes, we'd still be traveling in covered wagons. If somebody hadn't figured out how to describe computers, we'd still be using an abacus or adding up columns of numbers with pencils and paper. And so on. In the Industrial Age, we learned that there is a set of descriptive representations required to describe a complex industrial product including, among other things, drawings, functional specs, bills of material, etc., that is, *architecture*.

Regarding change, once you get a complex product created and want to change it, you start with the architecture: the drawings, the functional specs, the bills of materials, etc. If you have no architecture and you want to change something (building, airplane, computer, etc.), there are only three possible options: (1) You can change it by trial and error and see what happens. This is the high-risk option, in that you could make a rather small change and potentially cause irreparable damage. (2) You can reverse-engineer the architecture, the drawings, the functional specs, the bills of material, etc. to serve as a basis for changing it. That takes time and costs money. (3) Or, you could scrap the whole thing and start over again, building a new, changed version. The point is, architecture is the baseline for changing anything that is already in existence, and if you have no architecture, you are either going to have to create or recreate the architecture or risk scrapping the product.

In the Industrial Age, industrial products were increasing in complexity and changing. If we (humanity) had not figured out how to describe complex industrial products, we still would be in the Industrial Age and we would not have Boeing 747s, 100-story buildings, ocean liners, supercomputers, etc. It has only been in the last 50 years or so that we have figured out how to exploit these very sophisticated descriptive representations of industrial products to produce "custom products, mass-produced in quantities of one for immediate delivery."* This idea of "mass customization" is still relatively new even in manufacturing. However, as the Information Age wears on and customers want (or need) their products to be integrated to their unique requirements in very short periods of time, I expect that mass customization will be the rule, not the exception, for industrial products and enterprises.

In the Information Age, it is not only the industrial product that is increasing in complexity and changing, but also the enterprise. The question for the Information Age is, what is architecture relative to enterprises? This may well be the issue of the century. In fact, I wrote an article at the turn of the century entitled, "Enterprise Architecture: The Issue of the Century" (Zachman, 1997).

I would submit, if you (the enterprise) do not have an Enterprise Architecture strategy, you likely don't have a strategy for addressing orders-of-magnitude increases in complexity and orders-of-magnitude increases in the rate of change. I am confident that complexity and change are the characteristics of the Information Age, and that "the Enterprises that can accommodate the concepts of Enterprise Architecture are likely to be the survivors and those that don't are likely to be the rest" (Zachman, 1997).

I have spent more than 35 years of my professional life trying to figure out what architecture looks like relative to enterprises. If I have done anything of value, my contribution has been in the form of a framework, a framework for Enterprise Architecture. The framework for Enterprise Architecture simply defines what Enterprise Architecture looks like. How I figured this out is not mysterious. I went back to the Industrial Age products and tried to understand what architecture was relative to industrial products, and then I simply assigned enterprise names to the set of design artifacts that were created for describing anything, including enterprises.

---

* This is the definition of "mass customization."

It turns out that architecture is architecture is architecture. It doesn't matter what the architecture is for: buildings, airplanes, automobiles, computers, whatever. The underlying order of the descriptive representations is the same. This is a very, very brief discussion of a very complex subject.* In fact, I have written an entire book (Zachman, 1987) on this subject. However, for the purposes of this chapter, briefly, the descriptive representations (the architecture) fall into a two-dimensional classification system.

The Interrogative dimension, a single abstraction of the following:

> WHAT the product is made of: the material composition, the parts that have to be in inventory to create the product, the bill of materials
> HOW the product works: the transformation of raw material and energy, the functional specs
> WHERE the parts are located relative to one another: the geometry, the drawings
> WHO does what work: the operating instructions
> WHEN do things happen: the machine cycles, the timing diagrams
> WHY do they happen: the engineering design objectives

The Audience dimension, a single audience for whom each Interrogative is framed:

> SCOPE: setting the boundary, the limits of each abstraction
> OWNER: the needed concepts of the end result, the Requirements
> DESIGNER: the systematic logic to realize the concepts, the Schematics
> BUILDER: the technology constructs to build the product, the Blueprints
> SUB-CONTRACTOR: the production tool configuration for the Components
> OPERATOR: the end result—this is no longer architecture (i.e., a description); it is an instance of the Product, the end result

This two-dimensional classification system is typically depicted as a framework with the Interrogatives (abstractions) appearing as the columns and the Audience perspectives appearing as the rows. Because each column (Interrogative) is unique and varies independently from all the other columns and because each row is unique and varies independently from the row above and from the row below, the framework, the Zachman Framework, is not simply a matrix. It is a schema, a

---

* Boeing 747s are complex, and architecture for Boeing 747s is complex. Enterprises are even more complex than Boeing 747s and, therefore, Enterprise Architecture is going to be a very complex subject. People tend not to want to hear that enterprises are complex, but I would be less than honest if I didn't point this out. The whole reason for engineering anything is to make whatever you are engineering as simple as possible—but no simpler. ("Everything should be made as simple as possible, but no simpler."— Albert Einstein)

"normalized" schema. Only one fact can go in one cell, that is, one "meta-entity" can only be classified in a single cell.*

Although I learned about the underlying schema empirically by looking at the engineering design artifacts, the descriptive representations of Industrial Age products, my interest was in Enterprise Architecture, so I simply assigned enterprise names to the same engineering design artifacts that were relevant for describing airplanes, buildings, computers, anything. Figure 13.1 is the framework for Enterprise Architecture, the Zachman Framework as it presently is depicted.

The meta-entities and the meta-meta-entities have appeared at the bottom of each cell of the Framework since its inception. I have changed some of the words since I first created the graphic around 1980. The schema itself has not changed, nor will it ever change. In fact, the classification on either axis of the framework has been employed by humanity unchanged for hundreds if not thousands of years. There are two reasons for my changes of some, actually few, of the words in the graphic. First, our understanding of the schema in 1980 was limited, and some of the words I selected did not accurately represent the classification concepts. Second, and unfortunately, I came from the information community and therefore some of the words I selected came from my information systems vocabulary.† This has contributed to some of the misunderstanding of Enterprise Architecture as an information technology issue as opposed to the correct understanding that it is an enterprise issue.

Because each cell of the framework is unique and because it can contain only two meta-entities, the meta-entity that constitutes the focus of the cell description and its relationship with itself (the other meta-entity), I call each instance of a cell model a primitive model. The raw material for doing engineering is the engineering design artifacts for the complex product. For engineering an enterprise, the framework cell descriptions, the primitive models, are the raw material for doing enterprise engineering. In fact, I would observe, if there are no primitive models for any given enterprise, that enterprise has not been engineered. It has simply happened.

In contrast, implementations require components from more than one cell, composite models as opposed to primitive models. A primitive model is not

---

* For the nontechnical reader: you don't have to be intimidated by the words *schema, normalization,* or *meta-entity*. The schema is just a two-dimensional classification system that can be depicted in a matrix form, rows and columns. Normalization simply means that the classification system is "clean"—that is, there are no "apples and oranges" or mixtures in any cell of the matrix. And meta-entity is an abstraction that you need if you want to store something in a database. In the case of Enterprise Architecture, you *will* want to store the models in a database—trust me.

† We have been working with some linguists from SIL International for nearly five years to identify words that more accurately convey the concepts of the framework schema and to employ words that are more business-oriented than technology-oriented. In November 2005 we published the new standard meta model for the framework at www.ZachmanInternational. com. Although the new standards are available at no cost, they are distributed on a CD that contains my book among some other things, and the CD must be registered to be opened.

	DATA — *What*	FUNCTION — *How*	NETWORK — *Where*	PEOPLE — *Who*	TIME — *When*	MOTIVATION — *Why*	
SCOPE (CONTEXTUAL) / *Planner*	List of Things Important to the Business; ENTITY = Class of Business Thing	List of Processes the Business Performs; Process = Class of Business Process	List of Locations in which the Business Operates; Node = Major Business Location	List of Organizations Important to the Business; People = Major Organization Unit	List of Events/Cycles Significant to the Business; Time = Major Business Event/Cycle	List of Business Goals/Strategies; Ends/Means = Major Business Goal/Strategy	**SCOPE (CONTEXTUAL)** / *Planner*
BUSINESS MODEL (CONCEPTUAL) / *Owner*	e.g. Semantic Model; Ent = Business Entity, Reln = Business Relationship	e.g. Business Process Model; Proc. = Business Process, I/O = Business Resources	e.g. Business Logistics System; Node = Business Location, Link = Business Linkage	e.g. Work Flow Model; People = Organization Unit, Work = Work Product	e.g. Master Schedule; Time = Business Event, Cycle = Business Cycle	e.g. Business Plan; End = Business Objective, Means = Business Strategy	**BUSINESS MODEL (CONCEPTUAL)** / *Owner*
SYSTEM MODEL (LOGICAL) / *Designer*	e.g. Logical Data Model; Ent = Data Entity, Reln = Data Relationship	e.g. Application Architecture; Proc. = Application Function, I/O = User Views	e.g. Distributed System Architecture; Node = I/S Function (Processor, Storage, etc), Link = Line Characteristics	e.g. Human Interface Architecture; People = Role, Work = Deliverable	e.g. Processing Structure; Time = System Event, Cycle = Processing Cycle	e.g. Business Rule Model; End = Structural Assertion, Means = Action Assertion	**SYSTEM MODEL (LOGICAL)** / *Designer*
TECHNOLOGY MODEL (PHYSICAL) / *Builder*	e.g. Physical Data Model; Ent = Segment/Table/etc., Reln = Pointer/Key/etc.	e.g. System Design; Proc. = Computer Function, I/O = Data Elements/Sets	e.g. Technology Architecture; Node = Hardware/Systems Software, Link = Line Specifications	e.g. Presentation Architecture; People = User, Work = Screen Format	e.g. Control Structure; Time = Execute, Cycle = Component Cycle	e.g. Rule Design; End = Condition, Means = Action	**TECHNOLOGY MODEL (PHYSICAL)** / *Builder*
DETAILED REPRESENTATIONS (OUT-OF-CONTEXT) / *Sub-Contractor*	e.g. Data Definition; Ent = Field, Reln = Address	e.g. Program; Proc. = Language Statement, I/O = Control Block	e.g. Network Architecture; Node = Address, Link = Protocol	e.g. Security Architecture; People = Identity, Work = Job	e.g. Timing Definition; Time = Interrupt, Cycle = Machine Cycle	e.g. Rule Specification; End = Sub-condition, Means = Step	**DETAILED REPRESENTATIONS (OUT-OF-CONTEXT)** / *Sub-Contractor*
FUNCTIONING ENTERPRISE	e.g. DATA	e.g. FUNCTION	e.g. NETWORK	e.g. ORGANIZATION	e.g. SCHEDULE	e.g. STRATEGY	**FUNCTIONING ENTERPRISE**

© John A. Zachman, Zachman International

Figure 13.1 The framework for Enterprises Architecture (The "Zachman Framework".)

implementable. A composite model is made up of components from more than one primitive model. Implementation is manufacturing, not engineering. Primitive models are for engineering. Composite models are for manufacturing.

Maybe a useful metaphor for the framework is the periodic table. It was around 1890 that Mendeleyev published the periodic table, a two-dimensional classification of the chemical elements of the universe. The periodic table classified all of the possible elements even though many of the elements had not yet been discovered. The elements themselves do not exist as elements in nature. In nature, the elements, the primitives, only exist as compounds, that is, as composites of more than one element. The elements of the periodic table are the raw material for doing chemical engineering. Creating compounds is chemical manufacturing. Manufacturing is not engineering. Before Mendeleyev defined the periodic table, there were chemicals (compounds) but there was no chemistry. It was alchemy. Nothing was predictable or repeatable except by personal experience. The Enterprise Framework implications of this metaphor are that although the enterprise is made up of composite implementations, they were not likely engineered. They were created by trial and error based on the experience of the implementers.

If you assume the most robust case, that there is a many-to-many relationship* between any one meta-entity in any one cell and all the other meta-entities in the row as well as a many-to-many relationship between any one meta-entity and the meta-entities of the cell above and the cell below, and if you had populated a data base with primitive models for some enterprise, then you could create virtually any composite implementation for that enterprise simply by (late) binding the primitive components together. That is, you could "mass-customize" the enterprise at the click of a mouse. You could satisfy the demand for virtually any enterprisewide implementation at the point in time the enterprise discovered they needed that implementation.

Please remember that this is a very brief discussion of a very complex subject and that it will likely take some period of time to accumulate some (and possibly, someday, all) of the primitive models. However, hopefully this gives you a sense of the enterprise possibility for addressing orders-of-magnitude increases in complexity and orders-of-magnitude increases in the rate of change by engineering the enterprise (the primitive models) and assembling the enterprise to order (building composites) on demand.

At the time I published the second *IBM Systems Journal* article on my framework in 1992 (Zachman and Sowa, 1992), we felt that Business Rules were classified in the WHY Column (Column 6) and the SYSTEM Row (Row 3). In fact,

---

* For nontechnical readers: a many-to-many relationship simply means that there are two different things that are related to one another but that vary independently of each other. For example, Employees and Positions. They are different. They are related. And, they vary independently.

I named the Column 6, Row 3 cell "e.g., Business Rule Model."* Subsequent to that publication, we have learned much about primitives and composites as well as about Business Rules, and today, I would observe that the focus for identifying and defining the Business Rules may well still be Column 6, Row 3, but the Business Rules themselves are likely complex composite constructs relating meta-entities from more than one cell. Had we known what we know today when the "GUIDE Business Rules Project Final Report" was published in October 1997,† we probably could have anticipated the composite nature of the business rule simply by observing the meta-model described in the report. Clearly, there were meta-entities that would be classified in cells other than simply Column 6, Row 3. Further, the Row 2 Business Rule meta-model that was published in the October 2000 report by the Business Rules Group in October 2000 ("Organizing Business Plans: The Standard Model for Business Rule Motivation") also included meta-entities that would be classified in columns and rows other than and in addition to Column 6, Row 2. The body of knowledge in Enterprise Architecture as well as in Business Rules is presently exploding. There is no better time to be involved in these vital enterprise issues.

I don't think there is any question about whether an enterprise is going to do Enterprise Architecture or not; that is, it is not going to be optional if an enterprise intends to be viable in the Information Age. The only question is, when will they start working on Enterprise Architecture, because there potentially is a lot of work to do—and at the point in time the enterprise is going to need it, it is going to be too late to do it! Business Rules may well be a good place to start working on it.

The original version of this chapter was published in Barbara von Halle and Larry Goldberg's book *The Business Rule Revolution* (von Halle and Goldberg, 2006).

---

* This is consistent with Column 6, Row 3 of the Zachman Framework shown in Figure 13.1.
† Both Barbara von Halle and I were contributors to that report. The project likely spanned more than five years and was probably the first formal publication on the subject of Business Rules.

Chapter 14

Opportunities in Enterprise Architecture

Contents

The Decision Model in EA 331
   The Decision Model in the Zachman Framework 331
      Column 6, Row 1: Scope 334
      Column 6, Row 2: Business Model 334
      Column 6, Row 3: System Model 338
      Column 6, Rows 4 through 6: Technology Model, Detail
      Representation, and Functioning Enterprise..339
      The Benefits of Positioning the Decision Model in the Zachman
      Framework for Enterprise Architecture...340
      Business Governance, the Decision Model, and Row 2 Artifacts 340
   A Summary of the Capabilities of a Decision Model Tool............................341
   The Decision Model and Other EA Approaches in General 343
   The Decision Model in the Federal Enterprise Architecture
   (FEA) Program 343
   The Decision Model in TOGAF 346
The Decision Model in System Architecture...349
   System Architecture 351
      Historical System Architecture 351
      Current System Architecture 352

The Role of the Decision Model in Multi-Tiered System Architecture
with an ESB...354
The Decision Model in MDA...354
The Decision Model in Service-Oriented Architecture......................355
Summary...356

This chapter explores the role of the Decision Model in Enterprise and Systems Architecture and features for a Decision Model tool. The latter includes the means by which the Decision Model is the basis for automatic generation of business logic in business systems.

Because the Zachman Framework for Enterprise Architecture (EA) is the EA standard, the chapter begins by positioning the Decision Model in that framework. This includes the connections between the Decision Model and other framework artifacts. The chapter also investigates two major representative EA methodologies and the opportunities the Decision Model offers to practitioners of these methodologies.

Drilling into System Architecture, the chapter explores the role of the Decision Model in Model-Driven Architecture (MDA): OMG's specification for architecture models that can be transformed into working systems. It is here that the Decision Model offers significant opportunities for delivering models to generate decision services. In both enterprise and systems architecture, the Decision Model is a solution that has not been available to the architect. This chapter is appropriate for enterprise and systems architects or readers who are familiar with the Zachman Framework, or who have read Chapter 13.

The Decision Model provides a significant opportunity for advances in information technology. One obvious opportunity is the emergence of a Decision Model tool that enables creation and maintenance of Decision Models by businesspeople with point-and-click convenience.

However, a related, and perhaps best, use of the Decision Model is to serve as the foundation for automatic or assisted deployment of business logic into digitized business systems. Fully realized, this opportunity implies that the business logic contained in a Decision Model is automatically generated into business system code. This direct generation of code ensures the greatest degree of fidelity of the business system to business requirements, potentially reducing development and testing time, cost, and risk. Other opportunities flow from this level of automation. These include introduction of feedback loops that measure business outcomes against business objective and provide autonomic, heuristic adjustment in the business logic while the system is in operation. This is called "adaptive control and optimization," and is the realm of an advanced practice of Business Decision Management (BDM) (or Enterprise Decision Management [EDM])*.

But such opportunities represent the finish line for the Decision Model in information technology. This chapter first explores the role of the Decision Model in every aspect of information technology to provide an appreciation of the full scope of opportunity. Fortunately, there is a mechanism called enterprise architecture (EA) for understanding every aspect of an enterprise and its information technology. The techniques of EA lead to decomposition of the enterprise, identification of where business logic currently guides the business, and a means for determining where Decision Models should be deployed.

As this chapter journeys through EA, the opportunity becomes apparent for a Decision Model tool (or perhaps tools).

The Decision Model in EA

Architecture is defined as "the fundamental organization of a system, embodied in its components, their relationships to each other and the environment, and the principles governing its design and evolution" (ISO, 2007). In the case of EA, the system is an operating business.

The goal of EA, then, is to define an operating business by decomposing it into its basic components, determine how they relate to each other, and define standards and guidelines by which they work alone and in unison. Also, because information technology is a crucial aspect of operating businesses today, EA addresses the delivery of enterprise components in information technology, when doing so is appropriate.

Operating businesses today are complicated, and so the representation of an operating business's components usually requires an EA framework that encompasses different types of components and their connections to each other. The goal of this chapter is to position the Decision Model within EA to leverage it across all components of an operating business.

The Decision Model in the Zachman Framework

The original EA Framework was invented by John Zachman, who is referred to as the father of EA. The Zachman Framework for Enterprise Architecture (i.e., the

---

* Chapter 19 has a detailed explanation of the ideas and methodologies of EDM.

Zachman Framework) remains a principal reference for most EA approaches. Its utility and longevity proves that it is a complete decomposition of an enterprise into its constituent interrogative perspectives (i.e., who, what, where, how, when, and why) and audience perspective (i.e., planner, owner, designer, builder, subcontractor, and operator). This chapter refers to the interrogative perspectives as dimensions and the audience perspectives as views.

The Zachman Framework is not a methodology for developing EA for a particular enterprise. That role is played by other EA approaches such as the Federal Enterprise Architecture (FEA), the Department of Defense Architectural Framework (DoDAF), The Open Group's Architectural Framework (TOGAF), and others. But all of them derive from the original idea of, and most provide a mapping to, the Zachman Framework. It follows then that the Zachman Framework is an obvious starting point for positioning the Decision Model within EA. Most audiences will be able to map this positioning into their chosen approach for EA.*

The Zachman Framework for Enterprise Architecture consists of six columns representing the dimensions and six rows representing the views, and therefore, 36 cells. Each of the 36 cells contains content that is unique to the cell and cannot (i.e., must not) be found in any other cell. In other words, the Zachman Framework is a normalized schema of EA artifacts because it disallows unnecessary duplication of content among cells. Zachman calls the cell content primitives. Primitives connect orthogonally to all primitives in the same row and to primitives immediately above and below them in the column.

This book's modification to the Zachman Framework, shown in Figure 14.1, positions the Decision Model in Column 6. Only three of the six Zachman Framework columns are included in this figure, to illustrate connections from the Decision Model to artifacts in those columns. Although there are connections from the Decision Model to artifacts in the columns not included, the connections from the Decision Model to the columns for WHAT (Data) and HOW (Function) are most interesting. To the right of the modified Zachman Framework in Figure 14.1 is an annotation representing the correlation to the Object Management Group's (OMG) Model-Driven Architecture (MDA) stack (Frankel et al., 2003) discussed later.

To leverage the full potential of the Decision Model, Figure 14.1 contains necessary modifications to the cell titles and meta-entities of the first three rows of Column 6 in the original Zachman Framework. The other rows and columns need no modifications for the Decision Model. The positioning of the Decision

---

* The Zachman Framework for Enterprise Architecture is described in detail by John Zachman in Chapter 13.

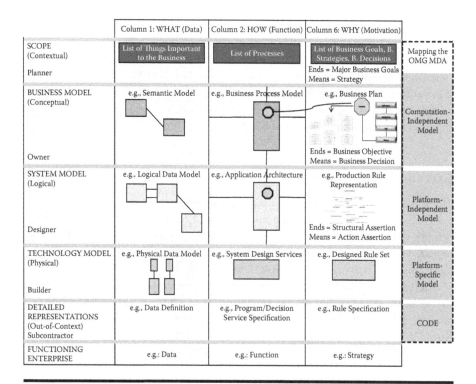

	Column 1: WHAT (Data)	Column 2: HOW (Function)	Column 6: WHY (Motivation)	
SCOPE (Contextual) Planner	List of Things Important to the Business	List of Processes	List of Business Goals, B. Strategies, B. Decisions Ends = Major Business Goals Means = Strategy	Mapping the OMG MDA
BUSINESS MODEL (Conceptual) Owner	e.g., Semantic Model	e.g., Business Process Model	e.g., Business Plan Ends = Business Objective Means = Business Decision	Computation-Independent Model
SYSTEM MODEL (Logical) Designer	e.g., Logical Data Model	e.g., Application Architecture	e.g., Production Rule Representation Ends = Structural Assertion Means = Action Assertion	Platform-Independent Model
TECHNOLOGY MODEL (Physical) Builder	e.g., Physical Data Model	e.g., System Design Services	e.g., Designed Rule Set	Platform-Specific Model
DETAILED REPRESENTATIONS (Out-of-Context) Subcontractor	e.g., Data Definition	e.g., Program/Decision Service Specification	e.g., Rule Specification	CODE
FUNCTIONING ENTERPRISE	e.g.: Data	e.g.: Function	e.g.: Strategy	

Figure 14.1 The Decision Model in the Zachman Framework. (Source: Adapted from John Zachman's "The Framework for Enterprise Architecture (The Zachman Framework)" and Frankel et al., "The Zachman Framework and the OMG's Model Driven Architecture." BP Trends Whitepaper, 2003. Used with permission.)

Model in Column 6 is aligned with Zachman's positioning of business rules in Column 6:

> "At the time I published the second *IBM Systems Journal* article on my Framework in 1992 (Zachman and Sowa, 1992), we felt that Business Rules were classified in the WHY Column (Column 6) and the SYSTEM Row (Row 3). In fact, I named the Column 6, Row 3 Cell 'e.g., Business Rule Model.' Subsequent to that publication, we have learned much about primitives and composites as well as about Business Rules and today, I would observe that the focus for identifying and defining the Business Rules may well still be Column 6, Row 3 but the Business Rules themselves are likely complex composite constructs relating meta-entities from more than one Cell." (Zachman, 2006a).

Indeed, as he foretold, this chapter positions the Decision Model as a complex composite in Column 6, the WHY (Motivation) column.

The following sections examine each cell in Column 6, row by row, to understand the cell's unique content with respect to the Decision Model and corresponding features of a Decision Model tool. Although such an ideal tool does not exist at the time of this writing, readers will recognize the opportunity for adding such functionality to existing tools or seeking it in new, emerging tools.

Column 6, Row 1: Scope

The audience perspective for Row 1 is the planner for the purpose of setting boundaries on the business and scoping all or parts of it. Therefore, Row 1 represents primitives that are to be included in scoping an enterprise if all six dimensions are included in the scope. The role of the Decision Model in Row 1 is to contribute a mechanism for scoping an enterprise's Decision Models.

Cell Content. Row 1 in the Zachman Framework prescribes the creation of lists of items related to the column dimension. For Column 6, this includes business goals and strategies. So, naturally, Figure 14.1 modifies the Zachman Framework Row 1 Column 6 to include a list of business decisions. This is a list of business decisions within scope that support the goals and strategies in Column 6 and relates to lists in the other columns. In that way, the list of business decisions is connected to all items in its audience perspective. So, an initial list of business decisions at Row 1 may be driven by an understanding of the list of business processes, events, goals and strategies, for example.

Decision Model Tool. A Decision Model tool to support deliverables in Row 1 not only captures lists of business goals and strategies, but also of business decisions. The tool uses these lists to frame the Row 2 models so that the list of business decisions is connected to primitives in the row below them. Indeed, today, data modeling and process modeling tools integrate Row 1 lists with their Row 2 deliverables. A Row 1 Decision Model tool that maintains Column 6 lists is very useful to business leaders if it integrates Decision Modeling capability with business planning capability.

Column 6, Row 2: Business Model

The audience for Row 2 is the owner. An owner is a businessperson with ownership or stewardship responsibilities for all or part of the operating business. The purpose of Row 2 is to produce a business model that describes models and architecture relating to the use of products (or services) of the operating business. Therefore, the role of the Decision Model in Row 2 is to serve the business audience and describe the architecture relating to the use of business logic as it relates to the business's products or services.

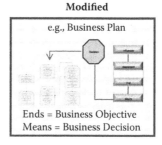

Zachman	Modified
e.g., Business Plan	e.g., Business Plan
End = Business Objective Means = Business Strategy	Ends = Business Objective Means = Business Decision

Figure 14.2 Modifications to Zachman Framework Column 6 Row 2. (Source: Adapted from John Zachman's "The Framework for Enterprise Architecture (The Zachman Framework)". Used with permission.)

Cell Content. Figure 14.2 positions the Decision Model in a modified cell for Column 6 Row 2 along with the Business Motivation Model (BMM),* as published by OMG. This figure shows these two models as a single, integrated model of the Business Plan, of which the Decision Model is the newly discovered component. However, the figure could also have depicted these as two separate models in the cell with a connection between them. Such a separation more easily allows each model, the BMM and the Decision Model, to evolve separately through the standards bodies and be adopted separately by practitioners.

For example, the BMM has already evolved through OMG over several years and hence has undergone scrutiny and refinements. On the other hand, the impact of the Decision Model on standards has only just begun and may proceed at a different rate among different players. Also, many practitioners have utilized the Decision Model in the absence of the BMM and probably vice versa.

Further, most likely the Decision Model in Row 2 has more connections to Column 6 Row 3 and its Row 3 representation to Row 4 than will the BMM. These connections will likely become more apparent as standards emerge in Row 3 for Production Rule Representation (e.g., for Rule Family rows) and in Row 4 for SOA (e.g., for Decision Model or Rule Family services).

The Decision Model in the Row 2 Column 6 cell contains the Decision Rule Family and its dependent Rule Families, together with the Conclusion and Condition Fact Types. Behind the Decision Model are its populated Rule Families. However, in practice, at any point in time, those Rule Families may not be populated or only partly populated. Hence, Rule Patterns may not be evident. Regardless, a Decision Model in Row 2, even before the Rule Families have been populated, has value in both business planning as well as in systems development methodologies, including agile and iterative development.

---

* The BMM is explored in greater detail in Chapter 6.

The Decision Model positions most appropriately in Row 2 because Row 2 serves a the business owner, a role concerned with a pure business perspective in the absence of design constraints. Therefore, positioning the Decision Model in this row emphasizes that the business logic within a Decision Model is a pure business perspective and its Decision Model structure simply reflects the inherent relationships within the business logic based on the logic itself, and not on design preferences or constraints. Further, the inherent relationships are easy for business-people (i.e., the "owners" of the business logic) to understand as the relationships are simply connections from conditions to conclusions, and nothing more than that.

Business process models in Column 2, Row 2 may be represented by a business process model diagram or use case model with business use cases or other techniques. Regardless, the positioning of the Decision Model in Column 6 implies that the business logic of business decisions referenced in Column 2 artifacts is not included in the Column 2 artifacts. Again, this is in line with the original Zachman Framework—the content of each cell is normalized and unique and should not be duplicated unnecessarily in any other cell. Therefore, there are orthogonal connections from the business process models of Column 2 Row 2 to the corresponding Decision Models in Column 6 of the same row.

Column 6 Row 2 may also contain artifacts representing other forms of the business logic statements in the Rule Families. For example, these include various ways to express business logic statements in a business-friendly manner, such as using SVBR or other customized grammar and vocabulary.

The content of Column 2—the WHAT (data) column—Row 2 is a semantic model of the enterprise. Loosely speaking, a semantic model is a representation of the information referenced throughout the enterprise. As such, a semantic model can take many forms, each of which has its own uses, and each of which is understandable to a business owner. The most common forms are a glossary of fact types and definitions, business object model, ontology, fact model, or conceptual data model. Therefore, the modified Zachman Framework prescribes that the fact types in the Decision Models of Column 6 be modeled in a semantic model of Column 1. Again, as the Zachman Framework implies, the semantic model and the Decision Model are unique models, and the content of one should not be buried in the other or found in any other cell. This means that embedding a diagrammatic representation of the business logic on top of a semantic model would not be compliant with the Zachman Framework because such a representation deploys only one kind of model to represent two framework dimensions. So, such a model is not pure in its separation of concerns. For this reason, it is very important for the Column 6 Row 2 cell to contain an artifact (or artifacts) that models the full aspect of business logic in the absence of a model of fact types. Likewise, it is very important that the Column 1 Row 2 cell contain an artifact (or artifacts) that models the full aspect of semantics (e.g., fact types) in the absence of a model of the business logic referencing them.

Applying the modified Zachman Framework for some projects may mean that a glossary of fact type names and definitions suffices as the Row 2 semantic model.

On the other hand, for other projects, it may mean creating an in-depth sophisticated semantic model, such as a business object model, for Row 2. Regardless, the management of the fact type definitions and any model of those fact types is the subject of Column 1, not Column 6. If the fact types in Decision Models in Column 6 have the same names as those in the Column 1 semantic model, the names can serve as the connection between those models. Otherwise, another way to materialize the connection between a Column 6 Decision Model and a Column 1 semantic model is needed.

Decision Model Tool. A Decision Model tool that supports the deliverables of Row 2, Column 6 enables the building and changing of Decision Models. The Decision Model tool also supports rich metadata around each business decision, Rule Family, condition and conclusion fact type, and inferential relationship. The metadata includes status information, stewards, Decision Model versioning, stakeholders, sources of information, implementation and deployment, outstanding issues, and dates relating to development. There would be a distinction between Enterprise Decision Models and project Decision Models, not to mention the ability to compare Decision Models and inherit portions of one Decision Model into another. The tool should also have a comprehensive reporting ability to provide and publish reports and views of business decisions, logic statements, and metadata on an ad hoc and routine basis.

A Row 2 Decision Model tool provides traceability from Decision Models to other artifacts in Row 2, such as business process models and semantic models, perhaps through integration with other tools. The Decision Model tool provides traceability to the lists of business decisions in Row 1 and to artifacts in Row 3. The Decision Model tool enables early assignment of Decision Models or parts of Decision Models to decision services.

A Row 2 Decision Model tool drills from a Rule Family icon in the Decision Model to its populated Rule Family. As a Rule Family is populated, the tool detects Rule Patterns as they emerge as well as provides automated analysis to determine compliance with the 15 principles of the Decision Model. In this way, the integrity of the business logic within the Rule Family is evaluated prior to testing. The tool enforces inferential integrity during Rule Family population.

The Decision Model tool is also capable of translating the business logic rows in a Rule Family into other forms, including natural language statements for use in regulatory filings, publications, and procedure documents. It may create these statements using a particular semantic business vocabulary and grammar such as SVBR. Ideally, business vocabularies in different natural languages are supported and generated.

Essentially, a Row 2 Decision Model tool houses a Computation-Independent Model (CIM)* of the important business logic of the enterprise, along with reasons for that importance.

---

* Computation-Independent Model (CIM), Platform-Independent Model (PIM), and Platform-Specific Model (PSM) are terms of the OMG as part of their Model-Driven Architecture (MDA), and are more fully described in the section titled "The Decision Model in MDA" below.

Zachman	Modified
e.g., Business Rule Model 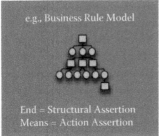 End = Structural Assertion Means = Action Assertion	e.g., Production Rule Representation 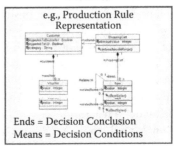 Ends = Decision Conclusion Means = Decision Conditions

Figure 14.3 Modifications to Zachman Framework Column 6 Row 3. (Source: Adapted from John Zachman's "The Framework for Enterprise Architecture (The Zachman Framework)". Used with permission.)

Column 6, Row 3: System Model

The audience for Row 3 is the designer, and the purpose of Row 3 is to produce a system model. A system model is a set of models and architectures used by engineers to mediate between what is desired in Row 2 for products and services and what is technically feasible. Therefore, the role of the Decision Model in Row 3 is to serve the designers in specifying feasibility while still being independent of specific technological solutions.

Cell content. Figure 14.3 shows that the artifacts in Row 3 Column 6 for the Row 2 Decision Model are a Platform-Independent Model (PIM) representation of its Rule Families. At the time of this writing, several organizations are working on such a specification,* including OMG, World Wide Web Consortium (W3C), and RuleML. Each organization has a slightly different focus, resulting in different flavors of approach. Other representations will likely emerge, and more than a single specification may well become widely used.

Decision Model Tool. To support the deliverables of Column 6 Row 3, a Decision Model tool transforms the Row 2 Decision Model into a PIM representation using one or more standard platform-independent languages. Acceptable transformations include models or languages that comply with specifications endorsed by standards bodies. The Row 3 Decision Model tool packages each Decision Model from Row 2 along with a link to the Row 2 semantic model of its fact types into a format that can be visually inspected, exported into standard files types, and imported into Row 4 technology to generate code. Because standards are evolving, and additional ones will emerge in future, the transformation routines that create

---

* These specifications are dealt with at greater length in Chapter 16, in the section titled "Production Rules".

these Row 3 artifacts will be configurable so that customized export requirements are met. Because of the rigor of the Decision Model and the mapping in Row 2 to the semantic model, this flexible transformation capability should be a readily attainable goal for the tool.

Column 6, Rows 4 through 6: Technology Model, Detail Representation, and Functioning Enterprise

The audiences for Rows 4 and 5 are the builder and the subcontractor. The builder and subcontractor produce detailed artifacts for designing, manufacturing, and assembling the target product or service. The audience for Row 6 is the real world because the business operates and interacts within it and externally. The role of the Decision Model in these rows is to materialize the designed, manufactured, and reusable executing business logic integrated with the real-world products and services.

Cell content. Beyond Row 3, the cell contents remain unaltered from the Zachman Framework. The PIM representation from Row 3 of Rule Families is implemented in Row 4 as components necessary for implementation,* whether automated or not.

Decision Model tool. A Decision Model tool that supports the deliverables of Row 4 produces a platform-specific model (PSM) of the PIM in Row 3. When major technologies adopt and support Row 3 standards for the Decision Model (i.e., when such technologies are able to consume standard PIM artifacts), the Decision Model tool will not need to produce this transformation, because the target technology will do so. At the time of this writing, however, this is not the case. Yet, a Decision Model tool that supports Rows 1 through 4 should produce output that can be consumed by specific target technology, and hence exported to and executed by different target technologies.

This transformation is straightforward if the target is a Web services implementation. In this case, the Decision Model tool provides a Web services wrapper to the decision service along with the appropriate code and artifacts required for implementation, such as the Business Object Model (BOM).

If the Decision Model tool provides the Row 4 PSM to the target technology, the Row 4 Decision Model becomes the source of the code. This means that the Decision Model tool should integrate well with life-cycle development environments such as Eclipse,† Microsoft's Visual Studio, and others.

For Decision Models not targeted for automation but used for guidance in manual processes, the Decision Model tool still supports Row 4 deliverables by

---

* See Chapter 16.
† Eclipse Open Source Community, www.eclipse.org.

producing the natural language statements as output from the Row 3 PIM. In this case, the Decision Model tool assembles and publishes these as a document or catalog. Indeed, at the time of this writing, early adopters publish (usually to the Web) the Decision Models and Rule Families for human execution and documentation, and for use as requirements by development teams. Both business and technical readers find these more readable than other documentation.

The Benefits of Positioning the Decision Model in the Zachman Framework for Enterprise Architecture

Prior to the Zachman Framework, the common approach to systems development was to build each system to meet only the particular needs of a specific business area or function, with little thought to the larger business scope. The Zachman Framework renders this thinking quite undesirable. The Zachman Framework reveals that a business is not simply a sum of its departmental organizations. Instead, it functions as an integrated system that is optimized when engineered as a whole. When the enterprise is engineered as a whole, its business systems are designed and operated as a part of that whole. Taking it one step further, today's businesses think and plan for systems of enterprises that are interconnected.

Over the last 20 years, the impact of the Zachman Framework on enterprise and system development has been profound. Most areas of development in business and information technology have been better understood through the lens of the Zachman Framework.

By positioning the Decision Model in the modified Zachman Framework, the business logic of an enterprise is connected to relevant views and domains of the enterprise, such as artifacts for a business plan, business processes, and enterprise ontology. Business objectives in the business plan connect to the business logic through business decisions, and in turn, to the implementation and deployment of corresponding Decision Models. Positioning the Decision Model within an enterprise framework produces a roadmap that delivers important business logic as business levers across the enterprise as a whole.

Business Governance, the Decision Model, and Row 2 Artifacts

There is an important difference that becomes evident between the evolution and governance of the data artifacts and the Decision Model artifacts when they are positioned in the Zachman Framework.

When dealing with the data dimension in Column 1, the database is populated with actual data values in Row 6,* where Row 6 represents the operating database in the enterprise.

---

* This is generally true: however, in some cases "reference data" in lookup tables may be populated earlier. Of course, metadata is part of the earlier row models.

On the other hand, when dealing with the motivation dimension in Column 6, the Decision Model is populated with actual business logic content in Row 2, where Row 2 represents the owner's definition of the business logic. The Decision Model may be implemented as a populated decision base (i.e., a physical storage of Rule Families) or decision service in Row 6, where Row 6 represents the operating decision base in the enterprise.

The difference is where population of values happens. Data values are populated at Row 6 because they are the result of actual enterprise operations. Decision Model values are populated at Row 2 because they are actual Business Decisions that are applied to actual enterprise operations. Further, the population of Decision Model content at Row 2 implies that business governance over the content of Decision Models relates to Row 2 and therefore fits into the owner's (i.e., business's) perspective as opposed to being part of a designer's perspective. This difference emphasizes a changing role of business (versus technical) people in taking responsibility for Decision Model content, possibly before the process of requirements gathering has begun. After all, the Decision Model content is a reflection of business policies and supports business objectives, regardless of process, data, decision service, or other designs.

It also follows that, when viewing the enterprise through the Zachman Framework, it is important to maintain the BMM along with the Decision Models so that the two models remain aligned and synchronized.

The specific content representing the implementation of Decision Models in Rows 4–6 of the Zachman Framework changes over time as technology trends mature. Later, this chapter covers current trends, such as SOA, and the implementation opportunities afforded by the emergence of the Decision Model.

A Summary of the Capabilities of a Decision Model Tool

As indicated earlier, positioning the Decision Model in the Zachman Framework provides a rich context for identifying important capabilities of a Decision Model Tool. Such a tool should support the functionality needed in managing Decision Models for each audience perspective in the Zachman Framework. It also should include linkages from Decision Model artifacts to relevant artifacts in other dimensions or columns. Table 14.1 summarizes these capabilities only for the three Zachman columns that appear in Figure 14.1. The first column in Table 14.1 summarizes support only for the artifacts pertaining to the Decision Model itself. The second and third column summarizes linkages from those artifacts to other artifacts in the same Zachman column and to others in the same Zachman row, different Zachman columns. The linkages to different Zachman columns imply that artifacts in those Zachman columns can either be created within a different tool for which there is an interface to the Decision Model tool or are created within the Decision Model tool itself.

Table 14.1 Capabilities of a Decision Model Tool

Decision Model Tool Supports:			
Zachman Row	Storage of Decision Model Aspects	Links to the Same Column	Links to the Same Row
1	Lists of business decisions	From the Row 1 business decisions to the corresponding Row 2 Decision Models and corresponding business planning models (e.g., OMG's BMM)	From the Column 6 business decisions to the corresponding Column 1 Fact Types for the conclusions and corresponding Column 2 Processes guided by the business decisions
2	Computation-Independent Decision Models (projectwide, enterprisewide, comparisons, inheritance, versioning, test cases, natural language representations, etc.)	From the Row 2 Decision Models to the Row 3 Platform-Independent Models and assignments to decision services	From the Column 6 Decision Models to the corresponding Column 1 Semantic Models (e.g., fact model, business object model, conceptual data model) and corresponding places in the Column 2 Business Process Models (via Decision anchor point)
3	Platform-Independent Models (in Platform-Independent Languages)	From the Row 3 Platform-Independent Models to corresponding Platform-Specific Models	From the Column 6 Platform-Independent Models to the corresponding Column 1 Logical Data Models or class diagrams and corresponding Column 2 Application Architectures
4	Platform-Specific Model for target technologies	From the Row 4 Platform-Specific Models to corresponding Business Logic Specifications	From the Column 6 Platform-Specific Models to the corresponding Column 1 Physical Data Models, class diagrams, component structure diagrams, and corresponding Column 2 System Design Services

Table 14.1   Capabilities of a Decision Model Tool (Continued)

	Decision Model Tool Supports:		
Zachman Row	*Storage of Decision Model Aspects*	*Links to the Same Column*	*Links to the Same Row*
5	Business Logic Specifications	From the Row 5 Business Logic Specifications to the corresponding Operating Code	From the Column 5 Business Logic Specifications to the corresponding Column 1 Data Definitions, class specifications, and to the corresponding Column 2 Program/Decision Support Specifications

Based on the positioning of the Decision Model in the Zachman Framework and corresponding Decision Model tool capabilities, it is worth examining the role of the Decision Model in other important enterprise architectural approaches.

The Decision Model and Other EA Approaches in General

Beyond the Zachman Framework are other widely practiced EA methodologies. They differ from the Zachman Framework in that they are not just a reference framework, but are focused on implementation. Consequently, they are methodologies. Many of these incorporate the Zachman Framework, whereas some have their own framework by which to decompose an enterprise. Nevertheless, a comprehensive EA has the following components:

■ A framework for decomposing the enterprise into its constituent concerns: dimensions and views.
■ A set of specifications for the models, that is, standards for producing the deliverables for dimensions and views.
■ The concept of developing the "as-is" enterprise architecture.
■ The concept of analyzing the as-is enterprise architecture, and developing a plan to reach a "to-be" enterprise architecture, based on priorities. This forms a roadmap or transitional plan. Sometimes the plan includes several interim states for the evolving enterprise architecture.

The Decision Model in the Federal Enterprise Architecture (FEA) Program

The Federal Enterprise Architecture (FEA), having evolved over several generations (and several changes of names and governance structures), is perhaps the most

Figure 14.4   FEA Services Component Reference Model. (Source: OMB, Office of E-Government and Information Technology, FEA Consolidated Reference Model Document Version 2.3, 2007.)

comprehensive of the major EA methodologies. Commissioned in February 2002, it became available in increments within a year or so. Today FEA is released as version 2.7, and there have been several years of practice.

The FEA is a based on a set of "reference models" that taken together form the classification schema of the enterprise.

The FEA, like some of the EA approaches, recognizes business rules somewhere in the approach, but without the maturity of recognizing business decisions and corresponding normalized Decision Models. In the FEA, Business Rules are defined in the "Service Component Reference Model" (SRM), (Figure 14.4), which "… Is a business-driven, functional framework classifying Service components that support federal agencies and their IT investment and assets" (OMB, 2007). These services are independent of business functions, and are intended to provide reusable application capabilities, components, or services (in the sense of Service-Oriented Architecture).

The Service Domains in the SRM are the following:

■ Customer Services
■ Process Automation
■ Business Management Services
■ Digital Asset Services
■ Back Office Services
■ Support Services

Within the Service Domain of Business Management Services is the Service Type "Management of Process" (Figure 14.5). This Service Type aims to "manage the enterprise processes that support an organization and its policies" (OMB, 2007).

The component Business Rules Management is categorized as a component within the Service Type of Management of Process, as shown in Figure 14.6. Business Rules Management as defined aims to "manage the enterprise processes that support an organization and its policies" (OMB, 2007).

Service Domains	Service Types	
Customer Services	• Customer Relationship Management • Customer Preferences • Customer Initiated Assistance	
Process Automation Services	• Tracking and Workflow • Routing and Scheduling	
Business Management Services	• Management of Process • Organizational Management • Investment Management • Supply Chain Management	
Digital Asset Services	• Content Management • Document Management • Knowledge Management • Records Management	
Business Analytical Services	• Analysis and Statistics • Visualization • Knowledge Discovery • Business Intelligence	• Reporting
Back Office Services	• Data Management • Human Resources • Financial Management • Asset/Materials Management	• Development and Integration • Human Capital/Workforce Management
Support Services	• Security Management • Collaboration • Search • Communication	• Systems Management • Forms Management

Figure 14.5   An Overview of the SRM. (Source: OMB, Office of E-Government and Information Technology, FEA Consolidated Reference Model Document Version 2.3, 2007.)

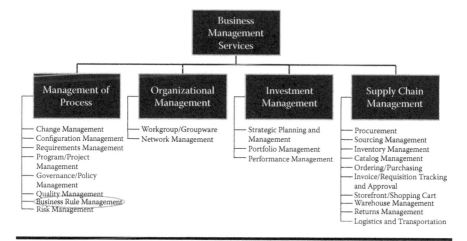

Figure 14.6   Business Management Services Domain. (Source: Adapted from OMB, Office of E-Government and Information Technology, FEA Consolidated Reference Model Document Version 2.3, 2007.)

It is within Business Rules Management that the Decision Model's capabilities would be deployed within the FEA. The Decision Model provides a specific and rigorous grouping of business rules relative to a business decision that guide processes in compliance with organization policies, such as those prescribed by the FEA.

Even better, the Decision Model provides a more precise, finer-grained relationship between the "organization and its policies" than seems envisaged in the FEA (or at least that is explicitly stated by the FEA). The Decision Model defines the relationship of the business decision (a more rigorous logical grouping of business rules undefined in FEA) to the business motivation, a concept that is not explicit in the FEA, but which is broadly defined and spread across the Business Reference Model (BRM) and the Performance Reference Model (PRM). Because the Decision Model assembles business rules in a logical and intrinsic business grouping, the Decision Model can be related to a specific policy or objective.

The performance of that policy or objective can be tested, and if adjustments need to be made, the set of related business rules to be adjusted are clearly delineated by the Decision Model. The FEA practitioner can therefore use the Decision Model to elevate Business Rule Management to the realm of Decision Management within the SRM. This is particularly useful when the Decision Model is deployed as a decision service (discussed later), with a defined relationship to the Business Reference Model and the Service Component Reference Model.

The greater opportunity, however, lies with the architects of FEA itself. If the FEA were to evolve to define a Decision Reference Model (i.e., DecRM, similar to the existing Data Reference Model (DRM) in FEA), the building of decision services as shared resources across the federal enterprise becomes possible. The new DecRM would provide the federal government with a significant improvement in agility as it would materialize a single source of business logic to share across the federal government. An approach to this amendment to the FEA is illustrated in Figure 14.7.

A Decision Model tool to support the deliverables of the FEA would federate the implemented Decision Models, so that they can be governed at the segment, line of business, and the federal level. This enables a project, line of business, or entire segment to create and manage the Decision Models, while making those models available across the entire federal government.

The Decision Model in TOGAF*

TOGAF is the architectural framework disseminated by The Open Group. It comprises several different components, the most visible being the "Architecture Development Method" (ADM). The ADM is a set of processes for creating an Enterprise Architecture methodology. In other words, TOGAF contains, in the ADM, the means of developing an Enterprise Architecture methodology, rather than being a complete methodology itself. The other two major components of

---

* TOGAF is a trademark of The Open Group.

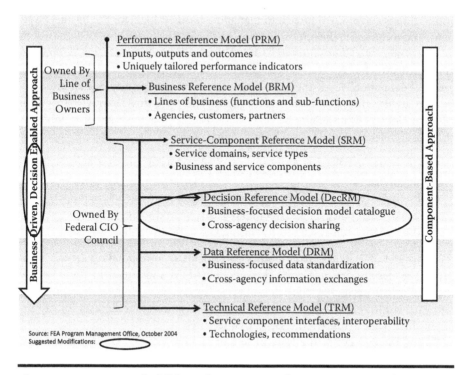

Figure 14.7 Suggested addition of a DecRM to the FEA. (Source: Adapted from OMB, Office of E-Government and Information Technology, FEA Consolidated Reference Model Document Version 2.3, 2007.)

TOGAF are the Technical Reference Model (TRM), which contains TOGAF standards for IT architecture, and the Standards Information Base (SIB), which is a "database of facts and guidance about information system standards" (The Open Group, 2007). This and other TOGAF knowledge bases enable organizations to create a customized EA methodology.

TOGAF does not have a comprehensive framework. Rather, it assumes that the practitioner will use an existing framework (e.g., the Zachman Framework) or develop one through the ADM. Regardless, TOGAF lacks a well-developed understanding of business logic or business rules management, and does not address the aspect of business logic in business modeling in any disciplined manner. For example, when discussing business modeling, a prescribed process within the ADM cycle, the TOGAF states: "Activity models can be annotated with explicit statements of business rules, which represent relationships among the ICOMs (inputs, controls, outputs and mechanisms/resources used)" (The Open Group, 2007).

However, the opportunity in TOGAF is to include the Decision Model, using a well-structured framework (e.g., the modified Zachman Framework) to create the Foundation Architecture. This makes good use of TOGAF's inherent flexibility while adding a rigorous approach to managing business logic for the business, systems, and technical architecture.

The Enterprise Continuum in TOGAF represents architecture, not as one specific destination but as a continuous scale of various scopes as destinations. Starting at the "Foundation" level, there are a set of architectural principles that are common to architectures across all organizations. There are three narrower scopes in which architectural principles become more specific to a given organization such that the architectures themselves become more customized:

- The Common System Architectures apply to most, but not necessarily all organizations.
- The Industry Architectures apply to specific industries, such as property and casualty insurance, or apparel manufacturing, and so on.
- The Organizational Architectures apply to a specific organization.

As each level of architecture embodies its principles, corresponding artifact templates and designs are developed through the ADM and stored in the TOGAF knowledge bases as illustrated in Figure 14.8. The Decision Model is an appropriate template within the foundation architectures as a common mechanism for capturing business logic across the TOGAF architectures.

Using the concept of the Enterprise Continuum in TOGAF, it is possible to use TOGAF to build Industry Architectures complete with Industry Decision Models. The latter might be at a skeletal, partly populated, or fully populated level. Regardless, individual organizations would augment the Industry Decision Models with proprietary business logic leading to the Organizational Architecture.

With this in mind, a Decision Model tool to support TOGAF stores multiple separate decision bases as templates, each related to a particular industry and each in skeletal, partially completed, or fully completed form. A particular organization simply copies the stored templates as a starting point for crafting a customized set of Decision Models.

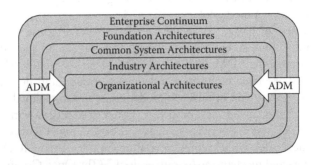

Figure 14.8   The Enterprise Continuum of TOGAF. (Source: Roger Sessions, White Paper: Comparison of the Top Four Enterprise Architecture Methodologies, 2007. Used with permission. http://www.objectwatch.com/white_papers.htm#4EA)

The Decision Model in System Architecture

Once an organization develops an EA, the goal is to deliver it in working form in technology solutions, as appropriate. Both FEA and TOGAF prescribe detailed methods and processes to translate the EA, as designed, through a transition state, into a "to-be" ideal state. In fact, the goal of EA methodologies, in general, is not to design the to-be architecture of a perfect future enterprise. Rather, it is to prioritize strategic challenges and appropriate IT investments to deliver technology solutions, the great enabler of the modern enterprise.

As indicated earlier, in the Zachman Framework, the technology delivery materializes by stepping from Row 3 through Rows 4 and 5 to Row 6. In other frameworks, there are different paths through the corresponding EA framework. In FEA, given the scope and size of the federal government, there is a functional (as opposed to political) segmentation of the organization as well as a hierarchy of implementation detail (Figure 14.9). In TOGAF, the EA revolves around the whole scope of "Requirements Planning," placing EA squarely in the software development life cycle (SDLC) process, as illustrated in Figure 14.10.

Whatever the approach, at some point, systems or applications are designed. Architects focus on the designs and implementation of systems fitting into the EA framework. Hence, there is a need for Solution, System, Application, Data—and presumably—the emerging Decision Architects.

Level	Scope	Detail	Impact	Audience
Enterprise Architecture	Agency/ Organization	Low	Strategic Outcomes	All Stakeholders
Segment Architecture	Line of Business	Medium	Business Outcomes	Business Owners
Solution Architecture	Function/ Process	High	Operational Outcomes	Users and Developer

Figure 14.9 FEA architectural levels and attributes. (Source: OMB, Office of E-Government and Information Technology, FEA Consolidated Reference Model Document Version 2.3, 2007.)

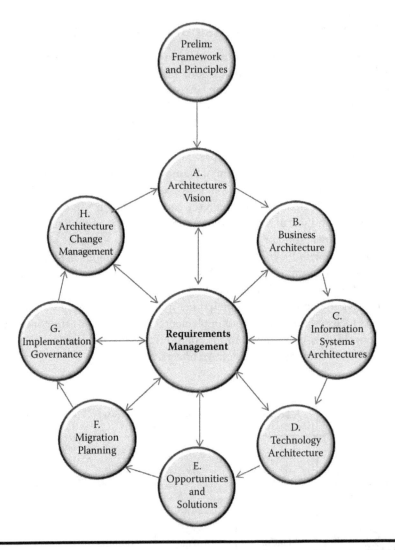

Figure 14.10   TOGAF ADM basic processes. (Source: The Open Group Architecture Framework (TOGAF) Version 8.1.1 Enterprise Edition. © Copyright April, 2007, The Open Group. Used with permission.)

This book uses the term systems architecture to mean the architecture for defining and delivering the enterprise as a deliberate system of systems, not as silo systems. At some point, such a broad system of systems transitions into the architecture of individual applications, but each is architected to participate with (and even enhance) the operations of other systems. (In some circles, people use the term application architecture to mean the architecture of a single application, sometimes isolated from other systems. Because the Decision Model offers advantages to larger scoped architectures, this book assumes that application architecture and systems architecture are two sides of the same continuum of architecture.)

System Architecture

Systems architecture occurs starting at Row 4 of the Zachman Framework, in the SRM and DRM of FEA, and in the "Information System Architecture" of TOGAF. In these respective layers, the software is engineered to connect to and reflect the models of the higher layers. As Ken Orr points out, "It turns out that coming up with an end-to-end solution—business strategy → working code (and back)—is an enormous undertaking, too much for even the largest, most sophisticated organization in the world" (Orr, 2007).

Historical System Architecture

The enormity of the undertaking referenced to by Orr is partly due to the complexity of the organization, but is also due to the complexity of systems created over the years. There are layers of code, varieties of programming languages, and generations of operating systems, not to mention a myriad of old and new software vendors.

A further complication is the narrow approach of systems development as it historically took place. As indicated earlier, prior to the acceptance of enterprise architecture, application systems were built to respond only to the requirements of departmental functions within the enterprise. This resulted in islands of automation separated by gulfs of "white space" among the departmental applications. These gaps were filled by manual tasks or connections among different systems, the latter with software interfaces that translate incompatible data formats and rationalize disparate data sources.

The solution lies in systems architecture, whereby all applications are viewed as a whole, single system. And this "system of systems" needs to be simplified by recognizing and implementing a separation of concerns. In the case of EA, such a separation is represented in the Zachman Framework for decomposing the enterprise into dimensions and views. In the case of system architecture, the separation involves the decomposition of application systems into constituent system functions. Ken Orr refers to these as dimensions (Orr, 2007), and identifies seven principle ones:

- Reporting/business intelligence (BI) dimension
- The database dimension
- The transactional dimension
- The security dimension
- The presentation dimension
- The workflow dimension
- The business rule dimension

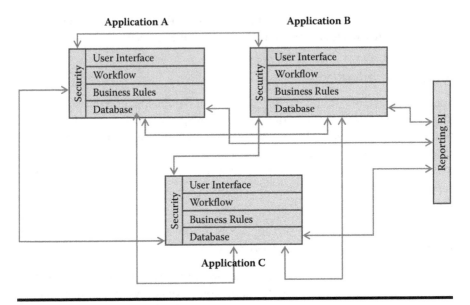

Figure 14.11   Legacy application structures.

Historically, each application included its own support for all dimensions, often without separating them. Thus, the code was not organized into logical patterns, therefore failing to deliver reusable modules.

Even on a small scale, the complexity can be seen easily in Figure 14.11. In this figure, three applications that, although well structured individually, connect to each other because each provides data and security information to others. The reporting dimension has been removed from the applications.* In this simple diagram, there are no fewer than eight separate interfaces, each having a proprietary interface on both ends. Imagine the complexity if the programs were not well structured, with security, data, and other dimensions not well separated. The complexity would increase even further if there were a need to share more dimensions than are illustrated. This is a simple case. In reality, a large enterprise comprises over 1000 applications, and perhaps many 1000s, resulting in unmanageable complexity.

Current System Architecture

In current system architecture, all the dimensions are separated into tiers. Figure 14.12 is a simplified view showing four "tiers" representing presentation services, business process services, application services, and database services. A device on the presentation layer connects to, initiates activity, or displays results from any of the business process tasks, which in turn calls application components in the

---

* Reflecting the historic fact that the reporting dimension became one of the first to be separated out of applications.

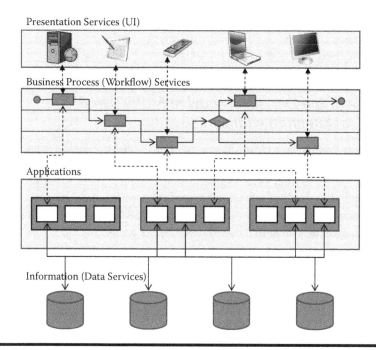

Presentation Services (UI)

Business Process (Workflow) Services

Applications

Information (Data Services)

Figure 14.12 Modern tiered architecture. (Source: Adapted from Ken Orr "Putting Data into SOA," Cutter Consortium, Business Intelligence Vol. 7, No 11. Used with Permission.)

application layer, which subsequently gets or sets data in the data layer. Each tier is well isolated from the internals of the others, and needs to be aware only of the information it needs to send to the next tier, and that which it receives.

In Figure 14.12, the number of connections among software pieces is still too many, adding unnecessary complexity to the architecture. The diagram shows that each UI component, workflow component, application component, and database has a direct connection to the component with which it is communicating.

Instead, architects can create a bidirectional universal switch, called a bus, to operate at the integration points between layers. The bus is a messaging system eliminating the point-to-point connections among software modules. In a bus world, each component connects only to the bus, sending and receiving messages to/from any component on the lower tier using that component's virtual address on the bus. Because each tier addresses only the tier below it, there are actually three buses: a process bus, an application bus, and a data bus. Together these buses comprise the Enterprise Service Bus (ESB).

The ESB does more than merely connect the components of the software together; it manages and maintains the state of transactions that are active across the bus, bringing stability to the relatively loosely bound pieces of the system.

A tiered architecture with an ESB allows separate architectural components to be changed or added to the system without perturbing the whole. Each new component need only know how to address the ESB to be able to fit into the system.

The Role of the Decision Model in Multi-Tiered System Architecture with an ESB

The Decision Model has a clear role to play in this tiered world. The application services tier is where the business logic of applications resides. In practice, this means that there is a correlation from Decision Models created by business analysts and the corresponding application components in the application services tier. So, there are architectural transitions for implementing the Decision Model in the application tier that are described in Model-Driven Architecture (MDA).

The Decision Model in MDA

In late 2001, the OMG began to pursue the development of MDA, leading to the publication of its guide to MDA (Object Management Group, 2003). The OMG was not alone. There has been a significant growth in model-based systems generation and related architecture work. "Business modeling serves the enterprise, but needs to couple directly to IT in order to deliver the goods" (Siegel, 2002). The notion of the architecture model of the system actually becoming the system is a future dream, and MDA is the beginning of its realization.

The OMG's MDA does not prescribe a particular EA. Instead, it is a set of independent but related models that represent the architectural path from business model to a model for a working system.

The general, simplest path is to start from a model that represents a business view and that bears no reference to system or implementation concerns. This is the controlling model, called the Computation-Independent Model (CIM). A process is applied to the CIM called a CIM-to-PIM mapping, which generates a Platform-Independent Model (PIM) from the CIM. The PIM is a model that represents a system view of the CIM, containing all information necessary to build an automated system of the model regardless of target technology platform. In other words, the PIM is independent of software vendor and product. Software vendors are expected to apply a process to the PIM called a PIM-to-PSM mapping in order to convert it into a model that represents a specific product's view and contains all the information necessary to convert the model into code that will execute on the vendor's product. This is called the PSM-to-Code mapping. The process is illustrated in Figure 14.13.

In practice, and to date, the dream of MDA has not yet been realized substantially. Several vendors have developed partial solutions, but there are impediments to a full realization. One barrier is that standards have not been developed yet that define a truly computation-independent, or even a PIM.

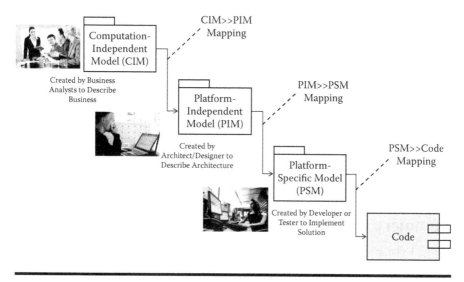

Figure 14.13   The OMG MDA Framework. (Source: Adapted from Frankel, David S., et al., The Zachman Framework and the OMG's Model Driven Architecture. Whitepaper, Business Process Trends, 2003. Used with permission.)

Relevant to the Decision Model is the Production Rule Representation (i.e., PRR). Because it is not yet released, vendors who support automation of business logic must start with platform-specific models (i.e., their own proprietary models). This is not in the full spirit of MDA. As standards mature, the hope is for the emergence of MDA tools through which the architectural transitions eventually become the system.

The Decision Model is a significant step forward for MDA because it enables the complete separation of business logic from all other concerns in the specification of a system. As such, the Decision Model is a CIM model of the business logic that can be specified and managed by the business.

The transformation of the Decision Model CIM to a PIM by an MDA tool would be relatively straightforward because of the highly structured Rule Families that are built in compliance with the rigor of the 15 Decision Model principles.

The Decision Model in Service-Oriented Architecture

More interesting than MDA for achieving model-to-system implementation is the advent of Service-Oriented Architecture (SOA). SOA views an application as a process-driven orchestration of services. In SOA, the focus is no longer the modeling of large-scale applications, but of finer-grained services. This enables models to be defined on a smaller, more manageable scale, with a clearly delineated role for the Decision Model, that of a decision service.

The concepts behind SOA are introduced in Chapter 5, and these concepts are examined in much greater detail in Chapter 15. The Decision Model is the model of the decision service as a component of a larger, composite service. Using the Decision Model, a designer predicts confidently the structure and complexity of the business logic behind a simple interface, which is all that the SOA architect need be concerned about.

By encapsulating the Decision Model behind a business decision into its own service, the designer of the larger service achieves a separation and externalization of the business logic from the larger service. This increases the flexibility of the design to meet the objective of the architecture.

Summary

The Decision Model represents an almost universal opportunity in modern Enterprise and System Architectures to represent business logic as a concern in its own right, separated from other different, but related concerns.

The Decision Model represents the declaration of independence of business logic from the other dimensions, and provides the ideal means for its architectural representation. That it fits well within the standard architectural approaches is not an accident, but rather a reflection of its inherent nature. The chapter summarized the ways in which this fit occurs:

- In the Zachman Framework, the Decision Model occupies Row 2, Column 6.
- The Decision Model is directly connected to the Business Motivation Model (BMM).
- The Decision Model is orthogonally connected in the Zachman Framework to the Semantic Models (such as the Business Object Model, Fact Models, and Glossaries) and the Business Process Models in Row 2.
- A Decision Model tool supports the Decision Model and its connections to artifacts in the row above and below in Column 6 and to artifacts in other columns of Row 2 of the Zachman Framework.
- In the major Enterprise Architecture Methodologies, such as FEA and TOGAF, the Decision Model plays a specific role that elevates the management of business rules and business logic to the maturity of Decision Management.
- In the OMG Model-Driven Architecture (MDA), the Decision Model is a Computer-Independent Model (CIM), and provides a platform for transformation to Platform-Independent Model (PIM).
- The Decision Model provides the ideal representation of a business decision for the implementation of a Decision Service.
- Within the Decision Model there is opportunity for finer-grained management of the business governance than is provided by an encapsulated decision service. Each Rule Family in a Decision Model may be governed by different departments.

- The structure of the Decision Model lends itself best to implementation in Business Rule Management Systems, because their production rule specifications bear a close, if not one-to-one relationship, to the rows within a Rule Family. This leads to the highest conformance between the business logic statement and its technical implementation.
- A Decision Model tool to support the Zachman Row 2, Column 6 properties provides the business user with all the requirements to build Decision Models. Such a Decision Model tool may also generate decision services.

Chapter 15

Service-Oriented Architectures

Mike Rosen

Contents

What Is SOA? 360
  Why SOA? 362
  Layered SOA Architecture 363
What Is a Service? 366
  A Word about Information Architecture 368
  Service Characteristics..369
  Service Size and Type 371
Service Roles 372
Designing Services...375
  Understanding Overall Context 377
  Flexible Service Design 378
Conclusion...380
Summary...380

As you have learned in the preceding pages, the Decision Model has a close, symbiotic relationship with Business Process Modeling (BPM). In this chapter the potential role for the Decision Model in SOA is explored.

There is no doubt that SOA is destined to be the architecture for the next decade, just as Web-based architectures predominated application development during the 2000s. All major software platforms and products are moving toward an SOA-based infrastructure built on top of an application and integration server platform in combination with Business Process Management (BPM) capabilities. In addition, major application vendors are spending billions of dollars to reengineer their product suites into collections of discrete services, tied together by processes, and executing on an SOA platform. Finally, the explosion of Software as a Service (SaaS) offerings is further fueling the hype and adoption of SOA.

SOA provides a better, more modular, and more flexible way to build enterprise solutions, and especially to support business processes. The steady march toward SOA is almost inevitable because it is being pushed and supported by all segments of the software industry. By default, it will deliver some value based on these attributes and the standards, tools, and frameworks that support it.

Although SOA will happen regardless, significant additional value from SOA is realized when services are reused across multiple business processes. The major packaged application vendors will manage this in their product suites, but many enterprises and projects will not succeed with significant reuse of their own custom services. There are many reasons for this; among them are the lack of architecture in IT organizations and a lack of understanding of the relationship between services, decisions, and processes. This book, and this chapter in particular, are aimed at addressing the latter issues.

What Is SOA?

The hype surrounding SOA over the past few years has spread confusion about the meaning of SOA as different "marketectures" compete for mindshare. In spite of this, some things are clear. SOA is not a product or a platform. SOA is not a technology, nor is it something you can simply purchase.

From an architectural point of view, SOA is an architectural style promoting the concept of business-aligned enterprise service as the fundamental unit of designing, building, and composing enterprise business processes and solutions.

Architecture is the fundamental organization of a system embodied in its components, their relationships to one another and to the environment, and the principles guiding its design and evolution (IEEE Standard 1471-2000). An architectural style is a family of architectures related by common principles and attributes. An architectural style provides a useful set of reasonable alternatives—not all alternatives—and coordinates them to work well together.

Let's begin by examining the architecture by looking at the relationship between BPM and SOA. Where does one leave off and the other begin, or what is the overlap between them? Business Process Management (BPM) empowers a business to align IT systems with strategic goals by creating well-defined enterprise business processes, monitoring their performance, and optimizing for greater operational efficiencies. Each business process is modeled as a set of individual processing tasks. These tasks are typically implemented as services within the enterprise. The BPM system provides a toolset that allows the business analyst to create process models using notations such as BPMN, and then performs the business process automation, or execution of the model, by invoking the services. Additionally, the BPM system provides monitoring and management capabilities.

One major complication is that enterprises want to leverage their existing systems and include them into the new business processes. Unfortunately, enterprises have tremendously complex IT environments that have evolved, often over several decades, using different platforms, different technologies, and different communication standards. This is a problem that enterprises have struggled with for years through a string of promising (or overpromised) technologies. Web services, the latest and current favorite, have the potential to solve these platform and communications issues and provide new interfaces (service wrappers) to those existing enterprise systems. This is convenient, because it is service interfaces that the BPM systems need to call when invoking the process tasks. But simply using Web services or wrapping existing applications as services does not qualify as a SOA.

Web services are a set of technologies for distributing business functionality in the form of services, such as the legacy system wrappers just discussed. On the other hand, SOA goes well beyond the details of connectivity or interface technologies to get to the "what," not the "how" of services. SOA is about enabling the independent construction of business-aligned services that can be combined into meaningful, higher-level business processes and solutions within the context of the enterprise. It's not so much about building a service; anybody can create a service, that is not the challenge of SOA. It is about enabling the enterprise to build the right collection of services. The real value of SOA comes when reusable services are composed together to create agile, flexible, business processes. Unfortunately, that does not just happen by itself.

In order for the composition of services to actually result in meaningful business processes, all of the services that are composed together need to share a variety of important characteristics. This requires that the architecture specify those important characteristics, including how services

- Have similar size, shape, form, function, and other characteristics
- Conform to enterprise standards
- Communicate at a technical level
- Communicate at a semantic level
- Support enterprise goals and strategy

(In this chapter, we focus on the first point, the form, function, and characteristics of services, but first a bit more on SOA architecture.)

Why SOA?

When an architectural approach is applied at the enterprise level, SOA can provide significant business value, including the following:

- Consistency—SOA allows us to have a single, common entry point into a process, task, or decision. In other words, it allows the business to provide consistent behavior regardless of the path taken to get to that behavior.
- Commonality—SOA allows us to have a single access point to common information that is spread across the enterprise. In other words, it provides the business with common, enterprisewide information that is consistent and coordinated. The most cited example of this is the "common customer," but there are many other opportunities to provide business value with common information.
- Modularity and flexibility—SOA provides an excellent mechanism for implementing modularity of business function, decisions, and information. When implemented well, those modules can be reused and recombined across multiple processes and scenarios. This provides the business with the flexibility and agility required to be innovative and competitive.
- Decoupled—SOA provides a mechanism for integrating business functions and information together, while at the same time minimizing the dependencies (or coupling) between them. In other words, independent business units, applications, etc., can work together, but continue to have their own schedules, life cycles, and business drivers.
- Manageability—SOA allows us to manage our business at the modular level by defining service level agreements (SLAs). In other words, we can set, monitor, and refine our business performance over time.

Layered SOA Architecture

BPM provides a wonderful abstraction for building business systems. But all too often, we see BPM being used to build higher-level, more efficient, but nonetheless siloed applications rather than contributing to an overall flexible, agile enterprise. This is where rules, decisions, and SOA come in. Business decision systems allow us to separate out business rules and decisions from a particular process so that the rule or decision can be applied consistently across multiple processes, and so that it can be easily managed and modified. SOA provides the application platform to host business decisions, and bridges between the business processes, the decision, and the operational resources, as shown in Figure 5.1 (Chapter 5). At the business-process level, it provides interfaces that directly support executing process tasks and decisions. But it defines those interfaces within an enterprise context to support consistency and reuse. At the operational resource level, SOA exposes existing capabilities as integration services. However, it doesn't do this by directly mapping existing applications as services. Rather, it provides new service interfaces based on enterprise semantic and functional requirements and maps them to the existing systems. Finally, it joins the processes and resources together through a layer of composable business services.

Together, BPM and SOA provide a perfect combination for enterprise computing. BPM provides the higher-level abstraction for defining businesses processes, as well as other important capabilities of monitoring and managing those processes. Services provide the functions, decisions, and information that support those processes. SOA provides the capabilities for services to be combined together and to support and create an agile, flexible enterprise. BPM without SOA is useful for building applications, but difficult to extend to the enterprise. SOA without BPM is useful for creating reusable and consistent services, but lacks the ability to turn those services into an agile, competitive enterprise.

Figure 5.1 (Chapter 5) shows a typical layered SOA architecture, with the following important concepts:

- **Processes:** High-level business functions, often spanning applications or lines of business.
- **Services:** Modular units of business functionality.
- **Integration:** Connection to and exposure of existing applications or data as services.
- **Existing Systems:** Existing legacy systems, COTS applications, and data that the enterprise wants to leverage.

But this representation of SOA is missing a key component of enterprises and IT systems, that of the information. To make the architecture more complete (and realistic), we need to add the appropriate informational abstractions, including the following:

- **Documents:** High-level unit of business information, such as a purchase order or an EDI document.
- **Semantics:** The underlying meaning of information that is exchanged in processes.
- **Transformation:** Conversion of information from one format or semantic to another.
- **Communications:** The ability of services to communicate with one another.

Figure 15.1 modifies the initial layered architecture to include two important concepts for each layer. On the left are the functional concepts that we use to construct systems and processes. On the right are the informational concepts that we use to pass, describe, or manipulate data at those different functional levels. In other words, we are explicitly recognizing the fact that enterprises are a combination of process and information. Each layer needs both abstractions. Yet, too often, SOA only focuses on the functional aspects, ignoring the important data concepts. From bottom to top, the layers are the following:

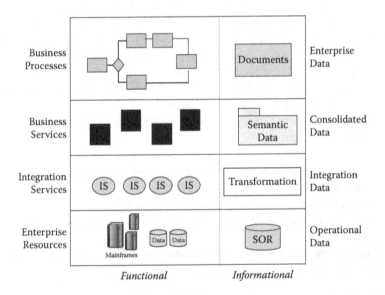

Figure 15.1   Architectural elements of SOA. (Source: Rosen, M., Lublinsky, B., Smith, K. T., and Balcer, M. J. (2008). *Applied SOA: Service-Oriented Architecture and Design Strategies.* **New York: Wiley. Used with permission.)**

■ **Enterprise resources and operational systems:** This layer consists of existing applications, legacy and commercial off-the-shelf (COTS) systems, including customer relationship management (CRM) and enterprise resource planning (ERP) packaged applications, and older object-oriented implementations. These applications provide business operations: transactions that represent single logical units of work in the enterprise's operational systems. Execution of an operation will typically cause one or more persistent data records to be read, written, or modified in a System of Record (SOR). Operations have a specific, structured interface, and return structured responses. Data at this layer resides in existing applications or databases.

■ **Integration services:** Integration services provide integration between and access to existing applications. The separation between the integration services and the business services is critical to maintaining a flexible enterprise environment. This often involves transformation of data and function between that which is desired at the business service level and that which is possible in the existing systems.

■ **Business services:** Business services provide high-level business functionality throughout the enterprise. This layer provides a service interface abstraction and integration of the layer below, breaking the direct dependence between processes and existing systems. Services are a managed, governed set of enterprise assets responsible for ensuring conformance to service level agreements (SLAs). Business services provide business capabilities through logical groupings of operations. For example, if we view Customer Profiling as a service, then Lookup customer by telephone number, List customers by name and postal code, and Save data for new customer represent the associated operations within the logical service. Note that all operations will not necessarily come from the same operational systems, or in some cases, the operations will be replicated across multiple similar systems. Thus, the business services provide a virtual implementation of related business operations. Business services operate on semantic data objects, virtual data that describes the information that must be shared or passed between services. It is often aggregated from multiple existing systems. Note that the business service layer will be composed of many different types of services, as discussed later in the chapter.

■ **Business processes:** A business process consists of a series of operations that are executed in an ordered sequence according to a set of business rules. Often, the business process is described in a business process model, such as those conforming to Business Process Modeling Notation (BPMN) and executed by a specialized Business Process Management System (BPMS). The sequencing, selection, and execution of operations is termed orchestration. Business processes provide long-running sets of actions or activities. They are composed of business services and typically encompass multiple service invocations. Business processes operate on business documents. The processes and documents are composed from the services and objects of the layer below, according to a business process model and a common semantic data model. The scope of these processes is often the entire enterprise. Examples of business processes are Initiate New Employee, Sell Products or Services, and Fulfill Order.

What Is a Service?

We looked at a basic, layered SOA and said that services are the fundamental unit for designing, building, and composing enterprise business solutions. So what exactly is a service? We define a service as a discrete unit of business functionality that is made available through a service contract.

The service contract specifies all interaction between the service consumer and service provider. This includes the following:

- Service interface
- Interface documents
- Service policies
- Quality of service
- Performance

One of the main differences between a service and other software constructs (such as components or objects) is that a service is explicitly managed. The quality of service and performance are managed through an SLA. In addition, the entire service life cycle is managed, from design to deployment to enhancements and maintenance. Figure 15.2 shows the major parts of a service.

There are two main aspects to the service itself. The top part of the service in the diagram is the service interface; the bottom part of the service is the service implementation. A service specifically separates the interface from the implementation.

The service interface specifies the service operations, that is, what the service does, the parameters that are passed into and out of the operation, and the protocols for how those capabilities are used and provided. A service typically contains several different, but related operations. The service implementation is how the service provides the capabilities of its interface. The implementation may be based on existing applications, or on orchestrating other services together, or on code written specifically for the service, or all of these. The important point is that how the service is implemented is not visible to the consumers of the service, only what the service does is. The producer of a service is free to change the implementation of a service, as long as it does not change the interface or the behavior. For example, a new service might be completely based on existing functionality in a legacy application. Once the interface contract is finalized, consumers can start to use the service. In the meantime, the producer may create a new, modern implementation, and retire the old legacy application, which runs on a platform that is no longer

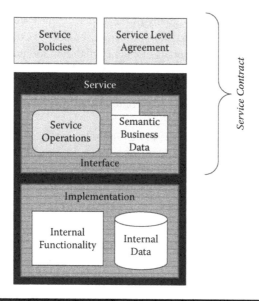

Figure 15.2   Components of a service. (Source: Rosen, M., Lublinsky, B., Smith, K. T., and Balcer, M. J. (2008). *Applied SOA: Service-Oriented Architecture and Design Strategies.* **New York: Wiley. Used with permission.)**

supported. Users (consumers) of the service may never notice the difference as long as the behavior and contract do not change.

In other words, we can think of the service interface as the point through which consumers (with needs) interact with providers (with capabilities). The interface defines the style and details of the interactions. The implementation defines how a particular provider offers its capabilities. This concept of a connection point allows design of more loosely coupled solutions.

There are also two different aspects to both the interface and implementation. These are the functions that are performed and the information that it is performed on. In other words, a service is a combination of a set of functional service operations, and the corresponding virtual business data that is passed into and out of the operations. Virtual business data is an abstraction of business entities (tied to an enterprise schema) that are independent of data storage or implementation. The service operation signature describes the parameters that are passed in and out of an operation. The information model (or enterprise schema) describes the structure and meaning of the virtual business data passed in and out.

The distinction between the virtual information in the service interface and the logical/physical data in the service implementation is critical. At the service interface level, what is important is the information that must be passed between services to enable and complete the business process. This is the information that must be agreed to and must be common between all the services that participate in the process. However, internally, many of these services have a different superset of the information, potentially in a different format. Luckily, we do not have to know or agree on all of the different details of the internal data models of all the services involved (which would be impractical if not impossible). Instead, the separation of interface from implementation (with regard to the information model) allows us to easily translate between the common (virtual) definition and the internal (physical) implementation.

The last important aspect of the service interface is the SLA. This specifies two important performance criteria about the service, the technical performance in terms of response time, throughput, availability, and reliability, and the business performance in terms of business units of work performed within a certain time frame and to a specific quality level.

A Word about Information Architecture

Now is a good time to clarify an important aspect of information architecture as it relates to services. We can describe the different types of information in terms of three layers: physical data (sources), domain (service) data, and semantic data. Physical data is the persistent enterprise data, usually preexisting. Domain data comprises the classes that encapsulate information needed to implement services. This uses the classic object/relational mapping. Semantic data is the information exchanged between service consumers and providers, and is often a nonnormalized view of domain data or data sources. The mappings between these three represent the mining of data for different purposes. The concept of separation of concerns isolates the service consumers, services providers, and persistent sources to provide more reusable, maintainable, agile solutions.

Figure 15.3 shows these relationships between the different types of data.

- Physical data—This is the data that is actually stored on disk. The details of how it is stored are described in a database schema. The schema is optimized for the performance characteristics and requirements of the particular data store.
- Domain data—This is the data that is used in the service implementation. It is described in a standard data model and describes all of the information that is used in the implementation of a service. It represents the private knowledge of the data. A subset of the data is the service's view of the common information. Service data is a view of the physical data and may come from one or more physical data stores.
- Semantic data—This is the data that describes the common understanding of business entities and information that must be shared between services. It is described in the shared information model and is closely aligned to the business model. It is used to describe information that is exchanged through service interfaces. Semantic data is a normalized view of the common data from all the different services.

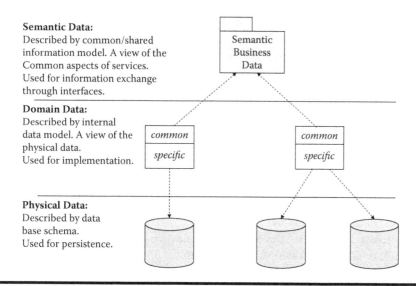

Semantic Data:
Described by common/shared information model. A view of the Common aspects of services. Used for information exchange through interfaces.

Domain Data:
Described by internal data model. A view of the physical data. Used for implementation.

Physical Data:
Described by data base schema. Used for persistence.

Figure 15.3   Types of information. (Source: Rosen, M., Lublinsky, B., Smith, K. T., and Balcer, M. J. (2008). *Applied SOA: Service-Oriented Architecture and Design Strategies*. New York: Wiley. Used with permission.)

Service Characteristics

In addition to the specific structure of a service, good services have specific characteristics:

■ **Modularity and Granularity:** In SOA, business processes are decomposed into modular "services" that are self-contained. Services themselves can be composed from other modular services and can be mixed and matched as needed to create new composite services.

Granularity is a quality of the functional richness for a service; the more coarse-grained a service is, the richer or larger the function offered by the service. Coarse-grained services provide a greater level of functionality within a single service operation. This helps to reduce complexity and network overhead by reducing the steps necessary to fulfill a given business activity; often this is accomplished by composing smaller tasks into a single coarse-grained operation. Fine-grained service operations provide the exchange of small amounts of information to complete a specific discrete task. An example of a coarse-grained service might be to price an insurance quote. A fine-grained service (which would be used by the pricing service, among others) might return risk information based on the postal code of the applicant.

■ **Encapsulation:** Services exhibit a strict separation of the service interface (what a service does) from the service implementation (how it is done).

Encapsulation hides the service's internal implementation details and data structures from the published interface operations and semantic model.

■ **Loose coupling:** Coupling describes the amount of dependencies between a service consumer and provider. Loosely coupled services have few, well-known, and managed dependencies. Tightly coupled services have many known, and more importantly, unknown dependencies. The degree of coupling directly affects the flexibility and extensibility of a system.

■ **Isolation of responsibilities:** Services are responsible for discrete tasks or the management of specific resources. A key characteristic of service design is the isolation of responsibility for those functions or information into a single service. This provides one (and only one) place for each function to be performed, providing consistency and reducing redundancy.

■ **Autonomy:** Autonomy is the characteristic that allows services to be deployed, modified, and maintained independently of each other and the solutions that use them. An autonomous service's life cycle is independent of other services.

■ **Reuse:** Together, modularity, encapsulation, loose coupling, isolation of responsibilities, and autonomy enable services to be combined into multiple business processes or accessed by multiple service consumers from multiple locations and in multiple contexts. In other words, services are shared and "reused" as building blocks in the construction of processes or composite services.

■ **Dynamic discovery and binding:** Services can be discovered at design time through the use of a design time service repository. Although it is theoretically possible to dynamically discover services at runtime, we have yet to see this work in practice.

However, service consumers can be dynamically bound to providers during runtime. In this scenario, the consumer asks the registry for a specific service and is routed and bound dynamically to the appropriate service provider. The dynamic binding of a service consumer to service provider enhances loose coupling and enables additional capabilities such as mediation. In more advanced implementations, the dynamic binding may be driven by the service policy.

■ **Stateless:** Service operations are stateless. This means that they neither remember the last thing they were asked to do, nor care what the next is. Services are not dependent on the context or state of other services, only on their functionality. Stateless services provide better flexibility, scalability, and reliability. (Note that this is typically a design goal, but it isn't always practical, for example, for long-running service interactions.)

■ **Self-describing:** The service contract provides a complete description of the service interface, its operations, the input and output parameters, and schema. The contract may also contain pre- and postconditions and constraints about the operations.

- **Composable:** Services can be composed from other services, and in turn, can be combined with other services to compose new services or business processes.
- **Governed by policy:** Relationships between service consumers and providers (and between services and service domains) are governed by policies and SLAs. Policies describe how different consumers are allowed to interact with the service, in other words, what they are allowed to do.
- **Independent of location, language, and protocol:** Services are designed to be location-transparent and protocol/platform-independent, in other words, to be accessible to any authorized user, on any platform, from any location (within reason).

Service Size and Type

We're often told that services should be coarse-grained, but of course, it's not that simple. There is no single, correct size (granularity) for a service. Rather, the right granularity depends on a variety of factors such as the following: Who are the intended users of the service (partners, business processes, other services)? What are the topology and performance requirements (LAN, WAN, etc.)? What is the intended scope of the service?

In any complex system or environment, we should expect to see a wide range of service types. Figure 15.4 shows a hierarchy of service types and granularity, including the following:

- **Enterprise business processes:** These business processes span the entire enterprise and can make use of the underlying services.
- **"Business" services:** Business services are the most coarse-grained services. Business services expose high-level, composed business functions to the enterprise. The functions and information match closely to the semantics and syntax required of business processes. Data integration services at this level support the consolidated data required by enterprise processes.
- **Domain services:** Domain services are medium-grained. They provide business-related services that are specific to a business domain, are used by many different business services in that domain (e.g., membership validation), but may not be exposed outside of the domain.
- **Utility services:** Utility services are the least coarse-grained. They provide lower-level services that provide common functionality across the enterprise (e.g., address book or part number validation).
- **Integration services:** Integration services expose existing applications as services for use by the rest of the enterprise, and provide consistent consolidated access to enterprise data that is spread across many different data sources. The granularity of integration services will be partially dependent on the existing

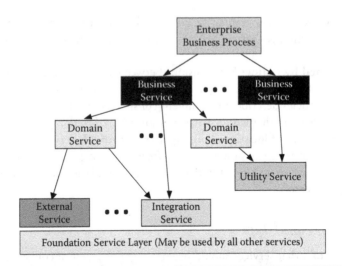

Figure 15.4 Hierarchy of service types. (Source: Rosen, M., Lublinsky, B., Smith, K. T., and Balcer, M. J. (2008). *Applied SOA: Service-Oriented Architecture and Design Strategies.* **New York: Wiley. Used with permission.)**

systems that they expose. Integration services typically involve transformation between the enterprise model and application model, both at a functional and informational level.

■ **External service:** External services enable access to systems and applications provided by suppliers or partners external to the enterprise (e.g. credit card validation, shipment tracking). The granularity of external services will depend on the particular service provider. Although traditionally these were relatively fine-grained, new Software-as-a-Service providers are creating a wide variety of services in all areas.

■ **Foundation service:** Foundation services provide fine-grained capabilities that are used in the construction of higher-level services, independent of any business domain (e.g., security, logging, and orchestration). These are the capabilities that we have traditionally called services, which supported infrastructures such as CORBA or COM. Unfortunately, we can't just stop calling them services, but we do need to distinguish between them and the business-related services listed earlier. These are sometimes also called technical or infrastructure services.

Service Roles

Another important consideration for services is independent of the size, scope, ownership, or construction of a service. That is the intended purpose, or role, of the service. To understand these different service roles, we can apply the architectural principle of separation of concerns. For example we have long applied the separation of data from logic as an important concept in constructing applications. This not only provides the opportunity for decoupling of the different concerns, but allows for specialized environments to implement them.

BPM is an example of separating out the workflow or schema of a business process from the rest of the logic so that the workflow can be executed and managed in a specialized environment, and so that the business can rapidly respond to changes by quickly modeling new processes. SOA facilitates this by providing business services as the basic building block of business processes.

Similarly, Business Decision Management (BDM) or Business Rules Management (BRM) is an example of separating out business rules or decisions from the rest of the application logic so that the rules and decisions can be executed and managed in a specialized environment and can easily be changed to support new business requirements. Again, SOA facilitates this by providing services that expose business rules and decisions.

Typically, we construct the service layer with three broad categories of service roles, as shown in Figure 15.5:

■ **Task services role:** Services that implement a business function, such as calculating the price of an insurance quote, or validating the format of an address, have this role. Service types ranging from discrete utility services to large business services can have a task service role. Smaller task services tend to be more general-purpose and provide greater potential for reuse. Business services types almost always play a task service role, are often large compositions of smaller services, and may be designed to support one or more specific

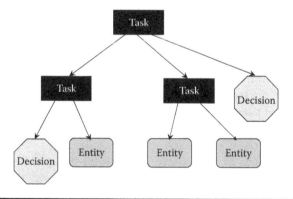

Figure 15.5 Service roles' usage and dependency pattern. (Source: Adapted from Rosen, M., Lublinsky, B., Smith, K. T., and Balcer, M. J. (2008). *Applied SOA: Service-Oriented Architecture and Design Strategies.* **New York: Wiley. Used with permission.)**

process. As such, they have less potential for broad reuse across processes (but this is okay, because they have been composed from other reusable parts).

■ **Entity services role:** Services that primarily manage access to business entities have this role. Examples of business entities are customers, policies, claims, etc., and correspond to major business information concepts. Entities are usually medium- to large-sized. Entities tend to be independent of any particular business process and, instead, are part of multiple different business processes. Entity services provide high levels of potential for reuse. Note that we are talking about business entities here, not low-level data schema elements.

In general, services with a task role are active and do something to deliver value. Services with an entity role support task services by adapting and providing information needed to implement the tasks. Care must be taken when designing entity services to avoid exposing internal data rather than business semantics.

■ **Decision services role:** Services that execute business rules to provide business decisions. An example decision service would be to approve creditworthiness. Services with a decision role generally provide yes/no answers to complex questions, or support frequently changing externalized rules, such as tax regulations. Decision services are usually composed into larger services and are small to medium in size. It is possible that service types such as business services, domain services, utility services, or even external services, may play decision service role, but usually services with a decision service role support those service types.

We combine these different service roles to provide flexible business capabilities that support the activities of business process. Best practices provide a variety of patterns, techniques, and tools for service composition that help us reduce dependencies, limit coupling, and maximize flexibility. Figure 15.5 provides a high-level illustration of a typical pattern designed to reduce dependency and increase reuse of entity and decision services. The pattern shows a service with a task role of orchestrating multiple services. Each supporting service provides access to one or more services with an entity, task, or decision role. A task service might make use of a service with a decision or entity role, but a service with an entity role is prohibited from directly invoking another service with an entity role.

Figure 15.6 expands the service layer of Figure 5.1 (Chapter 5) to include these additional concepts. As before, the tasks of the business processes are implemented by services (most often, task-focused service); high-level task-focused business services are composed of other, smaller services. Now, we can create new and different compositions of services using the richer set of process, entity, and decision service usage roles, combining the benefits of flexible, changeable rules, along with the benefits of modularity, flexibility, and reuse promised by SOA.

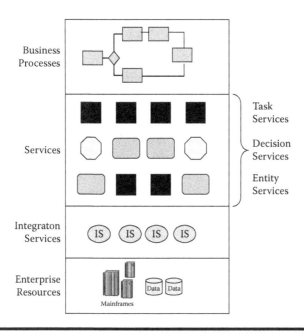

Figure 15.6   Expanded service layer. (Source: Adapted from Rosen, M., Lublinsky, B., Smith, K. T., and Balcer, M. J. (2008). *Applied SOA: Service-Oriented Architecture and Design Strategies.* **New York: Wiley. Used with permission.)**

Designing Services

One of the keys to achieving SOA success is creating a collection of services that can be combined together to support a variety of different business processes and scenarios. We often talk about having "loosely coupled" services, but how does that help achieve these goals? Loose coupling is important in reducing dependencies between services so that they can be used in different scenarios or to isolate the effects of changes. Two types of coupling are especially important in service inter-face design: data and functional dependencies.

Let's look at a simple example to illustrate these dependencies. Say, you have a service for insurance policy issuance. Among other things, to issue the policy, the service must update information about the customer, make a decision about underwriting, create the policy, bill the customer, and so on, as illustrated in Figure 5.2 (Chapter 5).

The policy issuance service coordinates all of these activities and then uses other services to help accomplish the processing. So, obviously, the policy issuance service is dependent on (coupled to) the customer service, underwriting service, policy service, and billing service. This is normal. So why don't you just implement all of these capabilities directly in the issuance services and be done with it? For two reasons: The first is because you want to be able to reuse the underlying capabilities in other high-level processes or services. The second is that policy issuance is not responsible for managing the customer, making underwriting decisions, managing the policy, or billing. It needs to use them, but it is not responsible for implementing them.

The customer service is used to manage access to customer information. It has the sole responsibility for providing, maintaining, and updating that information. You do this so that you can reuse the customer service in every place that needs to access customer data. But more important than the reuse of code is the isolation/centralization of access to customer information. Because there is only one way to access the data, the data is always consistent. So, although there are many services (order processing, billing, etc.) that need (are dependent on) the customer service, you understand and manage this kind of dependency through the use of patterns.

The same is true for the underwriting service, the policy service, and the billing service. You isolate these functions into their own services because you want to be able to use them for more than just issuance. Again, it is not just the reuse of the services that you're interested in. Good service design also provides consistency. By creating services to perform the underwriting, policy management, and billing functions, you can perform those functions consistently wherever they are needed. (Nothing is more annoying to customers than inconsistent results.)

The next logical question is, how do you decide what the services are? You use a combination of functional decomposition and information isolation. Back to the example in Figure 15.5, a functional decomposition of issuance led you to identify the underwriting, policy creation, and billing steps. Information isolation led you to identify customer and policy as shared information across the policy activities.

Of course, policy issuance is just one of dozens or hundreds of processes that need to be performed to run the business. So the problem of service design within an SOA needs to span many (or all) of these processes. In particular, you want to

- Avoid overlaps in function between services
- Avoid gaps in function between services
- Avoid duplication of data
- Coordinate access to data
- Have a single, consistent way of performing a given function

A key to achieving these goals is to keep the following questions in mind during the design of a service:

- Who is responsible for a given function? Where is that function used?
- Who is responsible for management of specific data?
- Who is responsible for defining and implementing specific rules?
- What step in the process owns the specific knowledge needed to perform a given task?

The answer to these questions helps to identify what the service should do and what it is responsible for. Just as importantly, it identifies what the service should not do, but rather depend on other services for.

Understanding Overall Context

To achieve these goals within the intended scope of the SOA, you must understand more than a single process, scenario, or use case. You must understand the overall context to which the SOA applies. The overall set of services within this context is referred to as the service inventory. This is where a business and domain model would come into play.

The SOA business model asks and answers the following questions:

- What business are you in (e.g., the domain model)?
- What are the goals and objectives of this particular business?
- What outcomes are needed to achieve those goals?
- How will they be measured?
- What capabilities and information are needed to achieve those outcomes?
- What processes, services, entities, and rules are needed to implement those capabilities?
- What existing applications provide basic capabilities and information that can support these?

The first four questions describe the business' requirements, while the rest describe the overall SOA context and provide the requirements for the service inventory. In other words, the service inventory describes the overall set of services necessary to support SOA within a context. In doing so, the inventory must identify:

- The overall scope
- Areas of service responsibilities
- Groupings of related services
- Task, Entity, and Decision services

The service inventory supports two major design time goals:

- It provides a mechanism for understanding the overall service context to aid in the selection of services for reuse. Specifically, what responsibilities does the service implement and how is it related to other services.
- It provides a mechanism for identifying the boundaries of responsibility of a particular service as a guideline for implementation of the service. This is critical in avoiding duplication of data and function across services.

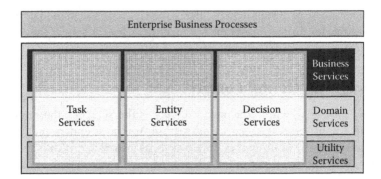

Figure 15.7 Service inventory template. (Source: Rosen, M., Lublinsky, B., Smith, K. T., and Balcer, M. J. (2008). *Applied SOA: Service-Oriented Architecture and Design Strategies.* **New York: Wiley. Used with permission.)**

Figure 15.7 shows a sample template for a service inventory. This sample shows how services might be organized according to service type and service role. In other words, the services are categorized across two dimensions: type—business, domain, utility; and role—task, entity, decision. Any given service falls in some intersection of these two dimensions. However, there are many different ways to organize the inventory. For example, it could also be organized by organizational structure, or business domain, or line of business. Of course, the template is just one way of visually presenting the information contained in the inventory. The same inventory could be presented in more than one view.

Flexible Service Design

If we think about some of the issues in reusing services, we quickly run into the problem that not every consumer of a service has the same configuration, is subject to the same business rules, has the same level of authorization and entitlement, or needs the same service level. So how do we go about making a service flexible enough to accommodate these different factors? We use the time-proven technique of indirection, or externalization. Rather than having these things hard-coded in the service itself, we design the service to get the information remotely at the appropriate time.

Figure 15.8 modifies our earlier diagram of a service to illustrate this technique. The service at the right of the diagram consists of the interface and implementation. This time, we show that the implementation requires certain resources and is subject to business rules and policies, all of which we want to be as flexible as possible in order to maximize the reusability of the service.

An external configuration mechanism, such as a file that is read at service start-up, or perhaps a configuration service, is used to point the service to the appropriate set of resources and rules to use. For example, if the service is for managing customer

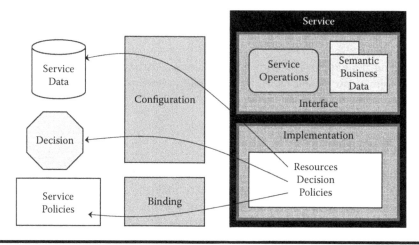

Figure 15.8   Designing In Service Flexibility. (Source: Adapted from Rosen, M., Lublinsky, B., Smith, K. T., and Balcer, M. J. (2008). *Applied SOA: Service-Oriented Architecture and Design Strategies.* **New York: Wiley. Used with Permission.**

information, we might point it to the ACME Customer Database. We could reuse the same service for the FOOBAR company just by changing the configuration file. Or, perhaps more likely, we might initially partition the database according to customer name, with one partition applying to customers with last names staring with A–L, and a second partition for M–Z. As the customer base grows, we could repartition the database into thirds, A–I, J–R, S–Z, or change to a geographical partition rather than an alphabetical one. We wouldn't need to change the service for this, just the configuration parameters.

The externalization of rules gives us similar flexibility in two areas. Consider, for example, our service that decides whether or not to underwrite a particular policy. If the rules for policy risk change, the changes are isolated in the lower-level risk decision service and don't affect the implementation of the underwriting service as a whole. Or, perhaps underwriting automobile insurance for commercial customers uses different rules than for individual customers. We could potentially use the same service for both types of customers by configuring the underwriting service to use a different risk decision service.

Again, the example may seem trivial. Why not just put a conditional statement into the code? Wouldn't that be easier? Easier, yes; better, no. What happens when we add a third or fourth type of customer with a different risk profile? Simple, just change the configuration, not the code.

Finally, there are many decisions to be made regarding entitlements, authorization, qualities of service, etc., that may affect how a particular consumer of a service is connected to a specific provider. The service's run-time policy allows us to externalize these characteristics and then intelligently apply them at binding time.

For example, Silver customers may be given a basic level of service quality, whereas Gold customers could be given a higher level. Rather than hard-coding these policies in the service, we have the service read them from the externalized run-time policy and apply them. Now, when we decide that we have to add a Platinum customer, with an even higher SLA, we don't need to rewrite the service; we just create a new run-time policy.

Conclusion

SOA has evolved over the past decade to create some of the most flexible applications in use today. Now, SOA is quickly becoming the architecture of choice for commercial software products and for custom application development. Yet, SOA remains difficult to master because success with SOA relies not on technology, but on architecture and design.

Overall, SOA applies a layered architectural approach to supporting business flexibility by separating business processes from operational resources. The trick to flexibility and the value delivered by SOA depends on the quality of the service layers that separates them. A simple "services should be large-grained" approach doesn't cut it. Services come in all sizes and shapes. The trick is knowing the characteristics of each type of service, when to use them, and how to design services to support the important characteristics of encapsulation, isolation of responsibility, flexibility, modularity, composability, autonomy, and loose coupling.

Still, that is not enough for success. Size matters, but knowing how services should be used is just as important. Services play three basic roles in supporting business processes: tasks, entities, and decisions. In other words, SOA provides a modern implementation approach to Decision Models that integrates decisions into the overall enterprise and makes them readily available for business processes. Enterprises that understand the value of business decisions, and use them effectively through an SOA platform, will be steps ahead of their competition. Will you?

Summary

The most important concepts covered in this chapter are the following:

- SOA is an architectural style promoting the concept of business-aligned enterprise service as the fundamental unit of designing, building, and composing enterprise business processes and solutions.
- SOA gets to the "what," not the "how" of services. In order to create meaningful business processes, the architecture needs to specify several important characteristics, including how services
  - Have similar size, shape, form, function, and other characteristics
  - Conform to enterprise standards

- Communicate at a technical level
- Communicate at a semantic level
- Support enterprise goals and strategy

■ The value of SOA includes the following:
  - Consistency—Regardless of the path taken to the service, it behaves in the same way.
  - Commonality—A single access point to common information spread across the enterprise.
  - Modularity and flexibility—Modules can be reused and recombined across multiple processes and scenarios.
  - Decoupled—Independent business units, applications, etc., can work together, but continue to have their own schedules, life cycles, and business drivers.
  - Manageability—The ability to manage our business at the modular level.
■ BPM without SOA is useful for building applications, but difficult to extend to the enterprise. SOA without BPM is useful for creating reusable and consistent services, but lacks the ability to turn those services into an agile, competitive enterprise. We integrate these two through a layered architecture (and, importantly, its informational contents) that consists of the following:
  - Business processes and enterprise data (documents)
  - Business services and consolidated data (semantic data)
  - Integration services and integration data (transformations)
  - Enterprise resources, existing systems, and operational data (online data)
■ A service is a discrete unit of business functionality that is made available through a service contract that specifies all interaction between the service consumer and service provider, including the following:
  - Service interface
  - Interface documents
  - Service policies
  - Quality of service
  - Performance
■ A service is explicitly managed (unlike components or objects) through an SLA.
■ The two major aspects of the service (which are specifically separated) are the
  - Service interface, which specifies
    • What the service does
    • Parameters to be passed to and from the operations
    • Protocols to be used
  - Service implementation, which is how the service provides the capabilities, and may be
    • Based on existing applications
    • Orchestrating other services together

- Based on code written
- All of the above

■ The service implementation may be changed once the service is deployed, replacing older code or retired implementation. The users (consumers) of the service may never notice the change as long as the behavior and contract do not change.

■ At the service interface, the information passed between services must be agreed and be common among services to enable and complete the business process. The internal data model of the services is independent, and therefore allows us to easily translate between the common (virtual) definition and the internal (physical) implementation.

■ The SLA specifies two important performance criteria about the service:
  - The technical performance in terms of response time, throughput, availability, and reliability
  - Business performance in terms of business units of work performed within a certain time frame and to a specific quality level

■ There are three layers of information relating to services:
  - Physical data—Data that is actually stored on disk, described in a database schema, and optimized for performance.
  - Domain data—Data that is used in the service implementation. It is described in a standard data model, is a view of the physical data, and may come from one or more physical data stores.
  - Semantic data—This is the data that describes the common understanding of business entities and information that must be shared between services. It is
    - Closely aligned to the business model.
    - Used to describe information that is exchanged through service interfaces.
    - A normalized view of the common data from all the different services.

■ In addition to the service characteristics, good services must also display the following specific characteristics:
  - Modularity and granularity
  - Encapsulation
  - Loose coupling
  - Isolation of responsibilities
  - Autonomy
  - Reuse
  - Dynamic discovery and binding
  - Stateless
  - Self-describing
  - Composable
  - Governed by policy
  - Independent of location, language, and protocol

- There is a wide range of granularity of services, based upon a hierarchy of types:
  - Enterprise business processes: Business processes that span the entire enterprise and can make use of the underlying services.
  - "Business" services: The most coarse-grained services that provide composite business function, for example, "Policy Issuance."
  - Domain services: Medium-grained services used throughout, but within the domain, for example, "Customer," and generally used by business services.
  - Utility services: The least coarse-grained, for example, "item number," "phone number," etc. May be enterprisewide.
  - Integration services: Expose existing applications as services. The granularity of integration services will be partially dependent on the existing systems that they expose.
  - External services: External services enable access to systems and applications provided by suppliers or partners external to the enterprise (e.g., credit card validation, shipment tracking). The granularity of external services will depend on the particular service provider.
  - Foundation services: Foundation services provide fine-grained capabilities that are used in the construction of higher-level services, independent of any business domain (e.g., security, logging, and orchestration).
- Service roles—The intended purpose of role or a service, allowing for service specialization:
  - Task role services: Services that implement a business function (typically composed of other services).
  - Entity role services: Services that primarily manage access to business entities (e.g., customers, policies, claims, etc.).
  - Decision role services: Services that execute business rules to provide business decisions (e.g., approve creditworthiness).
- Combine these service playing different roles to provide flexible business capabilities that support the activities of the business process, using best practices and patterns to help to reduce dependencies, limit coupling, and maximize flexibility.
- One of the keys to achieving SOA success is creating a collection of services that can be combined together to support a variety of different business processes and scenarios:
  - Avoid overlaps in function between services.
  - Avoid gaps in function between services.
  - Avoid duplication of data.
  - Coordinate access to data.
  - Have a single, consistent way to perform a given function.
- To achieve these goals, keep the following questions in mind during the design of a service:

- Who is responsible for a given function? Where is that function used?
- Who is responsible for management of specific data?
- Who is responsible for defining and implementing specific rules?
- What step in the process owns the specific knowledge needed to perform a given task?

■ Create a service inventory to understand the overall context in which the SOA applies. This requires an understanding of the business and domain models. The inventory should support two major design time goals, that is, provide mechanisms for the following:
   - Understanding the overall service context to aid in the selection of services for reuse
   - Identifying the boundaries of responsibility of a particular service as a guideline for implementation of the service
■ A service inventory can be organized in a useful matrix of service types and service roles.
■ Flexible service designs are created using indirection, or externalization of variable parameters and rules. Externalization of rules permits flexibility in policy and in customization.
■ SOA provides a modern implementation approach for Decision Models that integrates decisions into the overall enterprise and makes them readily available for business processes.

Chapter 16

Specifications, Standards, Practices, and the Decision Model

Contents

The Importance of Specifications and Standards...387
    What Are Specifications and Standards?..387
How Do They Relate to Current Practices?..388
Practice #1: Business Planning...388
    The Business Motivation Model (BMM) Specification..............................388
    The BMM and the Decision Model...389
Practice #2: Business Process Modeling 389
    The Business Process Modeling Notation Specification (BPMN) 390
    BPMN and the Decision Model 390
    Unified Modeling Language (UML) Specification 390
    UML and the Decision Model..391
    Integration of BMM, BPMN, Use Cases, and the Decision Model.............391
Practice #3: Information (Fact Type) Modeling..391
    A Glossary of Fact Types 392
    Fact Model 392
    Data Model 396
    Business Object Model 397

Information Models and the Decision Model 398
    Is a Fully Populated Glossary Necessary before Developing the
    Decision Model? 399
    Information Model Standards and Specifications.................................... 400
Practice #4: Business Logic and Business Rule Modeling................................. 400
    Semantics of Business Vocabulary and Rules Specification (SBVR) 400
        Overview of SBVR...401
    SBVR and the Decision Model 402
        How SBVR and the Decision Model Can Be Used Together...................403
        Top-Down and Bottom-Up Decision Models Using SBVR.................... 404
        The Decision Model Is Independent of SBVR.. 404
        Translation from SBVR to Rule Family 404
    Decision Trees.. 406
    Decision Trees and the Decision Model 406
    Production Rules 407
    Production Rule Specifications and the Decision Model 407
Practice #5: Information Systems Development Approaches 408
    The Role of Business Logic.. 408
    Information Systems Development Approaches and the
    Decision Model 409
        General Opportunities 409
        Component Testing...410
        The Decision Model in Agile Methodology 411
        Documentation... 411
    STEP Business Decision Methodology Approach 412
        A Brief Description of STEP 413
        The Decision Model Doesn't Mean a New Methodology......................... 415
Practice #6: The Decision Model and System Transformation Methods............416
    The Fundamentals of System Transformation...416
    A Common Shortcut 418
    System Transformation and the Decision Model 418
Summary.. 420

A natural question is how the Decision Model relates to current standards and best practices. This chapter explores the most common of these. It specifically emphasizes opportunities for improving them or how they are used. It is not meant to be exhaustive, but to touch only on those standards and best practices most common in, and most relevant to, Decision Model adoption.

The chapter starts by defining what is meant by standards and specifications and their importance. It proceeds to discuss the standards and specifications within six important areas of business practice and the likely impact of the Decision Model on these practices.

Readers may find it useful to investigate the influence of the Decision Model on industry standards, specifications, and common practices for two reasons. The first reason is that the Decision Model enhances usage of these standards and specifications because it fills a gap they don't address. The second reason is that the Decision Model itself may serve as a foundation for development of additional standards and specifications.*

The Importance of Specifications and Standards

What Are Specifications and Standards?

Roughly speaking, standards and specifications are principles or descriptions of how something is done or measured. They are established by an authority, common practice, or a level of consent. The publication of standards and specifications allows practitioners to benefit from the expertise of the bodies that establish them and to do so in a commonly acceptable manner. Adherence to standards and specifications promotes consistent communications and interoperability of final products, if appropriate. There is a difference between a standard and a specification.

A formal standard is a set of explicit specifications for a practice or artifact published by an international or national standards body. Examples of such bodies include the International Organization for Standardization (ISO), National Institute of Standards and Technology (NIST), International Electrotechnical Commission (IEC), and American National Standards Institute (ANSI). A de facto standard is a specification promoted by an industry group, or a single vendor that is so widely practiced as to be accepted as the norm. An example of a formal standard is SQL, which is both an ANSI and ISO standard.

A specification is a publication by an industry group, or a vendor consortium, often for the purpose of achieving adoption by standards bodies or of becoming a de facto standard. Examples of consortiums are Object Management Group (OMG), Organization for the Advancement of Structured Information Standards

---

* A useful future standard or specification may be a Decision Definition Language by which Rule Families are defined in much the same way that a Data Definition Language defines relational structures. Such a Decision Definition Language would include syntax for naming a Rule Family and defining its condition key, conclusion, and inferential keys, for example.

(OASIS), RuleML.org, and World Wide Web Consortium* (W3C). Examples of specifications include OMG's Semantic of Business Vocabulary and Business Rules (SBVR) and Production Rule Representation (PRR).

How Do They Relate to Current Practices?

The Decision Model plays a role in many different practices spanning areas of business management to systems development. This chapter considers the following six practices that benefit from the Decision Model:

- Business planning
- Business process modeling
- Information modeling
- Business logic and business rule modeling
- Information systems development
- System transformation

In some of these practices, multiple standards and specifications abound, as well as vendor practices. This chapter discusses, at a high level, each practice and one or more related standards or specifications for each, as appropriate. The objective is to review how the Decision Model in conjunction with these standards and specifications offers improvement in the related practice.

Practice #1: Business Planning

Business planning is an activity undertaken for the purpose of influencing the future of an organization in meeting the goals of its stakeholders, taking into account its resources and constraints. The practice varies widely, ranging from the informal, perhaps spontaneous, calculations on the back of a napkin for business start-ups, to the regular, highly formalized process often pursued in large enterprises.

The Business Motivation Model (BMM) Specification

The Business Motivation Model (BMM) is an OMG specification addressing the practice of business planning. The BMM was originally proposed by the Business Rules Group (BRG), an industry consortium of practitioners with an interest in business rules. The purpose of the BMM is to provide the basis for tools to support the creation of business plans for business enterprises. In other words, it is a meta-model for business planning.

---

* W3C is an international consortium consisting of member organizations drawn from all the major industry vendors and associations, a full-time staff, and the public, who work together to develop Web standards. W3C's mission is "to lead the World Wide Web to its full potential by developing protocols and guidelines that ensure long-term growth for the Web." Tim Berners-Lee, the inventor of the Internet, is a Director of W3C.

The "as-is" diagram in Figure 6.3 (Chapter 6) contains a high-level representation of the current BMM. Because business planning aims to produce a roadmap for business success, the BMM provides a set of concepts by which a planner records, tracks, and traces how Ends are to be achieved through Means. The concepts in the BMM delineate different kinds of Means and different kinds of Ends. The diagram shows these major concepts, organized into the following:

- Vision, Goal, and Objective, which together make up the End
- Mission, Course of Action, and Directive, which provide the Means
- Assessment, which makes a judgment on the outcome of End, based on the Means and the impact of Influencers

The Course of Action is realized through Directives, which include Business Policy and Business Rule. The Course of Action, particularly the Strategy, guides business process and connects the BMM to business process. The BMM does not recognize the concept of business decision, but it does contain the concept of business rule. Business rules are not organized into a model in the BMM but are considered to be modeled externally. Such a model is thought by the BMM authors as likely to be a set of business rules that implement a particular Course of Action.

The BMM and the Decision Model

The Decision Model is a model of a set of business rules that implement a Course of Action. The Decision Model is also the means by which the Course of Action controls a business process. The Decision Model, therefore, is a complementary model to the BMM. The relationship between the BMM and the Decision Model is set out in detail in Chapter 6.

Practice #2: Business Process Modeling

Business process modeling, a component of BPM, is the modeling and graphical depiction of business processes for the purpose of process improvement, shared understanding, and business planning.

Business process modeling approaches include symbols for representing different kinds of activities and various options for sequencing them. For example, some activities are to occur in a specific sequence, whereas others are to occur in parallel, and so forth. Business process modeling, often known by other names, is a practice that has a long history and became more formal with the introduction of early flowchart approaches decades ago. The practice of modeling business processes became very popular with the advent of Michael Hammer's Business Process Reengineering approach and continues today in various forms of BPM approaches. There are numerous methodologies and notation for representing sequential business activities.

The Business Process Modeling Notation Specification (BPMN)

A de facto standard in business process modeling is the OMG specification, Business Process Modeling Notation (BPMN). Chapter 17 discusses this specification and the mechanisms by which it is currently evolving to distinguish between procedural and declarative tasks. As detailed in Chapter 17, BPMN is evolving to include a new kind of task currently proposed as a Business Rule Task, to indicate a task involving execution of one or more business rules.

It is the proposed Business Rule Task that can be the placeholder for an entire business decision and its corresponding Decision Model. Acceptance of the proposed Business Rule Task or a version of it into the BPMN specification will represent a step forward from the current situation, where no distinction is made between a process task and a business logic task.

BPMN and the Decision Model

The Decision Model offers a significant evolution of business process modeling and BPMN in three ways. First, it supports the clear distinction and separation between the procedural nature of process tasks and the declarative, nature of decision tasks. Second, the Decision Model represents a uniform structure by which business logic is organized into a larger, more complex, fully declarative, and normalized collection of business logic. Third, this book proposes that the connection between a business process model and a Decision Model be an anchor point called business decision and not a link to individual business rules (or business logic statements). That's because maintaining individual links becomes impractical to manage and really isn't necessary.

Unified Modeling Language (UML) Specification

The Unified Modeling Language (UML) is an OMG specification for a graphical notation for defining, visualizing, and documenting software systems. Although UML is an OMG specification, it has a storied history, being the union of three separate and competitive vendor offerings. Over time the vendors, coalesced under the umbrella of Rational Software (now IBM), developed a nonproprietary, single version of the notation (hence "Unified" in the name). The UML 1.4.2 specification is an international standard, ISO/IEC 19501-205 Information Technology—Open Distributed Processing.

The focus of UML is software development, and therefore, it is not generally directly concerned with business process modeling for shared business understanding. UML diagrams are generally encountered in Row 3 and Row 4 of the Zachman Framework, lower levels than the Decision Model.

However, UML has a range of diagrams, including activity and use case diagrams that can, and are used to, depict sequential business activity. In fact, a common practice is to develop business use cases, and this is doubtless a Zachman Row 2 activity, as would be any activity diagrams derived from those business use cases.

UML and the Decision Model

Currently, in UML, the use case consists of a sequence of steps performed sequentially. Business rules or logic that is required at any step is simply annotated in the step. To leverage the Decision Model, a use case step should be designated as a "decision step," and assigned the name of the Decision Model that connects to that use case step. This would provide the opportunity to separate the decision logic from the use case description and manage it separately and appropriately.

A similar case for externalization of business logic can be made for activity diagrams and other sequential diagram classes within UML.

Integration of BMM, BPMN, Use Cases, and the Decision Model

Obviously, business planning is a very important practice because it aligns Means and Ends. Most business plans involve implementing or improving business processes whereby business decisions in those business processes are part of that alignment (the Course of Action and the Directive). So, it follows that there should be a connection among these three models. This integration makes it possible for a business to create business plans, define business processes according to those plans, and deliver business decisions that guide business processes aligned with business motivations (i.e., the value system).

Figure 16.1 illustrates one way to achieve the integration.

The relationships shown in Figure 16.1 among the Business Motivation Model, the business process model, and the Decision Model complete the path from business planning to execution. These relationships are explored in greater depth in Chapter 6.

Practice #3: Information (Fact Type) Modeling*

For the purpose of this chapter, information modeling is the structural representation of vocabulary. Vocabulary is defined as "a structured set of terms and other symbols together with their meanings and relationships among them, for use by a business community" (Object Management Group, 2006). Because the terms in this definition

---

* This chapter uses the term *information modeling* in the broad sense of representing facts or information, as opposed to representing processes or business logic or other modeled aspects.

are the fact types in a Decision Model, the models in this section can also be referred to as fact type models because the goal is to create a structure of fact types.

Information models are used for a range of purposes (and audiences), the most popular purpose being the foundation of database design.

There are various styles and preferences to represent the nouns, noun phrases, and connections among them in a model. The styles differ mostly in three areas: the intended audience, the primary purpose each serves for that audience, and the way each represents facts for the purpose and audience.

The most common types of information models are the following:

■ Fact model
■ Data model
■ Business object model

The practice of information modeling, although more recent than business process modeling, has a long and rich history. Therefore, there are varying approaches, notations, and standards.

Of interest in this chapter is the relationship of information modeling to the Decision Model, rather than to related specifications or standards. The most atomic element in the Decision Model is the fact type, and this same element occurs in most information models. The next few sections briefly review the different model types, and then summarize their potential relationship to the Decision Model.

A Glossary of Fact Types

A glossary of fact types for Decision Modeling is neither a standard nor a specification. It isn't even a model in the truest sense of the word. It is simply a managed list with an entry for every fact type or literal value in a Decision Model. There are currently no industry specifications or standards, and most glossaries are maintained in look-up table format in spreadsheets or databases.

The benefit of creating a glossary of fact types is that businesspeople, rather than business analysts or technical people, are at ease with maintaining and consulting a dictionary-like form of the glossary, and it provides rigor to a corresponding Decision Model. That is, specific modeling skills are not needed, especially if the fact types are not overly complex. An example of a Fact Type glossary for a Decision Model may be found in Table 7.7 (Chapter 7). If a fact type in the glossary becomes complex or there is a need to clarify its context with other fact types, a fact model may be useful. Examples are provided in the next section.

Fact Model

A fact model is a model of vocabulary and is used to impose rigor on a vocabulary. It represents the noun phrases in a full vocabulary that can be used in business

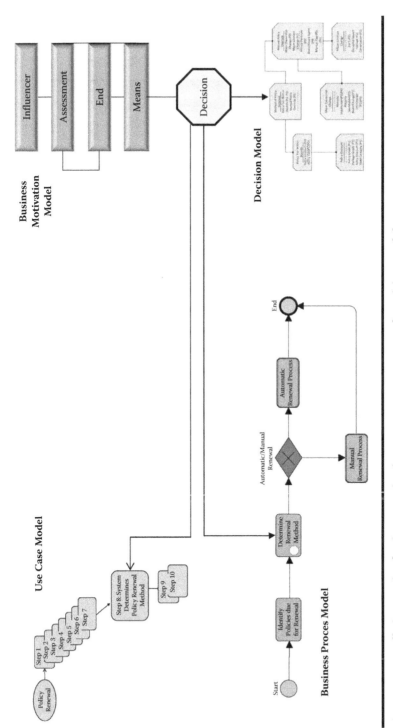

Figure 16.1 Fully integrating business motivation, process, use case, and Decision Models.

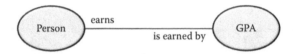

Figure 16.2 Sample fact model.

logic statements or business rules. Fact models depict subjects (the nouns or noun phrases) and predicates (the verbs or verb phrases). A fact model is a very rigorous model for representing fact types because it defines not only all nouns participating in a fact type but also the verb phrases among them that give the whole fact type a full context. A fact model includes those connections on the fact model diagram itself. Essentially, for the sake of a simple explanation, a fact model is a special way of diagramming a subject as a noun phrase and a predicate as a verb phrase.

Figure 16.2 depicts a very simple fact model in simple notation. It contains two nouns or terms. These are Person and GPA, and each is shown as an oval. It also contains a fact type that connects these terms. The fact type is shown as a line between the ovals with the verb phrases "earns" and "is earned by." (Some notations illustrate the fact type as a box between the lines.) The full fact type is "Person earns GPA" and "GPA is earned by Person."

In this case, one of the nouns, GPA, has a value that is the result of a computation. Once the formula is known for computing its value, this fact model may be extended to include other terms and connecting facts that are used in its formula.

Figure 16.3 illustrates a fact model consisting of four noun phrases. These are Person, First Name, Eye Color, and Date of Birth. It also contains three verb expressions. These are labeled "is called by/is given to," "has an/is of," and "is born on/is birthday of." These connect the nouns or terms appropriately into fact types. In a rigorous fact model, the connections are named in both directions.

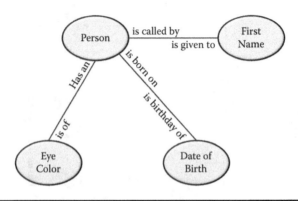

Figure 16.3 Fact model of four terms and three fact types.

Notice that all of the nouns are represented by the same shape (i.e., ovals), so there is no distinction between a noun that is a business concept (e.g., Person) and one that is a property (e.g., Eye Color, Date of Birth, First Name).

Some fact types can be very complicated. The more complicated fact types are those that need significant context to give them precise meaning. Such complex fact types are typically those that represent the following:

■ A function or mathematical formula on fact types to produce another fact type's value
■ Traversal of connections among fact types
■ Logic executed on a "cluster" of related fact types

A formal fact model can be very helpful for clarifying these kinds of noun phrases.

Consider the fact type of "First Name of Dependent of a Member covered by a Plan governing a Claim." When there are a lot of OF's or possessive nouns in a fact type name, there are likely to be many facts or relationships to uncover, model, name, and define, and some are hidden (i.e., not even mentioned) in the noun phrase. In this case, the fact that a Claim is submitted against a Plan did not appear in the name of the fact type.

Figure 16.4 shows a fact model using simple notation to provide full context for this fact type.

Here is another example of a complex fact type: Maximum Amount Due of Unpaid Order for a Customer over the past 12 months.

This is complex because its full context involves a combination of relationships or connections among fact types along with additional logic execution. The logic execution includes processing for a maximum amount, determination of unpaid status, and doing so over the past 12 months. One possible way to model this fact

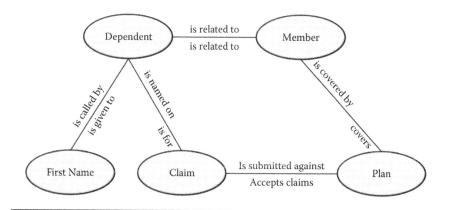

Figure 16.4   Modeling a complex fact type.

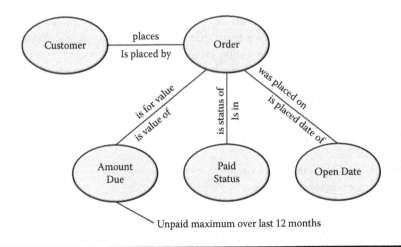

Figure 16.5 Adding execution logic to a complex fact type.

type is shown in Figure 16.5. Fact modeling techniques such as object-role modeling (ORM) exploit similar techniques to provide comprehensive fact modeling that supports a form of constraint logic.

In a fact model, every constituent noun appears with all of its associated fact types, each such association as a structural element. A fact model is, therefore, a very rigorous way of representing vocabulary because it exhibits a more detailed structure of fact types than do data and object models. The audience for a fact model is a business person or business analyst because it aims for precision in expression only, without technology considerations.

Data Model

By data model, this chapter refers to a logical data model that represents a logical data structure, independent of how it is physically stored in a target database technology. As such, it consists of data entities (similar to business concepts, such as Customer, Product), attributes (such as properties of a business concept, like Credit Rating of Customer), and relationships (representing connections from one entity to another, such as Customer places Order). Nouns and noun phrases that represent business concepts become entities and are modeled as boxes. Nouns and noun phrases that are properties of business concepts become attributes and are placed inside the boxes.

Therefore, a data-oriented model names the relationships among entities, but not the connections from an entity to its attributes. Also, attributes are placed inside the entity typically for those attributes stored in a database.

Figure 16.6 depicts a sample logical data model, using simple notation, showing the context behind the fact type of Person's GPA. A data model typically only

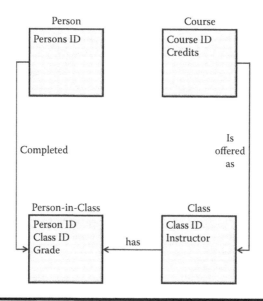

Figure 16.6   Sample data model.

shows fact types to be stored in a database. So, GPA is not there. However, the pieces for knowing the GPA are shown because they are stored in a database, along with data relationships among them. Here, a business concept of Course has two properties (i.e., Course ID, Credits) and is related to its possibly many classes, which is a business concept with two properties (i.e., Class ID and Instructor) that is related to its possibly many business concepts of Person-in-Class, which has three properties (e.g., Person ID, Class ID, Grade person received in the Class). Person is a business concept containing one property (i.e., Person ID), but is likely to contain Person Name, Person Eye Color, and Person Date of Birth. This model utilizes lines to show relationships among business concepts, putting the properties inside the boxes.

The primary purpose of a logical data model is to serve as a starting point for database design. Thus, the audience for it is a data modeler or database designer. However, it can also serve to validate a Decision Model whose fact types are represented by entities, attributes, and relationships. A logical data model may not fully suffice if it does not include fact types that are not stored in a database.

Business Object Model

The business object model does not contain technology-related considerations. As such, it is a model of objects (sometimes called object classes and similar to business concepts, such as Customer, Product), properties (similar to properties of a business

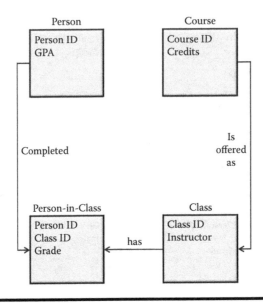

Figure 16.7 Sample business object model.

concept, such as Credit Rating of Customer), and relationships (representing connections from one object to another, such as Customer places Order).

A business object model names the relationships among objects, but properties are placed inside an object. Unlike most logical data models, business object models include properties that are not necessarily stored in a database. Refer to Figure 16.7 as a sample business object model showing the context behind the fact type Person's GPA. Unlike the previous data model, Person's GPA appears as a property of Person, whether or not it is stored in a database. The model may also depict the fact types for calculating the GPA, although these fact types are not shown in this figure.

The primary purpose of a business object model is to serve as a starting point for software design. In some respects, it is much like a data model, but it also serves as a means of creating object classes that interact with one another in a software implementation. Thus, its audience is a software designer or developer. However, it can also serve to validate a Decision Model whose fact types are its object, properties, and relationships. It is a very common adjunct to a Decision Model when such Decision Models are to be implemented in object-oriented technology.

Information Models and the Decision Model

The development of an information model of any kind is often a significant effort.

In practice, the decision of whether to create a formal information model (in addition to a glossary) as well as selection of a particular type of vocabulary model (fact, object, or data) may and should vary from project to project. Sometimes this decision will be driven by the rigor required in the vocabulary to yield accurate and precise business logic statements, how skilled or trained the audience is in vocabulary model rigor, or risk assessment of cost versus precision.

In many cases, a Decision Model, aimed at a pure business audience, can be supported with a glossary alone, sometimes with an information model for clarity. For Decision Models that will be automated (in a BRMS or not), a formal information model (usually object oriented or data oriented or both) will be needed for technically oriented purposes, not so much for business purposes. Also, frequently, for reasons external to the development of the Decision Model, an information model may already exist, or is intended to be developed, as an asset of the enterprise (or of a specific project). In these cases, the Decision Model should interface with it through the glossary. In other words, the Decision Model should contain fact types that are recognizable to the business audience, not those recognized only by technical people. When developing an information model, every fact type in the Decision Model should be defined in the glossary, and every fact type in the glossary, should be in such a model.

Is a Fully Populated Glossary Necessary before Developing the Decision Model?

The building of the Decision Model will certainly proceed quicker if a standard, agreed-upon information model or glossary is in place. However, this is hardly ever the case, and it is often impractical to require the creation of one before creating the Decision Model.

Instead, creation of a glossary or information model can occur in parallel and iteratively with the population of the Decision Model. This is a highly suitable approach for the highest productivity. In fact, a Decision Model can be created with a partial glossary before the Rule Families are fully populated, so that an initial information model, and perhaps automated prototype, can also be developed early.

The scope of a Decision Model, by definition, is a business decision. In other words, a Decision Model contains only the business logic required to reach a conclusion for the conclusion fact type and nothing more than that. This means that there is an information model for each business decision, not necessarily one for the entire project. Of course, there may be an information model for an entire project for the purpose of database design or software design, but a Decision Model does not require one. In practice, this means that an information model or glossary can be delivered for each business decision rather than aiming to deliver a project- or enterprisewide glossary or information model first. Subsequently, the glossaries and information models for the Decision Models within a project can be integrated and cross-referenced to project or enterprise glossaries and information models.

Information Model Standards and Specifications

There is a wide array of standards and specifications within the information modeling practice that have to do with the notation and methods for modeling vocabulary. All of these should, in principle, be able to connect to the Decision Model by mapping to the fact types in the glossary.

Practice #4: Business Logic and Business Rule Modeling

Prior to the publication of the Decision Model, the terms business rule modeling or business logic modeling meant the capturing of business rule statements and connecting them to information models or organizing them as a new subtype of requirements. These phrases did not refer to organizing these statements into a distinct model of their own.

Because the past focus has been on individual business rule statements, not on a normalized model of them, current specifications have aimed at ways of expressing business rules using templates, keywords, or prescribed grammars. The adoption of such specifications is beneficial because project and organizations will express business rules (and business logic) in similar ways. Indeed, these specifications have led to the introduction of software that assists in authoring expressions that adhere to a specific grammar, which should improve the precision and understandability of the final expressions.

The Decision Model, however, is not concerned with how such expressions are articulated, but rather with how they should be grouped in a rigorous way. So, the introduction of the Decision Model can also lead to new kinds of modeling tools or new functionality added to existing modeling tools, including those mentioned earlier that support rigorous business rule authoring.

It seems obvious that the practice of business logic and business rule modeling needs both perspectives to come together. That is, it needs a common mechanism for creating a normalized structure of business logic statements and business rules. And it also needs a common mechanism for articulating instances of those normalized structures in an industry-acceptable manner. There is a specification addressing the latter, discussed in the following section.

Semantics of Business Vocabulary and Rules Specification (SBVR)

SBVR is a specification published by OMG in 2006. This specification is valuable because it elevates business rules to the attention of the business audience, not just as a deliverable for technical audiences. SBVR "… is conceptualized optimally for business people rather than automated rules processing, and is designed to be used for business purposes, independent of information systems designs" (Object Management Group, 2006).

Overview of SBVR

SBVR provides a context for the meaning of a business vocabulary and its rules from a business perspective. As such, it includes a metamodel of the vocabulary to support business rules from a business, nontechnical perspective. SBVR is focused on the formal expression of the business rule statement, having a comprehensive set of grammar for the expression of such a statement.

In SBVR, consistent with the BMM, the business rule falls within the category of "Statements of Guidance." The categorization is structured in the hierarchy shown in Figure 16.8.

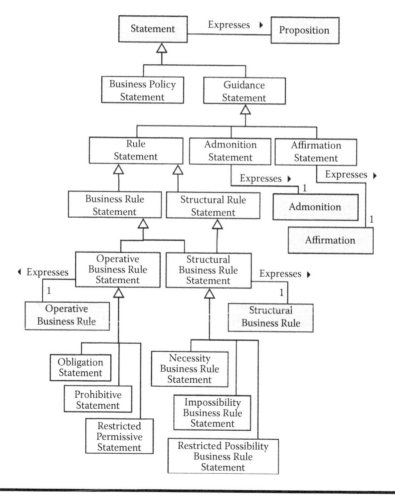

Figure 16.8 SBVR statements of guidance. (Source: Semantics of Business Vocabulary and Business Rules (SBVR) Interim Convenience Document, Object Management Group, Inc. © 2009. Reprinted with permission.)

The "Statements of Guidance" are made up of either business policy statements or business guidance statements. The latter covers "affirmation," "admonition," or "rule" statements. Rule Statements are expressed either as "operative" or "structural" business rule statements. Operative business rule statements are either an "obligation," "prohibitive," or "restricted permissive" statement, and express an "operative business rule" (which has "levels of enforcement"). Structural business rule statements are either a "necessity," "impossibility," or "restricted possibility" business rule statement, and express a "structural business rule." SBVR uses this classification of business statements to set the syntax for each business rule. The syntax is governed by the rigorous application of the semantics and the vocabulary.

The syntax of SBVR is complex, but very rich, and can encompass a wide range of business statements and logic. Here, to illustrate SBVR-type statements are some examples of business statements classified as operative business rule statements:

- Obligation statement:
  "If the drop-off location of a rental is not the EU-Rent site of the return branch of the rental, then it is obligatory that the rental incurs a location penalty charge."
  "A rental must incur a location penalty charge if the drop-off location of the rental is not the EU-Rent site of the return branch of the rental."
- Prohibitive Statement
  "It is prohibited that a rental is open if a driver of the rental is a barred driver."
  "A rental must not be open if a driver of the rental is a barred driver."
- Restricted Permissive Statement
  "It is permitted that a rental is open only if an estimated rental charge is provisionally charged to the credit card of the renter of the rental."
  "A rental may be open only if an estimated rental charge is provisionally charged to the credit card of the renter of the rental." (Object Management Group, 2006)

SBVR also includes a modeling capability for fact types, using Concept Diagram Graphic Notation. UML Notation may, as an alternative to the Concepts Diagram Graphic Notation, also be extended to represent SBVR-style vocabularies.

SBVR and the Decision Model

SBVR and the Decision Model play different roles and are used for entirely different purposes. It is important to review these differences to understand how the two can work together.

As indicated in the previous section, SBVR is a semantic schema for representing fact types and for expressing individual rules about the fact types. SBVR focuses on translating statements containing business rules and policies into a rigorous and precise articulation using parts of speech from natural language, not from programming languages.

The Decision Model, on the other hand, is a rigorous and graphical model for business decisions, the content of which is individual logic statements. The Decision Model groups together and represents all business logic about a single business decision based on normalization and other principles. It is a mechanism for ensuring that all of the business logic necessary to implement a business decision is complete and correct.

The rigor and distinct properties of the Decision Model's graphics are extremely important to its usage and value as a distinct asset. The Decision Model's graphical form is easily, quickly, and accurately able to be authored by business users with little or no analytical training. It also provides a graphic visualization of the business logic behind a single business decision. Within a Rule Family, the business rule is not represented by a complete natural language sentence, but as a row in a decision table adhering to first normal form at a minimum. This presentation of business logic has proved very accessible and has become popular with business users. The logic can be reviewed, in relation to the rest of the logic in the Rule Family, at a glance. Errors in logic, missing logic, and redundant logic are simple to spot. The graphical representation of the Decision Model also enables easy visual impact analysis of any change of business logic and enables changes to the business logic to be made by a very simple change to a single cell in the Rule Families or the addition (or deletion) of a single column or row.

Bruce Silver says that "collaboration around artifacts between business and IT demands a 'visual language' usable by both" (Silver, 2008). In this regard, the Decision Model has proved to be very effective and is not in conflict with SBVR. It simply is a means of putting SBVR statements into a larger business context (i.e., the business decision) and elevates them to higher levels of business management attention.

How SBVR and the Decision Model Can Be Used Together

It is natural that the Decision Model and SBVR can be used together. The Decision Model provides the visible structural organization of business logic statements, whereas SBVR provides a means for expressing each Rule Family instance as a natural language statement compliant with the SBVR specification. Conversely, SBVR statements can serve as input to populating Rule Families.

In many cases, there will be a one-to-one mapping from one SBVR statement to one instance in a Rule Family, but not for all cases. That is, sometimes one SBVR statement may translate into more than one Rule Family instance because first normal form for the Decision Model is sometimes more atomic than certain SBVR statements. The first normal form of some Rule Family instances renders the Rule Family closer to pieces of executable business logic than the SBVR representation.

In practice, the decomposition of some SBVR statements into more atomic first normal form versions in a Rule Family reveals that the atomic pieces themselves may actually change independently of the other pieces. And so, the business audience finds the first normal form very amenable to making such changes.

Nevertheless, any Rule Family in the Decision Model can be associated with a corresponding set of (one or more) SBVR statements.

Top-Down and Bottom-Up Decision Models Using SBVR

One way to develop a Decision Model is to first create a set of SBVR statements (e.g., derived from policies, fact models, business process models, or use cases) and subsequently organize them into normalized Rule Family structures. Obviously, this approach starts with the details (i.e., SBVR statements) and derives the normalized structure from them (i.e., Decision Models).

Another way to develop a Decision Model is to first identify condition and conclusion fact types, organize them into normalized Rule Families, and subsequently translate each instance into corresponding SBVR statements. Clearly, this approach starts with a preliminary guess at the structure (i.e., Rule Family headings) and derives the details from it (i.e., SBVR statements).*

The Decision Model Is Independent of SBVR

It is important to point out that the Decision Model does not require that SBVR be applied to its contents. Other ways of expressing its content are acceptable as far as the principles of the Decision Model are concerned. So, the Decision Model is independent of SBVR or any other future specification or standard. However, if SBVR becomes a well-practiced and popular specification, there would be advantages to expressing Rule Family content using SBVR. This is especially true if SBVR-supported software tools become widely used. The next section explores the representation of SBVR statements in a Rule Family.

Translation from SBVR to Rule Family

Some of the SBVR statements given earlier contain references to fact types with phrases such as "rental," "driver of the rental," "barred driver," and "renter of the

---

* Historically, in creating early data models, there were two general approaches in practice. The bottom-up approach was to first identify data elements and subsequently apply normalization principles to them to arrive at a normalized data model. The top-down approach was to first take a guess at the normalized structure (i.e., a preliminary entity-relationship diagram), populate it with data elements according to normalization principles, and refine it. Most data modeling practitioners today prefer the top-down approach. As data modelers became more experienced, they were able to take a guess at a reasonable normalized data structure faster. The same may prove true for experienced decision modelers.

Table 16.1   Rule Family for SBVR Statements

		Conditions				Conclusion	
Rule Pattern	Rental's Driver	Rental's Estimated Charge				Rental	
1	Is	Barred				Is	Not Open
2			Is provisionally charged to	Renter's Credit Card			Is	Open

rental." For use in a Rule Family, they are renamed to Rental, Rental's Driver, Barred Driver, and Rental's Renter.

Table 16.1 illustrates a partial Rule Family populated from two aforementioned SBVR statements (and using the already-described naming conventions) that lead to a conclusion about whether or not a rental is open. From this representation, there are two Rule Patterns. Immediate questions surface from inspection of the Rule Family:

- Is there a difference between a Rental's Driver and a Rental's Renter? The glossary, fact model, data model, or object model should have definitions for these fact types.
- What other statuses are possible for a Rental's Driver—not barred? Anything else? Again, the glossary, fact model, data model, or object model may provide the answer.
- Are there other rows, possibly with other condition fact types, that lead to an open rental? To a rental that is not open? These questions arise when the SBVR statements are translated into a Rule Family representation where gaps in the business logic become quite evident.
- What does it mean for a rental to be open or not open? Again, the glossary, fact model, data model, or object model should provide the answers.

So, organizations may use SBVR and SBVR-based software to provide natural language expressions of their business statements. From here, organizing those business statements into Decision Model structures allows these organizations to manage the related business decisions that drive their process models and to easily automate these business decisions as automation software evolves. No matter what grammar is used to state each Rule Family row in natural language, its representation is always the same: conditions leading to the single conclusion.

There are other ways to elicit business rules or business logic that involve a graphic representation. A common way is the use of decision trees.

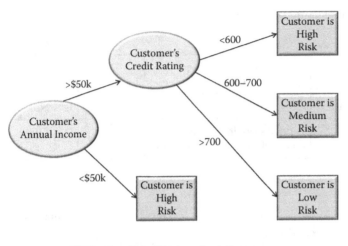

Four Actual Business Logic Statements:
- If Customer's Annual Income < $50k THEN Customer is High Risk
- If Customer's Annual Income > $50k AND Customer's Credit Rating <600 THEN Customer is High Risk
- If Customer's Annual Income > $50k AND Customer's Credit Rating BETWEEN 600 AND 700 THEN Customer is Medium Risk
- If Customer's Annual Income > $50k AND Customer's Credit Rating >700 THEN Customer is Low Risk

Figure 16.9   An example of a decision tree.

Decision Trees

A decision tree is a graphical representation of logic with a symbol for the antecedent (condition), the consequent (conclusion), and a directed line between them (Schreiber et al., 2001). The idea of "modeling" the relationship from conditions to conclusions is not a new one, and is often used in informal decision analysis.

Today, in practice, a decision tree is a very popular metaphor for drawing out and capturing logic in the manner illustrated in Figure 16.9. The figure shows two condition fact types (Customer's Annual Income and Customer's Credit Rating) and four possible conclusions for the same conclusion fact type of Customer's Risk. The figure suggests that Customer's Annual Income be tested first before testing Customer's Credit Rating. So, decision trees are a procedural representation of logic that this book proposes is better represented declaratively.

Decision Trees and the Decision Model

The diagram actually reduces to the four declarative business logic statements listed in the figure. Decision trees and similar representations are not part of the Decision Model, because they imply perhaps an unnecessary sequence of execution of conditions based on the arrows in such a graph. That's not to say that such representations are not useful for eliciting a set of conditions leading to conclusions, particularly when there are a limited number of nodes in the tree, because the decision tree provides easily accessible visual value. Once the elicitation is complete, however, the decision tree can be translated into and maintained as Rule Families because these are technology and processing independent, allowing flexibility and easier maintenance over time. If useful, decision trees can be saved and correlated with their related Rule Families.

Whether business rules and logic statements are expressed in SBVR, represented in decision trees, or cast as normalized business logic in a Decision Model, there is a need for a representation that is close to automation, understood by technical audiences but still technology independent. The next section addresses this need.

Production Rules

Work is proceeding on standards for business rule expressions that can be used across multiple platforms. Such a standard would be a prerequisite for MDA and interoperability, as today each BRMS has its own proprietary language. The shorthand name given to such a standard is Production Rules.

At this time, at least two groups are working on specifications for a standard form of expression of Production Rules. OMG is developing a specification called Production Rule Representation (PRR), and W3C is developing a specification called Rule Interchange Format (RIF). An "open standards" group called RuleML. org is working in parallel with W3C. OMG explains the division of labor as follows:

> There is an overlap in scope between W3C RIF and PRR, and they share the goal of rule interoperability, albeit for different stages of the software development lifecycle. The division of labor is
> - OMG PRR focuses on the standard metamodel definition and modeling of production rules (and possibly other rule types) with an XMI-compliant interchange format for UML based modeling tools.
> - W3C RIF focuses on a Rule Interchange Format suitable for the real-time "Web" and users of "Web technologies" such as XML. (Object Management Group, 2007)

Because it will be a while before the overlaps and specifications are clarified, vendors appear to be "watching with interest" before developing support for these production-oriented rule representations.

Production Rule Specifications and the Decision Model

The PIM form of business logic is useful to the Decision Model as it is a standard by which the Decision Model logic may be transformed into executable code.

The transform of Decision Model logic into production rule standards is dependent on the finalization of those standards, and significant technical work that will then need to be completed to create those transforms.

Because of the simple but rigorous structure of the Decision Model, developers should not have difficulty in creating a lossless transformation into a target form. All of the business logic constructs in the Decision Model are available in both the PRR and RIF, and vice versa.

All of the specifications and techniques discussed in this chapter so far are subsets of the larger practice: that of developing entire information systems.

Practice #5: Information Systems Development Approaches

This practice covers the process that enables the development of information systems from their conception to deployment. It includes the systems development process, methods of managing the process, and prescriptions for the work products.

The goal of the practice is to reduce the risk attached to building systems, which today are necessarily large and complex, involve many people, various roles, and often evolving technologies.

This is a broad practice embracing a wide range of disciplines. This chapter deals only with areas influenced by the Decision Model.

The Role of Business Logic

The evolution and maturation of systems development has resulted in the separation of concerns, new roles, hybrid roles (part business and part technical), modeling tools, requirements tools, change management tools, generations of software, and sophisticated academic degrees in computer science.

Despite such sophistication, the complexity (and politics) of the systems development process itself has not yet given adequate visibility and importance to the underlying business logic in the systems. Most conventional methodologies refer to "business rules," but these are either developed early in the requirements gathering (so it takes a long time) or are developed later because they are perceived as design details (so technical people solicit or construe them). In either case, they are usually created from an interaction between software developer and business person.

On the horizon then, is another significant improvement by which business logic or business rules is recognized as a true concern worth of full separation and management. This is an approach in which a businessperson articulates the business logic in a rigorous (but not difficult) form as input to the system requirements or design. For this to be possible, the business logic must be accessible to authorized business users so that they may author, review, and amend that logic within the systems development and maintenance cycle or within a shorter maintenance cycle.

Information Systems Development Approaches and the Decision Model

The Decision Model provides the means for the business to develop business logic in parallel to the development of the process models, use cases, business scenarios, other models and, in the case of agile methods, the code itself.

The development of Decision Models, potentially by businesspeople, changes the information systems development process. In some cases, businesspeople can and will lead the business process and decision modeling activities, at least to some extent, to ensure the accuracy of the business logic and the business process. If the Decision Model is easy to create, interpret, and maintain, it will be more likely that businesspeople will take control of the business decisions. The impediment will then be to find available business resources and who can invest their time in doing so. The impediment will not be that it is too difficult or that it requires technical skills.

Opportunities for related benefits based on experience are now explained in more detail.

General Opportunities

1. **The Decision Model can serve as an important deliverable very early.** In UP methodologies, the Decision Model can be delivered during the Inception and Elaboration phases and even incrementally within those phases. In UP (Unified Process) approaches, Decision Modeling fits most naturally as a part of the Business Modeling, Requirements, and Analysis disciplines. If done as part of Business Modeling, it is likely to invite much business participation. If done as part of Requirements, it is likely to involve a team of business analysts and businesspeople.

2. **The Decision Model can simplify business process models and deliver them quicker.** These improvements are possible when Decision Models are taken up in parallel with business process models, use cases, and UI design.

3. **In some cases, Decision Models can be created without any relationship to process flow, use case, or UI flow.** In other words, Decision Models can be driven by business motivation models, including business policy statements, in the absence of specific process, use case, or screen flow.

4. **Decision Models can define decision services for an SOA catalog.** Such services are designed for reuse in multiple applications and processes.

5. **Decision Models can evolve the role of business analysts.** Specifically, business analysts take on the creation, analysis, and maintenance of Decision Models, not to mention the administration of a Decision Modeling tool.

6. **Decision Models can lead to more effective utilization of technical and business resources, thereby saving time and money.** Consider that all systems development projects are complex by definition. Justifiably, they involve business and technical staff skilled in a wide variety of advanced expertise. The cost of such expertise is high, and various approaches for reducing this cost have been introduced over time, including balancing the usage of on- and offshore technical resources. The integration of Decision Models into systems development projects can shift responsibility from technical to business resources, put more emphasis on earlier deliverables, accelerate testing practices, and reduce software errors.

Component Testing

The Decision Model brings significant advantages in systems development methodologies in the area of testing and test script development.

Component (or program, or unit) testing in development projects traditionally takes place after that component has been programmed. The test script is designed to test the inputs and outputs of the component as a whole. Errors discovered during testing are fixed and retested, but because testing occurs after programming is complete, the fix may require significant rework. It is also difficult to be sure that all logic states are accounted for properly in the program code because logic errors may be corrected by other program code in the component.

The Decision Model offers improvements in these areas and can shorten the development and testing cycle in the following ways (the use of the Decision Model in testing is explored in Chapter 6):

1. **The Decision Model can serve as the source of test scripts before programming has completed.** Test scripts can be developed directly from populated Rule Families, even before programming has completed. Each Rule Family row may be tested to determine that the software leads to the correct conclusion for that given set of conditions. The development of test scripts for business logic testing becomes simple, as each row in each Rule Family becomes a discrete set of conditions to be tested. Enterprising developers could use the Decision Model as the source for automatic generation of test scripts.

2. **The Decision Model can reduce the need for full transaction volume testing.** Large transaction sets that are used in acceptance testing can be significantly reduced in scope when test scripts are able to fully exercise all the decisions in a system.

3. **The Decision Model can enable rapid test script changes.** In test scripts derived from Decision Models there is a direct, one to one, correlation

between test script lines and Rule Family rows. Consequently, when logic changes in the Rule Family, the lines in the test scripts that are effected can be adjusted with little or no additional analysis.

In summary, the separation of business logic from other concerns allows for earlier specification of test scripts, lower volume testing, more accurate testing, and greater traceability for making changes.

The Decision Model in Agile Methodology

One of the goals and benefits of agile methodologies is the delivery of smaller increments in shorter quantities of time. The Decision Model offers opportunities for smaller, earlier increments in shorter time for two reasons. First, it provides a separation of business logic as a discrete subset of a software component. Second, the Decision Model itself can be delivered in incremental pieces, where those increments can be tailored to the iterative nature of the specific project.

1. **The Decision Model can be the template for an early prototype of a component.** After the outline of a Decision Model is defined but before it is fully populated, an Agile developer can create a prototype of the software component containing the skeleton of the Decision Model. The component can be tested with "fake" condition and conclusion values. Discovery of the true business logic can take place in parallel with further development of the software. The business logic content can be completed in the software once the Decision Model is fully populated.
2. **Coding of the business logic can be done on a Rule Family basis,** because conclusion values for supporting Rule Families can be simulated without having to code all of the underlying logic. In this way, iterations of the software can be delivered to suit the complexity and scope of the project.
3. **The Decision Model can enable very rapid implementation.** As Agile developers become familiar with Decision Model structures, the developers will learn that the Decision Model enables very rapid coding using appropriate patterns of development.

Documentation

The Decision Model promotes shared understanding among business and IT audiences, and is easy to understand. Not only can it replace other forms of documentation, it can also serve as a tool with which to manage business logic changes. This can improve the quality of the business logic as it is understood by businesspeople and as it is deployed in the target software.

Table 16.2 summarizes the opportunities for improvement in information systems development methodologies and projects that are possible with the introduction of the Decision Model.

Table 16.2 Opportunities in Information Systems Development

- Businesspeople are more easily involved in creating and revising Decision Models.
- Decision Models can be delivered earlier (i.e., prior to design) in the development cycle or even before the systems development cycle.
- Decision Models can be delivered in increments, enabling agile development.
- Business process models and use case models are simpler.
- Decision models lead to reusable decision services in SOA catalogs.
- Utilization of important resources (i.e., business and technical experts) is more effective, needing fewer resources and far less time.
- Earlier test scripts can be written before programming begins.
- Earlier object models can be created before programming begins and even before Decision Models are populated.
- Increased quality in business logic leads to fewer errors.

STEP Business Decision Methodology Approach

At the time of this writing, one proprietary approach incorporates the Decision Model in incremental stages in a project and has been tested in practice.* This methodology is called STEP,[†] which is an acronym for

- **S**eparate the business decisions and their business logic from all other aspects, including process.
- **T**race the business logic from business motivation, to code and to manual processes.
- **E**xpress the business logic in a form understandable by all stakeholders.
- **P**osition the business logic for change.

STEP is designed to augment existing methodologies, not replace them, and adds an awareness of business decisions. STEP focuses on iteratively developing Decision Models together with process models and use cases as deliverables either within business requirements or prior to them. The approach taken for the fictional project in Chapter 7 is a good example of the tasks, deliverables, and roles in STEP. Figure 16.10 presents five high-level tasks of STEP, all of which contribute a particular aspect to an evolving Decision Model, denoted in its center.

---

* The hope is, of course, that many different methodologies will incorporate the Decision Model, expanding its usefulness.
† STEP is a licensed approach offered through Knowledge Partners International, LLC, of which the authors of this book are managing partners.

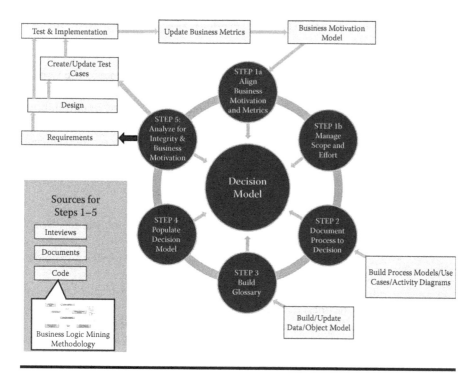

Figure 16.10   Five high-level tasks of STEP.

A Brief Description of STEP

There are five primary high-level tasks in STEP that represent an iterative process. These tasks are described in the following text.

- STEP 1a: Align Business Motivation and Metrics.

   A Decision Model effort begins with identification of the business motivation factors behind the project to justify the cost of the project and identify the means by which the success of the business decisions will be measured. The project may optionally utilize OMG's BMM as a means for capturing the business motivation factors. It is important that a preliminary list of anticipated business decisions be created and business goals for each of those business decisions determined. Where appropriate business objectives are set, based on business analysis and SMART principles. Doing this ensures that Decision Models are developed to the appropriate level of completion and in appropriate sets of increments for meeting the business motivations.

   The project, at the completion of STEP 1a, is supported by a full understanding of the goals of the project (to a granularity that is meaningful to the business) and the metrics by which it will measure those goals.

Contribution to the Decision Models: List of anticipated business decisions

■ STEP 1b: Manage Scope and Effort.

In STEP 1b, the scope and effort of the project are planned. The scoping activities include identification of stakeholders, definition of technology infrastructure requirements, establishment of roles and responsibilities, establishment of the team, development of a project plan and statement of work, implementation and customization of software tools, implementation of toolset standards and processes, development of a project office, and reviewing and accepting a project initiation process. The scoping activities unique to STEP 1b include the following:

- Identifying the sources for the business logic
- Creating high-level process models or use case models to discover where business decisions are to provide guidance
- Confirming business motivations and metrics to those candidate business decisions
- Identifying the target Business Decision Maturity level for each candidate business decision
- Allocating business decisions to project increments
- Developing an estimate of time, resources, and cost for the proposed business decisions

Contribution to the Decision Models: Business decisions anchored in high-level process models or use case models that provide insight into reuse of Decision Models and decision services

■ STEP 2: Document Process to Decision.

In STEP 2, more detailed business process models or business use cases are developed (according to a BPM methodology, if appropriate). Business decisions are anchored at appropriate places within these models. Sometimes, preliminary headings of fact types for Rule Family headings are identified. Typically, STEP is conducted in parallel with business process modeling efforts, and the decision modeling and the process modeling activities complement each other. This is illustrated in Figure 16.11.

Contribution to the Decision Models: More specific placement of business decisions in detailed processes and preliminary Rule Family structures

■ STEP 3: Build Glossary and Link to Object/Data Models.

Concurrent with STEP 2 and STEP 4, the glossary is created to properly define the fact types used in the Decision Model. The glossary may start from, or be mapped to, other vocabulary models.

Contribution to Decision Models: Glossary of fact types

■ STEP 4: Populate Decision Model.

Concurrent with STEP 3, the Rule Families are populated with conditions leading to conclusions.

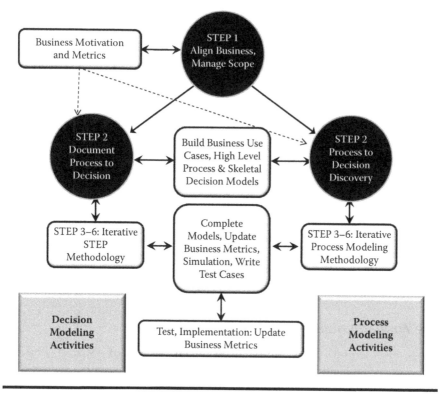

Figure 16.11 STEP and process modeling.

Contribution to Decision Models: Populated Rule Families

■ STEP 5: Analyze Rules for Integrity and Business Motivation.

   STEP 5 analyzes the Decision Model against the 15 principles. In this task, Decision Model test cases can be developed.

   STEP 1a through STEP 5 are iterated as the Decision Models in this increment evolve, and again as additional Decision Models are added in subsequent increments.

   At some point, a business governance and maintenance process for ongoing management of the business decisions is put into place.

Contribution to Decision Models: Decision Models in third normal form and aligned with business motivations and metrics

The Decision Model Doesn't Mean a New Methodology

The IT industry probably does not need or want a totally new methodology. Learning new methodologies is costly and time consuming, and change is difficult.

The good news is that, based on experience to date, the tasks behind STEP (or similar tasks with similar deliverables) are easily adapted to an organization's existing methodology. Sometimes, the deliverables can replace existing ones and can be created more easily and in less time.

Practice #6: The Decision Model and System Transformation Methods

System transformation is the process of reinventing a business system. Sometimes, the need for system transformation arises from a business reengineering effort that recommends a significant change in system capabilities. Sometimes, it is merely the movement of an existing system from an obsolete technology platform to a more modern one. Whatever the reason, system transformation is a complex undertaking, sometimes requiring more effort that it took to create the system in the first place. That's because it involves understanding the original system before reinventing it into something better.

The Fundamentals of System Transformation

The best way to understand the fundamentals and processes of system transformation is to review Figure 16.12, the SEI* "System Transformation Horseshoe." SEI explains the Horseshoe as follows:

> In its purest and most complete form (represented by the large outlined arrows), the first process recovers the architecture by extracting artifacts from source code. This recovered architecture is analyzed to determine whether it conforms to the "as-designed" architecture. The discovered architecture is also evaluated with respect to a number of quality attributes such as performance, modifiability, security, or reliability.
>
> The second process is architectural transformation. In this case, the "as-built" architecture is recovered and then reengineered to become a desirable new architecture. It is reevaluated against the system's quality goals and subject to other organizational and economic constraints.
>
> The third process of the horseshoe uses architecture-based development (ABD) to instantiate the desired architecture. In this process, packaging issues are decided and interconnection strategies are chosen. Code-level artifacts from the legacy system are often wrapped or rewritten in order to fit into this new architecture.
>
> For convenience we break the world of program understanding tools into categories according to the program, system, or design information

---

* Carnegie Mellon Software Engineering Institute (and design)^{TM}.

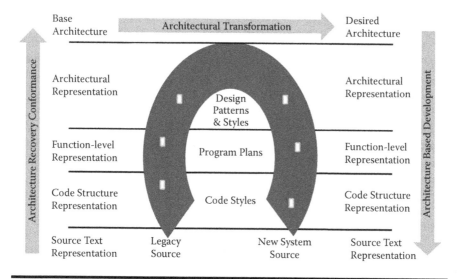

Figure 16.12 The System Transformation Horseshoe. (Source: Carnegie Mellon Software Engineering Institute (and design)™, http://www.sei.cmu.edu/ reengineering/horeseshoe_model.html © 2008 Carnegie Mellon University. Used with permission.)

they work with and the corresponding information that they produce. We break our knowledge schema into three distinct levels. The first, or base, is the code level, which includes the source code and artifacts such as abstract syntax trees and flow-graphs obtained through parsing and rote analytic operations. The second is the function level, which describes the relationship among a program's functions (calls for example), data (function and data relationships), and files (groupings of functions and data). Third is the concept level in which clustering of both function and code level artifacts are assembled into patterns of architectural level components.

The trip around the outside of the horseshoe represents the most abstract and purest form of reengineering. In practice there are two additional shortcuts that cut across the horseshoe and that enable one to get from the "as-built" system to the "as desired" system. These "shortcut" paths across the horseshoe can represent pragmatic choices based on organizational or technological constraints, such as reengineering tools available. In these cases our analysis process does not result in the system architecture representation, but in lower level artifacts that may be closer to the source code than the architecture. (Software Engineering Institute–Carnegie Mellon, 2008)

A Common Shortcut

In the past, one of the most popular "shortcuts" involved "mining" the business logic from the code, and then recoding it, without change, directly into new technology. A difficulty in this approach is determining the accuracy and completeness of the mined code. Generally, business logic is spread across many software modules. Frequently, some business logic may appear in several versions across a system. Resolving its accuracy is very difficult when it is in a chain of other business logic, scattered across the system. Other difficulties are analyzing the mined business logic to determine whether it is still valid and rationalizing technical names to business names.

System Transformation and the Decision Model

The process of digging through program code in search of business logic will never be very simple. However, the Decision Model simplifies the mined business logic representation for all audiences. The Decision Model is a deliverable that can achieve transformation from the low-level existing code to a high-level architecture, and it can provide significant improvement of efficiency over other methods of doing so. For example, as in the case of information systems development, a Decision Model unearthed from program code may, in some cases, be delivered in increments. Fact types can be gathered and arranged in preliminary System Rule Families. Such a Decision Model delivers a candidate component for SOA, and programmers can start to code for it. This means coding can happen much earlier than without the Decision Model.

Figure 16.13 depicts an approach, used with success, for mining business decisions from code. The diagram depicts the first four steps as a conventional business rule mining process, whether an automated tool is used or the process is done manually. Step 1 is the scoping, drawing the boundaries of the code to be mined. Step 2 process called "archeology" because the code is, as it were, unearthed to discover the main sources of logic from all the artifacts within the scope. Once the archeology is accomplished, the nature of the code unearthed will help determine the appropriate tools and techniques that will be used for the next step, the code and mining inspection. Step 3 includes slicing the code into segments that may contain business logic, inspecting them to mark and recover specific code snippets of buried business logic. Step 4 includes inspecting data structure definitions and sometimes database content in search of business logic. Steps 2 through 4 are frequently performed by various forms of software scanning tools and techniques that have become quite adept at discerning patterns, or links, of logic statements.

Step 5 is critical as it is where the Decision Model improves over other techniques. Step 5 introduces the notion of System Rule Families—representing the business logic and fact types found (either by hand or by automated tool inspection) in the existing code.

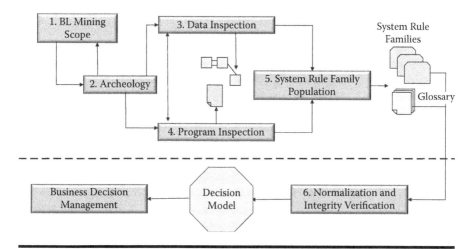

Figure 16.13   High-level depiction of mining business logic using the Decision Model.

Step 5 involves re-sorting the code snippets that have been identified into Rule Family structures for conclusion fact types that were discovered in the code. As the process continues, normalized System Rule Families emerge. These are called System Rule Families because they represent the inherent structure of the business logic as found in the existing system, which use the variables or fact types used by the system. They are not in business-consumable form.

Once the System Rule Families are fully populated (that is, the code has been fully examined), step 6 is the creation of a business-friendly glossary of fact types. The business-friendly fact types replace the system-oriented fact types in the System Rule Families. In this way, true Decision Models begin to emerge.

Naturally, in Step 6, the 15 Decision Model principles are applied to the evolving Decision Model, just as in any Decision Model project. When that analysis is complete and the principles are fully applied, the Decision Model is complete and ready to be implemented in the target technology.

The result of this decision-aware system transformation process constitutes half of the complete trip around the business transformation horseshoe. It delivers fully on an "architectural representation," at least for the logic of the system. Experience shows that it is no more difficult or time consuming to do so with Decision Models than if other "shortcuts" across the System Transformation Horseshoe had been taken. The Decision Model provides the means of achieving a high-value architectural result from System Transformation, at a cost that is potentially no greater than that which would have been paid for a lower-value deliverable.

The business value of using the Decision Model in system transformation is illustrated in Figure 16.14.

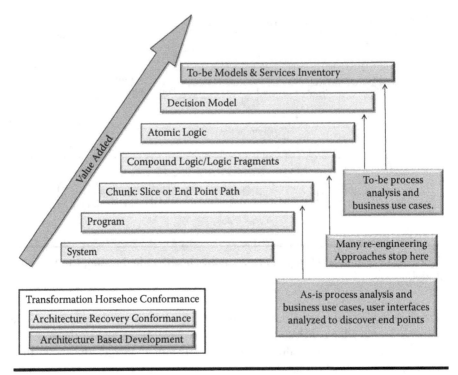

Figure 16.14   Value-added elements of system transformation.

Summary

This chapter describes a sample of specifications, standards, and practices relevant to the introduction of the Decision Model. All of these are valuable in their contributions to the advancement of information technology usage.

Yet, because the Decision Model reflects the inherent structure of business logic and separates it from all other concerns, it is independent of the standards in the practices discussed. The integration of the Decision Model into these practices appears to hold significant promise of adding value to the enterprise in the future.

Chapter 17

Integrating the Decision Model with BPMN

Bruce Silver

Contents

Introduction 421
The Role of BPMN 423
Integrating the Decision Model with BPMN 424
Summary 426

Introduction

The intersection of process design and decision logic design is confusing to beginners and experts alike. The fact that we still see debates about "BPM versus business rules" as rival approaches to solution development is illustrative of the problem. Neither the Decision Model nor the business process model encompasses all the business logic in an insurance claim, loan origination, or customer service solution. In fact, they define distinct and complementary aspects of that logic. OMG's Business Process Modeling Notation (BPMN), the de facto standard language today for business process modeling, describes an end-to-end process as a flow of tasks. BPMN does not define the business logic within each task, nor other details of the task implementation, but merely its relation in time to other tasks and events in the process: when the task starts, and what happens next when it's complete. In other words, the process model just describes the routing logic from step to step in a process.

Just as the process model externalizes the orchestration (flow) logic in the end-to-end solution, the Decision Model externalizes the decision logic. Decisions described by a Decision Model become, in the process model, a particular type of task, and each decision used in the business logic of a process solution is represented as a decision task in the process model. BPMN 1.1 distinguishes user tasks and service (automated) tasks, and BPMN 2.0 proposes to add a new "business rule" task type, distinguished by its own icon within the rectangular task shape. A decision task is not the same as a decision gateway, the BPMN diamond shape defining routing logic. Gateways have long been misused in process models to surface decision details in the diagram, a bad practice that is largely responsible for the market confusion over BPM and business rules as rival marketing techniques. In this chapter, we'll provide basic principles and rules of thumb for organizing process models to maximize agility, reuse, and governance of decision logic in BPM solutions.

Business Process Management (BPM) represents a particular perspective for describing and managing a business, not in terms of individual functions, operational units, or IT systems, but in terms of "end-to-end" business processes that cross those functional, organizational, and system boundaries. Because customers and trading partners view your company from the perspective of such end-to-end processes, managing your business—that is, optimizing business performance—from that perspective only makes good sense. But because most companies have organized their employees and IT systems around discrete functional units, changing to a cross-functional process view is not easy. The issues around moving to such a process perspective are at the core of BPM as a management discipline.

One of these issues, a major one, is simply documenting existing processes end to end. Frequently, there is no single "process owner" today, and each participant in the process may understand only his or her own fragment of it, so an end-to-end process model is usually a good starting point for any performance monitoring or process improvement effort. By providing a common visual language for understanding the entire business process, process models provide a business-oriented context for identifying problems in the current process, connecting them with specific activities, and suggesting potential improvements that can be captured in proposed to-be process models.

Process modeling does not attempt to capture all aspects of the business process, and does not purport to be a complete description of the process. Confusion on this point is central to the confusion on the intersection of BPM and business rules. Although there are many possible ways of describing the workings of a process, the term process modeling—at least as it is used in BPM—represents a particular way: a flow of activities leading from a well-defined start of the process to one or more well-defined end states of the process. An activity, a step in the process model, represents a bit of work done, an action. It is not a state, not a function, not an event.

Such activity flow diagrams, often drawn with activities organized in swim lanes representing various roles or organizations involved, have been a staple of business process modeling for two decades, and are familiar to business analysts and business architects. Although such swim lane flowcharts all share a generally similar look, modelers historically have not paid too much attention to any precise semantics behind the boxes, diamonds, and circles in their diagrams. Modeling tools that included such precise diagram semantics—to support simulation analysis, for example—suffered from the fact that there was no common standard. But today there is a common standard, and that fact is changing the role of process modeling in the BPM landscape.

The Role of BPMN

The Business Process Modeling Notation (BPMN), a vendor-neutral specification from OMG, has emerged as the de facto standard for business process diagrams. In BPMN, the shapes have precise meaning, with rules about what can or cannot be connected to what. BPMN goes beyond traditional flowcharts by describing the communications between the process and external parties, such as customers and service providers, and by describing how the process responds to events that may occur: an order cancellation in flight, a missed deadline, or an internal business exception.

The combination of familiarity to business and expressive precise semantics—attractive to IT—has pushed BPMN to the forefront of BPM's technology suite, because it lets process models do more than generate requirements handed off to IT. It lets the models serve as a continuous "business view" of the process throughout the implementation life cycle of an automated to-be process solution. It thus encourages a more agile iterative implementation style in which business and IT actively collaborate on process improvement, and for that reason BPMN has been adopted by BPMS vendors ranging from Lombardi, Savvion, and Appian, to BEA, TIBCO, SAP, Oracle, and Software AG.

BPMN's widespread adoption by the leaders in BPM Suite technology has put into sharper focus what exactly is in the process model and what is in the executable design created by IT, implementation properties layered on top of the model but not part of it. More precisely, what information is defined within the vendor-neutral standard and what is defined in vendor-specific tools? The short answer is that most process modeling tools use BPMN only to describe the abstract activity flow: the name of each step, maybe which role or organization performs it, when it starts, and what activity starts when it's complete. That's it. It does not describe the internal business logic, user interface, or data manipulation within a step, just the "orchestration" or flow logic. Those other details are part of the implementation design, but not part of the process model. Business input to the implementation design is frequently provided via other models, such as use case models, user interface mockups, and—of course—Decision Models, but those are activity details described outside of BPMN.

Integrating the Decision Model with BPMN

This suggests a specific and concrete way of integrating Decision Models with process models in BPMN. BPMN defines two types of process activities: A task is an atomic activity, meaning it has no subactivities described in the process model. A subprocess is a compound activity, meaning it contains subparts—tasks and subprocesses—and can be further described by expansion as a process flow of those tasks and activities. The BPMN standard lists several task types, which are frequently distinguished by icons within the rectangular task shape: user, meaning a human task; service, meaning an automated task; send, meaning a message to another process; and so forth. These task-type distinctions make the process diagram clearer to the beholder and allow the executable design environment to provide the implementation properties appropriate for that particular type of task.

In BPMN terms, execution of a decision described by a Decision Model is a particular type of task. You could call it a service task, but it would be better to define a new task type called decision, with its own icon to distinguish it from the generic service task type. The BPMN 2.0 specification, now under consideration in OMG, in fact proposes such a new task type, called a business rule task, so this is in keeping with the direction the standard appears to be taking in its next version, anyway.

Undoubtedly the Decision Model authors would prefer the term *decision task* to *business rule task*, but the term *decision* has an inherent conflict with another term by that name in BPMN. That conflict is another factor behind the confusion over the intersection of business rules and business process. In BPMN, a *decision gateway* is a diamond shape that defines a branch or split in the activity flow. Each path out of the decision gateway has an associated condition, a Boolean expression, which some people call a rule.

But a gateway does not "decide" anything; it just specifies the path taken by a process instance based on existing process data. If establishing that data value—Approved or Denied, for example—requires a decision, that decision must be made in a task prior to the gateway, either in a user task (human decision) or in a decision task (automated decision). Omission of this decision task is a common mistake made by inexperienced BPMN users. For example, it is not uncommon to see diagrams such as Figure 17.1.

An order is received, and if it is valid, the process goes to task A, and if not, to task B. But this is incorrect, because a gateway cannot make a decision. It cannot perform any kind of work, in fact. A gateway is pure routing logic; it enables paths in the diagram based on an expression of process data. It should be modeled as shown in Figure 17.2.

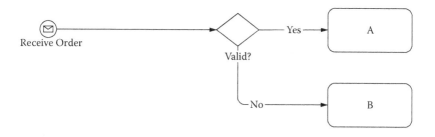

Figure 17.1   Misusing the gateway.

Here, Validate Order is the decision task. Its logic is described by the Decision Model. The gateway simply tests the output of the decision and routes the flow either to A or B based on the result. Some might argue that in Figure 17.1, the gateway is not "performing work" but simply evaluating a complex data expression involving elements contained in the received order. In a sense, that could possibly be true. But it would be bad practice, and in fact, a violation of the principle that business rules are inherently independent of the processes that invoke them.

In Figure 17.2, the task Validate Order invokes a decision defined in the Decision Model. Many other processes, such as for other types of orders, might rely on the same Decision Model. Managing decision logic external to process logic, and centrally for all processes, greatly improves governance and agility. Figure 17.2 allows the Decision Model logic to change without affecting the process that invokes it. And the Decision Model can make use of much more complex rule set logic than a simple gateway, which must be reduced to a hard-coded Boolean expression. For all of these reasons, the gateway in Figure 17.2 would not be called an expression of a business rule, just a routing rule, meaning explicitly defined at a single node in a process diagram. The term business rule in BPM—what we now want to call a Decision Model—is inherently defined independently of any particular process or node in a process.

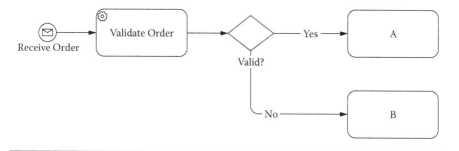

Figure 17.2   Proper use of the gateway.

Finally, you sometimes hear the argument from proponents of the Decision Model that it allows simpler process models. What they are referring to are process diagrams in which complex decision logic—let's say the Validate Order decision of our previous example—is expressed in the diagram not as a single gateway but as a complex network of gateways each of which makes a simple routing decision, such as: Is the CustomerId valid? Is the ShipTo address complete? Etc. A spider web of such simple gateways is required to flesh out the complete order validation logic. Complex decision logic translates into complex process diagrams using that approach, but it has the undeniable advantage of making the decision logic explicit in the diagram itself rather than "hiding" it in some linked external Decision Model. But the real problem with this approach is not complexity of the diagram but the same problems as Figure 17.1: hard-coded logic requiring a new process version when the decision logic changes; no centralized management of decision logic across processes or process nodes; and decision logic restricted to simple Boolean expressions. The Decision Model, integrated with the process model as in Figure 17.2, has none of these problems, and represents the correct way to integrate decisions with BPM.

Summary

BPMN, the OMG Specification, has become a de facto standard notation for BPM. The notation represents business activity in tasks and routing logic in gateways. The appropriate way to represent business decisions is through the use of an appropriately designated task, currently defined in the BPMN 2.0 draft as a business rule task type (this designation is given in order to differentiate it from the decision gateway). By representing the Decision Model with a specific task type and managing the logic separately, the business logic can be managed independently of the business process and reused across the enterprise.

Chapter 18

The Case for the Physical Decision Model

Daniel J. Worden

Contents

Introduction 428
Cataloging Decision Assets 429
MDM and Decision Models 429
Decision Metadata 430
Representing Physical Decision Metadata 430
Linking Decision Models 431
Decisions as Transactions 432
Covering the Decision 433
Physical Decision Models and Metadata 434
Decision Resources 435
Resource Considerations 436
Resource Profiles for Conditions 437
Resources and Representations in Physical Decision Models 437
Calculating a Discount Business Decision 437
Decision Models as Aspect Maps 438
Decision Models as a Transaction Map across Enterprise Resources 439
Summary 440

In the world of Data Architecture, there are logical data models and physical data models. Logical data models represent the data in a technology-independent manner, adhering to specific logical data modeling principles. Physical data models, sometimes called physical database designs, represent that same data in an implementation-specific manner. As such, physical data models take into account data availability, data volumes, transaction volumes, and data manipulation performance requirements.

This chapter explores the notion that the Decision Model as disclosed in this book has a physical counterpart, called a physical Decision Model. Further, this chapter provides insights into considerations that ought to become part of a physical Decision Model, especially in distributed environments.

The differentiation between logical Decision Models and corresponding physical Decision Models is important in preserving the business perspective and enables the delivery of optimum technology solutions.

Introduction

In Figure 1.2 (Chapter 1) a comparison was made between Decision Models and data modeling techniques. The discipline of describing data has for quite some time taken two distinct routes: the logical and the physical. Appropriately, the logical models of data lend themselves to depicting inherent data relationships, dependencies, and constraints. Physical models also add a distinct flavor by incorporating physical characteristics of the data such as data type and length. However, as database administrators (DBAs) can attest, there are additional technological features such as indexes that make the physical implementation of the data model a working database.

This chapter proposes the idea that the same holds true for Decision Models as well.

Additionally, the role of a physical Decision Model as a mechanism that leads neatly to integration of other models and organizational management techniques will be discussed. Specifically addressed is the ability of Decision Models to support Master Data Management (MDM) efforts, the ability of physical Decision Models to identify related SOA and Web resources, as well as the natural fit of Decision Modeling with aspect-oriented solution design with multidimensional separation of concerns.

By the end of this chapter, you should have a strong appreciation of the fact that Decision Modeling is an appropriate first step for enterprises seeking traction in their SOA, MDM, and IT realignment efforts. You will understand that a logical Decision Model (as disclosed in this book) is a gateway for innovation in subsequent and varied physical Decision Models.

Cataloging Decision Assets

A large portion of the value derived from the Decision Model comes from incorporating its principles into a practical set of methodological steps for delivering high-quality Decision Models. A methodology enhanced with such steps is agile and efficient, and it works. In moving from logical to physical Decision Models, there are a few additional steps that are needed to capture and convey the physical Decision Model elements. The first is an inventory of assets and creation of a glossary by name and description.

Many people outside the IT realm do not think of computing artifacts as assets. In all likelihood, programs and data probably should be formally classified as business assets. Increasingly, software and data are being capitalized and depreciated financially as corporate assets. But due to the highly technical nature of their construction, in a great many cases only a qualified IT technician can parse the data and program structures, comprehending what lies within.

The inventory step is required to extract the business value of code and data sources to identify them by a consistent, common naming convention.

The focus of a Decision Model is on the ultimate set of if-then-else logic forks that must be taken as a result of a combination of values in a given setting. It does not focus on how the business logic is presented, parsed, and executed as part of some software program. As fascinating as the discussion of logic cache and state buffers might be to some, this is not what is meant by a physical Decision Model. Instead, the physical Decision Model is a representation, a model and depiction, of "how" the decision is to be processed. It accommodates the realities of the deployment, and in fact, ensures that the logical model is not invalidated by such otherworldly concerns as "timeliness" and performance. The physical Decision Model is physical in that it points to a real-world environment.

MDM and Decision Models

The methodology for developing logical Decision Models has been refined over time into a proven, highly effective agile process. By extending the methodology to include the attributes of a physical model, some additional structure and notation is needed.

It is not necessary for those extensions to be developed from scratch. In fact, it is the discovery and exploration of decision elements that relate to existing systems that neatly ties physical Decision Models to other enterprise initiatives, such as MDM.

Many well-managed enterprises, large and small alike, have undertaken efforts to treat their entire collection of information artifacts as assets. The first step in managing these assets is to inventory and catalog them. This is completely consistent with the first steps of developing Decision Models. The Decision Model may take advantage of MDM inventory efforts already made, or the process can drive out the definition of data and services elements from the business perspective.

Physical Decision Models can be developed after, during, or before MDM classification projects are constituted. The resulting models provide important annotations for data scope, use, and approvals from the operational or business standpoint.

Decision Metadata

Decision Metadata is not "data about data." It is data about decisions. It describes the decision logic dependencies and resources required to support a decision, as defined by the business. Like MDM inventories, the decision Metadata may be identified from existing sources, or it can be defined abstractly during the logical decision modeling process. Once the decision Metadata is defined in the abstract, the corresponding implementations can be investigated as part of the detailed design of any systems solution that involves that decision.

Representing Physical Decision Metadata

Physical Decision Models address information assets, such as data and logic, which are most often already in existence. To support the assertion that the decision modeling process integrates well into other classification efforts such as MDM, and Information Lifecycle Management (ILM), it is reasonable to expect that decision modeling will leverage existing metadata classification schemes. Business decisions can be described as policies under Information Technology Infrastructure Library (ITIL) approaches, for example. The benefits from normalizing those policies (business decisions) can still be obtained, regardless of the terminology used to classify them.

For enterprises not already having such schemes in place, the physical Decision Models can build on work already done by the Dublin Core Metadata Initiative (DCMI), which in turn extends the Resource Description Framework (RDF) from the Worldwide Web consortium (W3C). These initiatives are providing tools for the semantic web, to allow machines to understand information assets as knowledge, not merely dealing with instructions for managing presentation of data.

To improve the ability of computing systems to take action on the basis of the semantic web, the information must be classified in a way the system can derive meaning from it. Review of existing application software, and representation of those data and logic elements as triples consisting of subject, object, and predicates, is an effective contribution to that objective.

Linking Decision Models

Where each logical Decision Model contains collections of unique combinations of true or false propositions leading to a single conclusion, physical Decision Models seek to capture additional properties and values. These convey contextual information in which the system will interpret the pattern and determine which policy to apply. The RDF allows for extension of their models to include scope and range of value information, as well as the potential to define types, which may be more or less immaterial to the business yet critical to systems integration or performance.

The DCMI core elements were originally defined as metadata for universally and uniquely describing information assets by title, creator, and type, among others. Extensions to the terms have emerged and a vocabulary built that allows classification of content across different media types. Business decisions are not content in that context, but the approach taken to defining metadata used by DCMI can be applied to include them. A cornerstone has been that each named entity or resource is uniquely defined by its associated properties. A description of the initiative in much greater depth can be found by exploring www.dublincore.org and by becoming involved with the DCMI.

The XML namespaces used by the DCMI allow classification of some information assets in keeping with those schemes used globally. Additional vocabularies, specific to a domain or enterprise, are developed and referenced also using XML. By harvesting business decisions from software already deployed, this approach allows slotting the data and logic into the appropriate vocabulary. Additional contextual information can be captured in private or special purpose ontologies designed to ensure the translation from the as-implemented decisions from code are not lost in the physical model.

A hierarchical representation of how the physical Decision Model properties can be classified is shown in Figure 18.1.

Decision models transcend rules and put them into a unifying context – the business judgment to be exercised. The physical Decision Model includes deployment considerations that might affect the process relying on the decision, such as performance, timeliness, or security.

Reverse engineering Decision Models from existing applications, as opposed to starting with a blank slate, means there may be a large number of implementation considerations that can be captured in the model. Generally, the logical model will not assume their availability or require them. However, behaviors such as logging, notification, timeouts, data latency, and exception handling are properties associated with a decision as implemented in software. The physical Decision Model, whether reverse engineered or newly designed from the outset, seeks to capture and associate such properties with the decision.

A key benefit of this is allowing developers of replacement systems to have the advantage of that information as they perform the design and specification

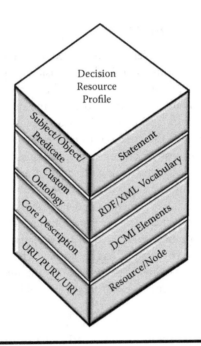

Figure 18.1 A hierarchy of Decision Model classification layers.

functions when creating the new software. Another advantage is the opportunity for the business to review the behaviors for purposes of validating it, or defining acceptable ranges within which the decision can be executed.

Decisions as Transactions

A physical Decision Model often exists within the confines of a transaction. That transaction may be (is likely to be) distributed across multiple resources and multiple geographies. The physical Decision Model is a deployment view of the conditions and conclusions that represent a set of Rule Families and Rule Patterns predicted as part of a Decision Model. The latency inherent in distributed heterogeneous computing, as well as the necessity of translating correctly the values and context of condition elements or conclusions, means that business must capture and convey expectations for performance as part of the transaction's definition.

In other words, it's not enough to model the route; the time allowed to cross the finish line must be defined before the crowd goes home.

As an illustration, perhaps the best way to encapsulate the value of a physical Decision Model is to revisit a little trick DBAs have been using for ages: covering the query in the index.

Covering the Decision

Indexes are, as is widely known, duplicate copies of selective real data. By creating these replicated sets, organizing them in alphabetic, date, numeric, or whatever sensible order, DBAs have provided queries with the speed they need to look up critical data quickly. In one example, a data query can be made on date of birth, where a decision is taken on the basis of age. Many of these kinds of considerations are most useful when dealing with millions of records. The same is true for the number of conditions and conclusions to be incorporated into a decision. When there are a great many elements to be encompassed, performance considerations become more challenging.

In the same way that a date-of-birth calculation can be translated to age, and that age informs a rental car rate, a credit rating can inform a decision to extend or decline a purchase on credit, or a frequent shopper membership type can affect the price or presentation of an option. Not every business decision maker has the luxury of time to establish all the ingredients of a good decision from scratch.

This is especially true of situations where information, say creditworthiness, must be obtained from outside sources, such as a credit reporting agency.

Decision Models have great applicability for representing not only the conditions and conclusions that represent the decision itself, but also the context in which the decision must be made. This context includes, of course, the maximum amount of time that an applicant, for example, must wait to be given a quote or a rate, or declined or referred to an agent. More than this, where other factors can affect the transaction, such as applicant status as a frequent customer, for example, these elements are also effectively rendered as Decision Models. This is shown in Figure 18.2.

In this example, it stands to reason that in the interests of efficiency, the process of validating the creditworthiness should be completed before transaction cost is incurred on the other decision elements. This is a typical perspective that an IT person might apply to the situation. After all, if the credit check is going to reject the applicant, why burn resources in the process?

However, from a business standpoint, say, the marketing perspective, only 15% of applicants are rejected, and the abandonment of the application due to delay is in excess of 40% when that delay is 2 min or more. As a result, it makes business sense to incur the cost of processing an application that may ultimately be rejected.

Sequencing of conditions to be satisfied is affected by the decision to be made. In this case, a cardholder with satisfactory credit history and either a gold elite status or attempting to purchase a promotional item within 10% of the limit may result in an approval. This may be already implemented in an existing application, in which case the sequencing can be depicted with a physical Decision Model element, or it may be the result of a new policy. This is shown in Figure 18.3.

From an application deployment standpoint, the preceding sequencing conveys to a coder that the first condition is better satisfied before the other two, but on

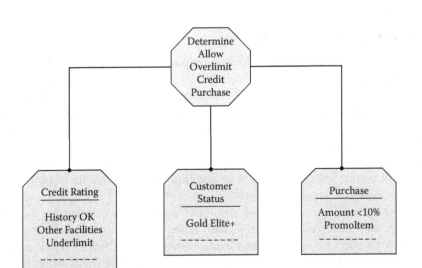

Figure 18.2 A logical Decision Model for allowing overlimit credit purchase.

satisfaction of it, the other two may be evaluated concurrently. This becomes particularly useful when SOA supports two distinct Web service resources to satisfy either condition.

The transaction then is not simply expressed as the algorithmic logic to be processed. The context and intersection of concerns becomes a critical part of the Decision Model. As referred to earlier, some enterprises express this information as metadata and capture or manage this data as part of their MDM initiatives. Many others may have coded it "once upon a time" in a legacy system. Physical Decision Models can facilitate the expression and validation of the business logic from both sources.

Physical Decision Models and Metadata

One of the cornerstone value propositions for MDM initiatives is to establish and administer SoR status for distributed data. Decision Modeling initiatives have direct applicability in advance of formal enterprise MDM efforts. Decision Models allow the business to define the latency that can be tolerated in arriving at a "good enough" business judgment on a case- and parameter-specific basis.

By intersecting each SoR (System of Records), and its replications in various distributed subsystems, with the decision processing an organization undertakes in an automated fashion, a set of appropriate computing resources is identified for each discrete decision. An application architect may use this as a business-validated resource pool when considering how best to align network topologies, server loads

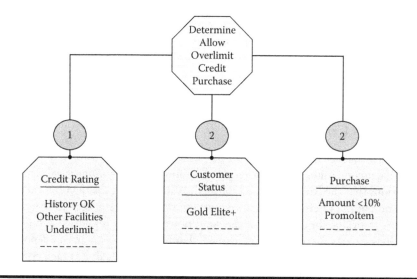

Figure 18.3   A sequenced set of rules to be processed as part of the overlimit decision.

and licensing, and many other indirect but real costs to supporting decision making with computing technologies.

An everyday example of this "good enough" processing is the use of a credit card to pay for less than $50 worth of gas at a service station. If the card swipe returns a valid status, it requires no signature. The transaction is thereby speeded up, and convenience can be sold as a differentiation from competitors. Filling up a transport truck appropriately requires more paperwork.

Extending the example, as the size of the application amount increases, so too does the amount of work required to approve it. Note that the low-, medium-, and high-risk assessments lead to significantly more diligence and investigation prior to approval, and in fact, could result in referring the application for person review. Represented as a use case, this set of main, alternate, and exception flows quickly becomes a long narrative, but as a Decision Model it can be taken in at a glance.

Decision Resources

The physical Decision Model begins to address the question of exactly how a particular set of logic will be applied to a given business judgment. This emphasis on execution allows for the introduction of critical elements needed for decision processing: its resources. When conditions and conclusions are the logical elements of the decision, effectively describing what it is, the resources identify from where specific resources will be obtained. The SoR designation fits here, as the purpose of a SoR is to establish the definitive version of a fact within the enterprise, or externally for the purposes of an enterprise transaction. The SoR is a resource that can be tied to the decision in order to establish how the consideration is to be resolved, using existing organizational assets.

Resource Considerations

The conclusion clause of a Decision Model is a unitary item for any given fact type. Each conclusion value is a result of a unique combination of values for the conditions that the Rule Pattern established. When looking for the physical implementation of the Decision Model, we must consider what resources are available to arrive at the value for each one of the conditions requiring resolution. To do that, we need resources. Accordingly, we can see that because the conclusion depends on the conditions and the conditions require values be established, it is each condition that has a resource profile.

A diagrammatic representation of a physical Decision Model resource is shown in Figure 18.4.

From the example in Figure 18.4, the resources describe the SoR for a PromoITem as the E3 (Inventory) system. Additional physical attributes that inform the decision include its location as InStore. Whereas the Logical Decision Model would likely differentiate InStore PromoItem from OnLinePromoItem, the physical resources for the decision element would identify the system by which the item status would be acquired.

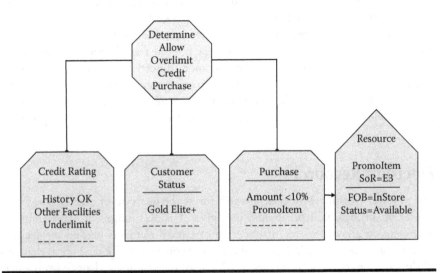

Figure 18.4   A decision resource.

Resource Profiles for Conditions

Taking the DCMI definitions as resource profiles for decision conditions makes sense. Not only can we use the MDM resource description to provide a unique address for each resource, but we can also collect metadata about the resource, including additional valid sources of resolving the request from caches or proxies. Combined with the asset inventory exercise referenced at the beginning of this chapter, the resource profile can be as slim as a list of names to be fleshed out at a later date, or an exhaustive catalog of Web services, interfaces, and constraints for obtaining definitive values in a SOA architecture. No doubt most organizations will range between the two extremes, depending on the proliferation of SOA efforts and enterprise application integration experience to date.

Resources and Representations in Physical Decision Models

There were two aims for physical Decision Models identified at the beginning of this chapter. The first aim was to show how Decision Models support abstraction of decision elements from existing production systems, without losing the optimum sequential ordering or other deployment considerations contained therein, including SoR and valid alternates. The second aim was to capture business concerns for such systems aspects as security and performance.

Calculating a Discount Business Decision

Let's say the decision to be modeled is whether a potential driver of a rental car qualifies for an additional discount on the basis of age and experience. We will represent these two considerations, and the conclusions supported by the facts in the Rule Family represented in Table 18.1.

Table 18.1   Business Decision to Calculate a Discount

	Conditions						Conclusion	
Rule Pattern	*Age is >55 years*		*Resource Profile*	*Accident Free*		*Resource Profile*	*Apply Safe Driver Discount*	
1	Is	Yes	Decision Resource Property/Value SoR=Siebel AltSource= JDEdwards	Is	Yes	Decision Resource URI=http:// www.DMV. com/WAS? driversrecord	Is	Yes
1	Is	Yes		Is	No		Is	No
1	Is	No		Is	Yes		Is	No
1	Is	No		Is	No		Is	No

In this view, the Resource Profiles reflect two levels of maturity. In the case of Age > 55 years, the example implies that all that is known is the SoR and a valid Alternative Source (AltSource), expressed here as the accounting system JD Edwards. Anyone who has worked with business users in a requirements gathering or joint application development setting should recognize that frequently a representative of the business will indicate that a particular source for data is used and has validity.

The Resource Profile for the Accident Free status implies that there is a working Web service accessible from the Department of Motor Vehicles. This example shows how the Decision Resource points to an external value that is required in order to arrive at the conclusion.

The physical nature of the Decision Model is the referencing to specific datasets, Web services, or systems of record that are required to validate the decision. By using named condition clauses, the Decision Model provides a means for the business to define advice for the coders of Web services or implementers of decisions and business rules in code. Advice in this context is defined as part of an Aspect-Oriented approach and refers to the steps that must be taken before finalization of the transaction A Credit rating or Accident Free status can be considered "advice" to the transaction.

When reverse-engineering the Decision Model from an existing production legacy application, control of flow information can be extracted during the evaluation, captured as part of the sequencing of the logic processing, and elaborated in the resource profile. By linking the resource profile to the condition and following the principles of conditions laid out as part of the Decision Modeling methodology, the resources available for a condition in the context of a particular decision can then be captured and documented.

To refer back to the notion of covering the query in the index, by associating resource profiles with conditions in context, different resources may be identified as suitable for the business purposes of a given judgment.

Decision Models as Aspect Maps

As well as integrating effectively with MDM and SOA initiatives, physical Decision Models provide an important context for programming under an Aspect-Oriented Software Development (AOSD) approach.

Aspect Orientation separates different areas of concern into related sets. Each set is treated in detail only when other concerns are abstracted away in order to support focus and clarity.

Business logic and associated rules are typically considered as one aspect. Systems security and performance considerations are two others.

It should be reasonably intuitive that although systems security is separate and distinct from business rules, the business itself has some security requirements.

They are not all driven by external regulation or industry practices. Some, but not all, will be a function of business differentiation or negotiated commitments to customers. These need to be captured and communicated by the business to IT implementers. The Decision Model serves as a highly effective way to accomplish this.

In the same way that the SoR or Alternate Sources of data to support conditions can be identified, so too can approvals, notifications, or dependencies that must be satisfied to arrive at a conclusion.

Aspect Orientation, similar to Object Orientation which came before it, is primarily a software engineering discipline. However, the business requirements form the foundation on which the other aspects rest. It is not necessary for operational business folk to understand or embrace Aspects. It is highly beneficial for the work done in Decision Modeling to support Aspects in the Solution Design. This is greatly assisted by fleshing out Decision Models to include Resource Profiles and other Physical Decision Model elements.

Decision Models as a Transaction Map across Enterprise Resources

The physical Decision Model allows representation of the various logical combinations in a Rule Family to be tied to specific computing assets to be accessed as part of assessing the conditions prior to coming to a given conclusion. By naming these conditions an Aspect-Oriented "advice," the Decision Model functions at a logical level. When the advice is obtained from sources identified by the metadata and meta rules as falling within parameters accepted by the business, the Decision Model can be navigated across multiple, distributed systems and services, each of which exists in its own silo of hardware, software, and communication resources.

A Decision Aspect allows the analyst to traverse the conditions and decision elements that contribute to a business judgment. Further, a Decision Aspect tied to physical resources that define the allowable ranges of latency for data validity and transaction duration provides the basis for documenting services orchestration from a business perspective.

The value of this approach is significant. The Decision Model can be used to model either existing or to-be business states or both. The logical Decision Model can be developed from a strategic end-in-mind perspective, or from an organizational break-fix view. The physical model may be defined alongside or afterward and can inventory assets or constraints imposed by legacy applications. Gaps or unfilled requirements for data or computing services could conceivably fall out of the review of the Decision Model as it relates to service orchestration. There will be situations when the logical Decision Model remains static while various physical Decision Models will evolve.

In each case, the Decision Model allows the analyst to work down from a strategic goal, up from an existing system, or across a set of systems that must be coordinated in a multiple phase transaction. This single model of the business logic, expressed as decisions and rules and organized as nested conditions and conclusions, brings together all aspects of software in a way that can be understood, communicated, and managed.

Summary

Physical Decision Models may be derived in either direction: forward from strategy and requirements or backward from existing working systems. While engineering Decision Models on an as-built, "already exists" basis, additional useful information can be obtained through the Decision Modeling process.

This chapter points to the kind of information that can be pulled as a starting point, or expressed as a sophisticated link to MDM catalogs. SOA assets as internal and external services can be depicted as resources that are aligned with conditions as part of a fuller description of a business decision.

The differentiation of the physical from logical Decision Models accommodates the deployment concerns of the business, and ensures that those expectations are captured and conveyed to those who will be building solutions from decision, data, and other models.

From this chapter it should be clear that Decision Models, either logical or physical, fit well within existing efforts in an organizations to gain control of data and software services.

By virtue of extracting the decision elements the business requires, Decision Models lay the foundation for SOA and enable improved IT alignment and productivity through innovations such as AOSD.

The theory underpinning Decision Models is sound. In practice, these models provide a Rosetta Stone for communicating the one overriding concern that affects everyone associated with the enterprise: the business and how it needs to work.

Chapter 19

Enterprise Decision Management and the Decision Model

James Taylor

Contents

Decision Services..442
Business Rules 443
Predictive Analytics 444
Adaptive Control and Optimization..445
Operational Decisions 446
Using the Decision Model with EDM..449
The Process..449
Finding the Right Decisions for EDM 451
The Decision Model as an Analysis Technique...................................452
Decision Models and Business User Control 453
Decision Model and Adaptive Control...453
Other Thoughts on Using the Decision Model..................................454
Conclusion..454

Enterprise Decision Management, or EDM, is an approach for automating and improving high-volume operational decisions. The complete definition has five crucial elements. This chapter focuses on operational decisions and the Decision Model.

EDM provides a formal, well-defined approach for taking the Decision Model and putting it into production alongside sophisticated analytics.

We should begin with a definition of Enterprise Decision Management:

Enterprise Decision Management is an approach for automating and improving high-volume operational decisions. Focusing on *operational decisions*, it develops *decision services* using *business rules* to automate those decisions, adds analytic insight to these services using *predictive analytics*, and allows for the ongoing improvements of decision making through *adaptive control and optimization*.

This definition has five crucial elements identified in italics: Operational Decisions, Decision Services, Business Rules, Predictive Analytics, and Adaptive Control and Optimization. Given this book's focus on the Decision Model, the first of these deserves its own section (see following text), but the others are each summarized first.

Decision Services

Although it is not essential to use a Service-Oriented Architecture (SOA) to deliver EDM, it is by far the most effective approach. Designing decision services and deploying them in an SOA makes the decision making you need available to applications and processes throughout your organization. Smart (Enough) Systems defines a decision service as follows:

A **decision service** can be defined as a self-contained, callable component with a view of all conditions and actions that need to be considered to make an operational business decision. More simply, it's a component or service that answers a business question for other services.

Decision services use your data and the insight derived from it for automated decision making. They also isolate the logic behind your operational decisions, separating it from business processes and the mechanical operations of procedural application code. A decision service represents a single point of decision making throughout all your systems and processes, so it allows you to focus resources on improving and even optimizing that decision (Taylor and Raden, 2007).

Decision services can be reused like any other service in an SOA. Decision services tend not to update systems of record—they simply make a decision—making them particularly easy to reuse across processes and channels. Decision services also eliminate the time, cost, and technical risk of trying to reprogram many systems simultaneously to keep up with changing business requirements. In an era where an increasing number of applications will be so-called Composite Applications made up from a mix of existing, new, and packaged components:

> A decision service can be used to provide a "brain" for your composite applications ... With decision services plugged into this approach; you can make these composite applications "smarter" and less reliant on people for decision making. Sometimes this approach makes it easier to connect existing services, and sometimes it lets you take more advantage of the services you have (Taylor and Raden, 2007).

Decision services provide a framework for externalizing and managing decisions, but you must also automate those decisions in a new way—you cannot code your way into the future. Just as business rules are the building blocks of a Decision Model, so are they also the building blocks of decision services.

Business Rules

The use of business rules, and of a BRMS, to manage the logic in decision services is the next element of EDM. As we wrote in Smart (Enough) Systems, for business rules to be manageable:

> You need to be able to state them in a declarative way so that each rule is independent of the others and distinct so that it can be managed.
>
> You must be able to manage potentially very large numbers of rules. Managing large numbers means being able to version them, control access to them, and track changes so that you know how you got the rules you have.
>
> They must be represented so that both business and technical users can interact with the representation. Both groups must be able to read, edit, create, and delete rules so that business and IT can collaborate on rule management effectively.
>
> To deploy business rules, your IT department needs technology to turn these rules into executable code that runs in your application architecture. They also need support for testing, release management,

data integration, and the rest of their standard application development process. The most effective approach is adopting what's commonly called a **business rules management system (BRMS)**. This has a repository to store and manage business rules, rule-editing tools designed for business and technical users, a rule engine to execute rules in a system context. It also has pieces of technology to handle integration with data, deployment into different systems, and other essential functions (Taylor and Raden, 2007).

The business rules in these decision services might be derived from policies, from regulations, from expertise, or from the analysis of information.

Business rules may be represented as a set of rules—a rule set—but may also be represented using one of a number of graphical metaphors. For instance, in a decision tree, each leaf in the tree—each final outcome—represents a rule with each branch point being a condition in that rule. A decision table can likewise be considered in terms of a set of business rules, one per cell, where the conditions are the rows and columns of the decision table. Newer techniques, such as Directed Action Graphs, can also represent one or more rules. In all cases, these are representations of rules and are functionally equivalent to a set of rules that can be written. It should be noted that decision tables in this context are not the same as the decision tables used to represent Rule Families, as noted earlier.

Apart from the focus on business rules executable in software, EDM uses business rules in much the same way as the Decision Model. Each rule is declarative and distinct and, as a result, manageable. Most BRMSs manage business rules in rule sets, and there is more on how Decision Models, Rule Families, rule sets, and executable business rules can and should be used together later in the chapter.

Predictive Analytics

In EDM we talk about analytics adding insight to our decision services. The analytic approaches we use can be divided in many ways, but in Smart (Enough) Systems we describe two broad categories: descriptive analytics and predictive analytics.

> **Descriptive analytics** uses various techniques to improve understanding of the data, such as clustering, grouping, or segmenting information into useful categories. This can be used to segment (or microsegment) customers to treat each segment differently, to group products or suppliers based on reliability, or to identify products that are crossover purchases between categories, for example. The most common way to "operationalize" these models is to turn them into a set of business rules and then manage and implement them as described later in this chapter. In many cases, this method is sufficient for enterprise decision management.

Predictive analytic models, on the other hand, are designed to make predictions about a specific customer, product, or transaction, such as the likelihood of a transaction being fraudulent, a customer accepting an offer, or a delivery being late. Represented as mathematical models or equations, they are combined with business rules to make a decision.

For instance, if certain types of transactions are predicted to have a high likelihood of fraud, what's needed in an EDM approach are models that calculate the likelihood of fraud combined with rules about how to interact with customers, such as the risk of annoying a good customer or the risk of overlooking a fraudulent transaction. Rank-ordering customers in order to group them by likelihood of a specific behavior is a typical use for a predictive model (Taylor and Raden, 2007).

Many analytic models can be executed by being translated into business rules and loaded into a BRMS. In such an approach, each analytic model typically becomes a rule set. It is worth managing these models distinct from rules being created from judgment or regulations, but the execution approach can easily be shared. Examples of analytic models that can easily be represented as a set of business rules include the following:

■ Many decision trees are derived analytically, as in the development of statistically significant segmentation rules.
■ Score cards where a score is calculated additively from various characteristics and the value those characteristics have. Each set of characteristic-value pairs and the resulting increase in the score can be represented by a rule.

Other models, such as neural networks or regression models, are better represented using equations, whereas more sophisticated models, especially those involving constraint-based optimization, must be executed dynamically in a specially constructed engine such as a solver. These models, indeed all models, should not generally be represented using the Decision Model, and this is covered later in more detail.

Adaptive Control and Optimization

Any given decision service uses a combination of business rules and analytics that is focused on and appropriate for the specific decision. However, decisions are not always easy to measure—it can take a significant period of time for the impact of a decision to play out. This means that by the time we know how well a particular decision has worked, it is too late to gather information about how alternatives would have worked. To learn about a decision, you must create an environment where you can track the results of decisions to see which ones were effective and which ones were not. You must capture this information and be able to show how close your models were to reality and how effective your rules were. This process is called **adaptive control** and relies on something called champion/challenger:

> The most basic element of adaptive control is the champion/challenger approach, which involves developing a "challenger" approach to a decision that's different from the current or "champion" approach. The system implementing the decision runs a small percentage of transactions through one or more challenger approaches instead of through the champion approach. The approach that was used is recorded for comparison purposes, the consequences of the decision play out, and the data is captured. If a challenger approach shows better results (in whatever timeframe is appropriate for the decision), you can promote it to be the new champion. You can then design new challengers and test them ad infinitum. This process allows constant improvement in decisions with minimal risk. Some mechanism for constantly monitoring and improving the way a decision is made is critical because decisions are unlike other parts of an operational process (Taylor and Raden, 2007).

Adaptive control also extends to optimization and simulation in more sophisticated organizations and more complex decisions. The objective of the approach and techniques is ultimately to optimize a decision and to maintain an optimal response to changing circumstances.

Adaptive control requires multiple ways of making a decision—the "thought to be best" or champion and others with potential, challengers. These variations are all likely to be very similar in structure and content—they are alternatives for the same decision after all—and so the use of the Decision Model should be similar across all the approaches. For many challengers, the structure of the Decision Models used will be the same—only the rules will be different—while for some the structure will also need to vary.

One use of adaptive control is to test proposed structural changes to Decision Models to see what impact they will have on decisions when this cannot be assessed using historical data. The proposed structure can be developed and deployed as a challenger. If it outperforms the champion, along whatever dimensions are being considered, then it can be promoted to the champion.

Operational Decisions

In order to consider how EDM and the Decision Model can be used together, it is essential to understand the way decisions are defined.

What is a decision? When considering decisions, differentiating between types of decisions and the actual decisions is worthwhile. A type of decision might be

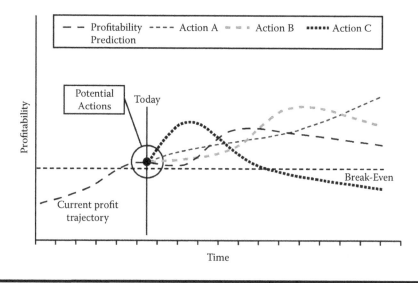

Figure 19.1 **Actions influence profitability in different ways. (Source:** *Smart (Enough) Systems,* **Prentice Hal, 2007. Used with permission.)**

"underwrite insurance policy" or "make cross-sell offer." An actual operational decision would be something like "underwrite James's insurance policy" or "make Neil a cross-sell offer." In this context, decisions have volume, not the types of decisions.

The Decision Model and EDM are both decision-centric approaches. They are also both focused on the definition of decision types so that each decision can be taken consistently and effectively. They differ in two ways:

■ EDM is focused on the **automation** and improvement of decisions, whereas the Decision Model does not differentiate between automated and manual decisions.

■ EDM decisions may contain a number of Decision Models as they combine procedural and declarative steps, whereas a Decision Model is purely declarative.

This has a couple of effects. First, it means that not every decision for which the Decision Model is relevant is also relevant to EDM. In Smart (Enough) Systems, we laid out some characteristics of a decision that would push one toward EDM as an approach:

■ **Volume**—Perhaps the most common characteristic of operational decision problems is that the number of decisions of a particular type you must make is high, so high you must automate it, or high enough that many front-line workers must make it on your behalf. Volume alone can cause problems or exacerbate another decision problem, such as compliance or risk assessment.

- **Latency**—Many managers now have more timely information about their business. If you can use this information to see trouble coming but can't change how you make decisions in time, you might have an operational decision problem. The latency between knowing something must change, and being able to change it probably comes from having systems or people processes that are hard to change quickly. This is often caused by the way operational decisions are handled.

- **Variability**—Try imagining nightmare scenarios and thinking about what approach you might take. Think about the systems and people interacting with associates. Decisions those systems and people affect that must change to reflect your new approach could well be operational decisions that, although not a problem now, would cause problems if the business climate changed suddenly.

- **Compliance**—Ensuring that decisions are made consistently by using the same set of guidelines and policies and being able to prove to regulators that the correct rules are in place and used for a given decision can be difficult, especially if the decision must be made in any sort of volume. Demonstrating compliance in every operational decision can be particularly time-consuming if the decision isn't automated correctly.

- **Straight-through processing**—"Straight-through processing" or "once and done" processing involves performing every step in a transaction or process without human intervention. A manual review that drags down response time in a process might be hiding a problem-prone operational decision. If you have a mostly automated process that hangs up on manual reviews, you might have a good candidate for an operational decision.

- **Managing risk**—A prime reason for having a person involved in a process is to manage risk, which is often all about making decisions that manage trade-offs or risks and rewards. A risk-centered decision that must be made quickly or in volume might be a good candidate for an operational decision.

- **Unattended**—With some transactions, there's no choice but to automate a decision. Without automation, there's no way to inject expertise or learn what works better and improve the decision; for example, there's no person who can make a decision in transactions on your Web site or at your ATM. These kinds of decisions are often good candidates for operational decisions.

- **Self-service**—Complex decisions are more common in self-service. No longer is it enough for a self-service portal to deliver a document or ask someone to call an 800 number when things get complex. Now you need to automate this decision so that customers can self-serve, even when the decisions involved are complex.

- **Personalized**—Any time you want to personalize interactions with associates, you're making a decision. For most organizations, these operational decisions can create problems because of the need to balance timeliness with personalization (Taylor and Raden, 2007).

Clearly not every decision, not even every operational decision, meets enough of these criteria to justify the use of the EDM approach. Although you might still use the Decision Model to understand and rationalize the decision, you would not use EDM to automate it.

The second consequence of the differences between decisions is a different approach to scoping. A business decision, suitable for automation and improvement using EDM, may contain a number of distinct Decision Models. For instance, a policy pricing decision might involve several Decision Models—eligibility, tiering, pricing—connected using a decision flow. Such a decision flow might also include steps that are procedural, not declarative, such as scoring a customer using a neural net. The linkage of multiple Decision Models together into a single operational decision that will be implemented by a Decision Service means that even if a decision being modeled with the Decision Model is suitable for automation, it may not map 1:1 to the decisions being discussed in EDM. Although the use of the words *decision* and *business rule* in both cases can be confusing, the two approaches have a different enough focus that this should not be a serious issue. Decision Model and Decision Service can be used to clarify the kind of decision, and Source Rule and Executable Rule can clarify the difference in rule usage.

Using the Decision Model with EDM

In many ways, the use of the Decision Model with EDM is very similar to the use of Entity Modeling with Information Management (see Table 19.1).

So, although using a Decision Model can be very effective in the context of EDM, it is not a substitute for EDM, and nor is EDM a substitute for using Decision Models. There is also likely to be a design step in which the understanding and specification of Decision Models is transformed/mapped onto a more systems-oriented view for use in EDM, similar to the design step that transforms an entity model into a database-oriented view.

The Process

Before detailing how the Decision Model and EDM can be used together from a process perspective, we should consider the basic EDM process. Here are the eight steps we outlined in Smart (Enough) Systems:

■ **Remove decisions from applications**—Decisions can't be managed effectively, or even automated effectively, while they're embedded in other applications. You must remove decision making from your applications.

Table 19.1 Comparison between Information Management and EDM

Information Management	Enterprise Decision Management
All sources of information can be described in terms of logical entities, their attributes, and their relationships.	All collections of explicit business logic can be represented using Decision Models.
Not all entities will be represented in databases or used in information systems.	Not all Decision Models will relate to decisions that are going to be automated.
Databases designed to implement entities might not implement a fully normalized entity model.	Decision services may implement multiple Decision Models, or none at all, or Decision Models with structure only, various combinations, and potentially not fully normalized Decision Models.
Not all information management is best described in a relational sense.	Some elements of decision automation and improvement, such as the inclusion of analytic models, do not lend themselves to specification using the Decision Model.
Entity models, and the formal relational model, its normal forms, etc., make for more accurate and more complete specification of information models.	Decision Models and their normal forms make it more likely that the rules derived from expertise, regulation, policies, and similar sources will be complete, accurate, and consistent.

- **Analyze decisions' potential for improvement**—Realistically, not all decisions lend themselves to the same degree of automation and management. Decisions offering the highest potential return should be addressed first.
- **Automate key operational decisions**—The key operational decisions, separated into what are called "decision services," can then be automated. Typically, this process involves a set of business rules developed from knowledgeable staff, regulations, policies, and perhaps legacy code.
- **Apply predictive and decision analytics**—Applying analytics brings insight derived from historical data to bear on your decisions. This step might take place in parallel with the previous one or come later, as a way to enhance decision making.
- **Give business users control**—At some point in the process, you will hand over control of all or some of the decision logic to business users in your organization. This change of focus is essential for ensuring maximum agility and collaboration.

- **Keep it simple as "intelligence" increases**—The more complex decision making becomes, the more important it is that the business can control the logic without too much of the complexity showing.
- **Focus on production performance requirements**—The decision process is running in production, so you must focus on performance and reliability the way you would for any operational system.
- **Manage change and evolve**—No decision is ever perfectly automated, or at least not for long. You must develop a mind-set of constant testing and refining the way you make these decisions (Taylor and Raden, 2007).

Although some of these steps are not impacted by the use of the Decision Model, many are. In particular, the Decision Model can help find the right decisions to which we can apply EDM, act as an analysis technique, play a role in how business users control rules, and more.

Finding the Right Decisions for EDM

One of the biggest challenges when adopting EDM is the need to become more decision-centric. Decisions must be removed from applications, identified, and managed. The definition of requirements, use cases, and other models must be adapted to separate out decisions and more formally define them. The Decision Model both supports this approach and provides some useful techniques for identifying, describing, and managing the definition of decisions.

One of the other interesting uses of the Decision Model when adopting EDM is in the estimation of potential ROI. Decision Models involving large numbers of rules, rules that change often, complex sets of Rule Families, and those where applying the normalization rules results in significant change will all tend to be good candidates for automation using EDM. Such decisions will typically show a higher ROI from the automation and ongoing improvement of decisions.

When a small group of Decision Models are often used together, there is the potential for the combination also to be a suitable decision for EDM purposes. As noted earlier, some EDM decisions involve multiple steps whereas some are sets of rules defined declaratively (specified by a Decision Model), and others are procedural or analytic. The understanding gained in creating the relevant Decision Models will make it much clearer which composite decisions of this sort are candidates for EDM.

An organization that uses the Decision Model to identify and describe the decisions that drive its business will have all the building blocks it needs when adopting EDM. It will already have found the decisions it can and should define formally, and it will be able to describe those decisions in a systematic and consistent way. Applying the criteria discussed earlier to find decisions suitable for automation with

EDM and some straightforward design decisions to group Decision Models into a single decision service is, then, all that is required to begin the process of automating and improving those decisions.

For example, one Decision Model discussed earlier is Determine Method of Policy Renewal. This has a number of Rule Families and rules where order is immaterial. However, an implementation of Policy Renewal Decision would have this as the first step and would then likely branch based on the resulting method of renewal, and continue with additional steps to handle the renewal itself. Some of these steps would also be defined using Decision Models (eligibility for a discount, for instance), whereas others might represent analytic models (risk scoring, for instance). All these steps would be packaged up as a decision service that could be used by applications and processes to automate renewal. The single decision, what method of policy renewal, might also be exposed as a decision service if it was sometimes needed other than as part of a full renewal decision. In this case, the Decision Model and decision service would have a 1:1 mapping.

The Decision Model as an Analysis Technique

Ensuring that the right rules are written, where those rules represent business expertise, regulations, or policies is essential to EDM. Although EDM focuses on the executable rules required to make a decision, there is a clear need to ensure that the correct rules are being defined. The Decision Model, with its techniques for checking completeness and consistency, is a great tool for this. Rules defined using a Decision Model will be easily translated into executable business rules as part of an EDM development project.

In general, most EDM implementations use a decision flow to describe the steps or tasks in a decision and then map specific steps or tasks to rule sets. Each rule set contains many rules that are executed either sequentially or declaratively depending on the kinds of rules and the degree to which ordering matters in those rules. Each rule set is likely to map to a single Decision Model. This is a consequence of the declarative nature of Decision Models: if the order of execution of rules within the Decision Model is to be immaterial (as it must be), then the execution of all these rules must be handled at run time as a single unit. Typically, a BRMS uses rule sets to manage this scope.

In many EDM projects, there are rule sets whose rules never stabilize long enough to be usefully analyzed: promotion rules, for instance, that might last only for a few hours and where many such rules are created, used, and removed every day. Although it is not generally useful to attempt to analyze an initial set of rules for such a rule set, it is important to understand the structure of these rules: what kinds of rules will be required. In these circumstances, the use of the Decision Model approach to finding the structure of the Rule Families and rules involved in the Decision Model can be very powerful. Giving a formal rigor to the definition of the kinds of rules to be required will make it much more likely that the environment developed to allow the rapid creation and modification of executable rules will support the necessary structural elements.

Decision Models and Business User Control

A core premise of EDM is that the business logic, the business rules, within a decision should be exposed to business users in a way that allows them to understand, manage, and evolve them. The power of the Decision Model to help business users understand how decisions are made, what rules are required, and to check those rules for completeness and consistency adds tremendous value. Business users who can manage both the requirements for their decisions—the Decision Models—and the execution environment of those decisions—using a BRMS—can truly take charge of their applications and the evolution of those applications to meet changing business needs.

Once a group of business users becomes familiar and comfortable with using the Decision Model to describe their rules, it would also be possible to develop a rules management environment that mimics the structure of the Decision Model. Essentially, the Decision Model would be used to navigate and manage the rules that were being executed. Whether this involved some automatic translation of the Decision Model to an executable format or the development of a user interface that allowed the rules being executed to be edited using a Decision Model-like interface is largely immaterial. The point is that a group of business users who come to understand the Decision Model have given you a ready-made design for the environment they need to manage their business rules in production.

Decision Model and Adaptive Control

The principle of adaptive control—the continuous improvement of decision making through constant challenging of the default approach—is critical to EDM. Decisions take time to play out, and the definition of a "best" or "correct" decision changes over time. Adaptive control helps manage both these challenges. Organizations using the Decision Model to specify their decisions may well find it easier to identify potential challenger approaches from the model. The possible combinations of rules within a Rule Family as well as the possible changes to structure within Decision Models and Rule Families will likely be more obvious in a formally modeled decision than they would otherwise be. As designing suitable challenger approaches is one of the harder elements of adaptive control, this will be very useful.

Other Thoughts on Using the Decision Model

The ability of the Decision Model to formalize the mapping of business logic to the motivation of an organization and to the measures tracked by the organization can also add value to EDM. EDM also values tracking how specific decisions impact key performance indicators and other measures, and the tracking over time of this impact. The Decision Model identifies the measures that should be considered when performing this mapping. Similarly, understanding the motivation for the current approach to a decision can be very helpful when deciding which decisions should be automated.

The integration of executable analytics and business rules in EDM is part of its power. Although the Decision Model is not a technique with much to offer to analytic practitioners, it does help formalize the rules that will use the analytic models. This will help analytic practitioners become more comfortable that the rules are being properly defined, and will provide a mechanism for a more precise discussion as to the kind of attributes and outcomes that should be delivered using analytic models.

Conclusion

There is only room in this chapter for a short discussion of EDM and its relationship to the Decision Model. Clearly, however, the two approaches are highly compatible and each adds much value to the other. EDM provides a formal, well-defined approach for taking the Decision Model and putting it into production alongside sophisticated analytics. The Decision Model provides a formal definition of the rules that are part of each EDM decision and helps ensure those rules are complete and correct.

Chapter 20

Introducing the Business Decision Maturity Model

Contents

Why a New Maturity Model?..457
    What Is a Maturity Model?...457
    The Current Opportunity in Business Logic 457
    The Previous Age of Software Crisis 457
    A Maturity Model Solution 458
The Original Maturity Model for Business Logic: The RMM 458
    The RMM as a Maturity Model...459
    What the RMM Was Missing..459
    The Impact of the Decision Model on Business and Technology 460
    The BDMM and Process (Not Model) Maturity.............................460
The Business Decision Maturity Model 461
    Unique Features of the BDMM 461
    The Characteristics of the BDMM Vectors 462
    Assessing the BDMM Level 463
Characteristics at Five Levels of the BDMM..464
    Level 0: None 464
        Business Value..464
        Business Architecture 464
        Business Governance 464

Level 1: Visible 465
    Business Value.. 466
    Business Architecture 466
    Business Governance... 466
Level 2: Agile 467
    Business Value.. 468
    Business Architecture 468
    Business Governance...470
Level 3: Aligned...470
    Business Value..470
    Business Architecture 471
    Business Governance...471
Level 4: Predictive...473
    Business Value..473
    Business Architecture 475
    Business Governance...476
Level 5: Autonomic 476
    Business Value..476
    Business Architecture 478
    Business Governance...478
Summary..479
What about the Quote 479

To exist is to change, to change is to mature, to mature is to go on creating oneself endlessly.

Henri Bergson, French philosopher

This chapter introduces the Business Decision Maturity Model (BDMM). The BDMM is a tool for aligning business objectives with the optimum Business Decision Management practices for achieving those objectives. It is similar to the Capability Maturity Model (i.e., CMM) because it defines various plateaus or levels of an organization's maturity related to a specific process. However, the CMM defines maturity levels for the process of producing software products. The BDMM defines maturity levels for the process of managing business decisions. This chapter defines BDMM maturity levels for the process of delivering, maintaining, automating, aligning, and leveraging important organizational Decision Models.

Why a New Maturity Model?

It is easy for a complex process to result in deliverables of poor or inconsistent quality. This is especially true when the process is not well defined, well communicated, well learned, or appropriately evaluated for quality. A maturity model provides guidance for such processes.

What Is a Maturity Model?

For the purpose of this chapter, a maturity model is a process improvement model used by organizations to identify best practices, improve process execution accordingly, and measure that improvement. When a process improves in certain predefined ways, it becomes more mature. To standardize incremental maturity, a maturity model typically delineates a fixed set of maturity levels where each maturity level is a well-defined destination on the way to achieving a well-established process.

There are maturity models for different kinds of complex processes. Some have been standardized as part of ISO 15504. This chapter introduces a maturity model for the process of Business Decision Management.

But first, the chapter starts with an obvious question: Why does Business Decision Management need a maturity model?

The Current Opportunity in Business Logic

Chapter 1 describes the opportunity to separate the business logic from other dimensions of system development and the significant advantages that would accrue from such a separation. In fact, this may become a necessity in today's world of fierce competition, strict and growing compliance requirements, global markets, and unforeseen threats.

Business logic, like software, is pervasive and powerful. It drives the business's decisions despite being invisible, and therefore should be managed properly. This situation represents the same opportunity that the years of 1965–1985 represented for software development. What were those opportunities, how were they were capitalized upon, and what might this mean for the opportunities of today?

The Previous Age of Software Crisis

The phrase software crisis was coined by F. L. Bauer at the first NATO Software Engineering Conference in 1968 in Gamisch, Germany. It refers to the process of creating correct, understandable, and verifiable program code. This process is difficult because of the complexity of the software development process and conflicting, changing requirements.

Many methodologies and techniques emerged to address the complexity of the software development process, but a significant contribution to taming it is the original and most well-known maturity model, generally referred to as the Capability Maturity Model (CMM)*. The CMM has evolved over time; today it is an accepted way to improve the quality of the software development process, with assessment tools to measure compliance with the CMM.

A Maturity Model Solution

With some similarities, separating the business logic refers to the process of creating correct, understandable, and verifiable business logic supporting a business decision whether or not the business decision is destined for program code or human execution. This process is difficult because of the complexity of defining and managing important business decisions and the necessity of changing the underlying business logic. It follows, then, that a maturity model aimed at the Business Decision Management process would be helpful in defining and charting improvement.

The Original Maturity Model for Business Logic: The RMM

There already exists a maturity model addressing the management of business rules that has proved useful in practice. It is called the Rule Maturity Model (RMM) (von Halle, 2006). The goal of the RMM is to provide a roadmap for advancing the process of business rule management from a poorly managed to a well-managed process.

The development of the RMM has an interesting history. More than ten years ago, a government agency requested an assessment of how other organizations, commercial or governmental, were embracing BRMS technology and related management processes. An initial survey of anonymous participants concluded that there was a wide range of complexity in such practices. Survey participants expressed an interest in a process improvement model for assessing their current and target maturity in the area of business rule management. Hence, the RMM was developed based on initial participants and refined through subsequent surveys. It has remained virtually unchanged until now.

---

* The Software Engineering Institute (SEI), a federally funded research and development center sponsored by the U.S. Department of Defense and operated by Carnegie Mellon University, developed the original capability maturity model—Capability Maturity Model for Software (SW-CMM)—and various other related maturity models, generally referred to collectively as CMM.

The RMM as a Maturity Model

Like other maturity models, the RMM has six maturity levels. These are numbered from 0 to 5. At RMM level 0, people in an organization are unaware that business rules have value. Yet, at RMM level 5, people use business rules as proactive business levers. At RMM level 5, organizations deploy business rules to gain momentum over the competition and react to anticipated events and futures. Therefore, each RMM level defines an alignment between organizational objectives and business rule management practices. Each RMM level implies corresponding advances in business rule awareness, roles, management processes, technology, and culture.* The RMM continues to be used by large and small organizations for individual projects or an enterprise scope (von Halle, 2007).

Although the RMM is useful for advancing from lower to higher levels of business rule management maturity, some organizations found it difficult to advance as quickly as desired. Of course, this is understandable. After all, advances in maturity imply organizational change, which is always difficult.

However, an interesting consideration arises. Is business rule management the correct focus for defining a mature business logic or business rule management process? In other words, is the concept of a business rule (or business logic statement) at too low a level to justify a high-level business management process?† The secret to quicker advances in maturity may be to elevate the management of business rules to the management of something of greater business magnitude and relevance—something executive management cares about, utilizes directly for business advantage, talks about, and which remains very tangible from inception to full development—the business decision, not the business rule.

The business decision is an orderly collection of business rules and business logic statements. However, the business decision is greater than the sum of its pieces. Practice proves that the business decision is the asset that the business really needs and wants to manage. Business rules and business logic statements are simply the details by which the business does so.

What the RMM Was Missing

The original RMM was missing a formal definition of and reference to the business decision. Yet, it turns out that executive management cares very much about important business decisions. This is even more so in changing and tumultuous business climates.

---

* A survey was conducted of a set of anonymously participating organizations across a range of industries; corresponding results were analyzed to determine the current and target states of maturity of business rule management (von Halle and Goldberg, 2006).
† In fact, one could suggest that specification of business rules has historically happened during design phases, not so much scoping, requirements, and analysis, because individual business rules are too detailed and distracting during those phases.

So, the business decision and the idea that it can be modeled for business consumption elevates the business rule management process to that of business decision management. From an organizational maturity perspective, this shift upward has a profound effect.

The Impact of the Decision Model on Business and Technology

Early experience with the Decision Model indeed confirms that the business decision and Decision Model are assets that gain higher business management attention. As such, it is easier to incorporate them earlier in business-driven projects, such as BPM, process improvements, and business transformation efforts. That's because business people easily recognize that business value is not found in the individual business rule or business logic statement, but in entire business decisions. Therefore, entire Decision Models (even without details) emerge as the asset that drives toward business objectives.

At the same time, the natural connections from the Decision Model to BMM, BPM, and SOA are so compelling that they elevate the management of business decisions to the status of critical technology assets or services. Not only that, but it becomes easier to incorporate Decision Models earlier in systems development projects and enterprise architecture projects. Again, an entire Decision Model (even without details) emerges as an asset that drives enterprise and system architecture in support of business objectives.

Thus, the impact of the Decision Model on business, information technology is significant enough to develop a maturity model focused on Business Decisions rather than business rules, and call it the Business Decision Maturity Model (BDMM).

The BDMM and Process (Not Model) Maturity

It is important to note that maturity models address the quality of the implementation of a process. Maturity models do not address the quality of a particular modeling approach, but only verify that it is carried out accurately.

So, the BDMM is not a measurement of the effectiveness of the Decision Model as a modeling approach. Instead, the BDMM is a measurement of the Business Decision Management process. The integration of Decision Modeling into this practice, however, elevates the status and importance of the business decision as a manageable asset worthy of its own management process. Thus, the BDMM measures the quality of the Business Decision Management process, where the goal is that a good-quality process delivers high-quality business logic behind business decisions. Improving the quality of business decisions improves the performance of the business itself.

Therefore, although the original goal of RMM was to advance the practice of business rule management, the goal of BDMM is to begin and evolve the practice of business decision management. This means advancing business decision governance to improve the quality and agility of business decisions. To date, the only way to do so in a rigorous manner is with the Decision Model.

The Business Decision Maturity Model

The high-level, diagrammatic summary of the BDMM is shown in Figure 20.1. It is important to note that, even though the model defines the maturity of the process, the titles for each given level of the BDMM (Unmanaged, Visible, Agile, Aligned, Predictive, and Autonomic) refer to the qualities anticipated in the Decision Models created at each level, and not the qualities of the process.

Unique Features of the BDMM

The BDMM has two unique features, which are based on experience gained in practice with the RMM. First, like the RMM, but unique among maturity models, the model incorporates a business value vector indicating the business consequence

Level 0 Unmanaged	Level 1 Visible	Level 2 Agile	Level 3 Aligned	Level 4 Predictive	Level 5 Autonomic
MINIMUM		Business Value			**MAXIMUM**
Risk of loss of business control is high. Risk of business change is high. Ability to predict business impact of change is low. Cost of change is high.	Risk of loss of business control & business change is lower. Cost of change is lowered. Ability to predict business impact of change is still low. Analysis of business decisions is possible, but is manual.	Risk of loss of business control greatly reduced at the project level; business change becomes possible through automated analysis. Ability to predict business impact of change is still low.	Risk of loss of business control greatly reduced across projects. Ability to predict business impact of change is improved. Consistency between business units improved. Cost of change and testing reduced further.	Firm control of business policy established. Ability to predict short-term futures, ability to assess the impact of change on the future is possible.	Optimize business policy to changing conditions in real time and against predicted changes in business models and metrics. Management focus on evolving business objectives and policy with a firm business control; the birth of the Agile Enterprise
IMMATURE		Business Architecture			**MATURE**
No business architecture; to speak of.	Informal Business Decision Management architecture.	Project level process and business decision standards established within broader architectural standards.	Cross project level process and business decision standards defined within broader architectural standards.	Detailed standards for process and Business Decision Architecture established and managed.	Continuous improvement of process and Business Decision architecture within the broader architectural process.
NOT PRESENT		Business Stewardship			**ENTERPRISE**
No stewardship.	Business Analysts lead business decision discovery for local logic development.	Integration of Business Decisions with use cases and process flows with business metrics.	Stewardship of business process and Business Decisions across project boundaries.	Stewardship of business process and Business Decisions at enterprise levels.	Full integration of process and Business Decision Management into business planning.
DECISIONS SHARED ACROSS: ← PROJECT LEVEL ONLY →		← PROJECTS →	←	ENTERPRISE	→

Figure 20.1 A high-level depiction of the Business Decision Maturity Model.

of each level within the model. Second, the model is adaptable for use with an architecture maturity model. Thus, if the organization is already using an architecture maturity model, the BDMM can serve as an adjunct for assessing close alignment between BDM maturity and architectural maturity.

The Characteristics of the BDMM Vectors

The BDMM can be applied to any organization or project of any size, complexity, and maturity. It provides three vectors for each level:

- Business Value. The Business Value vector identifies the relevant business consequence of a particular level of maturity in the Business Decision Management process. This is helpful when building a roadmap to, and weighing the risk/reward of, the investment in developing a given level of maturity. Determining the optimum level for a given organization is an important use of the BDMM. This vector is therefore the starting point for assessing the current or target maturity of BDM. That is, organizations use this vector to select a target BDMM level. From here, the other vectors define characteristics and measurement criteria for achieving that level. Each organization may customize a set of characteristics and criteria to measure the actual business value earned from a given level of maturity relative to the benefits suggested by the model.
- Business Architecture. The Business Architecture vector describes the maturity of the Business Decision Management process within the Business Architecture. This vector can be customized to align with the organization's business architecture practice. It may use baseline characteristics for architecture maturity as found in architecture maturity models. These characteristics would then need to be modified specifically for Business Decision maturity purposes. For illustration, this chapter references the U.S. DoC ACMM (United States Department of Commerce IT Architectural Maturity Model) framework, modified to take into account specific Business Decision characteristics.
- Business Governance. The Business Governance vector describes the maturity of the business governance of the Business Decision Management process and is measured against the characteristics specified for this vector. This is a separate set of characteristics for stewardship or governance in architectural maturity models.

Table 20.1 contains the primary characteristics of the Business Architecture and Business Governance vectors. Each characteristic is assessed at each level of the BDMM against a set of criteria. These criteria are set out by level from Table 20.2

Table 20.1   Characteristics of the Measured Vectors of the BDMM

Vector/Characteristic #	Characteristic
Business Architecture	
1	Senior Management Involvement (in architecture)
2	Operating Unit Participation (in architecture)
3	Architecture Communication (in architecture)
4	Decision Modeling standards and process
5	Process Modeling standards
6	Business Planning standards
7	Integration with specialized execution environments
8	Integration to Business Intelligence (BI)
9	Integration into methodology
Business Governance	
1	Senior Management Involvement in Business Decisions
2	Operating Unit Participation in Business Decisions
3	Business Planning/Decision Governance
4	Performance Stewardship

through Table 20.6. Should the organization already utilize an architectural maturity model, the BDMM characteristics may be augmented by those found in that maturity model. Table 20.1 uses three characteristics from the ACMM. (The augmentation characteristics may differ in practice, depending on the base architecture maturity model being employed by the organization).

Assessing the BDMM Level

A BDMM assessment is carried out by referring to the BDMM diagram and details, and scoring each of the Business Architecture and Business Governance characteristics to determine the extent of that compliance. The assessment is based on two separate judgments:

- A qualitative judgment, which is the extent to which the organization has developed processes and practices that match the characteristics of the specific level being assessed.
- A quantitative judgment, which is calculated by the breadth of implementation across the prescribed level of the organization.

These two judgments are maintained separately and are not combined in a single score. The qualitative assessment is critical in all levels, but the quantitative judgment is more important the higher the level in the BDMM. The risk of proceeding to level 3 before a sufficient number of projects, given the size of the organization, have demonstrated a level 2 proficiency would be a high risk. Similarly, a sufficient quantitative score for a level 3 would be a prerequisite to attempt a level 4 without significant risk. Finally, from level 4 to 5 it is presumed that the organization would be widely acculturated to Business Decision Management, and would be at a relatively high quantitative score. A detailed description of how to conduct such an assessment is beyond the scope of this chapter.

Characteristics at Five Levels of the BDMM

These are examples of the characteristics for each of the following six levels of the BDMM.

Level 0: None

At this level there is no awareness of business decisions as a manageable asset, and business logic is not formally managed or separated from code, documents, or individual knowledge.

Business Value

There is no business value in the Business Decision Management process existing at level 0. There is the adverse value due to the business logic being "lost" to the business. Lack of knowledge of the business decisions and their business logic presents significant risk to the business in a wide range of areas, and dramatically increases the cost of business change.

Business Architecture

There is no formal control or management process relating to the business decisions in the organization. No architecture relating to business logic or business decisions is present.

Business Governance

There is no business governance of or accountability for business logic.

Level 1: Visible

The general goal of level 1 is to gain visibility (hence the label Visible) of business decisions and their business logic. Such visibility allows stakeholders to know the content of the business logic behind the business decisions. Generally, at level 1 the visibility is relatively localized to specific areas of the organization, or even more typically, to a given project.

Table 20.2   Characteristics of the Business Architecture Vector of the BDMM for Level 1: Visible

	Business Architecture
1	Senior Management Involvement (in architecture): Limited management team awareness or involvement in the architecture process.
2	Operating Unit Participation (in architecture): Limited operating unit acceptance of the IT architecture process.
3	Architecture Communication: The latest version of the operating unit's IT architecture documentation is on the Web. Little communication exists about the IT architecture process and possible process improvements.
4	Decision Modeling standards and process: Ad hoc, localized Decision Modeling standards and process: loosely connected to process modeling standards.
5	Process Modeling standards: Ad hoc, localized decision modeling standards and process: loosely connected to decision modeling standards.
6	Business Planning standards: Ad hoc, localized business planning. Loosely integrated into Decision Model metrics.
7	Integration to specialized execution environments: No integration efforts; spreadsheets or simple repositories used for capture and storage.
8	Integration to Metrics/BI: Ad hoc reporting from data warehouse to support business decision modeling efforts.
9	Integration into methodology: Little or no integration into methodology.

Table 20.3 Characteristics of the Business Governance Vector of the BDMM for Level 1: Visible

	Business Governance
1	Senior Management Involvement in Business Decisions:
	Little to no management involvement.
2	Operating Unit Participation in Business Decisions:
	Only localized involvement in the business decision, with no operating unit involvement.
3	Business Planning/Decision Governance:
	Little or no business planning in relation to the business decision; any business policy is locally determined by subject matter experts (SMEs).
4	Performance Stewardship:
	The business analysts may undertake ad hoc, local testing of business decisions and business performance after discovery and implementation into process or code.

Business Value

At level 1, the organization discovers, documents, and models business decisions. This has the merit of enabling the organization, at a localized level, to develop a shared understanding of the business decisions that are operable. This improves communication between stakeholders and supports business continuity.

However, at this level, risk of loss of business control is high. Risk of business change is high. Although lower than level 0, cost of change remains high. Ability to predict business impact of change is low.

Business Architecture

There is no formal control or management process relating to the business decisions in the organization. No formal architecture has been developed to integrate business decisions into the organization's architecture. The minimum criteria for the Business Architecture characteristics for level 1 are shown in Table 20.2.

Business Governance

Business analysts lead business decision discovery for local business logic development. There is little or no business management awareness or formal interest in the business decision discovery process. Business experts are content to share their view of the business logic with business analysts who act on their behalf as its stewards.

Table 20.3 sets out the characteristics of level 1 business governance of the Business Decision.

Level 2: Agile

The overall goal for level 2 is to achieve agility, meaning that business decisions are not just known, but can be changed rapidly. Business decisions are implemented in technology, where the business logic of the business decisions has been externalized

Table 20.4   Characteristics of the Business Architecture Vector of the BDMM for Level 2: Agile

	Business Architecture
1	Senior Management Involvement (in architecture): Management is aware of activities surrounding the separation of business decisions.
2	Operating Unit Participation (in architecture): The operating unit is aware of the Business Decision Management approach.
3	Architecture Communication: The project publishes its architectural process and architectural deliverables in Web pages available to the operating unit.
4	Decision Modeling standards and process: A formal Decision Model standard and process is adopted by the project.
5	Process Modeling standards: A formal process modeling standard is adopted by the project.
6	Business Planning standards: A formal business planning standard is adopted by the project.
7	Integration with specialized execution environments: The architecture for the execution environment is harmonized to the Decision Modeling standard, and meets the objective of agility; that is, the logic in the Decision Models may be aligned to future changes to decision logic to meet the criteria of change velocity set by the project. A Business Decision repository is established with a formal glossary and traceability from business motivation and business policy all the way through to deployment.
8	Integration to BI: A formal process of feedback from BI reports, with performance adjustment to the business decisions, is defined and implemented.
9	Integration into methodology: A formal set of methods relating to Decision Modeling and implementation are defined and integrated into the project methodology.

and exposed such that the business analyst, or even business user, is able to rapidly change it. Typically, a BRMS is used. The business decisions at level 2 are normally localized to a project.

Business Value

The principal business value of level 2, as implied by its label, is business agility: to be able to effect rapid adjustments to business policy by making changes to the business logic in the relevant business decisions. This benefit is largely confined to the specific project, or projects, that implements business decision management. However, the management of performance means that the project is expected to assign the role of performance steward for business decisions, to set business performance targets for business decisions, and to track the performance of those decisions into the future.

Additional business value, localized to the project would be as follows:

- A greater degree of alignment between business policy, objective, and business decisions leading to business decisions that are not only more agile, but allow the organization, at the local level of the project, to better control its direction.
- More transparent decision making in the processes implemented at the project level.
- Lower-cost, higher-quality system development for the project, arising from the decision management approach.

So, risk of loss of business control is greatly reduced at the project level, and business change becomes possible through analysis. However, level 2 does not support the wider benefits of Enterprise Business Decision Management; this can only be achieved at level 3 and beyond. Nor does level 2 position the organization to easily predict business impact of change to future events and conditions. Anticipation of the future is achieved at level 4 and beyond. Level 2 is the precursor to level 3, which cannot be achieved until the organization has demonstrated the maturity to achieve a level 2 capability with more than a single project.

Business Architecture

Projects that achieve level 2 of the BDMM are expected to exhibit an architectural maturity that demonstrates a consistent ability to create, manage, and maintain business decisions that can respond to changing business objectives and conditions with the minimum of time or effort. Therefore, an architectural process, published on a Web site available to all project stakeholders, must be put into place that clearly defines processes and deliverables. Senior management, and the business unit, should be aware of the process and its capabilities.

Because level 2 assumes a significant degree of automation of the business decisions, the architectural process for business decisions and the architectural process for the implementation and deployment of those business decisions must be harmonized for each to support the other. Other important areas of harmonization between processes include those surrounding business intelligence and business planning. This is because the business decision will need to be structured to meet business objectives, must be measured against future business results, and will need to be capable of change as the objectives or the metrics change.

At level 2, the architecture is expected to demonstrate clear separation of the business logic dimension from the other dimensions. This is enhanced by the use of a Web services structure, a Service-Oriented Architecture for business decisions similar to the approach advocated in Chapters 5 and 15. This approach will also assist the transition to a future level 3.

Finally, at level 2, the formal methodology for developing business decisions must be integrated into the formal project methodology.

The business architecture characteristics of level 2 are summarized in Table 20.4.

Table 20.5   Characteristics of the Business Governance Vector of the BDMM for Level 2: Agile

	Business Governance
1	Senior Management Involvement in Business Decisions:
	Senior management is aware of the activities, and receives performance reports from performance stewards.
2	Operating Unit Participation in Business Decisions:
	The operating unit includes the project business planning and performance deliverables from project, and incorporates them into its business planning processes.
3	Business Planning/Decision Governance:
	Business analysts, working with performance stewards, lead the formal process of business planning and Decision Modeling.
4	Performance Stewardship:
	Performance stewards define performance definitions and performance reporting requirements from BI, and provide a formal process for Decision Model adjustment to performance. Performance stewards provide reporting to the project and organization.

Business Governance

In order to demonstrate level 2 compliance and capitalize on its capabilities, the business governance processes must be capable of developing the right business decisions and exercising the control and optimization of them over time. This means that the business decisions must be designed based on business objectives and their associated metrics, and must continually be monitored and adjusted for performance. Governance must be consistent across the project, and the business unit must fully support the project to meet these goals.

At level 2, it is sufficient for the governance process to be localized to the individual project, but the process must still be clearly defined.

The criteria for the business governance characteristics at level 2 are set out in Table 20.5.

Level 3: Aligned

The overall goal for level 3 is alignment of business decisions across projects, and prospectively, across business silos. This enables the reuse of business decisions, and—more importantly—positions the organization for higher-quality business processes as business decisions become aligned across the processes. There is significant business change implied between level 2 and level 3, as the governance processes cross organizational boundaries and become more challenging.

The alignment may commence at a project-to-project alignment of business decisions, and may progress to a wider scope. The benefits of level 3 become greater the more widely spread the alignment.

Business Value

The implementation of level 3 across significant operations of the business unit means that business decisions are reused across projects and functional boundaries; this enables a high degree of business alignment with all its attendant benefits.

This does not necessarily mean that business decisions are not localized, or even personalized. What it does mean is that local business logic is transparent to other stakeholders across the boundaries and that this business logic is governed appropriately by the correct stewards.

So at level 3, risk of loss of business control is greatly reduced, and the ability to predict business impact of change is improved. Consistency among business units is improved. Cost of change is reduced further, while development time in projects may be significantly reduced due to reusability of business decisions and a cross-organizational Business Decision Management process. Successful achievement of level 3 positions the organization to move to level 4, which provides a predictive capability.

Business Architecture

At level 3, the organization demonstrates that the maturity of business architecture that was achieved at the project level is implemented across projects, or even across an entire business unit or across several business units.

The need for widespread adoption of the architectural processes is paramount. Senior management and the entire operating unit will have to embrace the Business Decision Management architectural processes and standards for success to be achieved. For that reason, clarity in architectural processes and the widespread availability of the processes is essential. Business planning linked to consistent business intelligence practices, at the business unit level, enables management to develop and manage business decisions in a well managed process.

Level 3 processes have a significantly more complex set of challenges than level 2. There is almost always a heterogeneous systems environment with complex operating requirements, which is different from the simpler environment normally found at level 2. In this situation, a Web services approach is very helpful, if not obligatory. Using the patterns suggested in Chapter 15, this permits the creation of business decisions that can be used widely across one or more business units, but closely tailored to the circumstances of the use.

The specific business architecture characteristics of level 3 are summarized in Table 20.6.

Business Governance

The challenge for business governance at level 3 is to build processes that resolve or accommodate the conflicts that may occur when business decisions, business logic, and glossary fact types are defined by stakeholders across organizational boundaries. Notwithstanding these potential conflicts, the processes have to deliver business decisions that demonstrate consistency with business objectives and must respond to changing business conditions and metrics.

To meet these difficult criteria, the processes provide for a governance council to clarify and resolve difficulties across the business unit. This council reflects the widespread adoption of the Business Decision Management processes across the enterprise and the close involvement of senior management in the Business Decision Management processes. At the same time, performance stewards are responsible for tracking the business performance of the business decisions for the stakeholders and governance council, and seek changes where performance metrics indicate that business decisions may not be achieving their goals. These performance stewards may have localized as well as wider business unit responsibility.

A summary of the characteristics of level 2 are set out in Table 20.7.

Table 20.6 Characteristics of the Business Architecture Vector of the BDMM for Level 3: Aligned

	Business Architecture
1	Senior Management Involvement (in architecture): Senior management team aware of and supportive of the enterprisewide architecture process. Management actively supports architectural standards in Business Decision Management.
2	Operating Unit Participation (in architecture): The entire operating unit accepts and actively participates in the Business Decision Architecture process.
3	Architecture Communication: Architecture documents updated regularly on business unit architecture Web page.
4	Decision Modeling standards and process: Decision Modeling standards set and agreed across the business unit.
5	Process Modeling standards: Process modeling standards set and agreed across the business unit.
6	Business Planning standards: Business planning standards set and agreed across the business unit.
7	Integration with specialized execution environments: The architecture for the execution environment is harmonized to the Decision Modeling standard and is agreed across the business unit. The repository is provided with federation capabilities to establish local business decisions and business unit business decisions.
8	Integration with BI: A formal process of feedback from BI reports, with performance adjustment to the business decisions, is defined and implemented across the business unit.
9	Integration into methodology: A formal set of methods relating to Decision Modeling and implementation is defined and integrated into the project methodology across the business unit.

Table 20.7   Characteristics of the Business Governance Vector of the BDMM for Level 3: Aligned

	Business Governance
1	Senior Management Involvement in Business Decisions:
	Senior management is aware of the activities and receives performance reports from performance stewards. Senior management actively supports standards. Senior management adopts the Decision Model in their decision-making activities.
2	Operating Unit Participation in Business Decisions:
	Most elements of operating unit or enterprise show acceptance of or are actively participating in the Business Decision Management process.
4	Business Planning/Decision Governance:
	The business unit or enterprise creates a council-based governance system for business decisions and adopts a formal business planning process that integrates the Decision Model.
5	Performance Stewardship:
	Business unit or enterprise processes are implemented whereby performance stewards define performance definitions and performance reporting requirements from BI, and provide a formal process for Decision Model adjustment to performance. Performance stewards provide reporting to the business unit or enterprise.

Level 4: Predictive

The overall goal of level 4 is to be able to predict changes in the business environment and develop business decisions in response to anticipated or hypothesized business events and conditions.

Business Value

At level 4, the business reduces future risk by anticipating future conditions and preparing for them. The business is able to model future events and test the impact of changes in business decisions to meet those conditions. The business is able to react quickly to conditions across a business unit or enterprise. At BDMM level 2, the relationship between business intelligence and business decisions is limited to one or two projects. At level 3, this relationship is established across one or more business

Table 20.8   Characteristics of the Business Architecture Vector of the BDMM for Level 4: Predictive

	Business Architecture
1	Senior Management Involvement (in architecture): Senior management team directly involved in the Business Decision architecture review process.
2	Operating Unit Participation (in architecture): The entire operating unit or enterprise accepts and actively participates in the Business Decision architecture process.
3	Architecture Communication: Architecture documents are updated regularly, and frequently reviewed for latest architecture developments/standards.
4	Decision Modeling standards and process: Decision Modeling process is part of the culture.
5	Process Modeling standards: Process Modeling process is part of the culture.
6	Business Planning standards: Business Planning process is part of the culture.
7	Integration specialized execution environments: Decision Model structures become a standard part of the execution environment. A sophisticated tracking of business metrics against business decisions is established, with dashboards and warnings to management.
8	Integration to BI: The BI and decision environments are integrated into a single prediction/action/reaction environment. The environment is able to model business scenarios and evaluate the likely results of the application of certain business decisions.
9	Integration into methodology: The close relationship between business motivation, business metrics, business process, and business decisions is embedded into the methodology as a standard approach to all IT and planning activities.

Table 20.9   Characteristics of the Business Governance Vector of the BDMM for Level 4: Predictive

	Business Governance
1	Senior Management Involvement in Business Decisions: Senior management use business decisions as an integral part of their approach to management, and drive the "what-if" scenarios.
2	Operating Unit Participation in Business Decisions: The Decision Model is part of the culture of the operating unit and is an important lever in the operation of the business.
3	Metrics/BI integration into Business Decisions: The BI integration into business decisions is seamless, and there is constant monitoring and adjustment of decision logic against actual and predicted results.
4	Business Planning/Decision Governance: The Decision Model governance is integral to the management structure of the business unit.
5	Performance Stewardship: The performance stewardship of the Decision Models and Process models is integral to the management structure of the business unit; they lead efforts to predict future events, elicit the appropriate Decision Model changes for those potential events, and test the changes in the scenario models.

units, and so the business can adjust its business decisions against changing conditions across a wide business scope. This supports true BPM implementation of wide and long-running transactions (as detailed in Chapter 4). Level 4, a natural progression from level 3, provides a strategic agility, a broad control over policy implementation, and the ability to not only model future events, but also to prepare and tests responses to those potential events. This is the beginning of the implementation of adaptive control (discussed in Chapter 19) and a major step towards autonomic computing.

Business Architecture

The evolution of business architecture from level 3 to level 4 is focused on the relationship of the Business Decision Management processes to BI, because level 4 seeks to use the pervasiveness of the business decision across a wide business scope, achieved at level 3, as a means for predicting how to react to potential future events.

This requires an ability to model future events and carry out scenario planning using the Decision Models and BI tools to fashion the best possible business logic to use to respond to prospective changes. Important processes are those that enable the construction of business models and simulate results given certain business decisions under different circumstances.

Table 20.8 summarizes the criteria for the characteristics of the business architecture vector for level 4.

Business Governance

The business governance process at level 4 builds on the processes implemented at level 3, but includes governance processes to conduct and maintain business scenarios for future events. This expands the role of the performance stewards, who lead the effort to conduct simulations and elicit the correct business logic changes that may become necessary in the given scenarios.

Senior management is expected to become an integral part of the business planning and scenario modeling processes.

Table 20.9 summarizes the criteria for each of the business governance characteristics for level 4.

Level 5: Autonomic

The overall goal of level 5 is for time- and business-critical business decisions to respond to changing events without human intervention, at the "speed of business," based on algorithms and predictive models that control the business decision logic. This level is called autonomic, and ensures that the response of the business is both based on careful advance planning and instant adjustment. This is the evolution envisaged by Taylor and Raden in Smart (Enough) Systems (Taylor and Raden, 2007) and which they call adaptive control. For a complete discussion of the potential value of level 5, see the discussion of EDM in Chapter 19.

Business Value

At level 5, the business is capable of carefully planned, rapid, and continually improving reaction to events. This significantly reduces business risk and optimizes business opportunity.

Level 5 represents the full realization of BDM (or EDM), where there is a culture of decision management across the business unit and where decision management is constantly improving.

Business planning reaches a high degree of capability, and models that provide continuing guidance to business decisions are capable of making automatic adjustments to conditions without the need for human intervention. This reduces cost,

Table 20.10 Characteristics of the Business Architecture Vector of the BDMM for Level 5: Autonomic

	Business Architecture
1	Senior Management Involvement (in architecture):
	Senior management involvement in optimizing process improvements in architecture development and governance.
2	Operating Unit Participation (in architecture):
	Feedback on architecture process from all operating unit or enterprise elements is used to drive architecture process improvements.
3	Architecture Communication:
	Architecture documents are used by every decision maker in the organization for every business decision.
4	Decision Modeling standards and process:
	Decision logic is architected to respond to business metrics; Continuous improvement in Decision Modeling standards and processes.
5	Process Modeling standards:
	Continuous improvement in Process Modeling standards and processes.
6	Business Planning standards:
	Business planning provides predictive models to determine business logic changes that will have to be made in the event of changes in business metrics. Continuous improvement in Business Planning standards and processes.
7	Integration with specialized execution environments:
	There is an automatic feedback loop between the BI and Decision Model environments based on predictive models created in the business planning process. The specialized execution environment is continuously improved.
8	Integration with BI:
	BI provides the metrics to drive the autonomic capability and is continuously improved to support this effort.
9	Integration into methodology:
	The methodology is continuously improved to support the autonomic system.

Table 20.11   Characteristics of the Business Governance Vector of the BDMM for Level 5: Autonomic

	Business Governance
1	Senior Management Involvement in Business Decisions: Senior management is involved in building and optimizing the predictive models.
2	Operating Unit Participation in Business Decisions: All operating unit elements provide feedback on the decision logic optimization and potential future events.
3	Metrics/BI integration into Business Decisions: The BI and business decision environments are considered an integrated system.
4	Business Planning/Decision Governance: The Decision Model governance is integral to the predictive modeling and constant optimization of the decision logic.
5	Performance Stewardship: Performance stewardship is integrated into Business Planning/Decision Stewardship.

and even more importantly, reduces latency time between detecting an event and taking steps to react to those events.

Business Architecture

The evolution of business architecture from level 4 to level 5 requires processes that evolve automated algorithms and formulas to control business decisions against changing business results without external intervention. These automated routines are developed from the business models and scenarios created and tested in level 4, and are extended to enable them to be automated. Table 20.10 provides a summary of the criteria for each of the characteristics of the business architecture for level 5.

Business Governance

The level 4 business governance is extended even further in level 5, where the focus is to design, then constantly verify the continuing accuracy, relevance, and optimization of the autonomic business decisions. This requires the close cooperation of senior management, performance stewards, and the governance councils. Table 20.11 contains the criteria for each of the characteristics of the governance objective for level 5.

Summary

The quality of a business is related not only to the quality of its business processes and software infrastructure but also to the quality of the business decisions that drive both of these.

To ensure the best possible decision making, a process improvement maturity model aimed at business decision management is helpful. Organizations use this maturity model to assess current state and a realistic target state, and how to achieve the latter in step-by-step increments.

The most important ideas in this chapter are the following:

- A maturity model is a process improvement model used by organizations to identify best practices, improve process execution accordingly, and measure that improvement.
- A maturity level is a well-defined destination on the path to achieving a well-established process.
- There already is a maturity model addressing the management of business rules that has proved useful in practice.
- Practice proves that the business decision is the asset that the business really needs and wants to manage. Business rules and business logic statements are simply the details by which the business does so.
- So, the business decision and the idea that it can be modeled elevate the Business Rule Management process to that of Business Decision Management.
- The BDMM can be applied to any organization or project of any size, complexity, and maturity, and is simple to use.

What about the Quote

The quote at the beginning of the chapter discloses that maturation implies creating oneself endlessly. Today's business world places strict demands on agility and compliance. A critical way in which a business goes on creating itself endlessly, even reinventing itself, is through redefinition and testing of new Decision Models underlying important business decisions.

Chapter 21

The Decision Model and Enterprise 2.0
Enabling Collaboration

Brian Stucky

Contents

The Search for Agility 482
Problems with the Status Quo 483
   The Business Gap 483
      Business-Centric Approaches and Forgetting IT 483
      Fitting a Square Peg (Rules) into a Round Hole (Requirements) 483
   The Technology Gap 484
      IT-Centric Approaches and Forgetting Business 484
      Only the Rich Get Richer 485
   The Organization Gap 486
      The Idea of Purple People 486
      Tearing Down the Silos 486
What the Decision Model Can Do for Us Now 487
   A Framework for Collaboration 487
   A Prescription for Organization Structures: Everyone Is Purple! 488
What the Decision Model Can Do for Us Later 489
   Where Are We Headed? 489

How Does the Decision Model Help Us?..490
   Finding Buried Treasure 490
   Decisions on Demand..491
Final Thoughts 492

Organizations wishing to embrace the Decision Model often recognize its value, but are not optimally positioned to realize the benefits. This often happens for two critical reasons: the inability to truly represent requirements in a format that facilitates analysis by both technical and business units, and a corporate organizational structure that hinders efficient cooperation and communication. These factors will become even more crucial as Web 2.0 emerges with the promise of agile collaboration and information sharing. This chapter will discuss how these critical components must be addressed to create an environment that fosters acceptance of the Decision Model and, ultimately, enables Enterprise 2.0.

The Search for Agility

Business Rule Management Systems (BRMSs) and Business Process Management Systems (BPMSs) have long been advertised as the tools any organization should deploy to bridge the gap between business and technology in order to achieve true collaboration. Although this has been primarily a technology-based approach with respect to vendor platforms, there have also been methodology and business reengineering efforts that attempted to reach the same goal. There have been successes. However, more often than not that success is not replicated—if it is achieved at all—and many enterprises find themselves unable to claim true consistency in terms of their approach and implementation.

Our experience in working with organizations through the years has suggested several recurrent causes that time and again slow the progress and adoption of these approaches and technologies. These difficulties are not so much an issue with the platforms themselves, but instead reach back to even more fundamental elements: in business-centric approaches where core requirements are mishandled, in technology-centric approaches where the focus is only on information technology (i.e., IT) concerns, and finally, in the bloated organizational structures of these enterprises.

These shortcomings will soon become even more critical with the advent of Web 2.0 and the dawn of Enterprise 2.0. Why? Collaboration. Decentralization. Distribution. These are all aspects that both strongly suggest the need for technology platforms (like BRMSs and BPMSs) but will absolutely require it to be done in a way that facilitates collaboration.

There is hope! We believe the Decision Model may be the key to overcoming current deficiencies while at the same time moving us smoothly to the world of Enterprise 2.0. And with that we may even find some ways to attack other problems looming on the horizon.

Problems with the Status Quo

We have already alluded to several common problems that have slowed the growth and acceptance of what can be very powerful approaches for organizations wishing to become both collaborative and agile. This section will address the problems we have encountered most often in our work.

The Business Gap

A common approach to looking at rules frequently focuses on more of a business modeling viewpoint that somewhat resembles business process reengineering. This methodology—often referred to as a Business Rules Approach—is most concerned with a vendor-neutral, top-down approach to describing a business, its processes, and the corresponding rules. Key to this approach is the complete and consistent delineation of all facts and terms needed to fully describe the business. Because it requires a complete analysis and definition of these elements, we often find a waterfall approach to development. Nothing else can be done until this initial business analysis is finished. This leads to a few problems.

Business-Centric Approaches and Forgetting IT

The first drawback to this approach should be fairly obvious: modeling complex processes (much less an entire enterprise) is extremely difficult. Because the model must be complete and consistent, consensus must be reached across the organization. Seemingly simple concepts—for example, what is a taxpayer?—suddenly become lightning rods for debate and a never-ending series of meetings and analysis. Ultimately, many organizations fall into the dreaded "paralysis by analysis" syndrome and find themselves many months and many millions of dollars down the road with little to show for it. Even if they do make it through this maze, another significant hurdle awaits.

Fitting a Square Peg (Rules) into a Round Hole (Requirements)

Should an organization manage to make it through the analysis, modeling, and documentation of their processes and rules, the question arises: now what? As we discussed, this approach is nearly always vendor neutral. Technicians anxious to begin development await the information they need to begin design. And what do they get? Process models. Spreadsheets of business rules that are not organized in a standard manner. Business terms describing the business. They receive a business requirements specification that in no way resembles the technical requirements specification they need. IT is now forced to either make their own interpretations or go back to Business and request a specification that they are ill equipped to create. Collaboration? Not so much here.

This point is worthy of more discussion because it can be argued that the traditional practice of requirements is quite broken. *CIO Magazine* said as far back as 2005 that "analysts report that as many as 71 percent of software projects that fail do so because of poor requirements management, making it the single biggest reason for project failure—bigger than bad technology, missed deadlines or change management fiascoes." This happens for a variety of reasons. Businesses often have difficulty deciding what they want or prioritizing if multiple efforts are being pressed. When they do know what they want, it is often something well out of scope or with a complexity that cannot be delivered. Most importantly, it is extremely difficult to represent business concepts in a format that IT understands. On the other hand, the technical side of the organization may try too hard to please and will subject the requirements to their own interpretation so they don't have to bother business. IT may also fail in setting realistic expectations so the business knows what can be reasonably achieved. Technicians frequently do not ensure user acceptance. A working system may look very different when viewed through business and technical eyes.

Trying to force a description of rules and process into these traditional requirements further complicates the matter. Modern BRMS and BPMS platforms are fantastic when it comes to representing, executing, and maintaining rules. However, their strength lies in being able to hand over a turnkey solution that only needs to be maintained. Getting it built right in the first place is a different matter.

The Technology Gap

Strictly technical approaches have fared only a little better. However, the majority of what have been termed successful business rule implementations fall into this category. In this case, projects relied heavily on the power of BRMS platforms and attempted to separate rules from application code in order to specify them in the formal grammar inherent to the selected BRMS. A very iterative approach was typically undertaken and ultimately produced systems in which rules could be independently persisted, executed, and managed. Some measure of agility was in fact delivered to the enterprise. But did it really deliver all that it could or should have?

IT-Centric Approaches and Forgetting Business

As with a business-centric approach, the technology-centric approach suffers from the same tunnel vision. Rather than striving to understand and model the business as completely and accurately as possible, these efforts relied heavily on technical expertise to get the job done. There was often a lack of understanding of key business concepts, most notably, language and processes. Instead, there was a rush to integrate a Business Rule Engine (BRE) and start executing rules as quickly as possible. Because there was little work done to set a solid business foundation, we've often seen a malady we've called the "Curse of Single Project Solutions."

By focusing only on an isolated project with no attempt to organize standards, establish a repeatable framework, or collaborate on enterprise consistency, we often find multiple "successful" efforts that bear no resemblance to one another. In this way, each new effort develops independently. The result is an enterprise with numerous unsynchronized BRMS efforts at best and potentially duplicate or redundant rules on various technical platforms throughout the enterprise in the worst case. Now any hope of consistency, and, ultimately, collaboration, is close to extinguished.

Only the Rich Get Richer

It should be no surprise that early adopters of a business rule approach have been major players in industries where markets are dynamic, competition is fierce, and policies are quite complex. Mortgage, insurance, telecommunications, and banking industries have all been active for quite some time. It is also clear that these have all been primarily large companies with a significant investment in IT and staff. In these vertical markets, agility is no longer a luxury but a mandate. However, many small and midsized companies simply cannot afford to take the plunge to purchase and implement a BRMS or BPMS. In the mortgage industry, some estimates have suggested that only 10% of the over 8000 lenders can afford the investment to acquire, implement, and maintain their own BRMSs.

Software packages offered by the leading BRMS vendors have eased technical barriers to entry in terms of both development and maintenance. But initiating a business rule or process solution is still an expensive proposition. In addition to software acquisition costs and maintenance, skilled business rule development resources are still a scarce and costly commodity relative to other IT and analyst staff.

Cost may not even be the most difficult obstacle to overcome. Business rule and process platforms currently available in the market are terrific at execution and management. The harvesting, analysis, and documentation of rules is a very different story. It is easily the most important of all the activities surrounding agile rule and process development. It also remains the least understood—something of a "black art" that only a few wizards truly understand. Again, bringing in costly experts to support and mentor the process is only an option for the largest of companies.

The Organization Gap

Technology and business gaps notwithstanding, many companies still cling to old hierarchical organizational structures that promote separation and facilitate silos. The irony lies in their frequent attempt to create an agile and collaborative environment by virtue of technology approaches. Without altering the inherent obstacles presented by these structures, they have little chance in succeeding.

The Idea of Purple People

We have noted that organizations have traditionally facilitated a huge chasm between technical and business resources. The only form of communication between the two is often requirements and, as we suggested earlier, they are rarely in a form that is understandable by both sides. With the modern BRMS offering a vehicle with which both business and technical analysts can communicate, we must consider whether either resource alone is sufficient.

The notion of purple people was born several years ago when we observed that business and IT were much like the red and blue used to color the states in maps of the United States during an election. Our ideal new resource would combine technical and business expertise; hence, the notion of a purple person. Although such individuals do not need to have deep technical knowledge, they should be to codify policy and express it logically in the forms of rules. Although they are not strictly business analysts, they must have a solid foundation in the business domain and be able to grasp business concepts. Business skills are more important, especially as the constantly evolving and improving BRMS provides more of the necessary technical features. However, the mix of business and technical skills is still critically important to attain long-term business rule management success. Without a means for communication that clearly bridges the gap, we mostly remain stuck with various shades of red and blue

Tearing Down the Silos

Too many organizations find themselves perpetually restructuring in an effort to truly find themselves. Sometimes this is the result of new management; other times it's simply an effort to regain an edge that they believe may have been lost. Regardless of the reason, the partitions are often created along artificial boundaries that have the unfortunate side effect of becoming permanent. When this occurs we run into several problems:

Ownership. The business and technology within a silo nearly always has implications for other silos. How is change handled here?

Subject matter experts. Where does their knowledge reside? Is it accessible outside the silo? Their knowledge may be imparted to the system created, but it is likely not in a format useable outside that system. And what happens when they leave the organization completely? Has their expertise been captured?

Consistency. You say "po-tay-to," I say "po-tah-to." If we're all talking about a potato, shouldn't we just say it? It is often amazing to see how members of the same organization can discuss the same business concepts but in a completely different language.

When an enterprise reaches this state, it is far too likely to complain that "we bought a BRMS, but we still aren't agile"! Is it any surprise, when it has to face the technology, business, and organization gaps we've just described?

What the Decision Model Can Do for Us Now

We have long argued that the optimal way to bridge the gap between business and technology would be with a true business decision management approach. This would be a business, rule, and decision perspective that reduces both the formality of an enterprisewide semantic model and the reliance on a strictly technical implementation. The business rules can be viewed within the context of a well-defined business process: the actual business decisions! With that framework in place, one can more easily evaluate and understand the following:

- The business processes of an enterprise
- The decisions needed to support those processes
- The business rules that comprise those decisions
- The requirements for management and governance of those rules

The Decision Model finally brings this to life with a rigor and general applicability that has been missing for far too long. And with it in place, we can now address the problems that have inhibited the search for the agile enterprise. We will only touch on these points here as the authors have provided complete detail on the Decision Model in the preceding chapters.

A Framework for Collaboration

Many of the justifications noted as prompting the creation of the Decision Model are symptoms of the wide chasm that often exists between Business and IT:

- There is no standard for representing business logic and supporting methodologies
- Technology alone cannot be the driver
- A representation format must be able to exist on its own
- A representation format must be easily understood by anyone

The Decision Model resolves these issues and now presents us with a much-needed means of collaboration by virtue of serving as an effective model for generating requirements that can succeed. In addition to the ever-present need to have scope defined and traceability maintained during any requirements process, we believe an effective requirements process must move from simply a textual decomposition to a system that

- Provides methods for the effective delivery of business modeling and requirements to alleviate or remove the communication gap between business customers and information technology providers by establishing a single consistent means of exchange
- Provide an effective tools suite to support project- and enterprisewide implementation of these methods
- Provide effective processes for change management, governance, and reuse of assets related to requirements and to business models, (for example, decisions)

By using the Decision Model as this means of exchange (and ultimately, as a tool), the requirements process can effectively describe the construction of the right business model. Costly errors will be minimized by correctly modeling the business to truly reflect the customer need. The new rigor placed on decisions (and their associated business rules) significantly enhances clarity and completeness of the business model. The corresponding requirements may now be developed to reflect the actual content of the business model while it in turn becomes the basis for a logical data model. Finally, test cases and scripts will be truly based on the content of the business model, so the notion of a correct system becomes an objective one.

With the Decision Model, business specifications and technical specifications can slowly merge to a uniform, consistent, traceable, and understandable form.

A Prescription for Organization Structures: Everyone Is Purple!

Some of these points will be saved for a later section when the model for Enterprise 2.0 is discussed. For the sake of this argument, we will assume the future enterprise begins to flatten and the dilemma of silos will begin to diminish over time. However, there are still two important points to make.

The first point is a question: does the Decision Model effectively make everyone a "purple person"? I'll give that a qualified yes. As the authors stress, we now focus on a representation and documentation format that is not driven by technology, focuses on business first, and is understood by anyone. I believe the many examples presented in the previous chapters clearly suggest a framework that both succinctly represents the business model while providing the technical rigor needed by IT to design and implement a system that clearly reflects the description. This certainly implies that many more people than ever before can consider themselves purple—or at the very least be able to communicate ideas back and forth in a common language.

This alone does not get the modern enterprise off the hook. We have long been proponents of establishing proper governance to ensure intelligent and consistent use of best practices, methodology, and technology. The Decision Model is no exception. Even within a flattened organizational structure, care must be taken—especially in the initial stages—to ensure success. Training, support, providing tiered service levels to projects and program initiatives that assist with effective and pragmatic implementation of methods, tools, and management processes will all be required. This group may eventually flourish to support Decision Managers who are responsible for overseeing the ongoing care and feeding of decisions, rules, and processes so that they will be used effectively across the entire enterprise.

What the Decision Model Can Do for Us Later

The future of technology and collaboration is becoming quite clear. Cutting-edge approaches by companies at the forefront of innovation (Google, Flickr, YouTube) have clearly shown the way. We will briefly discuss a few of these before looking at the very exciting possibilities for the Decision Model in this collaborative future.

Where Are We Headed?

Web 2.0 is not about any particular underlying technology, but instead focuses on new ways to get large numbers of people to come together to work, share, and build: in other words, to collaborate. The idea is strikingly simple yet incredibly powerful. Users create value when they are empowered. When networks are created (blogs, IM, interactive formats), the created value can be multiplied and shared. This value or competence can be capitalized upon and, when combined with previous innovations, results in yet another new innovation.

Although Web 2.0 will certainly bring great change to an external audience, many organizations will reap the benefits internally through what is being called Enterprise 2.0. It will reflect a radical departure in the way an enterprise is structured, communicates, collaborates, and, ultimately, innovates. The world of Enterprise 2.0 is open, dynamic, and on demand. Geographic boundaries will become nonexistent with global distribution. This transparent organization will be inherently agile—agility will no longer be an out of reach goal. Most importantly, for our purposes here, Enterprise 2.0 will not be IT driven. User control and business-driven technology will be its hallmark.

Lastly, we have an innovation that is rapidly becoming mainstream: Business on Demand. Issues with the current approach to software (buy, implement, maintain) are becoming even more apparent. Long-term costs with respect to software maintenance dwarf the initial purchase price. Ensuring availability and enabling disaster recovery are never-ending tasks. Measures to safeguard systems and increasingly complex security requirements become the overriding concerns. And if we make it through all of that, we must deal with the relatively simple task of ongoing change management and upgrades. The keys to any successful business are specialization and repetition: determine what we do best and do it over and over very efficiently. This is often automated to enforce consistency. However, more companies are moving that automation elsewhere to focus on what they do best while leaving the headaches of software behind.

How Does the Decision Model Help Us?

It has become increasingly clear that the Decision Model is "2.0 ready." Its very nature supports the goals of an open, dynamic, collaborative world. And with that in mind, we may find some very interesting approaches to handling problems on the horizon.

Finding Buried Treasure

In any organization, business rules likely exist in a variety of disparate sources, including legacy software systems, policy manuals, and in the heads of human Subject Matter Experts (SMEs). Further compounding this situation is the likelihood that differing interpretations and representations will result in inconsistencies, conflicts, and redundancies from the rules collected. As the authors noted very early on, "business logic" technology generally works, but

- It may be unknown.
- It's probably buried.
- It reflects an IT interpretation.
- It relies on IT resources that may no longer be around.
- It relies on IT resources that are all over the place.
- It needs SMEs who may no longer be with the organization.

We always tell the organizations we work with that they must plan for more time than they think it will take to go through what used to be called the "knowledge engineering" process: finding, documenting, and analyzing everything surrounding decisions. All of the points just delineated occur time and again. We frequently hear, "where did that come from?" or "why do they do it that way?" or "it's just the way the system works."

By the same token, we've also noted that organizations that have managed to succeed with a BRMS or BPMS technical implementation that was actually turned over to business had an interesting thing happen. Business became creative. Business became innovative. Because they could readily see exactly what was in the systems and had some control over management of it, new doors were opened that previously remained closed. We believe Web 2.0 adoption will result in the same kind of dramatic shift during the knowledge engineering phase. Imagine a companywide Wiki devoted to the capture and documentation of decisions and their related rules that is accessible to everyone in the organization. This would provide an incredibly powerful way to allow everyone to provide input, to capture the intellectual capital, and harness all the resources necessary to make the system right. Running around with spreadsheets, knocking on doors, and catching someone in the hallway is simply an inefficient process, yet it remains the commonly accepted means to handle this analysis.

We believe this may also be an important way to alleviate the expected issues associated with the retiring workforce. It is no secret that baby boomers are reaching retirement age. Rapidly. Those individuals (born between 1946 and 1964) number well over 80 million individuals, and they will start leaving the workforce in approximately six years. All facets of industry—particularly the government—are staring at the door as an incredible amount of intellectual capital gets ready to walk away. And because of all the reasons we've just discussed, when it leaves it leaves forever. The missing element is the means to capture and retain this information as a true corporate asset so that it can be maintained and made available for years to come. It must be in a form that is readily understood by anyone and is focused on the business. Again, the Decision Model coupled with Enterprise 2.0 may enable us to keep the spirit of SMEs alive as long as it's needed.

Decisions on Demand

We conclude with what may be the most powerful impact of the Decision Model. Enabling business rules and business process in the current market truly only helps large companies that are able to make all the necessary investments. So what of the little guy? As we noted earlier, they must be the most agile to survive in order to respond both to the market and their competition.

Service-oriented architecture (SOA) may technically enable the answer. If the obstacles to bringing rules to small and midsized companies are too great, perhaps they can be brought to the rules. Imagine a scenario where a third party responsible for rule management houses a completely transactional system for rule execution. When our small company has a business process requiring a decision, a call would be made to that service, which can execute the appropriate rules to render the necessary decision. Many industries have already established standards (ACORD [global insurance standards] and MISMO [mortgage industry standards] were each created to establish a foundation for common vocabularies, standards, and frameworks in their respective domains) so everyone can speak the same language. Customers would have access to this service only when they need it and just as often as they need it. This would allow smaller organizations to reap the benefits brought by increased agility while not requiring the large up-front investments needed for software and services.

This "Business/Decision on Demand" approach can result in a powerful mechanism to ensure industrywide consistency and compliance. Truly central repositories of decisioning will both move the traditional software headaches to those who wish to deal with it while letting Enterprise 2.0 have access to those things necessary to do what they do best.

Final Thoughts

The Decision Model truly comes at an important time in the evolution of agile technologies. Although the current technology approaches and methodologies have truly helped narrow the long-standing gap between Business and IT, the Decision Model finally brings them together. And it's just in time to complement the fast-arriving future of Enterprise 2.0 and Business on Demand.

Chapter 22

A Management Perspective

David L. Haslett and Tracy Williams

Contents

Awareness of Business Rules 493
A Cultural Change 496
The Decision Model as a Tool..496
What Does the Decision Model Bring to Business? 497
What Does the Decision Model Bring to Information Services? 499
Conclusion... 500

> Although the concepts of business rules and Business Rule Management are widely publicized and accepted, putting them into practice in the real world is not so straightforward. The adoption of Business Decision Management (and the Decision Model) requires vision, methodology updates, cultural changes, and a tangible way to measure added value. This chapter was written by practitioners from field experience in working with the Decision Model.

Awareness of Business Rules

If you have read much about business rules and Business Rule Management (BRM), you are undoubtedly aware of the merits of business rules and the disarray that business is in. There is always text explaining why it's important to capture, document, and manage business rules, about which there is little disagreement. However, these statements generally do not go far enough to detail the problem. In most organizations, the business staff proposes a project that eventually leads to IS staff meeting with business to specify scope and requirements. Along the way, business rules are gathered, sometimes documented and sometimes not. Eventually, a computer system is designed, coded, and implemented. Although formal training and many books have been written about business requirements and business rules, many IS and business professionals continue to struggle with the difference between business requirements and business rules. As such, neither is specified clearly enough to remove the ambiguity that leads to confusion and rework. After the appropriate approvals are given, the program code is written, tested, and implemented, and we expect and hope that the project has met its objectives. As we all know, expectations are sometimes met, but more often, they are not. We are then faced with having to correct the design flaws created by poor communication, inadequate requirements, and vague or misleading business rules.

The IS professional community has created many methodologies and techniques in its quest to improve quality and break this continuous cycle of repair and change, all of which have met with varying degrees of success. We are all engaged in the relentless pursuit to produce automated solutions faster and cheaper; quality is assumed and seldom expressed. Because of our direct experience with business rules and specifically the Decision Model, we suggest that the Decision Model and related techniques introduced in this book are a huge leap forward for business and business rules. Business rules, formulated correctly, are a gift to IS that will improve quality and reduce costs. The Decision Model and its techniques revolutionize business rules just as data modeling normalization techniques did for database management.

How important are business rules to business? Are business rules an asset worth managing? One should not answer a question with a question but allow us this one. Do you know of any piece of data that does not have a rule attached to it? Nearly every piece of business data is edited and validated before being placed in a database. Business rules primarily focus on core business rules rather than data integrity rules, but everyone understands data integrity rules, so it serves as a simple example.

Visualize an environment in which

- There is a Business Process Model with decision points identified for every business process, and enterprise business rules are articulated for those decision points in a manner that brings absolute clarity, no loose ends, no gaps in logic, and no assumptions.
- All rules have been validated to bring absolute credibility.
- Everyone in this enterprise uses terminology that has one, and only one, definition.
- All automated solutions are perfectly aligned with business decisions, corporate policies, and goals.

- All customer inquiries are answered with information supporting those business decisions.
- Changes to business practices start by examining and changing business rules, followed by procedural and automated system changes rather than the other way around.

How would this environment impact your organization? Of course, the perfect glasshouse does not exist; however, a mediocre goal yields mediocre results.

One might ask, "What is the value statement of such a lofty goal?" There are many aspects to discuss, but first let us look at application system testing. Most business testing activities create test cases from three sources: application documentation, reuse of test cases from prior projects, and intellectual knowledge. The goal is to test application features and functions to ensure the application is providing expected results. None of these three sources takes into account programming logic improvised by developers filling in gaps where the requirements and business rules were not clearly specified. It is common practice for development staff on tight schedules, with the best of intentions, using their own understanding of the projects' goals, to fill in gaps in requirements and business rules with their own interpretation, expecting the testing activities to validate or clean up misinterpretations. Many new features have been introduced to projects in this way, and many a project has seen its scope creep ever larger, in part due to these activities.

Again, the industry has spent millions of dollars on training, documenting best practices, developing automated tools, and dedicating staff to testing centers of excellence. This comprehensive effort attempts to ensure that IS has properly interpreted what business is articulating to them. IS staff using documentation created during the development cycle make a gallant effort to design an agile system, which produces expected results. After, or sometimes in parallel with the development and design cycle, business subject matter experts (SMEs) make a heroic effort to find or create test data that tests all potential business scenarios to ensure the system behaves as intended. They are testing rules they have communicated to IS, and IS has done its best to interpret. All are professionals doing the very best job they can to develop and test the system. Results are generally good; however, we have all grown to expect application problems that will be reported and repairs made for an untold amount of flow time after implementation.

Through the design and best practices of the Decision Model, decision points and their corresponding business rules are clearly communicated, removing all doubt about what business is expecting. We would suggest that application testing is the art of building test cases that test rules and decision points provided by business stakeholders to ensure the derived conclusions are correct. We are not going to suggest the Decision Model is the perfect answer. We will suggest it is a giant leap forward.

A Cultural Change

The reality of instituting business rules into an enterprise is that it is a cultural change. We would suggest that senior management support is a requirement for success. Establish an enterprise business rule team, sometimes referred to as a center of excellence, staffed with a variety of disciplines. A strong IS background is a must for all members of this team. It is important to purchase a business-rule-centric methodology that is both teachable and repeatable. Expect to spend some time training on both the methodology and business rule processes and tools. Do a lot of reading and join a professional organization. As you start working on project initiatives, we strongly suggest starting in a single business area and executing a series of small projects within that same business area, widening the scope and complexity slowly. Build on success. During the first 18 to 24 months, depending on the skills your staff brings with them, don't expect too much. During this period, establish your quality standards, your project deliverables, metrics you wish to capture, metadata you wish to capture, and all those other tasks we traditionally think of when establishing a new team (mission, vision). You will soon realize you need an enterprise repository for your decisions, rules, and terms; understand that not all rules need the discipline of Business Decision Management (BDM) processes. The BDM focus is on core business decisions that have a direct monetary impact, is strategic to the businesses goals and behavior, or affects the competitive environment. Remember that your customers see the business through its behavior and decisions made. Business knowledge is knowing the business rules. Knowing the businesses rules is to know the business. Think about it: your most valued employees are those with great skills and have the most business knowledge. Sharing the rules and terms with the enterprise empowers the entire enterprise.

The Decision Model as a Tool

The Decision Model is one tool within a large toolset having all tools focused on a single goal: to capture and manage business rules in a form understandable by business. During the documentation process, the Decision Model expresses rules in a visual structure to facilitate rule analysis and rule normalization. Rules in the Decision Model are formal rules documented in a decision table that adhere to the specified integrity principles. Once completed in this format, the natural language rules are a snap. This tool will shorten most business rule initiatives and improve quality of the rules. Its greatest impact is visual analysis, providing the ability to visually see gaps and overlaps in the rule family. The business rule analyst is not relying solely on analytical skills and knowledge.

For the business professional, the Decision Model expresses rules in a visual structure, so management can easily review all rules for any given decision point or any one conclusion. This visual representation greatly enhances analysis by business management, business analysts, and business rule analysts. While contemplating modifications to the rules, one can determine the impact of that change against all other business rules supporting a business decision. Making enterprise business rules and term definitions available to all business staff throughout an enterprise empowers the entire staff.

For the IS types, the Decision Model is similar to database modeling. A set of data tables represents a normalized data model for a given set of data. Each column is a defined data field, and each row contains business data. In a Decision Model, the columns are conditions or a conclusion, and the rows are rules. Each conditional rule clause is completed with an operator (e.g., =, <, >, ...), where the column and row intersects. In the decision table, all the rules (rows) are evaluating conditions that result in a valid value for the same conclusion header. When the decision table adheres to the integrity properties, then and only then is it considered a Rule Family. A Decision Model is a set of related rule families all working together for a single business decision. It follows then that for IS units practicing SOA, a Decision Model becomes a perfect service. Each service is dedicated to a single business decision supported by a Decision Model defined by the business for the business.

In the final analysis, rules must have credibility to have real value and that value comes from validation activities. There are many validation techniques, and we will suggest just a couple. All stakeholders must agree with the rule intent and verify all conditional values. Some rules harvested from manuals, intellectual knowledge, policies, contracts, and other such sources should be validated by building test cases to determine if the automated system is performing as expected. Enterprise rules can and should be reused across the organization, ever increasing the value and savings to the enterprise. Validated business rules created with business rule best practice methods result in credible rules bringing tremendous long-term benefits to the organization.

What Does the Decision Model Bring to Business?

Listed in the following text are seven benefits for the business of the Decision Model:

1. Visualization of business logic and business rules: This enhances the ability to identify erroneous or missing rules, conditions (column headings), condition values, errors in logic, and overlapping rules. The visual acuity of the structure helps to ensure that all attributes of a condition are surfaced, leading

to improved rule readability and accuracy. Business can expect rules to be maintainable and aligned with business requirements.

2. Improved efficiency of a business rule approach: The Decision Model is just one tool in the toolset, yet it brings clarity and predictability to the outcome of any business rule initiative. This single deliverable by business can ensure that business and IS programmers will arrive at identical conclusions, reducing assumptions, improving results, and reducing testing. Implementation of rules, in an automated or manual process, results in the processes being deployed correctly the first time.

3. A common understanding across the enterprise: The Decision Model creates an atomic form of business rules from which a natural language form of business rules is easily created. The intent is to express rules in a form more readily understood by all business staff. Making these two forms of business rules visible with a business terms glossary, through an enterprise repository to all staff, empowers the entire staff with the knowledge of the business. The investment and knowledge gained makes the enterprise repository an invaluable asset.

4. Easy assessment of change management impact: Whether you are making rule changes to adapt to changes in the marketplace or rolling out new products, you'll rarely change just one rule in the model. Changes may cross several models. The extent of the changes and their impact to business are easily understood. Changes to automated systems can be more accurately assessed and estimated. Implementation timelines and costs can be more accurately projected. This is especially true for organizations using SOA principles, where any one Decision Model is implemented as a service.

5. An entire set of Rule Families for a given business decision and their relationships to one another: The Decision Model notation is a graphical representation of the structure and information that is necessary to make a specific business decision. It is very helpful to management when they don't want or need to see the detailed rules for a given business decision, but need a high-level overview.

6. An easily understood structure from which logical test cases can be written: Every row in a decision table represents a set of conditions and a single conclusion. All rows in any one decision table have the same conclusion. Through analysis and normalization processes, all possible conditions for any one conclusion become a row in the table. Building test cases for each row in the decision table is not only much quicker and easier to create but ensures that all rules required for reaching the given conclusion are tested.

7. Improved testing results: We have discussed testing multiple times, so suffice it to say that the Decision Model will reduce your testing effort, improve outcomes, and reduce the cost of testing.

What Does the Decision Model Bring to Information Services?

Listed in the following text are five benefits for the IS function of the Decision Model:

1. Shorter development time: The business rule approach is not a substitute for gathering system requirements and making good technical design decisions. It does, however, facilitate the requirements and design as the business intent of the system is known, and depending on the types of rules, differing designs may be chosen. For example, rules that change frequently may be best placed in a rule engine (i.e., BRMS), and those that never or seldom change may be written in a traditional language such as COBOL, JAVA, or any other language of choice.
2. Improved testing and higher-quality outcomes: Fewer errors and shorter project run out ultimately reduce cost.
3. Solutions directly in alignment with business: The business intent is defined and well known by IS, and in a SOA environment, the services directly correlate with business decisions, goals, and objectives.
4. Facilitated SOA: One of the many challenges facing IS today is turning legacy applications into business services. A big part of that challenge is working with business to determine services worthy of the effort. The BDM approach delivers a business process model outlining business decision points. Business rules are defined for each business decision worthy of BDM techniques (not every business decision point is complex enough or important enough to require BDM). The metadata captured and maintained through BDM helps to provide vital metrics. These deliverables as well as the Decision Model and the extensive involvement of business are all necessary and helpful attributes in determining and designing good enterprise services.

   Just for clarity, the business rule approach and the Decision Model are not substitutes for gathering system requirements, do not design an automated solution, are technology independent, and do not conflict with the normal project system development life cycle (SDLC). A BDM approach does facilitate SOA, provides clear business logic through rule families, and clear separation between the enterprise business rules and their implementation.
5. Separation of business rules from implementation: Enterprise business rules must always be separated from their implementation. A tight link between rules and their implementation leads to a dual-maintenance situation, which we must avoid. Changes to the implementation of a rule, automated or manual, should not force changes to the underlying rule in the enterprise repository. Changing rules at the point of implementation generally bypasses the whole intent of BDM. Rule maintenance begins in the business units. Changes to a rule starts with business staff updating rules in the repository and then, for automated rules, writing IS projects for implementation.

Conclusion

By now you know that an ideal business rule environment is one where the documentation and analysis activities are a cooperative process between business and a dedicated enterprise business rule team, (i.e., center of excellence) and precedes the traditional SDLC of IS projects. Once specified, analyzed, and normalized, business rules are a deliverable from business to IS from which automated business solutions can be designed in an optimal SOA environment. We all know that the largest price for mining, harvesting, and documenting of business rules occurs when business rules have not been managed in the past. Once business rules are documented and managed, the cost per rule is dramatically reduced and the benefits to the business are tremendous. We are not aware of any wide-scale studies to determine the cost and flow time difference between an IS project following a full SDLC where business rules were not documented using a business rule approach versus projects where a business rule approach was properly completed. However, we suggest that when a BDM approach is followed and the business rules are properly managed, the IS project life cycles will be reduced.

Chapter 23

Better! Cheaper! Faster!

David Pedersen

Most systems development projects that don't use Decision Models seem to suffer from a common set of problems not with standing. This is despite the quality of deliverables and experience of the development staff. Learning about the Decision Model early in a project can significantly enhance the success of typical systems development projects. This chapter describes how principles of the Decision Model were applied late in a project, with important benefits.

The most important ideas in this chapter are the following:

- I had worked for three years on a global, strategic project on which we had completed comprehensive requirements and had chosen a good BPM vendor.
- We hired the most experienced consultants that the vendor had, but after two years of construction and testing, the product was not complete, and the project faced significant challenges.
- As a result I undertook research to discover the answers to the problems being experienced; I realized that the Decision Model was key to addressing many of my project issues.
- The BPM technology decision certainly was the right fit for this project, but development still could not keep up with the changes and additions and the complexity of the rules.

- We had built a business rules editor that gave business staff the ability to maintain a portion of the business decisions and business rules without having to take the application through a development cycle. This experience proved the value of the Decision Model even though we had not intentionally designed it to test this methodology.
- What we were lacking was the Decision Model across the rest of the system. The discovery of the Decision Model as a way to express the business rules in a platform-independent manner was a key missing component.
- When we updated a large portion of the program with new functionality, I separated business rules into Decision Models, resulting in an estimated 10% to 25% decrease in development time, while improving quality. If we had used the Decision Model, I'm confident that we could have cut our requirements and development time by as much as 50%.

I remember the first time I learned about the Decision Model. I had been working three years on a project to implement regulations and enterprise policies into our processes. These regulations and policies included independence, conflicts, risk management, financial risks, contracts, and a complex approval process. The global regulations and policies had to be augmented with local country policies and regulations across approximately 130 countries. Up to this point, these complex polices and regulations were implemented in a variety of automated and manual siloed systems.

I spent close to a year gathering and documenting the business requirements. The final business requirements, processes, and business rules document was about 100 pages long. Needless to say, outside of one other project, the requirements were one of the most thorough and complete documentation the company had ever prepared for a project (to the best of my knowledge). When I asked the programmers to rate the documentation, they often told me that they had never seen a project that had such thorough requirements. When we moved into the use case and functional requirements project phase, we exerted the same level of effort and exuberance. I'm proud of the quantity and quality of documentation; we wanted to do it right and leave no stone unturned.

After we had gathered most of the requirements, we turned our attention to searching for the best technology to implement these complex processes and rules. We decided that Business Process Management (BPM) software was a great fit. Out of the box it gave us great capabilities and tools to rapidly build and manage our processes. At the time of our search, I would say that the BPM market had just matured to the point where off-the-shelf software could implement a project of this size and complexity. We had a very thorough process for reviewing candidates, including a proof of concept, to select the best vendor for the job. The last step in this process was to check the vendor's references. One of the references told us that, while their project was very successful, it took much longer than planned. They told me that one of their biggest lessons learned was that you don't know what you don't know.

We moved into the construction phase with high expectations that we could build and test the application in a reasonable period of time. We hired the most experienced consultants that the vendor had and, after two years of construction and testing, the product was not complete. Something was wrong! I don't want to minimize the great accomplishments that the team had achieved, but we were not done and we had a long way to go. I reached a point where I needed answers to some very tough issues.

Armed with a long list of questions (which were the questions that I originally did not know that that I did not know), I began my search for answers. I realized that the Decision Model was key to addressing many of my project issues.

These issues included:

1. The amount of time and effort it was taking to communicate the business rules to the development staff was exhausting. Even though we received excellent marks for our requirements, I found that they often had difficulty identifying and interpreting the rules.
2. The product managers could no longer keep track of all the rules, which had become so complex that they were getting buried in the code.
3. The deployment team had to spend a lot of time with the core development team because they could not find the business rules they needed to support deployment.
4. It was difficult to trace policies and regulations to the requirements and vice versa. These connections were in my head, but it was difficult for other team members who had not been part of the project from the beginning to make these connections.
5. The rules were changing faster than development could change the code.
6. When rules changed, it became difficult to identify all the locations in the application that would have to be updated.
7. We found missing and inconsistent rules.
8. Our Quality Assurance (QA) Testing function had difficulty writing effective test plans. They missed testing portions of the application because they did not understand the business rules.
9. We were significantly behind schedule.
10. Once the application was deployed, I could see that ongoing maintenance would be difficult because the rules had become so complex and numerous. They were also becoming buried in the code and documentation because we did not have a standard method for documenting them.

11. A maintenance cycle would be required every time a business rule changed in the process portion of the application.
12. Each time the executive sponsorship changed or when we added team members, it would take an extended period of time for them to get a working understanding of the business rules. In fact, I'd have to confess that most of the team members only had a working understanding of portions of the rules; very few had a good understanding of all the rules.

There were two main portions of this project, the Process and the Questionnaire. The Questionnaire implemented complex business rules that walked users through the complicated global and local policies, regulations, and risk analysis. Answers to questions triggered conclusion factors, subprocesses, and approval requirements. We knew that the questions would change frequently because of the nature of the policies, regulations and risks to the firm. We needed the system to be agile so the business could change the rules quickly. To address these requirements, we built a business rules editor that gave business staff the ability to maintain the questions (business decisions and business rules) without having to take the application through a development cycle.

The Process portion of the application turned out to be rather inflexible even though we had used the latest BPM technology. The BPM technology decision certainly was the right fit for this project, and it made managing the changes easier, but development still could not keep up with the changes and additions. The complexity of the rules was too much to manage.

This experience proved the value of the Decision Model even though we had not intentionally designed it to test this methodology. We needed to separate the business rules from the process and use a standard technology-independent method for documenting them that business people could easily understand. When I reflect on the effort put into the business requirements and functional requirements, I am convinced that using this methodology could have significantly reduced the time to gather and validate requirements and improve quality. We could have spoken a common language that would have made the rules clearer and more absolute. We would have had fewer missed rule interpretations, and changes could have been more predictable. It would have been easy for the business to take ownership of the business rules.

By this time, we were a long way into the development cycle, but I had the opportunity to take a step forward toward implementing the Decision Model when we updated a large part of the program with new functionality. I separated the business rules in each portion of the program that we were updating and documented them into rule tables. This step resulted in an estimated 10% to 25% decrease in development time. The rules became clearer, more absolute, and it made them easier for business and IT to understand. This also resulted in validation sessions becoming more productive because of the clarity of the details.

Acceptance of the Decision Model approach varied among the team; some understood it without any explanation and others were reluctant at first. The person who managed the deployment documentation told me that the Rule Families were easy to understand without any instructions. One developer said that this provided beter information, was easier to program now that all the rule permutations were documented and it would save significant time for development and QA. He said that it would result in a higher-quality product. Another developer initially resisted, but once he understood it, he said that the new business rule format was clearer, more absolute, and made more sense than writing them in natural language. This feedback was consistent with information I received from other companies who told me that staff (business and IT) may initially push back, but once they see the value, they get on board. Often the biggest opponents become the biggest proponents.

Because of this success I decided to roll up my sleeves and thoroughly research this and related subjects. I read a boatload of books and articles, and interviewed subject matter experts and companies that had implemented this methodology. Although this technology-independent method for documenting business rules turned out to be a key factor in my project, applying this in the context of the enterprise has amazing value.

My project depended on interfaces to other enterprise applications. Because these applications did not have a standard method for documenting business rules, the team spent a considerable amount of time meeting with other application owners to discover business rules. We found that rules given to us were not clear enough (even though we thought they were clear) and were frequently misinterpreted. We found that changes occurred in other applications, and my team did not find out about them until it was too late.

With all of my research and experience, I often reflect on this project and ask how much time could have been saved if I had known and implemented the Decision Model from the start of the project. I can say that I'm very confident that we could have cut our requirements and development time by as much as 50%. I know this sounds too good to be true (it does to me), but even if my estimate is double the actual this still would have saved millions of dollars.

Most companies today have evolved many different technologies, and many different programming standards over decales. This has resulted in the inability to map IT systems to the business decisions and the organization's objectives. Often, changes to decisions are not predictable. Implementing a technology-independent method for documenting business decisions that the business understands and maintains is a foundational cornerstone needed to remain competitive.

Bibliography

Abbott, E. A. (1884). Flatland. London, Seeley & Co..

Aeppel, T. (2007, March 27). Changing the Formula—Seeking Perfect Prices, CEO Tears up the Rules. Wall Street Journal, p. 1.

Ambler, S. (2007a). Agile Requirements Modeling. Retrieved October 8, 2008, from http://www.agilemodeling.com/essays/agileRequirements.htm.

Ambler, S. (2007b, January). Dr. Dobb's Portal. Retrieved September 24, 2008, from http://www.ddj.com/architect/196902703?cid=Ambysoft.

Anthony, R. (1965). Planning and Control Systems: A Framework for Analysis. Boston: Harvard Business School Press.

Beck, M. and Moore, A. (2006). The Business Rule Revolution. In B. von Halle, and L. Goldberg, The Business Rule Revolution (pp. 119–146). Cupertino, CA: Happy About.

Cantara, M. (2006). Forecast: Pure-Play BPM and BRE Software New License Revenue, Worldwide, 2005–2010. Gartner Group.

Charette, R. N. (2005, September). IEEE Spectrum. Retrieved October 2, 2008, from http://www.spectrum.ieee.org/sep05/1685.

Codd, E. F. (1970). A Relational Model of Data for Large Shared Data Banks. Communications of ACM, Vol. 13 (pp. 377–387). Association for Computing Machinery, Inc.

Cooper, R. (1998). Coordination Games. Cambridge , UK: Cambridge University Press.

Dataquest Insights. (2007). Worldwide Software Market for SOA, Web Services and Web 2.0, 2006–2011. Gartner Group.

Date, C. J. (2005). Database in Depth: Relational Theory for Practitioners. Sebastopol: O'Reilly.

Date, C. J. (2000). What Not How: The Business Rules Approach to Application Development. Reading, MA: Addison-Wesley.

Drucker, P. (1954). The Practice of Management. Harper & Row.

Encarta, "fact." (n.d.). Retrieved March 6, 2008, from http://encarta.msn.com/dictionary_/fact.html.

Fleming, C. C. and von Halle, B. (1989). Handbook of Relational Database Design. Reading, MA: Addison-Wesley.

Foote, B. and Yoder, J. (1999, June 26). Big Ball of Mud. Retrieved September 28, 2008, from http://www.laputan.org/mud/.

Forrester, J. (1961). Industrial Dynamics. Boston: The MIT Press.

Frankel, D. S., Harmon, P., Mukerji, J., Odell, J., Owen, M., Rivett, P., et al. (2003). The Zachman Framework and the OMG's Model Driven Architecture. Business Process Trends.

Hammer, M. (2007, April). The Process Audit. Harvard Business Review.

Helfert, E. (1962). Techniques of Financial Analysis. Dow Jones Irwin.

IEEE. ((Std 610.12-1990)). Standard Glossary of Software Engineering Terminology. IEEE.

IEEE-SA. IEEE Std 1471-2000 IEEE Recommended Practice for Architectural Description of Software-Intensive Systems. Standard, New, IEEE.

ISO. (2007). 42010:2007(E) Systems and Software Engineering—Recommended Practice for Architectural Description of Software-Intensive Systems. ISO/IEEE.

Kamer, C. (1997, Volume 4, #4). The Impossibility of Complete Testing. Software QA magazine, p. 28.

Kelly, N. (2007, August 20). High Failure Rate Hits IT Projects. Retrieved July 22, 2008, from http://www.computing.co.uk/computing/news/2197021/failed-projects-hit-half-uk.

Merriam-Webster Online Dictionary "between." (n.d.). Retrieved April 2, 2008, from http://www.merriam-webster.com/dictionary/between.

Merriam-Webster Online Dictionary "complex." (n.d.). Retrieved April 2, 2008, from www.Merriam-Webster.com/Complex.

Merriam-Webster Online Dictionary "flexible." (n.d.). Retrieved April 2, 2008, from http://www.merriam-webster.com/dictionary/flexible.

Merriam-Webster Online Dictionary "in." (n.d.). Retrieved April 2, 2008, from http://www.merriam-webster.com/dictionary/IN.

Merriam-Webster Online Dictionary "model." (n.d.). Retrieved October 4, 2008, from http://www.merriam-webster.com/dictionary/model.

Merriam-Webster Online Dictionary "stable." (n.d.). Retrieved April 2, 2008, from http://www.merriam-webster.com/dictionary/stable.

Merriam-Webster Online Dictionary "wisdom." (n.d.). Retrieved November 15, 2008, from www.merriam-webster.com/wisdom.

Nolop, B. (2007, September). Rules to Acquire By. Harvard Business Review, pp. 129–139.

Object Management Group. (2007). Business Motivation Model (BMM) Specification. OMG.

Object Management Group. (2003). MDA Guide Version 1.0.1. OMG.

Object Management Group. (2006). Semantics of Business Vocabulary and Business Rules. OMG.

Sessions, Roger. A Comparison of the Top Four Enterprise Architecture Methodologies. White Paper, Austin, TX: ObjectWatch, Inc., 2007.

OMB, Office of E-Government and Information Technology. (2007). FEA Consolidated Reference Model Document Version 2.3. OMB.

Open Group, The. (2007). The Open Group Architectural Framework (TOGAF) Version 8.1.1, Enterprise Edition.

Orr, K. (2007). Putting Data into SOA: Data Virtualization, Data Buses, and Enterprise Data Management. Cutter Consortium.

Reeves, J. (1992). What Is Software Design? C++ Journal.

Rosen, Michael, Boris Lublinsky, Kevin T. Smith, and Marc J Balcer. Applied SOA: Service-Oriented Architecture and Design Strategies. New York: Wiley, 2008.

Rothenberg, J. (1989). The Nature of Modeling in Artificial Intelligence, Simulation, and Modeling. In L. E. William, K. A. Loparo, and N. R. Nelson, The Nature of Modeling in Artificial Intelligence, Simulation, and Modeling (pp. 75–92). New York: Wiley.

Schreiber, G., Akkermans, H., Anjewierden, A., de Hood, R., Shadbolt, N., Van de Velde, W., et al. (2001). Knowledge Engineering and Management: The CommonKADS Methodology. Cambridge, Massachusetts and London, England: The MIT Press, A Bradford Book.

Senge, P. (1990). The Fifth Discipline. New York: Doubleday.

Siegel, J. (2002, October 15). Making the Case: OMG's Model Driven Architecture. www.SDTimes.com.

Silver, B. (2008, July 16). BPMS Watch—BPM and Its Enemies. Retrieved July 22, 2008, from http://www.bpminstitute.org/articles/article/article/bpms-watch-bpm-and-its-enemies.html?tac=105i.

Snowden, D. J. and Boone, M. E. (2007, November). A Leader's Framework for Decision Making. Harvard Business Review, pp. 69–76.

Software Engineering Institute—Carnegie Mellon. (2008). Reengineering: The Horseshoe Model. Pittsburgh: Carnegie Mellon University.

Steiner, G. (1972). Comprehensive Managerial Planning. Oxford, OH: The Planning Executives Institute.

Stuart, R. and Norviq, P. (2003). Artificial Intelligence A Modern Approach. Upper Saddle River, New Jersey: Pearson Education.

Taylor, J. and Raden, N. (2007). Smart Enough Systems: How to Deliver Competitive Advantage by Automating Hidden Decisions. New York: Prentice Hall.

The Open Group. (2007). The Open Group Architecture Framework. The Open Group.

Tilman, L. T. and Phelps, E. (2008). Financial Darwinism: Create Value or Self-Destruct in a World of Risk. New York: Wiley.

Toffler, A. (1970). Future Shock. New York: Random House.

Toffler, A. (1990). PowerShift. New York: Bantam Books.

von Halle, B. (2002). Business Rules Applied. New York: Wiley.

von Halle, B. (2006). The Essential Business Rule Roadmap. In B. von Halle and L. Goldberg, The Business Rule Revolution (pp. 3–22). Cupertino, CA: HappyAbout.

von Halle, B. (2007, July 6). The Rule Maturity Model: Five Steps to an Agile Enterprise. Retrieved September 9, 2008, from http://www.intelligententerprise.com/showArticle.jhtml?articleID=200900717.

von Halle, B. and Goldberg, L. (2006). The Business Rules Revolution. Cupertino, CA: Happy About.

Wikipedia. (2008, September 5). Requirement. Retrieved September 24, 2008, from http://en.wikipedia.org/wiki/Requirement.

Wordwebonline "Decision Table". (n.d.). Retrieved April 13, 2008, from Wordwebonline. http://www.wordwebonline.com/search.pl?w=decision+Table (accessed April 13, 2008).

Zachman, J. A. (1987). A Framework for Information Systems Architecture. IBM Systems Journal, Vol. 26, No. 3.

Zachman, J. A. (2006). Enterprise Architecture: Managing Complexity and Change. In B. von Halle and L. Goldberg, The Business Rule Revolution (pp. 43–58). Cupertino, CA: HappyAbout.

Zachman, J. A. (1997). Enterprise Architecture: The Issue of the Century. Database Programming and Design.

Zachman, J. A. (2006, April). Exclusive Interview with John Zachman. (R. Sessions, Interviewer) IASA—International Association of Software Architects.

Zachman, J. A. and Sowa, J. F. (1992). Extending and Formalizing the Framework for Information Systems Architecture. IBM Systems Journal.

Index

A

ACMM (Architectural Maturity Model), 462
Activity models, 113, 347
Adaptive control, 442, 446, 453
ADM (Architectural Development Method), 346–48
Agile (methods)
  Agilists, 114–15, 136
  artifacts in, 114
  development approach, 114
Agile, BDMM level 2, 461
Agility
  BPMN, 425
  business, 11, 38–39, 468
  in business process, 44, 50, 59, 66, 425
  in FEA, 346
  improving business governance, 10, 461
  in SOA, 362
  in Web 2.0, 489
Alignment
  between Business Motivation and Metrics, 413
  between business policy objects and business decisions, 468
  between organizational objectives and business rule practices in RMM, 459
  of business decisions across projects, 470
  in business solutions, 499
  improved IT alignment though AOSD, 440
Ambler, Scott, 114–15
American National Standards Institute, see ANSI

Analytics
  combination of business rules and, 445
  models, 450, 452, 454
  production alongside Decision Model, 454
ANSI (American National Standards Institute), 387
AOSD (Aspect-Oriented Software Development)
  business logic in, 113, 117–18, 438
  modeling, 112
  productivity, 440
Architectural
  Development Method, see ADM
  process, 471
  representation, 356, 417, 419
  standards, 461, 472
  style, 98, 360–61, 380
Architecture
  Applications, 350–51
  in BDMM
    architectural maturity models, 461–62
    architectural process, 465, 477
    business architecture, 463–65, 467, 469, 472, 474, 477
    communication, 463, 465, 467, 472, 474, 477
    execution architecture, 467, 472
  Business
    in BDMM, 461–68, 471–72, 477–78
    in TOGAF, 350
  Enterprise, see EA
  Federal Enterprise, see FEA
  IEEE Standard 1471-2000, 360
  information, 368
  Information Systems in TOGAF, 329, 347–48, 350–51
  ISO Definition of, 331

511

models, 330, 354
planning for a Decision Model, 141
relationship between SOA and BPM, 361
Service-Oriented, see SOA
services, 380
System, 16, 330, 349, 351–52, 460
in system transformation, 416–17
in Zachman Framework, 325, 334, 338
Aspect-Oriented Software Development, see
　　AOSD
Atomic
attributes, 282
business logic, 17, 30, 303
business rule, 10
cell, 179, 306
Decision Model, 206
Decision Model vs. SBVR statements,
　　403–4
decomposition necessary, 281
heading in Rule Family, 206
logic expression, 178, 186, 206–7
meaning of, 281
operand, 179
row with more than one conclusion
　　is not, 188
row-and-column intersections, 281
uncombined pieces, 206
Audience perspectives, 323, 332, 334, 341
Automated systems
building of, 7
CIM model to build, 354
data storage for, 275
decision tables in, 172
design of, 5
policy renewal case study, 141, 148
SOA in, 92
test cases for, 497
whether or not Decision Model in, 8
Automation
appropriate, 54
in BDMM level 2, 469
business decision suitable for, 449
business logic separation for, 8
business processes as targets for, 4
no choice without, 448
Decision Models not targeted for, 339
of decisions, 447
degree of, 450
EDM candidates for, 451
in Enterprise 2.0, 490
impediments created by, 81
most appropriate technology for, 17

opportunities from level of, 330
policy renewal case study, 141
regardless of forms of, 17
representation close to, 407
Autonomic, 331
BI provides metrics for, 477
business governance for, 478
characteristics of Level 5 of BDMM, 477
Level 5 of BDMM, 461, 476

B

Backward-chaining, 225–26, 229–30
BDM (Business Decision Management)
and adaptive control, 331
adoption of, 11, 84, 373, 462, 493,
　　496, 499
analysts projected sales of, 11
approach, 84, 467, 487, 499–500
and BDMM, 457, 462, 468, 472, 476, 479
best practices in, 84
and BPM, 40, 64
center of excellence, 84
as critical technology assets, 460
Definition of, 83
insights into the future of, 88
process, 457–58, 460, 462, 464, 473
and SOA, 373
and system transformation, 419
tools, 88–89
See also EDM
BDMM (Business Decision Maturity Model)
characteristics of vectors, 462–64
high level summary, 461
Level 1, 465
Level 2, 467–69
Level 3, 472–73
Level 4, 474–75
Level 5, 477–78
as measurement of BDM process, 460
as roadmap toward BDM, 84
Beck, Michael, 133–35
BI (Business Intelligence)
Analyst, 144–45
in BDMM, 469
and Decision Model, 477
dimension in system architecture, 351
in legacy application structures, 352
reporting dimension, 351
resulting from relational way of thinking,
　　276
in the SRM, 345

Big Requirements Up Front, see BRUF
BMM (Business Motivation Model)
    and business decisions, 389
    as business plan, 113, 119, 342
    and business rules, 119, 389
    connecting to business process, 389
    and the Decision Model, 120–23, 129,
        262, 389, 409
    Integration of BMM, BPMN, and the
        Decision Model, 122, 137, 391
    as model of motivation, 111, 119
    OMG Specification, 388–89
    and SBVR, 401
    in the Zachman Framework, 335, 341,
        356, 388
Boone, Mary E., 42–43
BPM (Business Process Management)
    and BDM, 40, 64
    and BPMN, 426
    and business objectives, 78
    and business rules, 422
    and Decision Model, 425–26, 460
    and end-to-end processes, 422
    growth in, 11
    Integrating SOA, 360–61, 363, 373, 381
    systems, 361
BPMN (Business Process Modeling Notation)
    adoption of, 423
    as de facto standard, 390
    decision gateway, 68
    and the Decision Model, 390–91
BPMS (business process management system)
    and agility, 482
    and Business Process, 365
    executing business process, 365
    in the mortgage industry, 485
    and planning for Decision Model,
        141, 162
    turned over to the business, 490
    and Web 2.0 collaboration, 482
    and workflow rules, 34
BPTrends, 355
BRE (Business Rule Engine), 185, 225, 485,
    see also BRMS
BRM (Business Reference Model), 77, 100,
    346–47, 361, 373, 493
BRMS (Business Rules Management System)
    backward-chaining through Rule
        Families, 225
    in BDMM, 468
    business being creative with, 490
    and Decision Model, 136

deploying business rules in executable
    environment, 444
executing analytic model in, 445
forward-chaining through Rule Families,
    225, 468
to manage logic in Decision Services, 443
mortgage lenders that can afford, 485
planning for future, 141, 162
Proprietary language in, 407
rule sets in, 452–53
rules that many be best placed in a, 499
still not agile with, 487
as tool to bridge gap between business and
    technology, 482
in Web 2.0 collaboration, 482
whether Decision Models execute in, 399
see also BRE
BRUF (Big Requirements Up Front), 114, 138
Business alignment see Decision Model,
    Principles, # 15: Business alignment
Business analysts
    applying integrity principles, 249
    as audience for fact models, 396
    in BDMM, 468
    business process models created by,
        361, 423
    CIM created by, 355
    creating Decision Models, 410
    Decision Model teams, 143, 145, 354
    Decision Modeling tools for, 85–88
    leading business decision discovery, 461
    leading business planning and Decision
        Modeling, 466, 469
    role of, 164, 410
    testing business decisions, 466
    and visual representation, 497
    and Web 2.0, 486
    see also Business rules analysts
Business concept, 39–40, 61, 176, 395–97,
    484, 486–87
Business decision
    allocating to project increments, 414
    application platform to host, 363
    architecture process to support, 472
    augmenting awareness in existing
        methodologies, 412, 464
    automating in BDM, 40
    BDM focus on core, 496
    and BI environments, 478
    business unit, 472
    business value of, 37–38, 41–42, 61, 414
    business-critical, 61, 476

case study target, 57–58, 62, 128, 145–46, 148, 151
categorizing by business value, 38, 41–42, 56, 61–62
characteristics in BDMM, 57, 462
combining multiple into a single, 77, 122, 127, 302–3, 403, 497
complexity domain context of, 79
connector in Decision Model notation, 301, 309–10
creating preliminary list to capture business motivation, 413–14
delivered in manageable form, 140
event-based, 61
example of strategic, 51, 77–78
fact-based, 61, 77
importance in managing business process, 90, 456
modeling complete vs. incomplete, 44
with more than a single conclusion, 247
operational, 51
in operative context, 78
performance against business objectives, 80
in physical decision models, 433
and process models
    burying the logic in the process, 70
    discovery of business decisions, 143, 461
    process becomes agile when separated from, 80, 89
    process is simplified when sequence is removed, 77
    removing business decisions from procedural process flow, 68, 70, 77, 80, 89
services, 363
    see also Decision services
shape, 26–28, 203, 301, 309–10, 312
standards, 461
support for operational vs. strategic, 51–52, 77, 442
volume of, 51
in Zachman Framework, 334
Business Decision Management, see BDM
Business Decision Maturity Model, see BDMM
Business domain, 371–72, 378, 383, 486
Business goals see BMM
Business judgment, 431, 435, 439
Business logic
    business rule modeling and, 400
    and business rules, 31

changes in
    Decision Model supporting, 265, 411
    evaluating impact of, 29
    heading vs. cell, 182
    predictive model determining, 477
    region specific, 151
    sequence of execution, 280
in classical functional requirements, 117
complexity, 42, 52, 54–57, 59–62, 146–47, 151
declarative, 95, 154, 215, 220
errors in, 236, 241, 250, 252, 256
independence of, 216, 228–29, 279
model of, 8, 15–16, 169, 277, 299
as rows in Rule Family, 28
separation from other dimensions, 7
in SOA, 95
statements
    are declarative, 228
    atomic, 10, 30
    in the BMM, 119
    in BRMS, 357
    in business process models, 73
    and complexity in business decisions, 41–43, 47, 59–60
    not containing ORs, 205
    and expressions of business rules, 400
    grouping into structures, 170
    and information models, 399
    maintaining links to process models, 390
    natural language form, 20
    needs no grammar, 206
    and SBVR, 403
    unconditional, 184, 192
testing, 130
Business metrics
    Decision Model traceable to, 34, 52, 263
    integration with Decision Model, 461, 474
    measure effectiveness of Decision Model, 62, 83, 149, 263
    measuring against predictive models, 477
Business model, 134, 488
Business motivation, see BMM
Business Motivation Model, see BMM
Business object, 39, 144, 176
Business object model
    as artifact in web services, 339
    as formal structural model of fact types, 175
    includes properties not necessarily in data model, 398

as information model, 392
as starting point for software design, 398
structural differences from other models, 209
not technology related, 397
in Zachman Framework, 336–37, 342, 356
Business objectives, see BMM
Business performance
    and Business Decision Principle 15, 262
    of business decisions, 96, 471
    of Decision Model, 96, 163
    Decision Model contents influence, 234
    and performance stewards, 466, 471
    and SLA, 362, 368, 382
    see also Business metrics
Business performance metrics, see Business metrics
Business plan, see BMM
Business planning, see BMM
Business planning models, see BMM
Business policy statement, see BMM
Business Process Model
    in agile methods, 136
    and BDM approach, 499
    and business decision projects, 122, 146, 151, 153–56, 162–63, 204
    and business decisions, 26, 66, 70–73, 75, 77, 88–89, 264
    business rules in, 118–19
    and business scenario testing, 134
    connecting to the business decision shape, 26
    and data validation rules, 32
    and decision modeling tools, 86–88
    never reveals all business logic, 70
    as procedural model, 67–70, 88, 216, 220–21
    and process improvement, 65
    and requirements, 113
    role of the process modeler in, 143
    and routing logic, 421
    scope of, 145
    and SOA, 365–66, 499
    in STEP methodology, 414
    and traceability to other models, 34, 122, 124, 137, 391
    in Zachman Framework, 325, 333, 336–37, 342, 356
Business Process Modeling Notation, see BPMN
Business processes
    automating, 4, 162
    in BDMM, 461, 474, 479
    and BMM, 122, 389, 391
    and BPMN, 422–24, 426
    in a business rules approach, 483
    combining into one common business process, 154
    as component of BPM, 389
    decision aware, 66
    and Decision Model, 11, 43–44, 64, 67, 73, 77, 409, 487
    developed in project example, 153
    distinctions between business decisions and, 67–68, 70
    example of Customer Trip, 65
    excellence alone is insufficient in, 78
    non-operational, 77
    in operative context, 45, 50, 57–58
    in requirements, 106, 117
    smart decisions behind, 80
    in SOA, 95, 361–67, 442, 491
    in system architecture, 352–53
    in testing business scenarios, 134, 137
    in Zachman Framework, 325, 334, 340
Business Reference Model, see BRM
Business requirements
    and Agile methods, 114, 136
    in Aspect Orientation, 439
    and business logic, 118
    business rules in, 494, 498
    and decision services, 443
    generating code from, 330
    include Decision Model, 84, 87
    in SOA, 373
    in STEP methodology, 412
    and tools, 86–87
    traditional, 170
Business Rule Engine, see BRE; see also BRMS
Business Rule Management System, see BRMS
Business rules
    and adaptive control/optimization, 445
    adoption of, 8
    analysts, 496–97
        see also Business analysts
    approach, 485, 498–500
    atomic, 10
    awareness of, 459, 493
    and BMM, 120–23, 388–89
    as business logic, 6, 31
    and business requirements, 117–19, 484, 493–95
    center of excellence, 496
    and Decision Model, 4, 15, 75, 487, 490, 496–500

and decision services, 443–44
and EDM, 442, 445, 454
in FEA, 344
modeling, 388, 400
models, 119, 325, 327, 333, 338
and operational decisions, 450
and physical Decision Model, 438
in predictive analytics, 444
in production, 453
and RMM, 458–60
the role of, 408
as separate dimension, 6–7, 12
in SOA, 352, 363, 365, 373, 491, 499
statements, 6, 400–401
structural, 401–2
in SVBR, 401–3, 407
task in process, 122, 129
task type in BPMN, 422, 424–26
and testing business scenarios, 134–35
in TOGAF, 347
in UML, 391
in Zachman Framework, 319, 325–27, 333
Business Rules Group (BRG), 119–20, 327,
    388
Business service layer, 99, 365
Business service level, 365
Business service types, 347
Business services
    and Business Processes, 94
    coarse grained, 371
    composable, 363
    large, 373
    layer, 99
    types, 373
Business statements, 15, 17, 183, 402, 405
Business strategy, 325, 335, 351
Business systems, 12, 330, 340, 416
Business Tactic, 26, 122, 129
Business term, 175–76, 484, see also Fact type
Business transactions, 49, 56, 147
Business unit, 144, 461, 468, 470–73, 475–76,
    482
Business units of work, 368, 382
Business use cases
    in Agile methods, 114, 116, 136
    in business requirements, 107, 137
    and business rules, 118–19
    and Decision Models, 122, 124, 412
    examples, 109, 126–27
    identifying business decisions, 143
    integrated with other models, 393

in STEP methodology, 414–15
in system transformation, 420
and system use cases, 111
in UML, 391
in Unified Process, 110
in Zachman Framework, 336
Business vocabulary, 302, 337, 388

C

Capability Maturity Model, see CMM
CEP (Complex Event Processing), 45, 50
CIM (Computation-Independent Model), 337,
    354–56
CMM (Capability Maturity Model), 456, 458
Codd, Edward F., 7, 273, 275–76, 280,
    285, 300
Columns, conclusion, 18, 28, 218–19
Computation-Independent Model, see CIM
CRM (Customer Relationship Management),
    320, 345, 365
Customer Relationship Management, see
    CRM

D

Data
    physical, 368–69, 382
    semantic, 364, 368–69, 382
Data model
    attributes do not reflect interim
        decisions, 22
    best for data validation rules, 33
    conceptual, 336, 342
    connection points to Decision Model, 129
    decision model not addition to, 15
    declarative nature of, 216
    as information model, 396
    normalized, 404, 497
    physical, 128, 325, 333, 342, 428
    relational model as, 277, 298
    SOA Service internal, 368–69, 382
    standard, 368, 382
    structural model of fact types, 175
Data model, Enterprise, 128
Data Reference Model, see DRM
Database
    constraints as business rules, 31
    does not contain interim decisions, 22
    in layers of SOA, 95, 365
    properties not stored in, 398

technology, 7, 275
  in Zachman Framework, 340
Date, C. J., 275, 278, 281–82, 285
DCMI (Dublin Core Metadata Initiative),
    430–31
Decision, see Business decision
Decision Definition Language, 387
Decision elements, 426, 429, 433, 436–37,
    439–40
Decision gateway, 422, 424, 426
Decision management, see BDM; see also EDM
Decision Metadata, 411, 430
Decision Model
  as intellectual template, 14
  normal form, 281, 302
  notation, 13, 25, 301–2, 498
  Physical, 427, 430, 433–34, 439–40
  Principles
    # 1 Tabular, 171
    # 2 Heading, 173
    # 3 Cell, 178
    # 4 Row, 181
    # 5 Conclusion, 188
    # 6 Conditions, 191
    # 7 Connection, 199
    # 8 Declarative Heading, 217, 229, 306
    # 9 Declarative Body, 221
    # 10 Declarative Inferential
        Relationship, 223, 229, 307
    # 11 Rule Pattern Transitive
        Conditions, 235
    # 12 Consistency, 241
    # 14 Inferential Integrity, 256
    # 15 Business alignment, 261
Decision modeling
  artifacts related to, 88
  in BDMM, 460, 469
  declarative nature, 216
  and glossary, 392
  in project example, 143
  standards, 465
  in STEP methodology, 414
  Tools, 29, 87–88, 334, 337–38, 341
  in Unified Process, 409
Decision Resources, 435–36, 438
Decision Rule Family, 27–28, 202, 304,
    309–10, 312
Decision services
  in a composite service, 97–98
  in decision modeling tool, 337, 339, 357
  in EDM, 442–44, 449–50, 452

in FEA, 346
in MDA, 355
in project example, 162
in SOA service role, 95–96, 99, 374–75
in SOA services inventory, 101, 377, 409
Decision shape, 68, 73, 220
Decision steps in business use cases, 122, 124,
    127, 129, 391
Decision tables, 15, 24–25, 35, 172, 444,
    496–98
Decision tasks, 66
  and BPMN, 390, 422, 424–25
  in business process layer, 95
  connecting process model to decision
      model, 122, 124, 129
  containing decision icon, 73
  in decision aware processes, 66
  in Decision Modeling tool, 87
  declarative business logic, 220
  separated from process tasks, 66, 68
  in SOA, 99
Decision trees, 15, 266, 405–7, 411, 445
Decision word, 310, 312
Declarative, 16, 70, 211, 213
DecRM (Decision Reference Model), 346–47
Department of Defense Architectural
    Framework, see DoDAF
Dependent Rule Family, 256–57, 268, 270,
    305, 308, 311–12, 335
DoDAF (Department of Defense Architectural
    Framework), 332
Domain, see Fact type, domain
DRM (Data Reference Model), 346–47, 351
Dublin Core Metadata Initiative, see DCMI

E

EA (Enterprise Architecture)
  Decision Model in, 331
  and FEA (Federal Enterprise Architecture),
      344
  and methodologies, 330
  repository, 87
  and TOGAF (The Open Group
      Architectural Framework), 347
  and Zachman Framework, 317, 332
EDM (Enterprise Decision Management)
  adaptive control, 453
  in the BDMM, 476
  and business rules, 443
  Optimize, 453

and the Decision Model, 446, 449, 451–52, 454
referred to as BDM, 39, 64, 162, 331
and SOA, 442
Encapsulation, 369–70, 380, 382
Enterprise Continuum in TOGAF, 348
Enterprise data model, see Data model, Enterprise
Enterprise Decision Management, see EDM, see also BDM
ESB (Enterprise Service Bus), 353–54

F

Fact model, 113, 127–29, 175, 336, 391–92, 394–96, 404
Fact type
  as column heading, 182, 306
  conclusion, 187
  condition, 191
  in condition key, 193, 310
  correlating to anticipated metrics, 265
  definition, 43, 143–44, 160–61, 304, 337
  domain
    consistent with Decision Model scope, 248
    defined, 304
    values, 132
  in formulas, 201
  glossary, 127–28, 392, 414
  models see fact model
  as operand, 178
  in Rule Family shape, 310
  scope of domain values in Rule Pattern, 243
  unordered in heading, 217, 306
  values, 182
  in Zachman Framework, 336
Fact values, 28, 174, 304, 310
FEA (Federal Enterprise Architecture), 329, 332, 343–44, 346–47, 349, 356
First normal form, see Decision Model, normal form

G

Glossary, see Fact type, glossary, 113, 127–28, 392, 414, 419
Governance
  in BDMM, 461
  Business Decision, 80

of business logic in BPM solutions, 422
data vs. Decision Model, 340
Decision Model, 11, 162, 489
in example project, 143, 145, 163
IT, 11
provided by encapsulated decision service, 356
for Rule Families, 265
using BPMN gateway to improve, 425
GUIDE Business Rules Project Final Report, 327

H

Hammer, Dr. M., 389

I

IEEE (Institute of Electrical and Electronics Engineers), 106, 361
ILM (Information Lifecycle Management), 430
Inferential
  dependencies, 31, 73, 235, 238, 249, 304, 307–8
  keys, 202, 291, 299, 304, 310, 387
  relationship line, 301, 309, 311
  relationships, 199, 206, 208, 223, 229, 256, 305–7
Information Age, 7, 276, 320–22, 327
Information architecture, see Architecture, information
Information Lifecycle Management, see ILM (Information Lifecycle Management)
Information management, 449–50
Information model, 392, 398–400, 450
Information Systems Architecture, see Architecture, TOGAF
Information Technology Infrastructure Library, see ITIL
Institute of Electrical and Electronics Engineers, see IEEE
ITIL (Information Technology Infrastructure Library), 430

K

Keys
  foreign, 276, 279, 291, 299–300
  inferential, see Inferential, keys
  primary, 276, 279, 291, 293–95, 299

M

Mass customization, 322
MDA (Model-Driven Architecture), 112, 330, 332, 337, 354, 407
MDM (Master Data Management), 428–30
Metadata
    connecting Decision Models, 120
    in DCMI, 431
    in a Decision Model tool, 337
    in MDM, 434
    and physical Decision Models, 434
    as reference points in models, 113
    in RuleGuide, 85
Meta-entities, 324, 326–27, 332–33
Methodology
    BDMM, 463
    Business rules approach as, 483
    CMM, 458
    insights into Decision Model, 204, 227, 265
    physical Decision Model, 429
    references to business rule, 408
    requirements, 106
    search for agility in, 482
    STEP, 412
    Unified Process, 409
Model
    analytic, see Analytics, Models
    as a business requirement, 111
    connection points in, 112
    Decision, see Decision Model; see also decision modeling
    decision aware business process, 66
    Information, see Information Model
    maturity of process and not, 460
    need for a new, 8
    physical Decision, see Physical Decision Model
    prototype as, 114
    Relational, see Relational Model
    simple visual comparison of, 9
    in Zachman Framework, 330
Modeling
    business processes, 389
    decision, see decision modeling
    definition of, 111
    fact, see Fact model
    information (fact type), see fact model
    logic using decision trees, 406
    production rules, 407

    separate aspects, 112
    in Unified Process, 409
Moore, Art, 133–35

N

National Institute of Standards and Technology, see NIST
New Wisdom Software, 85–86
NIST (National Institute of Standards and Technology), 387
Normal forms, see Decision Model, normal form; see also Relational Model, normal form
Normalization
    Decision Model, 186, 205, 234, 280
    Relational Model, 7, 276, 280
    Zachman Framework, 324
Notation
    Business Process Modeling, 426
    data model, 396
    Decision Model, 10, 204, 302, 315
    fact model, 394–95
    information modeling, 400
    Physical Decision Model, 429
    process model, 361
    Unified Modeling Language, 390

O

Object model, 22, 128–29, 144, 396, 405, see also Business object model
Office of E-Government and Information Technology, 344–45, 347, 349
Office of Management and Budget (OMB), 344–45, 347, 349
OMG (Object Management Group), 332, 335, 338, 354, 400, 407, 423
The Open Group's Architectural Framework, see TOGAF
Operand, 19, 43, 129, 178–79
Operational decisions, 40, 49, 52, 66, 442
Operative context
    defined, 42
    each business decision has an, 41
    ordered domain, 43
        complicated context, 46
        simple context, 37, 43, 52–53, 58, 60–61, 78

unordered domain, 43
chaotic context, 49
complex context, 37, 47, 60–61, 78, 81
usefulness of Decision Model based on, 49
Operator (logical), 19, 43, 178–79, 205, 305, 313, 497
Optimization (of business decisions), 122, 331, 442, 445–46, 470, 478
Orr, Ken, 3, 5, 7, 351
ORs, 191–93, 288

P

Parker Hannifin (PH), 80–82
Physical Decision Model see Decision Model, Physical
PIM (Platform-Independent Model), 337–40, 342, 354–56
Pitney Bowes, 77–78
Platform-Independent Model, see PIM
Principles, see Decision Model principles
PRM (Performance Reference Model), 346–47
Procedural approach, 211–12, 214–15, 227

R

RAD (Rapid Application Development), 114
Raden, Neil, 40, 49, 51–52, 54, 66, 476
RDF (Resource Description Framework), 430–31
Relational Model, 4, 7, 273, 281, 289–91, 293–97
first normal form, 281, 296
second normal form, 297
third normal form, 294, 297
connections in, 291
functional dependency, 289
identifiers, 290
Resource Description Framework see RDF
RIF (Rule Interchange Format), 407–8
RMM (Rule Maturity Model), 318, 455, 458–61
Rosen, Michael, 92–95, 99
Rule Family
cell, 178
combined Decision, 259
condition fact types, 191
Decision, see Decision Rule Family
defined, 305
heading, 173
no hidden meaning behind sequence, 224

no implied sequence of rows, 222
inferential relationship, 199
Rule Interchange Format, see RIF
Rule Pattern
condition key, 244
condition key coverage principle, 231
defined, 313
Empty Conclusion Cell Principle, 168
Fully Empty Condition Key, 168
introduction, 25
Overlapping Condition Key Coverage, 231
Partial Condition Key Dependency, 168
Partially Empty Condition Key, 168
Role, 24
Transitive Conditions Principle, 231, 235, 269, 307
unconditional, 194
RuleGuide, 86
RuleML.org, 388, 407, 430

S

SBVR (Semantics of Business Vocabulary and Rules Specification), 386, 400–404, 407
SDLC (Software development life cycle), 116, 349, 499–500
Semantics of Business Vocabulary and Rules Specification, see SBVR
Service Level Agreement, see SLA
Service-Oriented Architecture, see SOA
SLA (Service level agreement), 362, 365–66, 368, 371, 381–82
SME (subject matter expert), 117, 466, 486, 490–91, 495
SOA (Service-Oriented Architecture)
and BDMM, 469
and the Decision Model, 96
and Decision Services, 442
decisions on demand, 491
plan for, 162
service inventory, 95
what is, 92
Software Engineering Institute (SEI), 416, 458
SOR (System of Record), 364–65
STEP Business Decision Methodology Approach, 412
Subject matter experts, see SME
System architecture, see Architecture, system
System of Record, see SOR
System transformation, artifacts, 417
System use cases, 110–11, 137

T

Term, business see business term
Test cases, 104, 117, 129–31, 137–38, 162, 495
Toffler, Alvin, 320–21
TOGAF (The Open Group's Architectural Framework), 332, 346–47, 349–51, 356

U

UML (Unified Modeling Language), 390–91
Unified Modeling Language see UML
Unified Process, see Methodology, Unified Process
Universal model of business logic, adoption of, 8

Use cases, see Business use cases; see also System use cases

V

Value chain, 65

W

Web 2.0, 482, 491
Web services, 162, 361, 437–38

Z

Zachman Framework, 319, 347, 349, 351, 356, 390
Zachman Framework for Enterprise Architecture, 330–32, 340, see also Zachman Frameworkv